The Mycenaeans
and Europe

The Mycenaeans and Europe

A. F. Harding

*Department of Archaeology,
University of Durham, Durham, UK*

1984

Academic Press
(Harcourt Brace Jovanovich, Publishers)
London   Orlando   San Diego   San Francisco   New York
Toronto   Montreal   Sydney   Tokyo   São Paulo

ACADEMIC PRESS INC. (LONDON) LTD
24/28 Oval Road, London NW1 7DX

United States Edition published by
ACADEMIC PRESS INC.
(Harcourt Brace Jovanovich, Inc.)
Orlando, Florida 32887

British Library Cataloguing in Publication Data

Harding, A. F.
  The Mycenaeans and Europe.
  1. Mycenae (Ancient city)
  I. Title
  938′.8   DF221.M9

ISBN 0–12–324760–8
LCCCN 83–73404

Typeset and printed in Great Britain
at The Pitman Press, Bath

Preface

The original study that forms the subject of this book was undertaken for a Ph.D. dissertation for the University of Cambridge entitled "The Extent and Effects of Contact between Mycenaean Greece and the rest of Europe". This work was carried out between 1969 and 1972 and the degree awarded in 1973. In the years following that several articles drawing on the contents of the dissertation appeared, but it has been felt wise to delay publication of a longer work until certain aspects of the subject were clarified by the progress of research. Even now it is possible to predict that in ten years' time the situation will be much clearer.

The resulting book differs from the dissertation in many ways, and has essentially been completely rewritten for publication. The organisation of the book is different from that of the thesis, the chapters dealing with general rather than specific categories of evidence. Some sections have been added, notably chapters 1, 2, 8 and 10; other sections have been dropped, particularly the more indigestible catalogue-type reviews of material. I have only provided lists of objects in a few instances, and these appear either in the Notes at the end of the chapters or in the Appendices. Deciding what to illustrate was difficult, and I am aware that there will be disagreement over my choice; yet to illustrate all the material that could be considered relevant, or that is discussed here, would have necessitated a greatly expanded set of figures that would have extended the book very considerably.

It is a pleasure to be able to express my thanks to those who have helped in the conception and creation of this book, particularly to Professor J. M. Coles (my research supervisor), Dr Jan Bouzek and Dr Oliver Dickinson. Dr Bouzek gave me a warm welcome as a student in the Institute for Classical Archaeology of the Charles University, Prague, of which he was Acting Head, when I studied there for nine months in 1970. He has freely shared his wide knowledge with me and though we differ on many points has always been a source of encouragement and constructive criticism. Dr Dickinson has read almost the entire text in draft and made many helpful comments and suggestions, most of which I have adopted; he has also advised me on all matters relating to Mycenaean pottery. For this help I am deeply grateful.

Others who have greatly assisted me by reading parts in draft and making comments are Professor J. B. Rutter, Mr C. C. Haselgrove, Dr W. J. Tait, Mrs H. Hughes-Brock, Mr S. E. Warren, Dr J. Henderson and Dr E. Macnamara, to all of whom I should like to express my thanks. Other help, in the form of discussion, information, provision of books and off-prints, etc., has been supplied by: C. W. Beck, M. Benzi, G. Bergonzi, A. M. Bietti Sestieri, K. Branigan, H.-G. Buchholz, H. W. Catling, S. Deger-Jalkotzy, M. L. Ferrarese Ceruti, K. Goldman, C. M. Guido, N. G. L. Hammond, V. Hankey, B. Hänsel, J. R. Harris, O. Höckmann, K. Kilian, F. Lo Schiavo, P. Mountjoy, J. D. Muhly, I. Panajotov, R. Peroni, S. Piggott, F. Prendi, D. Ridgway, J. Riley, R. Rottländer, N. Sandars, S. Sherratt, T. Smith, A. M. Snodgrass, L. Vagnetti, K. Wardle, P. M. Warren, S. E. Warren, and T. Watkins.

Undertaking a research topic of this nature has entailed visits to many museums, and I should like to thank the staff of museums in many countries for help and courtesies over a long period. In particular I should like to express my thanks to Dr J. Sakellarakis, formerly of the National Archaeological Museum, Athens, the single most important collection studied for the purpose of this book. I should also like to thank the Directors and staff of the British Schools in Athens and Rome for their many kindnesses.

On the production side, I am glad to be able to acknowledge the parts played by Keith McBarron and Yvonne Brown, illustrators, Tom Middlemass and Trevor Woods, photographers, Jean Towers, who expertly typed the manuscript, and Dr Janet Levy for her invaluable help in compiling the index. Without their excellent service the task would have been much harder. Lastly, I must thank my family for their forbearance during the writing of the book and the research trips which preceded it, and especially for their help in the final stages.

Durham, March 1984 A. F. Harding

Contents

Contents

Abbreviations

The following is a list of abbreviations that are used in the references cited in the *Notes* section of each chapter

A. General

Antiq.   Antiquaries, Antiquarian
Arch.   Archaeology, Archaeological (or equivalent in other languages)
EBA   Early Bronze Age
Ges.   Gesellschaft
Inst.   Institute
Int.   International
J.   Journal
Jb.   Jahrbuch
LBA   Late Bronze Age
LH   Late Helladic
Mag.   Magazine
MBA   Middle Bronze Age
MH   Middle Helladic
Mitt.   Mitteilungen
NM   National Museum
Proc.   Proceedings
Soc.   Society

B. Journals and monographs

AJA   *American Journal of Archaeology*
Annuario   *Annuario della reale scuola archeologica di Atene*
Arch. Delt.   *Archaiologikon Deltion*

Arch. Eph.   *Archaiologiki Ephimeris*
BCH   *Bulletin de Correspondence Hellenique*
BPI   *Bulletino di Paletnologia Italiana*
BRGK   *Bericht der römisch-germanischen Kommission*
BSA   *Annual of the British School of Archaeology at Athens*
Cyprus and Crete   *Acts of the International Archaeological Symposium, The Relations between Cyprus and Crete ca. 2000–500 B.C.* (Nicosia 1978), 1979
Eastern Mediterranean   *Acts of the International Archaeological Symposium, The Mycenaeans in the Eastern Mediterranean* (Nicosia 1972), 1973
Inv. Arch.   *Inventaria Archaeologica*
Jb. RGZM   *Jahrbuch des römisch-germanischen Zentralmuseums Mainz*
Not. Scavi   *Notizie degli scavi di antichità*, Accademia nazionale dei Lincei
PBF   *Prähistorische Bronzefunde*
Slov. Arch.   *Slovenská Archeológia*
Sov. Arch.   *Sovetskaja Archeologija*

□ 1
Introduction

When Heinrich Schliemann excavated the Shaft Graves of Circle A at Mycenae in 1876, he found in some of them "an enormous quantity of amber beads". Not only did he recognize them for what they were, he also realized that they bespoke far-reaching trade, for amber does not naturally occur in Greece. Wishing to determine the origin of the beads, Schliemann submitted some of them for chemical testing, first to Xaver Landerer of Athens, and later to Otto Helm of Danzig.[1]* While the former, whose methods remain quite unknown to us, decided that the amber was of Sicilian origin, the latter pronounced that it was Baltic, and, therefore, evidence of a trade that stretched right across Europe. Helm's method was to heat the amber and to collect and weigh the crystals of succinic acid which formed in the neck of the retort: if the amount was between 3 and 8% of the total, then the amber was held to be Baltic. These methods have long been regarded with suspicion by chemists, but the notion that much of the amber found in the Bronze Age Mediterranean is of Baltic origin has held the field ever since, receiving apparent confirmation from new methods devised by Curt W. Beck in the 1960s. More than anything else, the amber of Mycenaean Greece has promoted the idea that the Mycenaean Greeks were in contact, perhaps regular contact, with the barbarian world beyond their borders.

Since that time, many other categories of object, and even whole sites, have been linked with the supposed Mycenaean–barbarian trade (Fig. 1). Between the 1950s and the early 1970s new categories of evidence were constantly being introduced into the discussion—sometimes, it must be admitted, on the flimsiest of grounds, and only because received opinion held the link to be genuine and indisputable. This trend was strongest in two areas, Britain and central Europe; it should be recorded that Aegean specialists have been much more

---

* Superscript numbers refer to numbered notes at the end of each chapter.

reticent in proclaiming the existence of such links. It was in Britain that doubts were first expressed in print, by Colin Renfrew in 1968 in a much-cited paper. That the factual foundation for the arguments presented in it was not altogether secure mattered little in view of the influence the article exerted. Its appearance prompted reappraisal on both sides: active questioning of received ideas by research workers willing to break out of the established mould, and an entrenchment of attitudes by those who had worked to build up the links. In this conflict of ideas the development of radiocarbon dating techniques, and in particular the arrival of the first tree-ring and Egyptian historical calibration curves, played a major part. The investigation of these matters which is presented in this book also arose from this period of questioning, though it must be admitted that originally the links were examined in a far more positive spirit than is the case today.

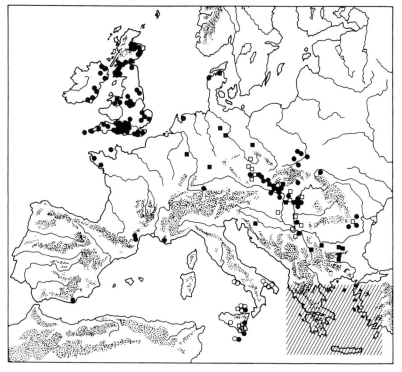

FIG. 1 ☐ Distribution map of objects of Mycenaean origin or inspiration in Europe according to S. Piggott, *Ancient Europe*, 1965. ○, Pottery; ■, metalwork; ☐, spirally decorated bone and antler; ●, faience beads.

In the late 1960s it rapidly became evident that nothing less than a complete and thorough survey of all the relevant classes of evidence would suffice to untangle the threads that formed the complex net wound round the whole question of Mycenaean–barbarian links. Even then it was far from clear that definite answers would be forthcoming. The reasons were not hard to seek: so much of the evidence adduced by protagonists of the contact theory was of a nebulous nature, based almost entirely on subjective stylistic criteria or unfounded allegations of provenance. Against these arguments it was, and remains, extremely hard to bring irrefutable proof that any other interpretation of the archaeological configurations in question was applicable. To a large extent much of the evidence still remains capable of the interpretation originally assigned: it is largely a question of personal taste which explanation is preferred. Some still think that a totally positive view of all the alleged connections between Greece and barbarian Europe can be taken; others are sceptical about parts of the evidence but see the totality of the picture as favouring at least a general connection; still others are completely unconvinced and will concede that only a minimum of contact took place. Different observers find different lines of explanation in archaeology satisfactory: these viewpoints can never be totally reconciled. What can and must be attempted is as objective a survey as possible of the evidence on which the alleged connections are based.

The scope of this book is the Late Bronze Age Minoan-Mycenaean world on the one hand and those areas north and west of Greece with which contact is believed, or alleged, to have existed on the other. In effect this means most of the rest of Europe. The bulk of the discussion affects sites and finds made on the mainland of Greece (or at periods subsequent to the decline of Minoan civilization, and so the tendency is to refer to Mycenaean or Mycenaeans), but Crete is also included in so far as it is affected by contacts with Europe. In general this seems not to have occurred to a very great degree: Crete was apparently much more within the East Mediterranean ambit than was mainland Greece, and—except towards the end of our period of study—had little or nothing to do with the west and north. In general, material earlier than the Late Bronze Age is not included, because it is too sparse to be useful and in many cases alleged contacts are highly dubious anyway.[1a]

A word—and an apology—must be included about the use of the term "barbarian" to describe the Bronze Age of Europe outside Greece. This is purely a term of convenience, and intended to be accurate only in the sense that all the cultural groups in question were non-Greek. It is certainly not intended to denote any kind of spiritual, moral or cultural impoverishment on those to whom it is applied. In some areas, indeed, notably the central Mediterranean, it would seem to have been only the scale of the political units involved that made the inhabitants different, on a cultural level, from those of Mycenaean Greece.

History and development of contact theories

> The fact that many of them [faience beads] resemble in colour, form and material, numbers found in Egypt appears first to have been vaguely recognised by the Rev. J. Skinner in 1826.[2]

Certainly by the end of the nineteenth century Bronze Age faience was regarded as being definitely of Egyptian origin. I have already alluded to the debate over amber, which had a brief vogue in the last quarter of the nineteenth century and then settled down to a firm conviction that all amber found in the south of Europe was of Baltic origin. Naue's catalogue of Pre-Roman swords included Greek swords in his group II, thus tacitly implying that such material was either imported or made in a common tradition with the European.[3] In 1904 Schmidt examined material from the Aegean basin and the Danubian area in an article entitled "Troja-Mykene-Ungarn. Archäologische Parallelen"; he discerned influences both in ornament and ceramic form which, in his view, linked the two areas at various stages of the Bronze Age.[4] By the time that Mötefindt published the Nienhagen cup in 1912, he was able to do so under the title "Eine neue Parallele zu den Bechern von Mykenae und Vapheio".[5]

Naturally the development of theories concerning contact between Greece and Europe in the Bronze Age was dependent on the quantity and quality of archaeological work carried out in each area. In Greece, little had been done, and nothing systematic, prior to the discovery of the Shaft Graves in 1876. Thereafter the tempo of archaeological discovery increased. Schliemann had already excavated at Troy by this time (1870–1873, 1878–1879); Tiryns soon followed (1884–1885), as did Orchomenos (1880–1881). Tsountas worked both in the Cyclades and in Thessaly in the latter part of the last century, laying the foundations for work such as that on Melos (1896–1899). In the early years of the twentieth century many new sites were dug: Knossos and Phaestos, Vapheio, Salamis, Kakovatos, Korakou, as well as renewed work at Mycenae and Tiryns. By the time that Wace started (and published) his investigations at Mycenae, and the Germans theirs at Tiryns, a picture of Mycenaean civilization had already been built up which has remained the basis for our understanding of the phenomenon. Further landmarks on the way to a more complete understanding of the nature of the Greek Late Bronze Age were the excavation of cemeteries of chamber tombs at Mycenae, Prosymna and Dendra, of non-palatial settlements such as Asine, Zygouries, Eutresis, Malthi and others (on Crete, Gournia, Vasiliki, Tylissos etc.), and—most important of all—the finding of the Mycenaean archives in the palace at Pylos (Epano Englianos). Since the Second World War, a huge proliferation of archaeological work in all areas has filled in many of the gaps left by earlier workers. Of particular importance for the present study have been the finding of the Bronze Age shipwreck off the southern Turkish coast at Cape Gelidonya, the excavation of two Late Bronze Age settlement sites in central Macedonia (Assiros and Kastanas), the continuing evidence from Mycenae of northern and western connections (such as the finding of an Italian axe mould in 1952), and the recognition of non-Mycenaean pottery in certain late Mycenaean sites (the first to be published was a vessel from Lefkandi).

The development of Bronze Age studies in "barbarian" Europe has also proceeded at different speeds and with different emphases. In most areas, early barrow-digging produced a good general idea, but very little detailed knowledge, about the material culture of the period, or the sequence in which it proceeded. By comparison with Greece the amount of material from secure stratified contexts was very small, and that from totally unknown circumstances very large, a situation that continues to give problems even today. The landmarks along the way to the development of the Bronze Age as we know it, are rather those of synthesis and publication than those of excavation and discovery. In the case of the Wessex culture, for instance, much of the relevant material had been found early in the last century, as with Colt Hoare's finds from Bush Barrow and other graves in the classic barrow cemeteries. But the Early Bronze Age barrows of Wessex were not appreciated for what they are until the 1930s, when first Beck and Stone published their study of the faience beads, then Stuart Piggott assembled and studied all the relevant groups, and finally Merhart set the amber spacer beads in their true perspective.[6] Since the Second World War, work has been done on the details of the typological and chronological sequence, and there has been some debate about the precise affinities of faience, amber and other material, but only one work—that of Sabine Gerloff—has provided a major new synthesis from which to embark on a detailed study.[7] The story of the development of Bronze Age studies on the Continent is similar in outline, even if the chronology is different.

The desire to be able to tie in the archaeological sequence in the "barbarian" world with that of the "civilized" East led to the exploitation of whatever chronological links were available. First Montelius, and later Åberg, constructed the entire framework of European prehistory around such cross-connections.[8] Others, such as Childe, were more interested in what such connections could tell us about the nature of the societies in question. Of the works of these three authors, Childe's were by far the most influential as far as the development of theories of contact were concerned, especially with the publication of *The Danube* in 1929, but also in other papers—"The Minoan influence on the Danubian Bronze Age", for instance, published in 1927, or "The Orient and Europe", published in 1939.[9] It was surely the influence of works like these which prompted the identification of the Roşiorii de Vede sword as Mycenaean (which it patently is not) in 1935.[10]

Another influential work which appeared early in the story was the famous article by J. M. de Navarro in 1925, "Prehistoric routes between Northern Europe and Italy defined by the amber trade".[11] At this time, chemical analysis already favoured the idea of a Baltic origin for the amber of Italy and Greece, and Navarro's article set out to define just how the amber may have travelled. By charting finds of amber in Bronze Age contexts (as well as earlier and later ones) he attempted to show that the most likely routes were down the great river valleys of central Europe and over the Brenner Pass to the head of the Adriatic, or else eastwards into the steppe zone. Comparable work on this detailed level has never been attempted since, and Navarro's postulated routes have remained the basis for all later investigation. A comparable synthesizing article was that by C. F. C. Hawkes on double-axes (especially double-axe ingots), published in 1937.[12]

Finally in the pre-war period we may mention those "area studies" which threw light on the archaeology of especially important zones of prehistoric activity. Piggott's assembling of the Wessex grave material has already been mentioned; another was that of Heurtley for Macedonia, a synthesis of work carried out mainly by him in the 1920s and 1930s at various sites in central and west Macedonia, a key area for the understanding of the Mycenaean border zone and its influence beyond.[13]

After the war the study of Mycenaean foreign contacts, and the notion of far-reaching connections with the barbarian world, grew to vast proportions. The 1950s and 1960s were characterized by several different types of article bearing on the question of contact.[14] First there is the study of particular classes of material, such as Buchholz's studies of double-axes, of copper ingots, and of arrowheads; Catling's work on Type II swords in the eastern Mediterranean, as well as his more general corpus on Cypriot bronzework; Coles and others on shields; Cowen on the earliest European swords, and Sandars on Aegean swords and knives; Hachmann on amber spacer-plates, and more generally on bronzes decorated with supposedly Aegean motifs; Jacobsthal on pins; Merhart on various classes of sheet bronze objects— vessels, armour and so on; Mozsolics on horse harnesses and on gold and bronze finds from the Carpathian basin; Snodgrass on arms and armour; Stone and Thomas on faience beads; Tihelka on model wheels; and Milojčić on "late" bronzes. By the mid-1960s the study of specific classes of material was thus well-developed; fittingly at the end of that decade came the first volumes of the influential series *Prähistorische Bronzefunde*, which will eventually place the study of at any rate bronzework on a secure and systematic footing. A number of valuable volumes affecting the subject under review here have already appeared. Through the 1970s studies and corpora have continued to appear, so that now, in the early 1980s, there are few categories of evidence for which at least some systematic study has not taken place.

A second broad tradition that concerns us is that of area studies. Since the Second World War, and especially since the mid-1960s, more information has been available from areas formerly poorly known or inaccessible, as well as systematic work on material from easily accessible areas. In the former category we may place the publications of Islami, Prendi and Korkuti for Albania, and the massive synthesizing tomes of Hammond (see p. 239); or recent work on the prehistory of Greek Macedonia, Thrace and Epirus (see p. 237); or other areas of the Mediterranean such as Sardinia (p. 252). In the latter category come corpora such as Gerloff's for Bronze Age Britain or Aner and Kersten's for the Nordic area.[15] The combination of these two trends means that very few areas, and those small ones, are now a blank on the map of the European Bronze Age. For our purposes, one may mention certain areas of Bulgaria especially, which remain poorly known. There are, of course, many regions for which we could hope for still better information.

Lastly in this survey of the literature and research we come to those works written specifically to investigate the whole question of connections between Greece and the barbarian world in the Bronze Age. A good many of these have now been written, which is perhaps the more remarkable in that all say essentially the same thing and repeat the same facts—or semi-facts. The first of these appeared in 1952, and was a brief survey by Werner, based principally on artistic motifs.[16] In 1966 two articles appeared dealing with the subject, quite independently, but both published in Czechoslovakia: one (much the shorter) by Piggott, the other by Bouzek (the first lengthy and at least partly systematic treatment of the subject).[17] Various contributions by Branigan started to appear around 1970.[18] The massive book by Gimbutas, *Bronze Age Cultures in Central and Eastern Europe*, which appeared in 1965, also dealt with various aspects of the matter, though more as an aid to chronology than anything else. Finally, several articles by Vladár have dealt with the whole question of East Mediterranean connections with the Carpathian basin: these rest principally on the evidence of artistic motifs, though other material has been dragged in too.[19]

The original work for this survey was started in 1969, and finished in 1972. It can be seen, therefore, that the main basis of literature was already in existence before or during its completion. Relatively little that bears directly on the subject has appeared since that time, as preoccupations have shifted to other areas of research. This is not to say that no up-dating was necessary to convert a doctoral dissertation into a book: a great deal was required, and the resulting book differs in many important respects from the dissertation. But conceptually the notions of contact that were current in the 1960s remain current today in many quarters. It has to be one of the prime tasks for the future to bring about a shift in attitudes towards the material evidence and what it is capable of telling us. To some of these problems I return below.

Is the problem a real one?

It will be evident from the above that the history of this question goes back a long way, and has remained firmly entrenched in the literature in spite of several attempts to displace it. Longevity may mean something, but the history of thought is littered with the ruins of debates about problems that seem quite unreal to us today, and which we would never consider problems at all. Our first task should be to decide whether the matter under discussion might not fall into this category. To decide if this is the case, we must be able to show that at least some of the alleged connections between Greece and Europe were real ones, and that there is a case to answer for more far-reaching contacts.

The tradition of seeing Mycenaean connections as of great importance for cultural as well as chronological matters goes back, as we have seen, to Montelius. Why does it exist? The simple answer, which would be given by adherents of the notion of contact, is that it exists because the connections exist. The sceptic would maintain that these connections are much less evident than has often been supposed, or even (in some cases) do not exist at all. I do not wish to forestall here the discussion in later chapters, but no secret need be made of the fact that certain categories of evidence seem to be above suspicion for the demonstration of contact. One of these is amber: the evidence of the amber spacer-plates cannot be made to evaporate by an effort of will. Another is the evidence of bronzework from around 1200 B.C., which showed many similarities in Greece and the European continent and seems to bespeak common smithing traditions. On the other hand, many of the pieces claimed to show contact palpably do nothing of the sort: a fine example of this is the architecture of Stonehenge, which has been alleged to show the influence of Mycenaean architectural traditions. This was mainly because of the carvings of "Mycenaean" daggers on the great trilithon; otherwise there is nothing except its circularity which links Stonehenge to Mycenaean Greece. Indeed, at the time it was erected the Mycenaeans had little skill in dealing with monumental stone. Connecting the two things was an absurdity, but an absurdity that found favour among a wide circle for a period of time. Much the same can be said for a number of other claimed "connections".

The force of fashion and tradition is perhaps especially strong in the world of scholarship, and nowhere more so than in prehistoric, or ahistoric, archaeology. The relation between material culture and the events, thoughts and processes of the past is a difficult one which is considered in Chapter 2 (p. 17). All too often it is forgotten that the basis for any statement about the prehistoric past is the evidence of material things, which may have little to do with mental states, ethnic affinities, or activities other than those of subsistence and industry. The significance of that evidence needs to be constantly questioned, and only those assumptions made about past human activity which rigorous testing will bear out. In the present case, these essential lessons were passed over, admittedly because there was no tradition of carrying them out: archaeology was an "arts" subject, which dealt with the workings and products of the human mind and thus considered itself above the rigorous procedures of the "sciences". There was also without doubt an element of romanticism present, especially since the Mycenaeans were shown to have been Greeks, or, more accurately, to have spoken Greek. The civilization and culture of Classical Greece is universally seen as the main forerunner of European civilization as we know it, and each western nation sees itself as the natural inheritor of Greek values and virtues. The Mycenaeans may not, in our eyes, have shared fully in those qualities but they are undoubtedly viewed by some as the rough-hewn blocks out of which the Classical Greeks were made. They also employed the services of skilled craftsmen, and had a predilection for gold and other precious materials. Mycenaeans and Minoans alike are thus romantic subjects in themselves, and the story of their discovery is romantic: who would not secretly wish to have the luck of Schliemann or Arthur Evans? As the picture of Mycenaean foreign relations was built up, with their distinctive pottery being found in Egypt, Anatolia, the Levant and Italy, it was perhaps natural that they should be sought also in the "barbarian" world. That pottery provided chronological security, but it provided more than that: it gave a link with the "civilized" world which in some way seemed to reflect well on the "barbarians" of the area under investigation. It is perhaps small wonder then that the habit of seeing Mycenaean objects lurking in every museum of central Europe become so well established. Determining to what extent the habit was merely the product of fashion, and to what extent a genuine reflection of the prehistoric past, is one of the prime tasks of this book.

The archaeological problem

If contacts between Mycenaean Greece and the barbarian world *did* exist, one must ask how they would manifest themselves in the physical record of the human past. That record consists almost entirely of artefactual material which may be more or less closely associated with particular contexts on particular sites. In Greece rarely, and in the Near East frequently, there is the additional evidence of archival material. For Greece, the Linear B tablets tell us nothing at all about trade and commerce with the outside world, and only about internal trade by implication. The Near Eastern sources are, of course, much more informative in this respect, but their bearing, if any, on the problems of northern and western contact may be questioned. It is the artefactual material which one is left to deal with.

The subjective nature of the problem is also a difficult obstacle to rational evaluation of the likelihood of contact. Much of the evidence is based on stylistic considerations which are not capable of objective assessment, let alone proof. A prime example is the claimed connection between the Aegean and the Carpathian basin as shown by the series of bone and antler objects ornamented in spiraliform or related designs akin to certain objects in the Shaft Graves and elsewhere. It is certainly possible to chart the occurrences of the designs in question, as is attempted in Chapter 7. What is not possible is to understand the significance of the recurrence of identical or similar motifs in widely separated areas.

Nor is agreement possible as to what constitutes "identity" and what "similarity", even though the terms themselves do not appear to be ambiguous. "Identity" ("absolute sameness", *Concise Oxford Dictionary*) means that there is no essential difference between two things (one could not say "no difference at all" simply because one *is* talking of two things, and two things cannot be one thing); "similarity" (likeness, mutual resemblance) implies no more than a notion of stylistic comparability. In terms of craft production, where one is talking of the output of single workshops or even single craftsmen, the two terms merge imperceptibly. It is unlikely that two objects will be absolutely the same in any situation where mass production is not involved: it is, after all, the true hallmark of craft industries that identical objects are *not* produced. But every artist or craftsman has certain tricks and habits which betray him to the practised eye; this is the basis for stylistic attributions in the art world. It is not, then, the overall artefact which is identical with another artefact, it is certain details of form, decoration or execution which lead to the supposition of a single origin. This does not mean, however, that wherever identical artistic motifs appear they have to be attributed to a single workshop or artistic tradition: far from it. It is obvious, though it needs stressing, that the same designs can and do appear in many different places and at many different times, without any connection between them whatsoever.

This whole problem of identity *versus* similarity will recur many times in this book, and wherever possible, attempts have been made to provide full documentation of the range of options open to craftsmen at given periods and places, and the range of solutions which they favoured. We may perhaps briefly foreshadow here some of the contentious issues, as examples of the type of problem which studies of this sort inevitably present.

Much the most famous is the supposed connection that linked the artistic conventions of Greece in the Shaft Grave period and those of Transylvania in the Early Bronze Age. Very similar motifs do indeed appear on objects in both areas, motifs that are executed in similar ways (by the use of compasses) and conform to the rules of a similar syntax. The medium on which these designs are expressed, however, is rather different in each area. What is more, the stylistic repertoire can be seen to be related to the general range of motifs available to the cultural group in question, for example on pottery. Sober consideration reveals that production by the same craftsman or men is out of the question; the problem is to assess the significance of the similarity.

Another famous group of pieces are the amber spacer-plates found in Greece, central Europe, Denmark, France and Britain. Here detailed examination of the pieces showed that both in form and in function two quite separate types of spacer were involved: one mainly found in central Europe, the other found in Britain and in Greece. In this case the material and the type of working seem so extraordinarily alike that a supposition of an identical origin is warranted. The consequences of such a notion are profound.

Finally we may look at the bronze industry of Europe in the twelfth century B.C., which provides evidence of a very different type of contact between widely separated areas. It was not that the entire bronze industry in each area became identical, but that certain forms were widely adopted. These include particularly weapons (sword, dagger, armour, spear) but also a certain number of ornament and tool types (fibula, pin, knife etc.). In the preceding centuries bronze-working traditions in Greece were *sui generis* and bore little resemblance to those of continental Europe. The same, *mutatis mutandis*, was true of other areas, such as Italy, Spain, or the Soviet Union. In the twelfth century B.C., on the other hand, the various traditions converged, and an object made in Greece is frequently not distinguishable from one made in Italy or central Europe. The reason for this is not clear; at least in the case of weapons it would seem reasonable to suppose that functionally superior forms were being copied—on the assumption, that is, that they were not invented in Greece in the first place. Where tools are concerned, a considerable degree of conservatism can be tolerated—the more monolithic the system, the greater the tolerable degree. But with weapons of war, on which the very survival of the system and society depend, the most up-to-date or at least (not necessarily the same thing) efficient system that can be afforded must be procured. It is hard to be sure to what extent the forms that the Mycenaeans did adopt in the twelfth century were actually superior, except in small details like hafting; it is by no means clear that sheet bronze body-armour, for instance, was any use at all, to judge from experimental evidence. Yet the Mycenaeans must have had good reasons for changing over to new forms of weaponry and armour, and in any case it is undisputed that the forms *are* in fact those one might term "European". It is not just a question of degrees of similarity to different objects hundreds of miles away; it is a question of a continuity of bronze-working traditions across the whole of Europe, the incorporation of Greece into a European "common market".

Chronology

Crucial to any discussion of possible links between the Aegean area and the barbarian world is the question of chronology. A prerequisite for the existence of direct links of any sort is that contemporaneity between events or processes can be demonstrated in the two areas. It does not, of course, follow that events that were contemporaneous had to be linked, but it does mean that events which were demonstrably not at least partly contemporaneous cannot have been directly linked. The problem lies in the fact that the chronologies used for the two different areas are of radically different types, and synchronisms are hard to establish.

The foundation for the absolute chronology of the Aegean Late Bronze Age was set out in detail by Furumark and others many years ago, and has been the subject of reconsideration by Hankey and Warren.[20] This is not the place to discuss the problems of Mycenaean chronology: suffice it to say that the general framework is clear enough, but the detailed attribution of phases to years B.C. is open to several sources of uncertainty. These stem partly from uncertainties in the Egyptian New Kingdom chronology (relatively minor) and partly from the lack of closely datable objects in closely datable contexts that are demonstrably close together in time: this latter is much the more serious problem.

Divisions of opinion in Egyptian New Kingdom chronology continue to abound, with no consensus yet in sight. Since discussion of these matters is quite beyond our present scope, and since the tendency is to "shorten" the New Kingdom, the lower range of dates given by Hankey and Warren are those followed here:

MM III	c. 17th to early 16th centuries
LM IA/LH I	c. 1550 ± 10–1490/80
LM IB/LH IIA	c. 1490/80–1440
LM II/LH IIB	c. 1440–1405
LM IIIA1/LH IIIA1	c. 1405–1375/70
LM IIIA2/LH IIIA2	c. 1375/70–1335/25
LM IIIB/LH IIIB	c. 1335/25–1190
LM IIIC/LH IIIC	c. 1190–?

The largest discrepancy from Furumark's chronology relates to the transition LH IIIB–C, which Furumark placed at 1230 B.C. He also put the end of LH IIIC at 1100, but the evidence for this is quite uncertain. Most authorities today put the start of Protogeometric around 1050.[21]

Although radiocarbon dates are available for some phases and areas of this period, it is at present not possible to reconcile them with the historical chronology—or, indeed, with each other. In any case, their standard deviations are considerably greater than the error factors involved in the Egyptian historical dating, and there can be no question at present but that the latter provides a more consistent framework.

The story is, of course, quite the reverse when we come to consider the barbarian world. Here there is no independent dating evidence except radio-carbon dates on which to base a judgement: such cross-dating as there is depends mostly on the Aegean and is in any case the subject of investigation of this book. It must be stated at once that the radiocarbon and traditional chronologies for central Europe (and thereby also for much of the rest of Europe) are in direct conflict. For reasons that will become apparent during the course of the book, I believe that much of the reasoning behind the traditional chronology is misguided. It is not that the radiocarbon chronology is automatically preferable so much as that the reasons for assuming certain synchronisms do not seem to me convincing. I have attempted elsewhere to show that argument is possible between the two modes of reasoning, but not on the evidence usually presented.[22] It has often been assumed, for instance, that European Br A2 should run parallel with the early Mycenaean period, on the basis of similarities between artistic motifs and productions in each area. Consideration of those similarities appears below (Chapter 7); in general they do not seem to me convincing, certainly not as convincing as other links which may be used that actually support the radiocarbon chronology.

While the status of radiocarbon calibration remains in a state of flux, no final answers to questions of radiocarbon chronology can be attained, but there can hardly be any question today of the correctness of the general principle of calibration. In the Anglo-Saxon world it tends to be forgotten that many Germans never have accepted radiocarbon dating as a viable method of dating, let alone calibrated dating. The influence of Milojčić, whose periodic fusil-lades against the advocates of radiocarbon dating in general and Renfrew in particular used to enliven the pages of *Germania*, lives on among his former students from Heidelberg, though few of them today are bold enough to attack the whole system as their master did. It is more than a little surprising in the 1980s that so many scholars in central Europe are prepared to ignore the laws of physics and stick by the subjective judgements of long tradition when it comes to matters of chronology and culture connections.

Thanks above all to a long series of dates from the stratified settlement site of the Padnal near Savognin (GR, Switzerland), the picture of the radiocarbon date bracket of the main Bronze Age periods down to Br D is reasonably clear (see p. 279).

The chronological systems in use in "barbarian" Europe can, and will, be used without absolute dates being attached to them: I return to absolute dating in Chapter 10. The system in most widespread use is that of Reinecke: developed initially for Bavaria, it has come to be applied to the whole of central Europe.[23] Reinecke first distinguished a *Bronzezeit* and a *Hallstattzeit*, and divided each into four (A–D). Subsequently, it became clear that Hallstatt C and D belong in fact to the Iron Age, while Hallstatt A and B, together with Bronze D, are commonly called the *Urnenfelderzeit* (Urnfield period). Most of the phases have now been subdivided into two or more subphases. In broad developmental terms, these phases line up as follows:

Bronze A (1, 2 and ?3)   = Early Bronze Age
                             (Únětice Culture and related)
Bronze B–C   = Middle Bronze Age
                             (Tumulus Cultures)
Bronze D, Hallstatt A (1, 2)
   Hallstatt B (1, 2, 3)   = Late Bronze Age
                             (Urnfield period)

For Hungary the system of A. Mozsolics will be used,[24] a six-fold sequence spanning the entire Bronze Age as follows:

	Phase	Bronzework	Archaeological cultures
Early Bronze Age	B. I		Nagyrév
	B. II	Komlod-Ercsi	Hatvan
	B. III a/b	Hajdúsámson / Kosziderpádlás	Füzesabony
Middle Bronze Age	B. IV a/b	Forró / Ópályi	Egyek/Piliny/ Tumulus
Late Bronze Age	B. V a/b	Aranyos / Kurd	Val I } Urnfield
	B. VI	Hajduböszörmény	Val II }

In peninsular Italy chronological divisions have usually been based on the sequence of pottery of the Apennine Culture which spans the entire earlier part of the Bronze Age. After 1200 B.C. it is replaced by material which was originally seen as being ancestral to "Villanovan" (named after the type-site, a series of Early Iron Age cemeteries near Bologna), and is thus called Protovillanovan. On Sicily and the Aeolian Islands, on the other hand, local culture names are used, and these can be placed relative to the Greek sequence by virtue of imported Mycenaean pottery in the same levels, thus:

Phase	Sicily	Aeolians	Greece
Early Bronze Age	Castelluccio	Capo Graziano	LH I–II
Middle Bronze Age	Thapsos	Milazzese	LH IIIA
Late Bronze Age	Pantalica	Ausonian I	LH IIIB–C

For northern Europe, the system developed by Montelius and modified by several other scholars is used: a six-fold division of the period, of which only Periods I, II and III affect us here.[25] Chronologies in other parts of Europe are either a series of local culture names, or rely on internal divisions quite distinct from those listed for central Europe, or else are attempts at relating one of the systems described to areas for which they were not designed. How all these systems relate to one another in terms of absolute chronology is a matter which Chapter 10 considers in more detail. Absolute dates are not given here, as they are derived from preconceptions which this book strives to abandon. Suffice it to say that traditional chronologies see a start to the Bronze Age perhaps around 1800 B.C., the Middle Bronze Age falling around the fourteenth century, and the Late Bronze Age from 1300/1250 B.C. on. In Müller-Karpe's scheme,[26] where each Urnfield phase is allotted one century (Br D = 1300–1200, Ha A1 = 1200–1100 B.C., etc.), the end of our period falls in Ha A2 in central European terms.

In view of the fact that the palace archives of Knossos and Pylos make no explicit mention of trade and traders, it might be thought that the importance to the Mycenaeans of overseas enterprise in the north and west is being over-estimated by the writing of so many articles and books, including this one, on the subject. In terms of economic importance, this is no doubt so, but the subject has loomed large over many years, colouring our view of Mycenaean foreign contacts in a very distinctive way. Whether that colouring is the right one is what we shall now be concerned to investigate.

Notes

1. The information in this paragraph comes from C. W. Beck, *Archaeology* **23/1,** 1970, 7–11.

1a. As for example with the alleged Balkan imports into Middle Helladic Greece, or the distribution of pottery claimed to be "Minyan" (Kilian, 1976, Abb. 4); I. Strøm, in Best and de Vries (1980, pp. 116, 122 n.15 with refs); cf. Dickinson (1977, pp. 36–37) for a suitably cautious view.

2. Beck and Stone (1936, pp. 203).

3. J. Naue, *Die vorrömischen Schwerter aus Kupfer, Bronze und Eisen*, 1903 (Munich, Piloty and Loehle).

4. Schmidt (1904).

5. H. Mötefindt, *Arch. Anzeiger* **1,** 1912, 99–103.

6. Beck and Stone (1936); Piggott (1938); G. von Merhart, *Germania* **24,** 1940, 99–102.

7. Gerloff (1975).

8. For example, O. Montelius, *Die typologische Methode. Die älteren Kul-turperioden im Orient und im Europa*, 1903 (Stockholm/Berlin, K. L. Beckman); N. Åberg, *Bronzezeitliche und früheisenzeitliche Chronologie*, 1930–1935 (Stockholm, Verlag der Akademie).

9. Childe (1927); *Amer. J. Arch.* **43,** 1939, 10–26.

10. V. Dumitrescu, *Dacia* **5–6,** 1935–6, 169–173.

11. J. M. de Navarro, *Geographical J.* **67,** 1925, 481–504.

12. C. F. C. Hawkes, *BSA* **37**, 1936–7, 141–159.

13. Heurtley (1939).

14. These studies are referenced in the appropriate part of the text.

15. Gerloff (1975); Aner and Kersten (1973–9).

16. Werner (1952).

17. Bouzek (1966); Piggott (1966).

18. K. Branigan, *Wilts. Arch. Mag.* **65**, 1970, 89–107; *Proc. Prehist. Soc.* **38**, 1972, 276–285; *Studi Micenei ed Egeo-Anatolici* **15**, 1972, 147–56.

19. Vladár (1973) and other similar articles.

20. Hankey and Warren (1974). I thank Dr W. J. Tait for helpful advice on Egyptian chronology.

21. For example, Snodgrass (1971, Ch. 3). Since Furumark's day the concept of a "Submycenaean" phase has gone out of fashion; some scholars urge that it should be abandoned (e.g. J. Rutter, *Temple University Aegean Symposium* **3**, 1978, 58–65).

22. Harding (1980).

23. P. Reinecke, *Germania* **8**, 1924, 43–4; Coles and Harding (1979, 24ff., 102–103n).

24. Coles and Harding (1979, p. 70, 108n.) for résumé.

25. Coles and Harding (1979, pp. 278–279).

26. Müller-Karpe (1959).

Approaches to prehistoric trade

Material culture and the archaeological evidence for trade

Since prehistoric archaeologists mainly have to deal with material culture remains, it is important to understand clearly the significance of those remains for the reconstruction of the past. Traditionally, heavy reliance is placed upon the precise form of artefacts, their exact find-spots, and the relation of form and find-spots to those of other comparable examples. Artefacts have been seen as characteristic of production traditions, and those traditions, the sum of which is usually called "culture", as distinctive of particular human groupings. This leads to a situation where the intervening steps in the argument are omitted and particular artefacts are taken as uniquely characteristic of particular human groupings: to the concept of "Beaker people", for instance. Where artefact distributions appear to correspond geographically to known or assumed tribal or ethnic groups, the name of the tribe or "people" is commonly assigned to the artefacts, thus "Illyrian", "Dacian" or "Mycenaean". The extent to which such correlations are justified depends on two aspects of artefactual material: its analytical characterization and its role in society as known from studied examples.

Analytical characterization

The simplest and most persuasive type of evidence, because objectively based, is that relating to the composition of materials or artefacts. A prime goal in recent artefact studies has been the analytical characterization of the objects. Such physical analysis, combined with typological study, has put such studies on a much more secure footing than hitherto, though it must be emphasized that suitable methods are not always available, or helpful.

17

A wide array of techniques is now available for characterizing the composition of materials. These techniques have worked best for unmodified raw materials, notably stone; the obsidian trade is an obvious example. Metals have proved less tractable, because of the changes they undergo during working; little certainty attaches to published claims for correlation between ore bodies and artefacts, though the recently developed lead isotope technique seems very promising. A considerable number of methods have been used for characterizing fabrics and clay types of pottery—these have led in some cases to unequivocal answers to questions about provenance and manufacture.

A decision in each case about whether a given composition pattern fits a particular source will usually rest on a number of factors, mostly statistical in nature. A prime consideration is the number and range of samples already tested. Especially in the early stages of an analytical investigation this has tended to be a stumbling-block: there is little use assigning an object to a particular source unless all potential sources have also been tested. Methods of comparing compositions vary. The student of prehistoric trade should be able to have access to the figures used as the basis for given attributions and an independent assessment attempted. On the whole, though, he now finds himself in a good position to discern which materials were in fact moved about in prehistory, though it is sometimes more difficult to decide whether human or natural agencies were responsible.

A raw material of particular importance in the period under review is amber. A variety of techniques have been used to characterize it, notably infra-red spectroscopy. Though opinions on the validity of analyses by this technique vary, it has provided numerous results that many people find credible. Analyses of Mycenaean ceramics outside Greece have been carried out relatively recently and most are not yet published; in the Levant and Cyprus, however, distinct composition patterns have been discerned and, in some cases, correlated with Greek sources. The situation with metals is uncertain. For the Bronze Age Mediterranean many analyses relate to finished artefacts, notably of the Early and Middle periods, but few to the Late Bronze Age. An exception is the ox-hide ingots which, however, metal analysis has so far signally failed to assign to particular ore sources—even as between, say, Sardinia, Greece and Cyprus. There are hopeful signs, though, that this situation may soon be resolved. Other materials, whether artificial like faience and glass, or natural like obsidian, have also been characterized, with varying degrees of success. We shall return to some of these problems in later chapters.

Unfortunately, several of the categories of evidence to be treated hereafter are not susceptible of treatment by such means. Chief among these are such matters as artistic techniques and influences, which relate to purely personal evaluations. Metal objects are also hard to treat by physical analysis, if only because by the Late Bronze Age the metal stock was probably mixed: it also seems to have derived from a large number of sources, large and small.

All these aspects of material culture can, however, be taken into account by the "anthropological archaeologist", for whom the objects which make up a population's material culture can be treated on several different levels. Such analysis has most commonly been on a simple empirical level, typically in modern situations believed to be structurally or technologically similar to the ancient ones that are the real centre of interest for archaeologists. In such cases, artefact distributions may be studied, to see how far they correlate with known geographical, ethnic or linguistic boundaries, or how their fall-off pattern reflects the social and economic conditions under which they were produced and put into circulation. The analysis has also extended, however, to the conceptual level, considering artefacts within a structural framework within which they operated as conscious or unconscious symbols, reflecting mental and behavioural states in their creators. In its extreme form this approach may resemble "palaeopsychology", against which L. R. Binford has eloquently warned us; but few would deny that artefact variability, as one of the principal problems facing archaeologists, must reflect—however weakly—behavioural patterns that can be approached both on a structural and on other levels.

The role of artefacts

Any artefact type can be examined from this point of view but pottery is especially interesting because of its ubiquitous occurrence in both archaeological and ethnographic situations, and because of the infinite variability of form, scale and fabric with which it can occur. As a result, great importance is attached by archaeologists to the study of ceramics, for the drawing of chronological, economic and "cultural" inferences. Pottery is regularly used as an indicator of chronological scale, but also of cultural and, therefore, ethnic and linguistic affinity, especially if geographically it appears to fall in the region of known historical groupings. This usage is, of course, quite different from, for example, "Attic" pottery which is defined as a technical and geographical type, whose place of manufacture is known, and which has no overtones of racial affinity. More often a class of pottery is named after the site or region where it was first identified, occurs most frequently, or is known to have been manufactured (e.g. New Forest Ware, Stamford Ware), but it is still commonly regarded in these cases as possessing a diagnostic value for determining who, in terms of ethnic, social or religious background, its makers were.

The discussion is far from being merely academic but bears directly and profoundly on many aspects of archaeological interpretation. Most traditional archaeology is written on the basis of assumptions such as these; that of the Aegean Bronze Age is no exception. We talk of "Mycenaean pottery", and mean by it a group of ceramic styles and fabrics of well known and defined type that occur on sites of the Late Bronze Age, mainly in the central and southern Aegean; because it is generally believed that the inhabitants of Greece at this period spoke Greek, we come to believe that the pottery is characteristic not merely of the Late Bronze Age material culture of Greece but actually of an ethnic and linguistic group, the "Mycenaean Greeks". Wherever it appears outside its "home area" it has then been assumed to represent the presence, in some form, of those same Greeks on foreign soil. But quite apart from the difficulty of defining what is meant by "home area" it is obvious that all one can really say about "Mycenaean" pottery is that it is a primary characteristic of the material culture of Greece in the Late Bronze Age. In itself it says nothing about the ethnic or linguistic affinities of its makers or users, and cannot be used as *prima facie* evidence for "Greeks" in non-Greek lands. This view contrasts markedly with the tacit assumption, adopted in most writings on the subject, that Mycenaean pottery is indicative of a unique culture and ethnic origin.

The further problem arises that under the term "Mycenaean pottery" are included a range of ceramic types, of which the characteristic painted wares only represent the fine end of the spectrum. Usually, however, it is these fine wares that were exported; the coarser wares for cooking and storage served domestic functions and had nothing to do with commercial activities. If one assumes, however, that there is a correlation between the geographical spread of material culture and socio-political units, then the presence or absence of the full range of ceramics is crucial. The significance of this point will be seen when we come to consider the question of "colonization" and the northern "border" of Mycenaean culture.

There are thus both positive and negative aspects of pottery distribution when correlations with human groupings are sought. Other aspects of pottery analysis also demand consideration. The sociology and economics of pottery production require a more sophisticated approach to the problem. Unfortunately such an approach has been applied only recently and there is no store of relevant literature yet available; nor can precisely comparable economic and political situations be found among present-day communities. Nevertheless, what is available suggests that pots are much more subtle in their information content than mere typological sequences would allow.

What evidence is there that pottery form is directly related to the affinity of either potter or user on group or ethnic level? Many studies of modern societies have shown that villages and even individual potters may produce distinctive pottery; this parallels, though it does not account for, ceramic variability through space in the archaeological record. Such variability may be derived from "microtraditions",[1] or from whim, or pure invention; equally, the nature of the "relations of production" and the method of reward for the labour undertaken, that is the socio-economic context, seem to be very important.

Studies of this topic in ethnographic contexts have produced markedly divergent results. One study, of a Fulani village in North Cameroon,[2] identified ten potters among the 113 adult women of Bé: seven of them were Fulani, two Gisiga and one Lame. (The majority of the Fulani pottery was utilitarian in nature, whereas the Lame potter was more accomplished.) Comparison of the cultural affinities of pots and inhabitants revealed that the latter were divided solely between Fulani (75%) and Gisiga (25%), whereas the 290 pots in the village broke down into 78.3% Fulani, 7.2% Gisiga, and 14.5% "other"—that is 42 pots of different cultural origin, mostly acquired either from visitors or from potters in outlying hamlets. Small-scale immigration, for instance of Gisiga women in marriage, has also broken the "normal chain of supply and demand", causing "temporary disruption in the relationship between material culture and total culture". The implications of this study appear to be that pottery styles and tribal affinities are closely linked, though a sizeable element of the pottery cannot be so correlated.

Other studies in the Baringo district of western Kenya[3] showed that some artefact distributions show clear boundaries, while others do not. Thus decoration on calabashes, which is the only element relating to home production, does not conform to social boundaries known to exist on linguistic and other grounds, but certain pot types do. Reasons for the latter are stated to include the strong pressures to conform, social competition and strain, leading to the stressing of distinct boundaries, and the symbolic value of certain items. Mass-produced items from outside the region, on the other hand, show no tribal correlation but occur in all the tribal areas. This situation is much more like that studied among the Lozi of Zambia, where a weakly-developed market system combines with a non-competitive socio-economic organization to produce lack of material distinguishability among different tribes of the same grouping.[4]

Analysis of American ethnographic data[5] produced similarly diametrically opposed results for correlation between language and material culture. On the one hand, study of cultural elements in a Yurok tribe in north-west California showed that tribes of different language shared in those elements as much as other tribes of the same language (including a confederate Yurok tribe); on the other, 20 Apache and Pueblo tribes showed a clear patterning of material culture, with a definite fall-off of culture elements from a core area where a common language was spoken.

A recent review article has listed many of the traditional approaches to the problem—usually speculative rather than based on any actual evidence—and indeed suggested various lines of enquiry which modern investigations render possible.[6] Such investigations relate not only to the behavioural meaning of pottery but also to technical factors: the discrepancy between the technical quality of the pottery and the degree of elaboration of its surface, for instance. Frequently the pottery that is technically best is artistically the least interesting and most stylized, whereas cruder wares may be treated to a much more elaborate and time-consuming process of surface decoration. This creates a situation where, to quote Hélène Balfet, the routine of the specialist leads to a "freedom from technical awareness", while at the domestic level of manufacture flexibility of functional and aesthetic adaptation is preserved, so that each object is a direct response to the needs and taste of its user.[7]

It is widely recognized that pottery production takes place in a number of different socio-economic contexts. Most authorities distinguish between the household or domestic context of production, the community context, and the regional context; or between unspecialized production for household needs, semi-specialized production by part-time specialists, often home-based, and fully specialized production by full-time specialists working in workshops solely used for that purpose.[8]

The nature of the clientele is also of crucial importance. Pottery made for use in one's own house does not *need* to show any special elaboration, certainly by comparison with that made for market sale. The presence of a market is widely reported to add flexibility to otherwise very constrained production incentives, as with the Indian contract system.[9] On the other hand it may also introduce selective pressures towards the creation of saleable pots—even tourist wares— which bear little relation to traditional pottery production. Even where markets are present, everyday pottery is widely found to be cheap and limited in distribution, with the result that potters are frequently poor, or of low status, or both.

Another artisan whose products are used by archaeologists as especially diagnostic of particular areas and periods is the bronzesmith, but such studies as have been carried out show that no one pattern of status or mode of operation is discernible.[10] The value of bronze goods for warfare, agriculture, daily life and religion suggests, however, that such goods could cross ethnic and language boundaries without difficulty. Typology of bronzes can be considered more likely to relate to workshop production ("industrial organization") than to any group affinity of their users, reflecting the work of different individuals or schools and the degree of contact between them.[11] Diametrically opposed to this view is the assertion that differences in the form of a metal type reflect symbolic distinctions which may be more or less stressed according to the degree of inter-group "conflict" involved.[12] The data on which this conclusion was based were admittedly puzzling: a study of Baringo iron spears showed that the products of different smiths were virtually identical, while the spatial patterning of spears of different origin tended to show group preference for the products of a particular maker. This study demonstrates elegantly the amount of information which metalwork typologies and distributions may reflect, but it makes the drawing of conclusions about metalwork in the ancient world almost impossible. Besides, though symbolic information may be contained in every aspect of behaviour, including artefacts, this approach takes too little account of large-scale production techniques such as became the norm during the Bronze Age, notably with the development of mould technology. This effectively meant that identical objects could be turned out to any desired quantity, so that while the original inspiration for axe types may have symbolic aspects, the distribution of axes that are demonstrably of identical origin (cf. Flanagan's "mould matrix analysis")[13] must relate to the location and mode of operation of the workshop involved, and the nature of the distribution mechanisms.

Most ethnographic studies of the correlation between artefacts and human populations have been concerned with tribal units of limited size. On the other hand, the nature of artefact distribution in the modern world clearly reflects commercial and political factors, not any aspect of language, race or group affinity. Neither type of society is an apt analogy for Late Bronze Age Greece, which appears to have incorporated political groupings much larger than tribe size, but smaller than state size; these notions are supported too by consideration of the internal organization of the presumptive "kingdoms" involved.

It is thus not easy to say which, if any, of the available sets of ethnographic data fits the Bronze Age situation best. Pottery production in Bronze Age Greece was clearly the result of full-time specialist activity, to judge from its technical competence and (as discussed above) its stylistic homogeneity or lack of adventurousness. On the socio-economic level, it would appear that production was either on a village workshop level or part of a centralized production system. Either way, mass production to high standards was pursued. Formal markets did not exist; production was therefore aimed at satisfying local needs or directed specifically towards the satisfaction of the requirements of central sites, such as palaces, perhaps by a contract system. The widespread homogeneity of Mycenaean pottery can perhaps most reasonably be seen to relate to the situation seen among the Lozi or the Hopi, where material culture is indistinguishable between tribes that have maintained different languages, religions and ceremonial patterns for hundreds of years. An interesting observation, made recently by Dr S. Sherratt, is that the Mycenaean pottery exported from Greece to both East and West appears to include a number of forms made especially for export to satisfy those "markets".[14] This may represent an example of the specific adaptation of artefact form under economic pressures to a specific supply and demand situation.

For the "barbarian" world, on the other hand, tribal organization is likely and the ethnographic examples studied more relevant, even though they are inconclusive. Virtually every study has made clear that even where a correlation between material culture and ethnic or linguistic groupings has been discerned, artefact types are by no means restricted to the areas in question, so that group boundaries are hard to discern by means of artefact distributions alone. Much discussion has taken place concerning methods by which such boundaries in artefact distributions can be distinguished.[15]

The analysis of ancient and primitive economies

Much has been written on the role of trade and exchange in relation to the development of forms of social and economic organization. Part of the discussion has been purely theoretical, and concerned, for instance, with the relevance of modern economic theory to "primitive" economies (the formalist-substantivist debate), while part has been concerned with the development of particular kinds of trading activity in "precolonial" situations. Relatively few authors have attempted to relate theoretical and anthropological perspectives directly to ancient trade, especially trade detectable only by means of archaeology.[16]

The standard approach by archaeologists to ancient trade has viewed it in modern commercial terms as a mechanism for the acquisition of desired goods by the provision of other goods, surplus to requirements. Little attention has been paid to the social or economic framework of such exchange, or its effects, though for Childe at least[17] trade served as a means of adaptation and change. In particular, he concerned himself with the nature of surpluses and their means of distribution through the system, though he did not attempt any detailed analysis of their socio-economic context. Adams has aptly termed the period of such traditional approaches the "era of impressionism in archaeological studies of trade and diffusion".[18]

Apart from approaches like these, which have been numerically preponderant, two main traditions have been influential in approaches to ancient and primitive trade. The first is Marxism. Since this approach is based on a view of the economy that is concerned essentially with the means and relations of production rather than with trade as an adaptive force, it is not surprising that this school of thought focuses on generalized aspects of trade within productive systems, treating its social ramifications as an integral part of the examination of the relations of production. Marx himself said:

> In the ancient world, the effect of commerce and the development of merchant capital always resulted in a slave economy . . . [or] in the [simple] transformation of a patriarchal slave system devoted to the production of immediate means of subsistence into one devoted to the production of surplus value.[19]

The other aspect of Marx's thought which directly concerned "archaeology" was his adoption of the concept of the "Asiatic mode of production". In Marx himself, and in Engels as well, these matters were not taken very far: hardly surprising in view of the state of archaeology at the time. Since the Second World War Marxist archaeologists have attempted to apply the principles of Marxist thought to archaeology, but some of the results have been crude, to say the least,[20] resulting in the shouting of empty slogans with little or no attempt to relate them to archaeology. Much more subtle and profitable are the approaches of the French neo-Marxist anthropologists, notably Maurice Godelier and Claude Meillassoux. Godelier, for example, has set the works of Marx and Engels in their historical perspective, finding their basic approach helpful still.[21] He views such matters as "surpluses" in terms of development in the productive forces: "social competition in class societies provides the major incentive to surplus production and, in the long term, leads indirectly to progress in productive forces", while recognizing that "surplus is destined partly for consumption by the ruling class (a consumption which takes markedly sumptuary forms) and partly for enterprises of collective interest, real or imaginary". Godelier asks such questions as "How is it that, in addition to inequality in the redistribution of the social product, there is an inequality in the control of the factors of production?", and takes their very existence as justifying Marx's thesis that "social inequality protects the collective interests of primitive communities and is an essential factor in their progress".

Meillassoux[22] has examined the question of "relations with a complementary economy" on the part of "community societies", distinguishing, on the basis of African examples, various types of resultant phenomena. Within such societies, which are in subsistence terms self-sufficient, the circulation of goods is carried on by the mechanisms of prestation and redistribution. When such a society comes into contact with another one possessing a desirable commodity it does not possess itself such as a metal like iron, Meillassoux predicts that it will take steps to protect the self-sustaining nature of its economy, which its social organization depends on. Valuables that are introduced are then fitted into the internal circulation mechanisms, becoming élite goods (Fig. 2). This leads to the situation where goods produced locally by the "juniors", i.e. non-élites, and having no value within the traditional circulation system, may acquire it when they can be converted by exchange into other commodities. If the metal is offered for exchange in the form of "low-value ingots", foodstuffs may even be an adequate exchange so that juniors too will have access to the exchange process, enabling them to acquire goods formerly indicative of high social status. This may result in various social mechanisms to preserve the status quo: class or caste prohibitions, for example.

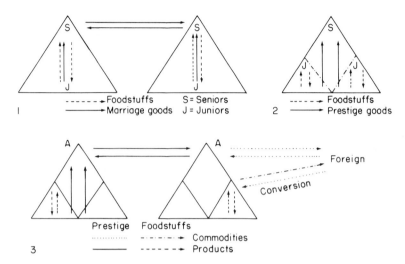

FIG. 2 ☐ Models for the circulation of foodstuffs, marriage goods and prestige goods within and between communities, according to Meillassoux (in Seddon, 1978). (1) Handling of goods associated with the rank of the person handling them. (2) Decentralization of control of staple goods, e.g. grain. (3) Conversion of ordinary goods into élite goods, e.g. by juniors with free access to foodstuffs, with entry into the community economy of goods exchanged between communities.

A final aspect of the Marxist approach to the economies of primitive societies which concerns us particularly here is the concept of the "Asiatic mode of production", originally developed by Marx and Engels and readapted and considerably refined by Godelier.[23] According to this approach, within primitive communities ownership of land is communal and organized on kinship lines, while state power, as the expression of the unity of these communities, controls the use of economic resources and appropriates part of the labour and production of the communities within it. This, for Marx, was one of the possible routes to class societies and states, and emerges when

> more developed forms of production allow a regular surplus, which is the condition for a more complex division of labour and for the separation of agriculture from manufacture . . . the existence of a surplus makes a more elaborate social differentiation possible and allows the emergence of a minority of individuals who appropriate a share of this surplus and thus exploit the other members of the community.

Projects involving large-scale cooperation, such as the great "hydraulic" projects of Egypt and Mesopotamia, would therefore offer scope for such exploitation via the need for decision-making and a central authority. The contradictory elements in such a model (community structures but an exploiting class, simultaneously a classless and a class society) are, allegedly, part of its attraction, and Godelier has related to this mode of production Creto-Mycenaean and Etruscan "monarchies", Black African Kingdoms, and pre-Columbian American states.

Marxist and neo-Marxist approaches to ancient and primitive economies thus lay stress above all on the concepts of labour and value within the framework of the relations of production. The role of primitive trade is specifically seen as a means of effecting alterations in the relationship between producers and consumers, and specifically leading to the formation of élites who achieved or consolidated pre-eminent status by means of great communal enterprises. In some respects such notions come close to the views held by modern anthropologists of very different political persuasions.

The other main tradition concerned with the nature of pre-market economies is Polanyi's substantivist viewpoint whereby economic activity is to a greater or lesser extent "embedded" in social relations.[24] In the absence of any clear indication about the way in which trade was carried out in the European and Aegean Bronze Age views on this matter must remain speculative, in marked distinction to Polanyi's own work which was based on historical and ethnographic sources, and for which the Ancient Near Eastern records were sufficient for arguments one way or the other to be fruitful. This is hardly the case in Europe. In Greece, a discussion of the social set-up discernible in the Linear B records might be helpful to an understanding of the framework within which trading occurred, but these matters are so disputed, and the indications of the texts so unclear, that such an exercise has no place here.

An economy such as that of Bronze Age Europe would today be labelled "primitive". Typical of such economies are the absence of market exchange, the "pervasive social control of production and distribution and the guarantee of subsistence livelihood through resource allocation and social right to receive aid in time of need".[25] Mycenaean Greece, on the other hand, with its evident lack of both money and markets, would probably qualify as an "archaic" economy in Polanyi's sense, the characteristic features of which are absent in primitive, kinship-organized societies and disappear with the widespread use of money.[26] Such features include voluntary communal work teams, "antichretic pledges", "status trading", and ports of trade—the last-named an important device, according to the Polanyi school, whereby traders could meet on politically neutral ground to carry on exchanges of interest and importance to adjacent, or distant, political units. Such places were often, but not always, on or near the sea, within easy reach of inland states and with very little territory of their own. Ports of trade in this sense have been discerned both in pre-colonial Africa, and, more important for our purposes, in the Eastern Mediterranean in sites like Ugarit and Al Mina.

The substantivist school distinguishes a number of different types of exchange.[27] Broadly, the distinction has been made between reciprocal exchange, redistribution, and market exchange. Reciprocal exchange, which Sahlins[28] has subdivided into generalized, balanced, and negative reciprocity, has been defined as "obligatory gift- and counter-gift-giving between persons who stand in some socially defined relationship to one another";[29] it includes all types of hospitality and kinship dues, ceremonial gift exchange, marriage transactions, as well as more strictly "economic" activities like barter and haggling. Redistribution entails

> obligatory payments of material items, money objects, or labour services to some socially recognized centre, usually king, chief or priest, who reallocates portions of what he receives to provide community services . . . and to reward specific persons.[30]

Market exchange, that is market exchange in "indigenous" or "aboriginal" communities (i.e. not in developed, "modern" economies), involves the socially neutral exchange of goods, usually for "economic" motives; it may involve the exchange of goods of the same or different kinds from surpluses accumulated at various levels of production, or it may involve money—"special-purpose money" in Polanyi's terminology, or "primitive money" in Dalton's—and prices—"equivalencies" in the substantivist jargon. It may be said immediately that there is no evidence for the use of market exchange in Bronze Age Europe, and even in the Ancient Near East, where trading was an old-established and important activity, the mechanisms developed seem to have relied rather on specialized forms of reciprocal exchange and redistribution than on the use of markets. A structure illustrating different levels and sectors within a primitive economy may be seen in Fig. 3.

Anthropologists of all persuasions, but especially the substantivists, have found the study of the development of trading links between widely separated areas which were subsequently brought into a "colonial" relationship, in Africa, for instance, useful. "Precolonial" trade in Africa has widely been regarded as offering useful analogies with Early Iron Age trade between the Mediterranean and the "barbarian" world during the period of Greek contact. Its lessons for the Bronze Age world are also potentially wide-ranging, though it is less easy to demonstrate their applicability. Two commodities above all, slaves and salt, were of crucial importance in African trading systems, though other minerals (copper, gold) were also vital. The slave trade, in particular, produced social and economic reactions of a very marked character: a "subtraction from the production of the agricultural communities, besides being an important cause of their disintegration";[31] it also led to political domination by those who conducted the trade. "In exchange for

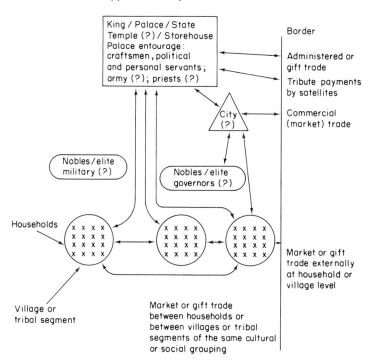

FIG. 3 ☐ Different levels and sectors within a "primitive economy", according to Dalton (1975).

slaves Europeans furnished primarily fire-arms and luxury goods which only benefitted this military aristocracy".[32] In the interior, on the other hand,

> trade was primarily based on goods produced by local peasants, since agricultural and craft products constituted the major part of the traffic. In return, internal commerce provided a commodity of great value—salt—which could be easily sold retail. The internal trade assured the complementarity of interregional exchanges and provided the peasant economies with labouring slaves who were to become the main productive agents of this interior commerce.[33]

Slavery came to rest, therefore, partly on trade and partly on aggression for ensuring its continuance. In Dahomey, by contrast, external trade was under the control of the king and his officials, and slaves came to be used in local palm plantations instead of exported, while at the same time old privileges were preserved by and for the ruling class "by taking over the new means of production and setting them to work for their benefit".[34]

A further product of trade, particularly trade in slaves, was the development of a military aristocracy, often of "foreign" origins but usually forming a distinct class, separated both socially and economically from the indigenous peasant groups. It depended for its survival on control of arms, whether by plunder or trade; only by pursuing warfare could it continue to exist.[35] Trade in other commodities, however, particularly trade in non-local commodities (i.e. those which do not compete with local goods and introduce an external value element into the local economy), favour the growth of specialist classes whose activities are related mainly to the movement of those goods, i.e. merchant classes. At the same time, in some situations trading expeditions could be carried out by the peasants themselves, procuring goods for their own use; such expeditions are "subordinate to the requirement of agricultural work. They are usually carried on in the dry season and therefore are limited in time since the participants must return before the beginning of the new farming season".[36] Even without the use of money commerce aims at maximizing returns on exchange operations—selling and buying at the most favourable times and places. The requirements of time, and of organization over large distances, mean that trading would naturally become a full-time pursuit. Traders need to exist in distant, usually alien, communities, and be separate economically, and hence socially, from the indigenous groups. In some cases, however, where trade and administration became closely linked, the barriers between trader and the rest of society became broken down, particularly where trading was open to all as in Ashanti.[37]

Trading patterns in the pre-colonial African context have also been set within other frameworks: geographical or economic, for example. A distinction between village and regional trade is possible at one level,[38] but more useful is Gray and Birmingham's distinction between an earlier "subsistence-oriented" trade and a "market-oriented" trade.[39] In the former,

> the exchange of goods makes virtually no impact on the subsistence economy nor does it generate a wide range of activities divorced from supplying the basic needs of subsistence agriculture . . . the significance of the exchange transaction remains intimately dependent on the social status of the parties concerned.

By contrast, in the latter,

> trade freed itself from these subsistence and kinship shackles, and . . . began to create a number of far-reaching economic innovations directly dependent on commercial opportunities . . . market-oriented trade . . . by itself generated new forms of wealth: a whole range of goods (e.g. ivory, slaves, cattle, wax) acquired new economic values which they did not possess in the subsistence economy. . . . Market-oriented, professional trade did not, however, produce in the pre-colonial period an economy integrated by the market principle. Most Africans continued to depend for their livelihood primarily on subsistence agriculture, and the production of vital foodstuffs was only very marginally affected by market demands.[40]

Trade at a subsistence level is exemplified, according to Gray and Birmingham, by Tonga trade,[41] where a variety of imported and indigenous items were exchanged over considerable distances within a defined network; yet the trade remained "geared to the subsistence economy", and had little impact on the socio-economic structure of society. A change from subsistence to market-oriented exchange is, according to Gray and Birmingham, to be seen in Lozi trade, which started off within a framework of redistribution or kinship exchange, and developed, with the arrival of large supplies of overseas products, notably cloth and arms, to a market-oriented system in which specialist traders by-passed the royal clearing-houses in the search for personal profit. It is argued, however, that long-distance trade was not a prerequisite for the rise of market-oriented economies, since the latter apparently sometimes developed without it.

The consequences of trade in a subsistence framework represent another of Gray and Birmingham's preoccupations. Its importance as a medium of communication suggests also to Fagan that technological advances may have proceeded along pre-existing trade routes.[42] The creation of a consumer demand for traded commodities brought about a range of possible implications, such as the ability to store wealth in realizable form more easily. Though this led to the accumulation of wealth in the hands of the few, political leadership appears to have played a very restricted role in the development of trade, supporting services usually being supplied by the traders themselves. Yet it is undeniable that many of the early African states owed their existence to the early development of trading networks. Especially in the case of mineral resources—in the African context salt and copper—proprietorial rights seem to have been established early and protected, often within the framework of state formation. The exploitation of animal and vegetable resources, on the other hand, was probably more a matter for variable activity over space and time (ivory, wax, rubber). Yet it was the slave trade above all which, according to Gray and Birmingham, enabled élites to acquire their positions as hoarders both of tangible wealth and temporal sway.

This discussion of models of trade and the examination of trade in the pre-colonial African context indicates that the role of trade as an adaptive force cannot be underestimated, particularly as far as the transformation of economies from "embedded" to "market-oriented" is concerned. Renfrew[43] has made some use of these approaches, drawing particularly on the concepts of reciprocity and redistribution (which he sees developing in the Early Bronze Age) to explain developments in Aegean exchange activity, and hence the diffusion of ideas within the area—trade serving as a means of innovation, and a variety of factors favouring the growth of trade. To a lesser extent some of these concepts have also been used by prehistorians of the Rome school, who have adapted generalized models of socio-economic structure to the case of Mycenaean external trade (Fig. 4).[44] It seems worth recording in passing that the function of redistribution in chiefdoms particularly has been called into question in recent years.[45]

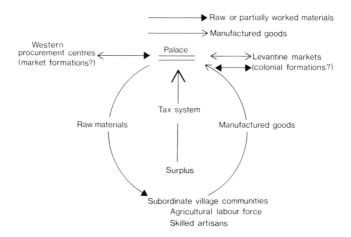

FIG. 4 ☐ Model of socio-economic structure in the Mycenaean palace system, according to Marazzi and Tusa (1979).

Trade in the archaeological record

While it is reasonable to suppose that trade between Bronze Age societies was of a reciprocal or redistributive nature, this in itself says little or nothing about the nature of archaeological configurations which would reflect such a situation. The worker who has concerned himself specifically with this topic is Renfrew, who has distinguished the following types of archaeological model for trade:[46]

    (a) down-the-line exchange
    (b) prestige-chain exchange
    (c) freelance commercial exchange
    (d) directional commercial exchange

A later article[47] attempted additions and refinements of these types of exchange within a substantivist framework (Fig. 5). In addition, Renfrew has distinguished "zones" within distributions: the "supply zone", where the user of a commodity is in direct access to a supply, commonly a short journey away; and the "contact zone", where goods are worth exchanging over much greater distances. Naturally, the latter is the more common type of distribution; the former is mainly found with very common materials or bulky items.

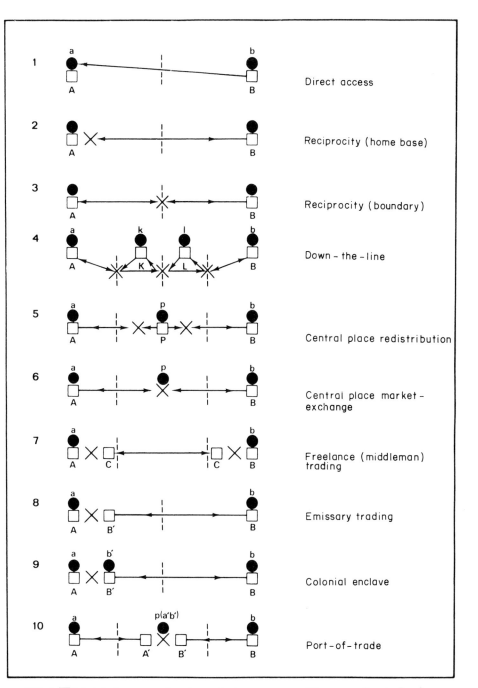

1		Direct access
2		Reciprocity (home base)
3		Reciprocity (boundary)
4		Down - the - line
5		Central place redistribution
6		Central place market - exchange
7		Freelance (middleman) trading
8		Emissary trading
9		Colonial enclave
10		Port - of - trade

FIG. 5 ☐ Models for types of exchange between communities, according to Renfrew (1975).

Renfrew has specifically mentioned several of the aspects of Mycenaean trade with which we shall be concerned in this book as falling in one or other of his categories. The amber trade he cites as an example of the prestige chain, early Mycenaean (and Late Minoan) trade as an example of freelance trade, and several aspects of later Mycenaean trade (LH III pottery at Scoglio del Tonno, Cypriot bronze ingots in Crete) as exemplifying directional trade. We shall have more to say about this in due course.

The potential of the archaeological record for identifying trade has been the subject of intensive investigation in recent years, but this is not the place to review such work.[48] The information latent in distributions of artefacts relates to a variety of processes, which ensure that the structure of the record is extremely complex. One aspect which can profitably be considered here, however, is the socio-economic structure of the Bronze Age societies we are concerned with: to this background to Bronze Age trade we now turn.

The background to trade in Bronze Age economy and society

Greece in the Late Bronze Age possessed a type and structure of society that did not to our knowledge exist elsewhere in Europe. It was more akin to societies, or at any rate economies, in the Near East than anywhere else. It is possible to say this on the basis of more than just material culture: the evidence of the Linear B archives fills out the bare bones of site and artefact-based archaeology on matters that would otherwise depend solely on speculation. Though there are naturally problems in reconciling the evidence from the two disparate sources, the combination of the two seems to give a good idea of the basic facets of Mycenaean life.

The evidence of buildings, graves and artefacts clearly indicates differential access to wealth of a most pronounced kind: graves of extraordinary richness (more at the start of the period), large-scale rectilinear agglomerative buildings reasonably interpreted as palaces, prestige objects that encapsulate rare materials and high-quality workmanship. The prevalence of weapons, at least on the mainland, gives an idea of the ways in which the powerful maintained, if not acquired, their prestige. But it is the tablets which bring home beyond all doubt the deep social divisions present in society, even if the precise nature of the offices and ranks recorded is not understood: the *wanax*, *lawagetas* and *heqetai*, the craftsmen and landholders, workers and slaves. More important for our understanding of the economic situation is the evidence for craft specialization and administrative functions. The richness and variety of Mycenaean material culture make it abundantly obvious that skilful and versatile craftsmen were on hand to produce the masterpieces in bronze, gold, faience, stone, ivory and other materials that are found in the Mycenaean world. But the population of Bronze Age Greece was probably large, and it was no doubt preeminently agricultural pursuits that occupied many in it. There must also have been masons and stone-carvers, mud-brick manufacturers, spinners and weavers, potters, fresco-painters, and many others. The tablets talk of some of these, and others whose existence could not be deduced from archaeology alone. They also make clear that although individuals were regarded as craftsmen in a particular field (e.g. smiths), they were also capable of owning—and therefore presumably working—land and being taxed, perhaps by virtue of that very ownership. The existence of an administrative set-up is also apparent: the tablets speak of the *korete* and *pokorete*, the *klawiphoros*, *moroqa* and *telestai*, who apparently range from regional governors to large landholders with only honorific functions. The very existence and subject-matter of the tablets implies, of course, several further occupations: scribes, accountants, quartermasters, tax-collectors and the like, no doubt controlled by palace officials who would assess tax liability, distribution needs and the palace requirements, and oversee the execution of the whole operation.

Rather more tenuous is the nature of Greek internal politics in the Late Bronze Age. Convincing reasons have been advanced for regarding Greece as having been divided up into provinces, roughly corresponding to those of the classical period (or the present-day), each controlled centrally by a major site, in some cases a palace. The relation of each province to the others is quite unknown, though the Homeric poems put Agamemnon, and therefore Mycenae, in a position of supremacy. In Homer, the Greeks are bound by not only a common language, but also by many ties of kinship, marriage and status obligation as well as by a common material culture (in so far as such things are recorded by the poet). It is clear that anyone from the Greek mainland or islands was regarded as a Greek; but even such near neighbours as Trojans were something different. Little idea can, however, be gleaned from Homer and other such sources about the nature of the Greek attitude to the "barbarian" world, which seems, indeed, to have lain beyond the ken of the Homeric heroes.

One of the remarkable things about the Linear B tablets is that no mention is made in them of trade or traders, even though such activities must have been carried on. Greece is variably provided with raw materials, a matter that is more fully discussed in Chapter 3. Especially with regard to copper and tin her import needs were, arguably, considerable and it seems likely that the copper (or bronze) which was being distributed to smiths at Pylos must have been brought in from outside the region. All the thousands of sheep recorded on the Knossos tablets must have produced a quantity of wool that would be far in excess of the requirements of Crete alone, and even if it was only exported to the islands and mainland, this is none the less a facet of the Bronze Age economy that is simply not recorded in the archives. Copper and tin were prime needs of the Mycenaean world; but other substances were also imported, such as amber, ivory and semi-precious stones.

From analysis of metals in the Pylos tablets, it seems fair to conclude that although not many people had access to any great quantity of metal, there was enough reaching Pylos for a sizeable smithing population to be kept at work (though it has been suggested that the figures indicate a severe shortage of metal at this period). Since metal was not hoarded in Greece in the same way that it was in Europe (at any rate it was not consigned to the ground), it is hard to say what the normal smithing stock or agricultural tool-kit was. It would be surprising, in view of the demonstrable capacity of the system to produce a large amount of high quality metalwork, if the lack of hoarded metal reflects a general lack of interest in metals and metal production.

Political and economic conditions in the "barbarian" world seem, on the evidence available, to have been rather different. Here we may first consider the scale of the units involved, for which a key factor is the capability of the terrain to support a given population. Life for most people in the Bronze Age was concerned with the daily round and common task of subsistence. The survival of settlements in particular spots—or even in whole regions—would depend on the ability of the inhabitants to feed themselves adequately; this was not the era of large-scale, long-distance foodstuff exportation—no shipments of North American grain when the harvest failed. Various responses to such a situation can be suggested, but one way or another the provision of cereals must have remained a crucial factor at all periods of later prehistory in Europe, ultimately a regulator of population in a Malthusian sense, but probably before then responsible for many more subtle shifts of emphasis in subsistence strategy as well as major dislocations in the settlement history of particular areas.

It is hard to know what size of economic unit might have been involved. In view of the fact that no sign of central places that might have served as exchange points is at all evident until an advanced phase of the Bronze Age, it would seem that the subsistence economy was conducted on an essentially local level. Such units, indeed, may not have surpassed the territorial size of a modern parish, though we might imagine that for certain particularly desirable commodities district or even regional exchange might be possible. The supply of raw materials like copper, on the other hand, cannot by its very nature have operated solely on this local level, and an element of longer-distance exchange, or procurement, must be envisaged. The impact of such commodities as copper is hard to assess; certainly its effect on the subsistence base may have been very restricted.

The people who operated within this framework remain extremely shadowy to us. By comparison with the situation in Greece, where a combination of Homer and Linear B makes the period seem almost historic, Europe is clothed in an impenetrable darkness as far as individuals are concerned. Yet the signs of individual achievement are there in the form of craft objects of various kinds; and evidence of achievement by corporate effort is present not only in the large-scale sites and monuments of the era, but also in the very procurement of raw materials of which we have been speaking. It is far from clear how copper procurement operated, but it seems likely that individual initiative was involved at least in the distribution of the ingots, if not in the actual mining and smelting operations. The smith, too, must have had a large degree of autonomy if the normal interpretation of smithing hoards is correct: stock, in the form of broken objects ready for remelting, would be left at various places presumably known only to the smith or his assistants, and collected again when the area in question was revisited. Both at the level of raw material distribution and that of dissemination of finished objects mechanisms for exchange were in operation. The extent of these mechanisms can perhaps be gauged from the distances over which metal is known to have travelled: Denmark, for example, has no native deposits of copper, but became one of the major consumers of the mineral. The nearest sources are in the Harz Mountains, some 350–400 km to the south. Such distances are by no means unusual, and if the ring ingots of the Early Bronze Age have been correctly interpreted as products of the Austrian (or at any rate East Alpine) ore sources, distances of 700 km or more were encompassed. Such a situation must imply regularized, if not regular, means of distribution.

But such exchange was of a rather general nature: copper was a universal desideratum, widely exchanged, and widely obtained. Objects of rare materials to serve as prestige objects, on the other hand, do not seem to have had a role to play in the same way. There are certainly cases of bronzes made in one area turning up in another: witness the English Channel shipwrecks or Irish axes, for example, which are quite widely disseminated on the continent in the Early Bronze Age, or a certain number of central European weapons which turn up in the northern area at the start of the Bronze Age. But this type of exchange seems to have been conducted on a rather generalized level; it does not indicate the long-distance specific directional exchange that is the main concern of this book. This may have much to do with the type of society which the European Bronze Age—and especially its early part—revolved around.

It is customary to talk in terms of tribal organization for the societies of this period, but little is known about how a "tribe" would manifest itself archaeologically. The division by American workers into band, tribe and state hardly provides us with the clarity of definition that we require, especially as those like Renfrew,[44] who have attempted to apply these categories to prehistoric Europe, have found that they do not appear to fit very well—particularly in the case of the Bronze Age. On the other hand, many of the criteria proposed by Service[50] for "chiefdoms" do seem to be present, such as the existence of the office of chief (visible in dress, activities and insignia of office), significant degrees of personal ranking, increase in population density, craft specialization, development of religion, execution of public works, and the rise of warfare. Whether a division into "group-oriented" and "individualizing" chiefdoms is helpful is a matter for discussion; there are other ways of dividing up the range of possible hierarchical structures that chiefdoms might encapsulate which could provide us with a more useful working model than these. In particular for the Bronze Age it might be helpful to distinguish between militaristic and non-militaristic chiefdoms (in the sense of display of martial materials); between those for whom display of wealth in general was of importance and those who either eschewed such parade or were unable to partake of it; between those able to draw on local resources and those compelled to import all prestige material; between those associated with specific ritual and religious activities and those not so associated; or several others. Examples of most of these kinds of distinction can be seen in "barbarian" Europe. Generalizations that do seem possible on the basis of such analysis as has been carried out support the notion that quite complex forms of social division were present already in Early Bronze Age populations, which did not, however, necessarily mark these distinctions with enormously different quantities of personal possessions. At least some Late Bronze Age individuals, on the other hand, did mark such distinctions in a most ostentatious way. At the same time it must be recognized that group organization probably varied considerably within barbarian Europe.

It is against this background that exchange between the Aegean and "barbarian" worlds must be seen. For all that the period is a prehistoric one, it seems clear that group organization in the two worlds was structurally quite different, if the archaeological materials from recovered sites are anything to judge by. It follows that the social and economic impact of exchange between the two worlds would also be different. To these matters we shall return in Chapter 10.

Conclusion

The framework within which trade or exchange takes place is very varied. Much depends on the nature of the social and economic institutions present in the areas in question, so that exchange may be regarded as either a social or an economic act, or both. To the extent that social consequences may flow from what starts off as purely economic acts (i.e. acts designed to improve access to supplies of particular commodities) all exchange has a social function, but some types have little economic background. Acts involving gifts by individuals, such as gift-exchange or potlatch, are classic examples of such exchange, and may be potent reasons for the appearance of goods in far-off places. Other cases where social rather than economic considerations are paramount might include such matters as "negative reciprocity" or coercion for the acquisition of personal wealth. The mechanisms by which goods are traded and luxury items accumulate in the hands of an élite might, on the other hand, be regarded as economic in origin. Archaeologically, it will naturally be very difficult to distinguish between them.

Many of the examples enumerated in this chapter relate more to sporadic exchange rather than organized trade. This latter was, however, certainly a regular feature of the Bronze Age world, at least in the East Mediterranean and in all probability elsewhere as well. In the Levant trade was carried out both by communities and by entrepreneurs, for whom the security of political institutions was an important consideration. Such activities were carried on in spite of the fact that neither markets nor coinage existed; instead, a whole series of other price-fixing mechanisms were developed to give stability to the system. As well as entrepreneurial activity of this sort there was commodity procurement by institutions, notably by palaces or palace-like centres in the Bronze Age Levant. This was presumably also the mechanism adopted by the palatial centres of the Aegean, where the absence of any mention of traders, though possibly accidental, is very striking.

It is demonstrable that exchange also played a role in the barbarian world. Here we are much more dependent on ethnographic and historical evidence to provide a framework; but there are signs, to which we will return, that at least some of the models developed are helpful and enhance our understanding of the impact of exchange in the Bronze Age world. It is to the specifics of that exchange that we must now turn.

Notes

1. W. Longacre, in I. Hodder, G. Isaac and N. Hammond (eds), *Pattern of the Past*, 1981 (Cambridge, Cambridge University Press), pp. 49–66.

2. N. David and H. Hennig, *The Ethnography of Pottery: a Fulani Case Study seen in Archaeological Perspective*. Addison-Wesley Module **21**, 1972, 1–29.

3. I. Hodder, in M. Millett (ed.), *Pottery and the Archaeologist*, 1979 (London, Institute of Archaeology, occasional publication 4), 7–23.

4. I. Hodder, in I. Hodder, G. Isaac and N. Hammond (eds), *Pattern of the Past*, 1981 (Cambridge, Cambridge University Press), pp. 67–95.

5. D. L. Clarke, *Analytical Archaeology*, 1968 (London, Methuen), 365ff., esp. 379ff.

6. I. Hodder, in I. Hodder (ed.), *The Spatial Organisation of Culture*, 1978 (London, Duckworth), Ch. 1, p. 11.

7. H. Balfet, in F. R. Matson (ed.), *Ceramics and Man*, 1965 (New York, Wenner Gren Foundation), pp. 161–177.

8. For example, C. L. Redman and J. E. Myers, in H. Howard and E. L. Morris (eds), *Production and Distribution: a Ceramic Viewpoint*, British Arch. Reports, Int. Series **120**, 1981, 285–307.

9. B. Saraswati, *Pottery-making Cultures and Indian Civilisation*, 1978 (New Delhi, Abhinav Publications).

10. M. Rowlands, *World Archaeology* **3**, 1971, 210–224; I. Hodder, *Symbols in Action*, 1982 (Cambridge, Cambridge University Press), pp. 59–68; D. A. Welbourn, *Arch. Review from Cambridge* **1/1**, 1981, 30–40.

11. M. Rowlands, *The Organisation of Middle Bronze Age Metalworking*, British Arch. Reports **31**, 1976; D. L. Clarke, *Analytical Archaeology*, 1968 (London, Methuen), p. 233. I. Hodder's earlier work was much more favourably disposed to an interpretation of metalwork distributions in group terms: I. Hodder and C. Orton, *Spatial Analysis in Archaeology*, 1976 (Cambridge, Cambridge University Press), 211ff.

12. I. Hodder, *Symbols in Action*, 1982 (Cambridge, Cambridge University Press), 59ff.

13. L. Flanagan, in M. Ryan (ed.), *The Origins of Metallurgy in Atlantic Europe*, n.d. (1980) (Dublin, Stationery Office), pp. 145–163.

14. E. S. Sherratt, in Best and de Vries (1980, p. 178).

15. For example, most recently T. Kimes, C. C. Haselgrove and I. Hodder, *J. Anthropol. Arch.* **1**, 1982, 113–131.

16. An exception is Adams (1974).

17. For example, in *Social Evolution*, 1951/1963 (London, Collins), 110ff.

18. Adams (1974, p. 241).

19. K. Marx, *Capital* III, 326 (English ed., Moscow, Progress Publishers, 1959).

20. For example, K.-H. Otto, in K.-H. Otto and H.-J. Brachmann (eds), *Moderne Probleme der Archäologie*, 1975 (Berlin, Akademie Verlag), pp. 11–27.

21. Godelier (1977, esp. 99ff).

22. C. Meillassoux, *Cahiers d'Etudes Africaines* **4**, 1960, 38–67 (reprinted in Seddon, 1978, 127ff., esp. 150ff.).

23. M. Godelier, in Seddon (1978, pp. 209–257).

24. As set out most clearly in Polanyi (1957).

25. Dalton (1967, p. 157).

26. Polanyi's essay on economic institutions in Mycenaean Greece concentrated specifically on the absence of money and consequent alternative systems of equivalence and apportioning: in C. H. Kraeling and R. M. Adams (eds), *City Invincible: Symposium on Urbanization and Cultural Development in the Ancient Near East*, 1960 (Chicago, Chicago University Press), pp. 329–350.

27. Dalton (1975, 91ff.) for a review of Polanyi's divisions; Hodder (1978); Renfrew (1975).

28. M. Sahlins, *Stone Age Economics*, 1972 (London, Tavistock Publications), 185ff.

29. Dalton (1967, p. 71).

30. Dalton (1967, p. 73).

31. Meillassoux (1971, p. 52).

32. Ibid.

33. Ibid., p. 53.

34. Ibid., p. 59.

35. Ibid., pp. 65–67.

36. Meillassoux (1971, p. 68).

37. Ibid., pp. 74–75.

38. J. Vansina, *J. African History* **3/3**, 1962, 375–390.

39. Gray and Birmingham (1970, p. 3).

40. Ibid., pp. 3–4.

41. M. P. Miracle, *Rhodes-Livingstone Journal* **26,** 1959, 34–50.

42. B. Fagan, in Gray and Birmingham (1970, pp. 37–38).

43. Renfrew (1972, 460ff., 493ff.).

44. Marazzi and Tusa (1979).

45. T. K. Earle, in T. K. Earle and J. E. Ericson, *Exchange Systems in Prehistory*, 1977 (London and New York, Academic Press), pp. 213–229.

46. Renfrew (1972, 465ff.).

47. Renfrew (1975, 42ff., esp. Fig. 10).

48. For example, D. L. Clarke (ed.), *Spatial Archaeology*, 1977 (London and New York, Academic Press); I. Hodder (ed.), *The Spatial Organisation of Culture*, 1978 (London, Duckworth).

49. A. C. Renfrew, in C. B. Moore (ed.), *Reconstructing Complex Societies*, 1974 (Cambridge, Mass., American Schools of Oriental Research, Supplement 20), pp. 69–95.

50. E. R. Service, *The Origins of the State and Civilisation: the Process of Cultural Evolution*, 1975 (New York, Norton).

☐ 3
Raw materials

Any society or culture dependent, as we are, on fossil fuel for the maintenance of everyday life must be all too aware of how unevenly the resources
of the Earth are distributed. For us it is a question of coal, oil and uranium,
but also some of the rarer minerals; for previous ages, dependent primarily
on wood and peat for fuel, the location of the useful minerals was crucial
(Fig. 6). This must also have been the case in the Bronze Age world,
especially after small local deposits of minerals like copper and gold had been
worked out. Since their Old World occurrence is extremely patchy, the
movement of such minerals over considerable distances must have been
inevitable in late prehistory. It is thus almost certain *a priori* that Mycenaean
Greece drew on raw materials from outside the Aegean basin; this represents
a potentially fruitful source of contact between it and other Old World
culture areas.

The main difficulty in considering the movement of raw materials is that of
characterization. Clay, stone and metal might all have been moved, but it is
hard to demonstrate this without each potential source being analytically
characterized. Different materials are more or less likely to be transported:
while it seems highly unlikely that clays would be moved over very long
distances, local, or possibly regional, movement is likely. The source of
many of the stones used for gem-making or Cretan stone vases is known,
and some stones, such as *lapis lacedaimonius* or *antico rosso*, are known to
have been imported into Crete. But though some stones were moved in this
way, the bulk of the evidence for raw material trade and transportation relates
to metal and to exotic materials like amber, *lapis lazuli* or ivory. In order
properly to assess the situation with regard to trade with the north and west,
the raw material needs of Greece must be considered as a whole.

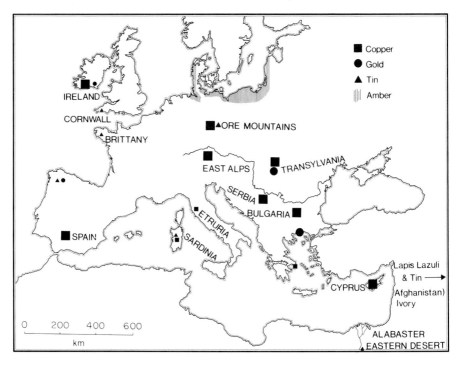

FIG. 6 ☐ Location of major deposits of various raw materials, as indicated. The map is not intended to be comprehensive, but rather to show some major options open to Aegean communities in the Bronze Age.

Metals

It is commonly supposed, though with what degree of justification is open to question, that metals were one of the most-traded commodities in the ancient world—and in the Bronze Age no less than in the Greek and Roman periods. This is largely attributable to the fact that the greatest metalworking centres (Greece, Hungary or Denmark for instance) are not generally well provided with metal ores and probably had to import most, if not all, of their metal. The assumption of importation has important implications for our understanding of the nature and extent of the foreign contacts of the countries in question.

In a Bronze Age context the metals involved would be copper, tin and gold; silver and lead were also used. The bulk of the discussion here will revolve around the first of these, as copper accounted for by far the greatest quantity of material; but tin and gold were also of great importance.

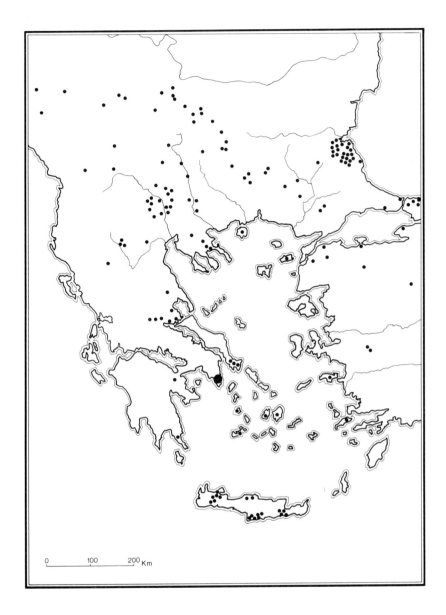

FIG. 7 ☐ Copper deposits in the Balkan peninsula and western Anatolia. Not all the sources were necessarily accessible with Bronze Age technology. The large dot indicates the Laurion source, proven analytically to have been in use in the Bronze Age. (After Branigan, 1974; de Jesus, 1980; Černych, 1978; Maczek, Preuschen and Pittioni, 1953.)

Copper in the Aegean *(Fig. 7)*

Substantial numbers of small deposits of copper are known from the Aegean basin. It has been concluded that Crete could have been self-sufficient in copper at least in the Early Bronze Age, if not later too.[1] This conclusion has been disputed by those who maintain, on the basis of re-examination of all known Cretan ore-sources, that Crete can never have produced very much copper, implying that most Cretan copper was imported even during the Early Bronze Age. Recent analytical evidence supports this conclusion.[2]

Sources of copper in central and southern Greece and the lesser islands are few and small. The Peloponnese and Boeotia are virtually devoid of sources; in southern Thessaly there is a number of deposits in the Othrys range between Lamia and Volos. Some of the islands (e.g. Euboea, Kos, Melos, Skyros, Naxos and Paros) have small deposits. On the other hand, the deposits at Laurion in Attica are claimed by some scholars to be big enough to have supplied most of the needs of the Bronze Age Aegean, though whether they did in fact do so is another matter.[3]

Northern Greece and the frontier areas have a number of copper sources which could have provided ample material for Bronze Age working. Macedonia, both Greek and Jugoslav, has a good many quoted sources; there is one on Thasos and three in Greek Thrace.[4] The Bulgarian sources are well-known and prolific, and copper is extracted even today in Albania.[5] There is, however, no evidence of large-scale working of these sources in the Bronze Age, and certainly no indication that they could have been supplying the main centres of central and southern Greece. On-site metallurgy, demonstrated at Kastanas and Assiros,[6] probably indicates no more than the exploitation of local sources for local needs.

Most observers have reached the conclusion that even if substantial copper deposits are present in the Aegean, much copper is none the less likely to have been imported during the Late Bronze Age. How can the source be discovered? There are two main lines of evidence: archaeological and analytical. The archaeological approach depends on artefact distribution and the evidence of metalworking, and is what we are chiefly concerned with here. The analytical approach deals with the characterization of copper objects and ore bodies by means of their impurity patterns. This method has not been used extensively for the Mediterranean Late Bronze Age and so the number of analysed objects is too small for characteristic patterns to emerge. Much more serious, however, is the failure to distinguish with any certainty the characteristics of particular ore-sources in particular finished artefacts, though advances by the lead isotope method should be recorded.[7] This connection must be made if the analytical method is to render the archaeologist any help in his task of defining ancient trade-routes. Even in central Europe, where the potential ore-sources are much better known, and the number of analyses much greater, such success as there has been in tying artefacts to sources depends on archaeological rather than analytical evidence, and experiments with the smelting of Rudna Glava ores provided results to sober the most optimistic observer.[8]

Copper sources of the East Mediterranean are much more prolific than those of Greece. The deposits of Cyprus are well known and have been much studied:[9] the major deposits at Skouriotissa and other places along the north side of the Troodos range contain millions of tons of ore and are still worked today. There is extensive evidence for Roman mine-working, and on-site metallurgy is demonstrated back into the Early Bronze Age.[10] Recent discoveries at Kition and Athienou bear out the extent and importance of smithing activities on Late Bronze Age sites,[11] while the famous Enkomi figurine standing on a model ox-hide ingot seems to symbolize the importance of Cyprus as a copper producer in the Bronze Age, as in later times.[12]

There are (or were) deposits of copper in Palestine and Sinai, the ancient exploitation of which is well proven. The recent investigations of Timna, near Eilat, have uncovered extensive Bronze Age workings which include deep shafts extending for hundreds of metres; the annual output of smelted copper has been estimated at 80 tons.[13] These sources are unlikely to have been supplying the Aegean, but they must have been crucial for the Near Eastern states and for Egypt. Documents from sites such as Ugarit and Ebla show how vast was the quantity of metal being traded in the second millennium.[14]

The inability to tie down artefacts to particular metal sources by analytical methods is the more unfortunate because, as we have seen, much of the metal entering southern Greece in the Late Bronze Age was arguably of non-Greek origin. Candidates for consideration are the sources in the east, the north and the west: one source can without controversy be assumed to have been exploited, namely Cyprus. To the question of how far other sources were used we shall return. But first we must consider the evidence for Greece's metal needs during the Late Bronze Age.

This evidence comes from artefacts themselves, and from references to metalworking and workers in the Linear B tablets. The former category is extremely hard to assesss. Late Bronze Age Greece is unusual by comparison with the other countries of Europe in that the quantity of hoarded metal was very small—small in absolute terms, but also small in comparison to the amount of metal deposited (or at any rate found) in graves. The main survey of these hoards, published in 1972,[15] listed only six (these are mainly founders' hoards, and do not include the great deposits of vessels and other pieces found in tombs in the early Mycenaean period). Even neighbouring Bulgaria, not notable for its richness in the Bronze Age, has produced to date at least 30 hoards, some of considerable size.[16] By contrast, the quantities of metal in graves were much greater in Mycenaean Greece: swords, spearheads and knives are frequently found, while occasional finds in early Mycenaean tombs of metal vessels in large numbers,[17] and of other objects, indicate that many tombs were originally much richer.

The metal needs in at any rate one province of Mycenaean Greece at one particular time can also be gauged from the Pylos Linear B tablets, which— if interpreted correctly—contain many mentions of smiths (ka-ke-u-si, $\chi\alpha\lambda\kappa\hat{\eta}Fες$) and copper/bronze (ka-ko, $\chi\alpha\lambda\kappa\acuteος$). The smiths sometimes crop up in the course of other business, but most important here are the allocations of bronze made to individual smiths in the Pylos administrative territory. The Jn series of tablets[18] list 274 smiths, concentrated in groups of up to 26 in places not otherwise known to have been of importance. Bronze is allocated to the smiths in quantities of up to 8 kg, with 1·5 and 5 kg being predominant. The total bronze listed in this way is 801 kg. Now tablet Jn 749 records simply a total of bronze, namely 34 talents 26 minae, which is estimated to be about 1046 kg, and some authorities have suggested that this is a totalling tablet recording the total amount of bronze in this particular distribution. This would mean that the number of smiths would have to be increased by about one-third in the allocation lists to account for the difference between 801 kg and 1046 kg; but since these are contemporaneous documents found in the same storeroom such a procedure is not as arbitrary as it might at first seem.

Two things about these figures are especially striking. First, the figure of 1046 kg, just over a tonne, is close to the estimated weight of the cargo of the Cape Gelidonya ship.[19] If that ship contained a typical load of metal, it would seem possible that the Jn allocations represent the distribution of a recently received cargo of metal of the quantity normally conveyed on an East Mediterranean merchantman. Secondly, the quantities of metal assigned to the individual smiths are very small. A total of 1·5 kg of bronze might make a good many arrowheads or ornamental plaques, but it would hardly go very far with larger objects, especially when a wastage factor (jets, runners, etc.) is taken into account. This has led some authorities to suggest that Pylos at the time of its destruction was experiencing an acute metal shortage, which is further borne out by tablet Jn 829, requisitioning bronze from local governors, allegedly to be made into spear and javelin heads.[20] One can think of a variety of other ways in which these documents might be explained, some perhaps equally plausible; yet supplies of metal were demonstrably arriving at Pylos (and presumably therefore at the other regional capitals of Greece and Crete) and being distributed to smiths in the local population. The need for metal was thus of importance to the Mycenaean economy at every level.

The copper trade

If Greece was receiving considerable quantities of metal from abroad the source of that metal must be sought. Apart from Cyprus and Palestine candidates might include the Balkan sources, Sardinia, Etruria, or even central Europe. Since analytical methods have not proved as helpful as one might have hoped, one is forced to rely on archaeological ones. Chief among these is the evidence of ingots. Here we enter a field much worked over and fraught with controversy, to which recent discoveries have nevertheless contributed greatly. The standard ingot form in the Aegean, as in much of the East Mediterranean, was the "ox-hide" or four-handled form (Fig. 8). These occur widely from Sardinia to Ugarit and (in depictions and model form) from Egyptian Thebes to the Black Sea[21] (Fig. 9). They are, however, most numerous—at least in full-size form—between Cyprus and the Peloponnese; Bass (1967) listed 75 on Cyprus, 31 on Crete, 23 in Greece and of course the 39 (plus fragments) on the Cape Gelidonya ship.[21a] This compared with two in Syria-Palestine, three in Asia Minor, four models (but also many depictions) in Egypt, and eight in the central Mediterranean.[22] The geographical spread is thus broad, and the centre of gravity of the form clearly Aegean; the Linear B tablets also depict them.

Recent finds have thrown fresh light on this problem. First, two ingots, one allegedly bearing Aegean signs, have been recovered from the Black Sea off Bulgaria, and a third from the hinterland of Burgas.[23] Secondly, excavation and re-examination of museum material has revealed many new fragments of ox-hide ingots in Sardinia (Fig. 8.7).[24] What, one may ask, were ingots with stamped or incised Linear A or Cypro-Minoan signs doing off Bulgaria or in Sardinia? Clearly they were not being imported there from Crete; rather the reverse. The fragmentary nature of many of the Sardinian pieces is interesting as it indicates that the ox-hide ingots were destined not solely for the Aegean market but were also—maybe at a rather later date—broken up and used locally. Identifying the source of the raw copper that was so used is thus a crucial question.

Provenance studies, based on metal analysis of ox-hide ingots, have not been able to solve unambiguously the problem of where the ingots originated. All of those analysed so far have proved to be of very pure copper, with no sign of alloying (as was once thought).[25] Most of the discussion of these analyses has revolved around their metallographic structure more than their impurity pattern. The indications of four ingots from Sardinia were that they had cuprous sulphide inclusions, not matte or oxide; they are thus from a sulphide deposit which—in the absence of a high manganese flux—was thought unlikely to be Cypriot. Equally it cannot yet be shown to be Sardinian. Sulphide inclusions were also detected in the ingots from Keos, Kyme, Ayia Triada and Antalya.

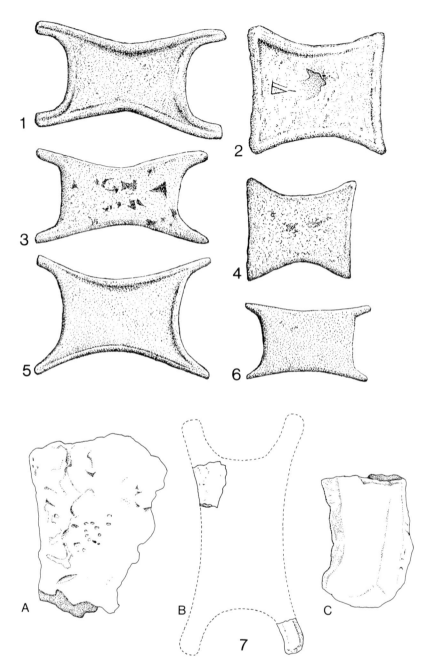

FIG. 8 ☐ Ox-hide ingots of various types. (1) Mycenae; (2) Ayia Triada; (3 and 5) Cape Gelidonya; (4) Antalya; (6) Enkomi; (7) Ossi (Sassari), Sa Mandra 'e sa Giua (A, C, two fragments; B, reconstruction). (After Buchholz, 1958; Bass, 1967; Lo Schiavo and Vagnetti, 1980).

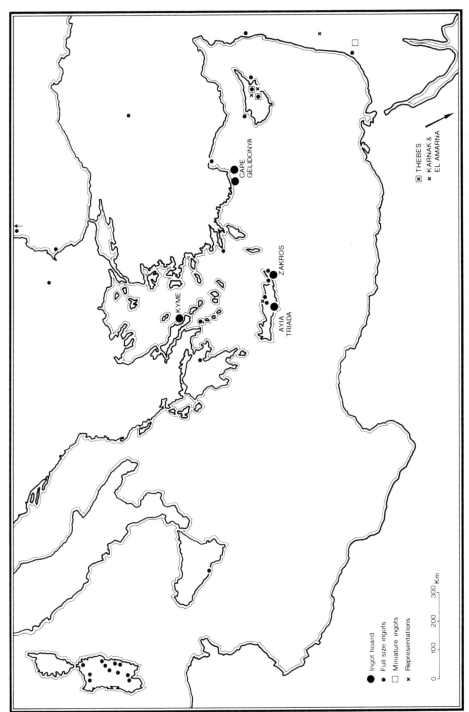

FIG. 9 ☐ Distribution of ox-hide copper ingots. (After Buchholz, 1959; Bass, 1967; with additions.)

CAPE
GELIDONYA

KYME

ZAKROS

AYIA
TRIADA

THEBES
KARNAK &
EL AMARNA

Ingot hoard
Full size ingots
Miniature ingots
Representations

0   100   200   300 Km

The same was true for the Cape Gelidonya ox-hide ingots, where the presence of copper sulphide, but little or no iron, suggests the use of a well-weathered ore. It is apparent, therefore, that elemental analysis of the ox-hide ingots has failed to provide any means of indicating provenience by the use of impurity patterns or—so far—by metallographic structure, though this remains a hope for the future.

At present the most suitable means of assessing the likely points of origin and destination of the ox-hide ingots are archaeological. On the one hand there is the evidence of a cargo ship sailing westwards to the Aegean from the East Mediterranean around 1200 B.C., laden with copper ingots and scrap. On the other there is increasing evidence for the presence of ox-hide ingots far from the Aegean: off the Bulgarian coast and in Sardinia, where they were locally used. Do the Bulgarian ingots indicate the transport of Balkan ore to the East Mediterranean? Given the presence of one ingot near Karnobat (behind Burgas) it is tempting to think so. The Aegean signs allegedly stamped on them cannot be regarded as decisive either here or in Sardinia, though they do presumably indicate that Aegeans were involved in their manufacture at some stage. The transport of copper ingots to Sardinia from the East Mediterranean would be as striking a case of coals to Newcastle as any one could find, but cannot actually be disproved. The Sardinian copper sources are substantial,[26] but no extraction sites are known to have been worked in antiquity. Yet copper objects are present in Sardinia already in the late Neolithic and Copper Ages, as they are elsewhere in Europe, and it is unthinkable that the great metal industries of the Nuragic period were not drawing on local sources. On balance, it seems most unlikely that the ox-hide ingots of Sardinia should have been imported.

How, then, did the metal trade (primarily in copper) operate? Here much depends on one's interpretation of the Cape Gelidonya shipwreck. Two opposing theses have been put forward.[27] The excavator has argued that the metal trade in general, and the Cape Gelidonya ship in particular, were operated by Syrians, who appear in a number of Egyptian tomb reliefs carrying ingots. The contents of the ship, moreover, showed it to have accumulated an eclectic collection of material, both personal and industrial, which would have made it at home in any Near Eastern port.

The contrary argument is that the introduction of Syrians and Phoenicians is irrelevant, that the copper trade has nothing to do with the later presence of Phoenicians in Sardinia, and that there is no other evidence for Semitic traders in the Aegean at this time. The Mycenaeans would have been perfectly capable of conducting their own metal trade, whose reciprocity would be shown by the finds of Mycenaean pottery in the areas exploited. At the time no Mycenaean pottery had been found in Sardinia, so it was asserted that

> the western trade represents a different type of operation . . . part of the amber trade between Northern Europe and the Aegean, an overland trade through

Europe which brought to the Aegean not only the amber of the Baltic Sea, but also the tin of Cornwall and perhaps even the gold of Ireland, along with the copper of Sardinia. This trade was not in the hands of the Mycenaeans who went no further west than the island of Sicily.[28]

Was the ox-hide ingot a distinctively Aegean type? Certainly it was the main, though not the only,[29] type used in the Aegean. But it was also, to judge from the frequency with which it is depicted in Egyptian tombs, well known in Egypt, and I have already alluded to its importance in Cyprus. The situation in the Levant is impossible to assess. The Cape Gelidonya ship contained few specifically Mycenaean objects (though on a ship one would not necessarily expect them), and an East Mediterranean origin is much more likely than an Aegean. This does not, of course, mean that all such trading was carried out by East Mediterraneans, particularly as far as the central Mediterranean is concerned. It is highly likely that Aegean ships sailed regularly up the west Greek coast to Italy and then on to Sicily and the Tyrrhenian Sea. Equally it cannot be ruled out that westerners sailed eastwards, though there is no representational evidence for ships in the west, and the relevant technology may have been less highly developed than in the east.

In summary, ox-hide ingots were the most common means of transporting raw blister copper in the eastern half of the Mediterranean in the Late Bronze Age. They were the main way in which raw copper reached Mycenaean Greece, but other areas used them as well. Finds of this type in the west and north probably indicate some of the directions to which Greece looked for the supply of essential raw materials.

The status of the other main copper sources of central and southern Europe (Fig. 7) is less easy to assess in the context of East Mediterranean metal requirements. The output of the Bulgarian and Serbian copper mines in prehistoric times must have been enormous, but there is no evidence that indicates unequivocally interest by Aegeans in these sources. Indeed, in most cases, evidence for Bronze Age (as opposed to Copper Age) exploitation is lacking. It has often been supposed that the metal sources of Etruria were a notable attraction for Mycenaean traders, but the evidence of a few scrappy sherds at Luni sul Mignone is hardly sufficient to demonstrate the extensive exploitation some have wished to envisage; nor is the evidence for exploitation by locals as convincing as one might wish.[30] The situation with the Alpine sources, on the other hand, provides a wealth of such evidence, as has already been touched on in Chapter 2. The detailed estimates of copper output in the Bronze Age for the Mitterberg mines, and extrapolation for the rest of western Austria, show that a vast amount of copper was entering the system. The means by which it was distributed, at any rate during the Early Bronze Age, was apparently the "ingot torc" or ring ingot. But the distribution of these ingots is almost entirely north of the Alps, and certainly does not seem to have penetrated far down the Balkans. There is no evidence yet that Alpine copper reached Greece in the Bronze Age. The same is true of the Transylvanian sources, where even less is known of the means by which the metal was extracted and distributed.

There is, however, one intriguing group of finds which deserve a brief mention at this point. It has long been known that ring ingots appear in small numbers in the Near East in the earlier part of the Bronze Age, and many scholars have supposed that a direct connection with the European series of ingots is likely. In view of the importance attributed to the ring ingots in central Europe, and the assumption that they are a means of transporting metal, these Near Eastern finds could be—and have been—taken as evidence that metals and metallurgical skills were moved between the two areas.

Penannular neck-rings occur in a dozen or so sites in Anatolia, Egypt, the Levant and Mesopotamia, at dates that seem to be within a couple of hundred years of 2000 B.C.[31] Closer investigation reveals, however, that not all these finds are of the same type, nor are they from secure contexts. In fact only six or seven finds are of ring ingots in the sense in which they occur in central Europe, and of these, only two are from what one might call secure contexts—though, as we shall see, dating those contexts is far from simple. Those two finds are Ras Shamra/Ugarit and Byblos, and in both cases, in spite of the assertions of the excavators, the context is far from clear. Much the most spectacular finds were those at Byblos, from the so-called Montet jar where 44 rings of bronze and silver were found, and from jar 2132. From the associations in these hoards a dating around 2000 B.C. seems assured, though opinions differ as to whether it should be a little before or a little after 2000 B.C.[32] By an amazing coincidence Schaeffer, whose excavations in the tumuli of the Haguenau forest in the 1920s had produced neck-rings of the standard European type,[33] also found them (or rather, a few fragments) at Ras Shamra, where one of his express intentions had been to sort out the nature of the link between central Europe and Byblos.[34] At Ras Shamra they are attributed to "niveau II", which is attributed to "Ugarit moyen I".

The remarkable thing about these finds is their identity with the European pieces. I have not seen them personally, but the illustrations, and the comments of those who have, seem to leave no doubt that these rings are indistinguishable from the European examples (Fig. 10). This fact led Schaeffer to propound his famous "porteurs de torques" hypothesis,[35] in which metal-using people entered the Levant at the end of the Early Bronze Age and then carried their skills and distinctive artefacts on into Europe. The destruction layers at the end of the Early Bronze Age, the finding of figurines wearing neck-rings and the contrast between artefact types of EB III and MB II all served to lend credibility to Schaeffer's hypothesis. More recently he has changed his ideas completely, insisting instead that the distinctive metal types (in addition to the neck-ring, the toggle pin) were brought from Europe to the Levant: *ex occidente ars*.[36]

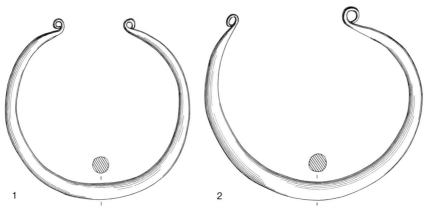

FIG. 10 ☐ Ring ingots from Byblos (1) and Moravia (2). (After Tufnell and Ward, 1966; Tihelka, 1965.)

While certainty on any of these points is impossible because of the nature of the material, the contexts and the excavations, a number of conclusions may be drawn. As far as one can judge, the form and size of the Syrian ingots corresponds to those of the European (Fig. 10). Ring-ingots do not appear elsewhere or at other times in the Levant; they are not a west Asian or East Mediterranean type. The sealed stratigraphical contexts of at least some of them in the Near East seem assured, and a date in the early second millennium B.C. is likely. None of these facts would rule out a derivation of the ring ingots from Europe; some, indeed, actively encourage it. It is certainly not necessary to subscribe to Schaeffer's views about population replacement to believe that this handful of bronzes could actually have been transported from central Europe to the Levantine coast. If the ring ingots were so transported they cannot indicate regular or large-scale contact; but their form is too precise and unusual to be dismissed lightly.

Tin

The problem of tin is not much nearer solution than it was 50 years ago. Sources in the East Mediterranean have often been suggested, and as often discounted.[37] A recent find that aroused much interest was the discovery of tin ingots in Haifa harbour (Fig. 11),[38] which would join the tin ingot of uncertain date from Falmouth harbour.[39] The tin question may not be soluble in terms of definite answers to specific questions, but we do know that tin was available in the Near East in plenty (assuming *annaku* is to be translated as "tin") and that the Cape Gelidonya ship contained a substance that may have been tin, probably in ingot form.[40] Tin sources in Afghanistan are now known to be plentiful,[40a] and alluvial sources, now worked out, have often been suggested. The early date at which tin bronze was being produced, and the apparent ease with which Near Eastern traders were able to obtain supplies, suggest strongly that local, or at any rate not distant, sources were available. Muhly has drawn attention to the close connection between tin and gold in alluvial deposits, and suggests that the Eastern Desert of Egypt, home of important gold deposits, is the best documented modern source of tin in the eastern Mediterranean or the Near East.[41] The potential importance of alluvial deposits is also shown by their hitherto unsuspected frequency in the ore-bearing zones of Saxony, which have sometimes been written off as far as Bronze Age exploitation is concerned because of the assumed difficulties of extraction.[42] Alluvial deposits in Anatolia have been quoted but seem less likely.[43] In spite of all the technological difficulties which the exploitation of these sources imply, we have little alternative but to accept that the difficulties were overcome.

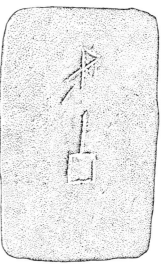

FIG. 11 ☐ Tin ingots from Haifa harbour. (After Maddin, Wheeler and Muhly, 1977.)

For what are the alternatives? There are small and inaccessible sources of tin in Tuscany and Sardinia, and richer deposits in central Europe, Iberia,[44] Brittany and Cornwall. While the former are geographically within the known range of Aegean commercial activity (as shown by pottery export) the latter are not—but here we enter the highly controversial field of the significance of certain objects allegedly of Mycenaean provenance found in the north-west. To this problem we return in Chapter 9. That tin was extensively worked in central and eastern Europe by the Late Bronze Age is evident not only by the vast amount of tin-alloyed metalwork in circulation but also by the finding of tin ingots in Transylvanian hoards of Ha A1 date.[45]

Gold [46]

It has often been stated that the Transylvanian sources may have supplied the Shaft Graves with at least some of their prodigious quantities of gold,[46a] but there is neither analytical nor convincing archaeological evidence for this: gold vessels and ear-rings in the Carpathian basin are hardly sufficient to prove the point (cf. below, see pp. 106, 112). Gold occurs in Greece in small quantities on Siphnos, Thasos and Euboea, the former being a proven source of lead and silver in the Bronze Age.[47] There are more abundant gold sources, including placer deposits, in Thrace and Macedonia and, since gold is widely present in the Earth's crust even if usually in minute quantities, it is quite likely that placer deposits may have been present in other areas of Greece as well. Gold sources in north-west Anatolia are often quoted. In any case, there are numerous gold deposits in the Near and Middle East[48] and it seems quite unnecessary to imagine that the East Mediterranean needed to import European gold. Yet the wealth in gold of Shaft Grave Mycenae was not available to contemporary Crete,[48a] and until more analytical work is carried out judgement is best withheld.

Other raw materials

Many other raw materials were reaching the Aegean during the Late Bronze Age, though not, perhaps, in large quantities. Chief among these are materials used for jewellery and fine art objects: amber and ivory are the best known and most prolific, but there are also various stones, including semi-precious ones, and such rarities as ostrich eggs. The material of principal interest to us here is amber, but in order to understand its context it is necessary to look at some of the other categories known to have been transported.

Ivory is a case in point. Although finds of Pleistocene elephants and mammoths have been made in Greece it is clear that elephants did not live there in the Holocene. The ivory used by Bronze Age Aegeans is, in any case, fresh, soft ivory and not the hard "petrified" ivory obtainable from fossil deposits.[49] It is not known for sure whether the ivory used in the Aegean is Asian or African. The Egyptians imported it from Libya, Ethiopia and Somalia, but also drew on Asian sources,[50] especially in the New Kingdom. Reliefs in the tomb of Rekhmire (c. 1470 B.C.) show whole elephant tusks being brought to

Tuthmosis III, interestingly enough by men from Keftiu. On balance, and especially in view of the artistic connections with the Levant, it is likely that the immediate source of the ivory used in the Aegean was the coastal cities of the Levant. This argument is further reinforced by stylistic considerations. Ivory objects carved in Mycenaean or mycenaeanizing ways occur at Ras Shamra and Tell Atchana: a number of pieces have been considered actual imports from the Aegean.[51]

Another raw material used in Greece, of distant but known origin, is *lapis lazuli*. Known sources lie in Badakhshan in north-east Afghanistan and, allegedly, in Iran.[52] It was widely traded in the ancient Near East from the late Ubaid phase, occurring at Tepe Gawra as early as Gawra XI or earlier, and in Egypt from the Gerzean.[53] In the later periods it is clear that north Syrian entrepôts could easily have serviced the entire eastern Mediterranean.[54] Little over 20 separate finds have been made in the Bronze Age Aegean, which indicates its rarity, and several of these are cylinder seals of oriental inspiration, if not origin.[55] The largest and most varied find comes from Kakovatos, where it is also among the earliest in the Aegean.[56] Room B at the "Kadmeion" site at Oidipou 14, Thebes, contained a jeweller's workshop with 73 fragments of *lapis lazuli*.[57] It is possible that faience and blue glass was often made in imitation of *lapis lazuli* (see p.105) and that blue glass was itself imported into Greece as a raw material for reworking.[58]

Other semi-precious stones are also assumed to have been imported into the Aegean area: carnelian, sard, amethyst and others,[59] while alabaster came from Egypt and perhaps some obsidian from Anatolia for stone vase-making.[60]

This leads us on to mention the most discussed material of all: amber. I consider this more fully in the next chapter, but it is necessary to consider here the origin of the amber found in Bronze Age Greece, since one thing is certain: it is not native to Greece. In that importation is assured, the effects on the economy might be thought to be the same, whatever the source; but as the most prolific European sources are also the most distant, special consideration seems called for.

Amber is a fossil resin, thought to derive from a now extinct species of pine deposited over geological time (mainly in the Tertiary age). It can occur in primary, secondary or tertiary situations; in the latter cases it may take the form of weathered pebbles of varying sizes. The chemical processes of its formation, and the means by which amber in the north can reach its present-day find-spots, have been extensively discussed.[61]

There are many sources of amber in the world, but we need to consider here only those of Europe and the Near East. The map of all naturally occurring amber in Europe is quite thickly covered (Fig. 12),[62] but this seemingly frequent occurrence is misleading. A great many of the finds in central, north-western, and eastern Europe in fact stem from the same geological sources, namely the Baltic and North Sea coastal sources, and were transported to their modern find-places by ice or sea action. Of the find-places which are not so derived, we may specifically mention spots in France, Switzerland, northern Spain, the Po valley of Italy, Sicily (the Etna area), Romania and the Levant. Of all these sources, however, by far the most prolific is the Baltic, accounting for the vast majority of European amber production in recent times. Numerically, amber of European origin is far more likely to be Baltic than anything else—and in prehistory we can probably rule out importation from other present-day prolific sources such as Burma.

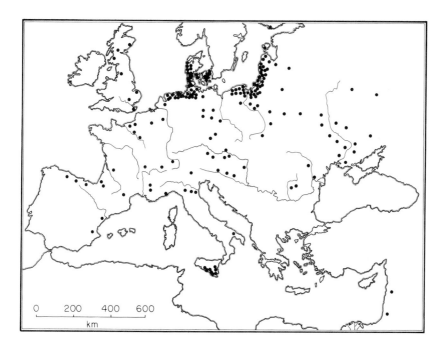

FIG. 12 ☐ Finds of naturally occurring amber in Europe. (After Rottländer, 1973.)

Ever since Schliemann's discoveries at Mycenae, chemists and physicists have been involved in trying to pin down the geological origin of those finds which are considerably removed from the nearest natural sources. It was not long before it was suggested that a way of telling apart Baltic from other ambers was by analysing their content of "succinic acid".[63] In the 1960s, it was demonstrated beyond all doubt that the succinic acid test was in itself unsuitable,[64] and new methods were sought.[65] Two groups started work more or less simultaneously: in the United States Curt W. Beck and his associates found that infra-red spectroscopy appeared to offer an unambiguous identification of amber types[66] while a team in Mainz demonstrated a clear differentiation between different sources by means of mass spectroscopy using field ionization.[67] One might have hoped that at this stage the matter could be satisfactorily resolved, especially in view of Beck's long series of analyses of Greek amber,[68] the majority of which purports to be geologically Baltic, but unfortunately even these methods have been called into question as a means of giving an unambiguous answer. According to Beck,[69]

> Infra-red spectra of amber are plots of absorbed radiation as a function of wavelength, and while they do give useful information about the chemical composition of the resin, they may for the purposes of provenience analysis be seen merely as fingerprints.

Characteristic of the "finger-print" for Baltic amber is the formation of the spectrum between 8 and 9 microns, which is said to show a particular "shoulder" diagnostic for the type, and found in both geological and archaeological specimens. The spectra of ambers from different sources are usually markedly different,[70] but even when they are similar can be distinguished by the presence or absence of the "shoulder".

Rottländer maintains, however, that the infra-red spectra do no more than demonstrate the existence in the specimen of succinic acid, which is not an inherent component of the amber but rather an oxidation product brought about by weathering:

> Ambers which "contain" succinic acid-anhydride exhibit the "Baltic shoulder" . . .. Baltic ambers which are without succinic acid do not exhibit the "Baltic shoulder" . . ... For the determination of origin of ambers *freshly* recovered from the sediment IR-spectroscopy is well-suited. With *archaeological* samples the weathering (diagenesis) which has taken place since the first recovery has to be taken into account.[71]

It is obvious that if these objections to Beck's method were to be proved correct, the results of the numerous analyses performed by the team would not prove what they purport to prove. But, as Beck says, "the provenience analysis of archaeological artefacts by infra-red spectroscopy is a purely empirical procedure, unburdened by any theoretical considerations" and the sheer quantity of analyses, performed on geological specimens and archaeological samples from the northern and central European area, where the use of Baltic amber may safely be assumed, makes it most unlikely that Rottländer's arguments can be taken seriously.[72]

Summary

The Bronze Age Aegean drew on a variety of areas for the various raw materials it needed. The case of *lapis lazuli* demonstrates that a far-reaching chain of exchange links connected Greece with remote areas of the Middle East; both this and ivory probably reached her in the first instance through the intermediary of Levantine ports. It is most unlikely that Aegeans went further than that, let alone to the sources themselves. The lesson for amber is probably that chains of exchange, as yet incapable of precise definition because of the paucity of finds, brought the material, some of it ready worked into beads, from the north and north-west to the Mycenaean trading sphere, perhaps to the central or conceivably the western Mediterranean if not actually all the way to Greece.

The case of metals is more difficult to pin down, but it is clear that the entire eastern half of the Mediterranean was involved in the transport of copper ingots from source to demand area. Greece was certainly drawing on Cyprus for supplies, and in all probability on Sardinia and other western areas as well, though each area also used the ingots for its own purposes. Gold was perhaps locally obtainable, and tin appears likely to have emanated from Near Eastern alluvial sources, not, as far as one can judge, from the distant shores of the Cassiterides.

Notes

1. P. Fauré, *Revue Archéologique* NS **1**, 1966, 47ff., Map 1; K. Branigan, *Copper and Bronze Working in Early Bronze Age Crete*, Lund 1968 (Studies in Mediterranean Archaeology **19**).

2. J. D. Muhly, in *Cyprus and Crete*, 90; Gale and Stos-Gale (1982, p. 15).

3. Map in Branigan (1974, p. 60). On Laurion, Gale and Stos-Gale (1982).

4. M. Maczek, E. Preuschen and R. Pittioni, *Archaeologia Austriaca* **12**, 1953, 68ff.; Hammond (1972, p. 13); Branigan (1974, 59ff., fig. 1).

5. Černych (1978); R. E. H. Mellor, *Eastern Europe, a Geography of the Comecon Countries*, 1975 (London, Macmillan), p. 307; cf. M. Shehu, *Report on the Directives of the 6th Congress of the Party of Labor of Albania for the 5th Five-Year Plan (1971–1975)*, Tirana 1971, pp. 52–53: the target figure for copper ore production in 1975 in Albania was 600 000 tons.

6. Assiros: *Arch. Reports for 1975–6*, 20, fig. 27; K. A. Wardle, *BSA* **75**, 1980, 253, pl. 22b. Kastanas: *BCH* **101**, 1977, 602.

7. For example, H.-G. Buchholz, *Berliner Jahrbuch für Vor- und Frühgeschichte* **7**, 1967, 189–256. Cypriot ores are there characterized as being tin-free, with either a Sb-Zn combination (as in the north-west of Cyprus) or an Ag-Au combination. Yet the Enkomi ingot analysed (over 98% copper) did not fit into any of these categories, and Early Cypriot metalwork analysed was very various in composition. For success with the lead isotope method, Gale and Stos-Gale (1982).

8. Cf. most recently Harding (1983), citing earlier work by Pittioni and associates; R. Tylecote, *Proc. Prehist. Soc.* **48**, 1982, 459–465.

9. Catling (1964, 18ff., Map 3); Muhly (1973, 192ff.), with further references.

10. At Ambelikou: P. Dikaios, *Illustrated London News*, 2 March 1946, 244–245.

11. Kition: K. Nicolaou, *Arch. Reports for 1965–6*, 31; V. Karageorghis, *Proc. British Academy* **59**, 1973, 10, 16ff.; id., *Kition*, 1976 (London, Thames and Hudson), 72ff. Athienou: T. Dothan and A. Ben-Tor, *Israel Exploration Journal* **22**, 1972, 201ff.; id., *Excavations at Athienou 1971–2* 1974, with illustrations (Jerusalem, Israel Museum).

12. C. F. A. Schaeffer, *Antiquity* **39**, 1965, 56–57, pl. XVIb; *Archiv für Orientforschung* **21**, 1966, 59–69. Cf. H. W. Catling, *Alasia* **I**, 1971 (Paris, Mission Arch. d'Alasia), pp. 15–32 for another comparable piece. Bass (1973, pp. 32–35) stresses the late date of the piece (twelfth century) by comparison with other pieces that are closely datable. Most recently, H.-G. Buchholz, *Cyprus and Crete* 84–85.

13. B. Rothenberg, Timna, *Valley of the Biblical Copper Mines*, 1972 (London, Thames and Hudson); P. Watson, *Illustrated London News*, March 1975, 39–40.

14. M. Heltzer, *Iraq* **39**, 1977, 203–211; P. Matthiae, *Ebla, an Empire Rediscovered*, 1980 (London, Hodder and Stoughton), pp. 181–182; L. Milano, *Studi Eblaiti* **3/1–2**, 1980, 1–21; A. Archi, *Studi Eblaiti* **4**, 1981, 129–166.

15. Spyropoulos (1972).

16. Hänsel (1976, 25ff.); Černych (1978, 248ff.); I. Panajotov, *Actes du IIe Congrès International de Thracologie* **I**, 1980, 105–111.

17. For example, Dendra, Asine, Nichoria, Tragana, Mycenae Shaft Graves and Chamber Tombs: Matthäus (1980a, 5–58).

18. Ventris and Chadwick (1973, 352ff., 508ff.); M. Lejeune, *Historia* **10**, 1961, 409–434; M. Lang, *Hesperia* **35**, 1966, 397–412.

19. Bass (1967, p. 163). The ship carried 34 whole and five half ox-hide ingots weighing between 8·5 and 25 kg, and at least 75 kg of fragments, a total of around 735 kg; 29 bun ingots and a related piece, average weight 3 kg, total 90 kg; 19 slab ingots, average 1 kg, total 19 kg; probably 3 tin ingots, at least 16 kg and probably much more; and 257 miscellaneous bronze objects.

20. Chadwick (1976, p. 141).

21. From the extensive literature: H.-G. Buchholz, *Prähistorische Z.* **37**, 1959, 28–39; Bass (1967, 57 ff.). Notable new finds: Kaş shipwreck (n. 21a); mould from Ras Ibn Hani, *CRAI* 1983, 249–290 (reference from J. D. Muhly).

21a. The *New York Times* for 30 October 1982 reported the finding of another Bronze Age shipwreck with around 50 copper ingots off the Turkish coast near Kaş; I owe this information to the kindness of Professor J. D. Muhly.

22. Buchholz (1959) listed other pieces, mostly without reliable context or provenance. Chief among these are 17 pieces from Sorgono, Sardinia (infamous from D. H. Lawrence's *Sea and Sardinia*!), attributed without further details to the "ältere Eisenzeit". The miniature ingot in the Evans Collection at Oxford alleged to come from Makarska, Dalmatia, is rightly treated with scepticism by L. Vagnetti, *Studi Ciprioti e Rapporti di Scavo* **1**, 1971, 203–216.

23. B. Dimitrov, *Int. J. Nautical Arch.* **8.1**, 1979, 70ff., fig. 3; Buchholz (1983, pp. 54, 128 n. 47, Abb. 11). J. Bouzek quotes M. Lazarov, *Pot'nalata flotilija, očerk za podvodnata archeologija*, 1975 (Varna, Biblioteka Neptun), pp. 43–57 (not available to me). Cf. Panajotov (1980, p. 177).

24. Lo Schiavo *et al.* (1981); Zwicker *et al.* (1980).

25. Summary in J. D. Muhly, *Cyprus and Crete* 87ff. Buchholz (1959, 11f.); T. S.

Wheeler, R. Maddin and J. D. Muhly, *Expedition* **17**/**4**, 1975, 31–39; Tylecote (1976); M. S. Balmuth and R. F. Tylecote, *J. Field Arch.* **3**, 1976, 195–201; Muhly *et al.* (1977); Zwicker *et al.* (1980).

26. References in Muhly (1973, p. 362 n. 32).

27. Bass (1967, pp. 52–83, esp. 75ff.); Bass (1973); J. D. Muhly, *Berytus* 1970, 19–64, and Muhly (1973, 185f.); Muhly *et al.* (1977).

28. Muhly (1973, p. 185).

29. Cf. the Mycenae Poros Wall hoard, which included fragments of both ox-hide and other types: F. H. Stubbings, *BSA* **49**, 1954, 295; Spyropoulos (1972, p. 50, fig. 107). Kea: Tylecote (1976, p. 164). Arkalochori: N. Platon, *Cyprus and Crete* 102–103, fig. 1.

30. G. Barker, *Landscape and Society: Prehistoric Central Italy*, 1981 (London and New York, Academic Press), pp. 172–173; L. Cambi, *Studi Etruschi* **27**, 1959, 415ff.; A. Sestini, in *L'Etruria Mineraria*, Atti del XII Convegno di Studi Etruschi e Italici (1979), 1981, 3–21, for discussion of Etrurian sources.

31. O. Tufnell and W. A. Ward, *Syria* **43**, 1966, 210f.; C. F. A. Schaeffer, *Ugaritica* **II**, 1949, 49ff.

32. M. Dunand, *Fouilles de Byblos* **I**, 1939 (Paris, P. Geuthner), p. 153, no. 2255, pl. LXIX; P. Montet, *Byblos et l'Egypte*, 1928 (Paris, Geuthner), 111ff., esp. 123; Tufnell and Ward, *op. cit.*; W. A. Ward, *Egypt and the East Mediterranean World 2200–1900 B.C.*, 1971 (Beirut, American University), p. 63. J. D. Muhly writes (letter of 21 June 1982): "I am now convinced that none of the hoards containing "torques" can be earlier than ca. 2000 B.C. This would include the "Montet Jar" and jar 2132 from Byblos".

33. (C.) F. A. Schaeffer, *Les Tertres funéraires préhistoriques dans le Forêt de Haguenau. I. Les Tumulus de l'Age du bronze*, 1926 (Haguenau, Imp. de la Ville), pp. 67, 70, fig. 31M, 32B.

34. *Ugaritica* **II**, 1949, 117.

35. *Op. cit.*, 49–120.

36. C. F. A. Schaeffer-Forrer, *Ugaritica* **VII**, 1978, 475–551.

37. O. Davies, *J. Hellenic Studies* **49**, 1929, 89–99 (Krisa/Kirrha); G. A. Wainwright, *Antiquity* **17**, 1943, 96–98 (Byblos area) and *Antiquity* **18**, 1944, 57–64; S. Benton, *Antiquity* **38**, 1964, 138; R. J. Forbes, *Studies in Ancient Technology* **IX**, 1964 (Leiden, Brill), 134ff.; J. E. Dayton, *World Archaeology* **3**, 1971, 49–70; J. D. Muhly and T. A. Wertime, *World Archaeology* **5**, 1973, 111–122.

38. R. Maddin, T. S. Wheeler and J. D. Muhly, *Expedition* **19/2**, 1977, 44–47, fig. 23; T. S. Wheeler, *Temple University Aegean Symposium* **2**, 1977, 24–26. M. Artzy, *Bull. Amer. School Oriental Res.* **250**, 1984, 51–55.

39. A. Way, *Arch. J.* **16**, 1859, 39; H. James, *Arch. J.* **28**, 1871, 196–202; A. Fox, *South West England*, 1964 (London, Thames and Hudson), 116f., pl. 60; Muhly (1973, pp. 246, 410 n.73).

40. Bass (1967, pp. 82–83, 171–172); Maddin, Wheeler and Muhly (1977) for a sceptical view.

40a. S. Cleuziou and T. Berthoud, *Expedition* **25/1**, 1982, 14–19; T. Stech and V. Piggott (in press).

41. J. D. Muhly, *Iraq* **39**, 1977, 76; cf. Muhly (1973, p. 259; 1976, pp. 102–103).

42. Muhly (1973, p. 256); L. Baumann, *Trans. Inst. Mining & Metallurgy* **82**, 1970,

B9–24; C. Shell, in M. Ryan (ed.), *The Origins of Metallurgy in Atlantic Europe* (Proc. Fifth Atlantic Colloquium), n.d. (Dublin, Stationery Office 1980), pp. 255–256. The density of Bronze Age settlement in the general area of the tin deposits might point to early exploitation of these sources, but I. Pleinerová, *Památky Archeologické* **57**, 1966, 341, fig. 1 and **58**, 1967, 24–25, sees little connection.

43. Muhly (1973, p. 257; 1976, p. 100).

44. L. Monteagudo, *Die Beile auf der iberischen Halbinsel* (PBF IX, 6), 1977 (Munich, Beck), 16ff., n.2, where an Iberian origin for Aegean tin is suggested.

45. M. Rusu, *Dacia* **7**, 1963, 184, refers to "ingots of pure tin in the hoards from Gusteriţa (II), Uioara de Sus etc.", and stresses that for these two, with those from Şpălnaca, Dipşa and Band, over 300 kg of tin was necessary. In his view this indicated connections with Bohemia-Saxony, "for no occurrences of tin were known in the territory of Romania". Tin is not mentioned at Gusteriţa or Uioara by Holste (1951) or Petrescu-Dîmboviţa (1978), but the latter does mention ?tin beads in the Cioclovina hoard (p. 118) and pieces of tin in Şpălnaca hoard II (p. 128).

46. R. J. Forbes, *Studies in Ancient Technology* **VIII**, 1964 (Leiden, Brill), 163ff.; J. D. Muhly, *Temple University Aegean Symposium* **8**, 1983, 1–14.

46a. For example, most recently E. Davis, *Temple University Aegean Symposium* **8**, 1983, 32–38.

47. N. Gale and Z. Stos-Gale, *BSA* **76**, 1981, 169–224.

48. Forbes, *op. cit.*, 157ff., fig. 33, but cf. the caution of A. Hartmann, *Prähistorische Goldfunde aus Europa*, 1970 (Berlin, Mann), p. 14, n. 37.

48a. E. Davis, *op. cit.* (n.46a).

49. J. Sakellarakis, *To elephantodonto kai i katergasia tou sta mykinaika chronia*, 1979 (Athens, Greek Arch. Soc.), 8ff.

50. W. Helck and E. Otto (eds), *Lexikon der Aegyptologie*, 1975 (Wiesbaden, Harrassowitz), **I**, p. 1225; Lucas and Harris (1962, pp. 32–33).

51. H. Kantor, *J. Near Eastern Studies* **15**, 1956, 166–171; *Archaeology* **13**, 1960, 18–19; J.-C. Poursat, *Les Ivoires Mycéniens*, 1977 (Athens, Ecole française), 142ff.

52. G. Herrmann, *Iraq* **30**, 1968, 21–57, esp. 22–29; Lucas and Harris (1962, 398ff.).

53. Ibid.; J. Crowfoot Payne, *Iraq* **30**, 1977, 58–61.

54. V. I. Sarianidi, *Archaeology* **24**, 1971, 12–15.

55. *Lapis lazuli* was the most common stone used for the cylinder seals found in Greece: H.-G. Buchholz, in Bass (1967, pp. 158–159).

56. K. Müller, *Athenische Mitteilungen* **34**, 1909, 276–277, fig. 1, 295–296, fig. 12. I am very grateful to Helen Hughes-Brock for help with the *lapis lazuli* and other jewellery.

57. S. Symeonoglou, *Kadmeia* **I**, 1973 (Studies in Mediterranean Archaeology **35**, Göteborg, Åström), pp. 66–69, figs 267–269.

58. Foster (1979, pp. 5, 33).

59. Lucas and Harris (1962, 386ff.) for presumed sources in Egypt; in the Aegean the field is unresearched.

60. P. M. Warren, *Minoan Stone Vases*, 1969 (Cambridge, Cambridge University Press), pp. 125–126, 135–136. Some of the largest pieces of rock-crystal may also have been imported (p. 137).

61. For example, most recently Rottländer (1970, 1980–1); K. Gripp, *Offa* **28**, 1971, 47–54.

62. Rottländer (1973, p. 12, fig. 1).

63. O. Helm, quoted in Rottländer (1970).

64. For example, W. La Baume, *Schriften der naturforschenden Gesellschaft in Danzig* **20**, 1935, 5–48.

65. Beck (1970).

66. C. W. Beck, E. Wilbur, S. Meret, D. Kossove and K. Kermani, *Archaeometry* **8**, 1965, 96–109.

67. G. Mischer, H.-J. Eichhoff and Th. E. Haevernick, *JbRGZM* **17**, 1970, 111–122.

68. Summarized by C. W. Beck, in Harding and Hughes-Brook (1974, pp. 170–172).

69. *Op. cit.*, p. 170.

70. Cf., for example, N. Negroni Catacchio, *Sibrium* **9**, 1967–9, 377–387.

71. Rottländer (1973, p. 11).

72. I would like to thank both Professor Curt W. Beck and Dr R. C. A. Rottländer for helpful discussions of this matter. Since the problem is basically a scientific one, I can offer no real contribution, but the number and unequivocal nature of Beck's results, together with their reliance on purely empirical procedures, seem to me overwhelmingly more persuasive than Rottländer's complicated hypotheses involving "diagenesis" from abietic acid. Rottländer's contention that all Baltic amber is "weathered" (i.e. redeposited) and therefore shows the "Baltic shoulder" is weakened, if not invalidated, when one realizes that other archaeologically important European ambers (Sicily, central Italy, Romania) are similarly "weathered": they occur in river beds.

□ 4
Trade in luxury goods

Georg Karo's catalogue of the contents of Shaft Grave Circle A at Mycenae runs to 956 entries, many of them multiple. Leaving aside the pottery (around 50 items), much of the rest consists of high-quality material in metal, semi-precious stone and faience. Of these, a surprising (and frustrating) number are unparalleled in Greece—or indeed anywhere at all. The 18 or so occupants of Circle A were, if they really did own all these objects, enormously wealthy. Such objects, rare both in themselves and in their materials, give us some picture of what prestigious people were able to accumulate at one period of the Bronze Age, and epitomize for us the concept of luxury goods.

What constitutes a "luxury good"? There can be no simple answer to this question as the matter is essentially subjective: one man's luxury is another's necessity. In the context of the two economic systems sketched at the outset we may interpret luxury goods as meaning those items not related directly to basic subsistence and survival. Thus, while copper ore should not itself be regarded as a luxury item, some copper or bronze objects, i.e. those that transcend the needs of every day life, should be. Foodstuffs in general one imagines to be necessities; but not those foodstuffs which are intended merely to please the palate or numb the senses. It is clearly impossible to draw an objective dividing-line between "necessary" and "luxury" goods, for in practical terms the distinction between what is indispensable for the continuance of life and what is not is a meaningless one.

More fruitful might be an approach based on such factors as rarity, distance from source, attractiveness and "work value". Some of these factors are hard to evaluate. The scarcity or otherwise of a material or object is related to the availability of supplies and suppliers, a chain in which distance from source is crucial. Thus *lapis lazuli* is known to have come from a single, very distant group of sources. Blue glass was allegedly made in imitation as a substitute, the sincerest form of flattery here serving as the best indication of value. Amber similarly came from distant, even if not certainly defined, sources, while gold was perhaps limited more by the inability of available local sources to satisfy demand—a case where product desirability was more important than scarcity resulting from difficulty of access to supplies.

Of a quite different order is "work value", that is value imparted to a material or object by means of work, that is to say, elaboration by a craftsman. The most mundane of objects can take on an exotic appearance in this way. Figured vases are a good example of this: the fine figured kraters, formerly thought to be of Cypriot manufacture because of their prevalence in Cyprus and the Levant, show how a vase-painter's craft could transform an everyday mixing-bowl of no special value into a prized and sought-after art object. The elaboration of the hilts and pommels of swords and daggers in the early Mycenaean period is another example. A rapier was a rapier, but the splendid pieces found in the Shaft Graves were more than this.

In other cases, a special social—even political—context added rarity and therefore, presumably, desirability to objects. The cartouche of Seti II on the type II sword from Tell Firaun added a significance to a weapon of war which we cannot fully appreciate.[1] Some of the objects in the Shaft Graves seem to represent more than simple ostentation: what, for instance, is the significance of the ivory zig-zag cylindrical mounts in grave Iota? Why were certain people provided in death with golden face masks? Why did the ability shown by the occupants of the Shaft Graves to accumulate exotic objects from distant sources not continue into later periods? We shall return to some of these problems later.

The most obvious use to which luxury imports are put is personal adornment. There is a great mass of material to be considered under this general heading, so it will be convenient to divide the discussion up into the various groups.

Amber

I have already (Chapter 3) devoted some space to the general question of amber importation, specifically the source or sources of the amber found in Bronze Age Greece. Here I wish to consider the uses to which that amber was put, the distribution and chronology of its importation into Greece, and the implications of the existence of an "amber route".

The early period: distribution of amber in early Mycenaean Greece

By far the largest quantitites of amber in Bronze Age Greece occurred in the Shaft Graves of Mycenae, dating to LH 1. This raises the question whether amber appeared there suddenly, as if out of the blue, or whether there was already a tradition of amber importation in earlier stages of the Bronze Age. Mrs Hughes-Brock and I in 1974[2] found no certain evidence for importation into Greece prior to the Late Bronze Age, though elsewhere in the East Mediterranean and Near East there may have been a little. In Egypt other fossil resins had been in use since the Badarian, but amber proper does not appear until the XVIIIth Dynasty. There are no certain cases in Anatolia, though Dorak Tomb II, assumed to date around the third quarter of the third millennium B.C., was reported to contain an amber macehead. Further east, amber was found in a grave at Tell Asmar (ancient Eshnunna) in the Diyala valley of Mesopotamia; it is assumed to date to the time of the Northern Palace, near which it lies, the main level of which is dated *c.* 2450–2350 B.C. This is at present the earliest attested amber find in the Near East, though as far as I know it has not been examined by an amber expert to see whether it is not rather some other resin. Amber, probably of the earliest second millennium B.C., also occurred at Assur and Hissar level IIIC, though the same reservation applies here.

In Greece, there are no reliable indications of amber earlier than the Shaft Grave period, and its appearance at that time must therefore be seen in connection with the general phenomenon of the Shaft Graves and the extraordinary way in which their occupants contrived to acquire new wealth in all sorts of forms. Indeed, it would only be natural to expect a certain amount of

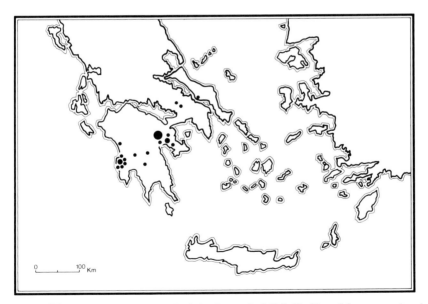

FIG. 13 ☐ Distribution of amber finds in Greece in LH I–II. Size of dot proportional to number of separate finds at each find-spot.

amber prior to that period, as the result of haphazard exchange mechanisms, possibly drawing on amber sources such as those of Sicily, Romania or the Ukraine. Not until the Shaft Grave period, however, were those mechanisms elaborated.

Figure 13 shows the distribution of amber in Greece in the early Mycenaean period. As can readily be seen, it is almost entirely concentrated in the Peloponnese, and above all at and around Mycenae and along the west of the Peloponnese. In LH I and II amber occurs on 14 sites in 36 different finds; the number of pieces known is in excess of 2500, giving a frequency per find of 70 pieces. (Compare by contrast the situation in LH IIIA, when the frequency is only 8·33 pieces per find, or in LH IIIB–C, when it drops to a mere 2·91.) In the Shaft Graves alone, more than 1560 beads were found. Over 500 pieces came from Kakovatos in Triphylia, the only sizeable find outside the Mycenae and Pylos areas.

The earliest of these finds are those from Shaft Grave Omicron[3] and the Pylos "Grave Circle",[4] dating to the very end of the Middle Helladic and beginning of the Late Helladic, i.e. c. 1550 B.C.

The great majority of the amber beads found in the Shaft Grave period are simple rounded beads, often lopsided, best described as "flattened spherical". Sometimes these are flattish, with a small hole, in which case they may be called "discoid"; sometimes they are more like a quoit, in which case they are referred to as "annular". Figure 14 shows a selection of the main shapes represented.

There are also some oddities. A few pieces are unperforated. Mycenae Chamber Tomb 518 produced an amygdaloid amber seal, of purely Mycenaean character. Other seals came from the Athens Agora, Pellanes and Routsi, the first two a little later in date. At Kakovatos are various unique shapes: ring pendants, figures-of-eight, and triple circles (Fig. 15). Most remarkable of all are the "spacer-plates", found at Kakovatos, Peristeria, Pylos Grave Circle, and—in greatest quantity—Mycenae Shaft Graves Omicron, IV and V. These consist on the one hand of D-shaped or trapezoidal end-pieces with converging perforations, on the other of rectangular central plates with parallel borings, at least some of which have V-perforations between the main borings. We shall return to the significance of these pieces shortly. Finally, there is the celebrated gold-bound disc from the tomb of the Double Axes at Knossos, which, though LM III A1 in date, it is convenient to take here.

The archaeological origin of amber

We have seen that amber in Greece must have been imported, and further that geologically most of it is "Baltic". Scientific analysis ceases to be of help at this

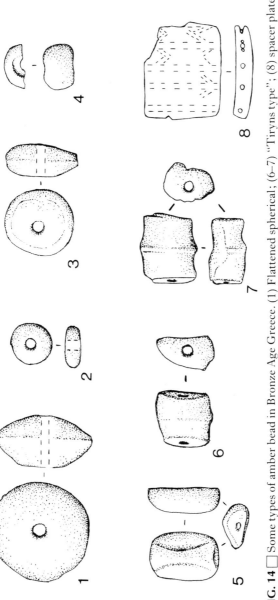

FIG. 14 ☐ Some types of amber bead in Bronze Age Greece. (1) Flattened spherical; (6–7) "Tiryns type"; (8) spacer plate.

point, for it is capable of distinguishing only the ultimate origin of the material, not its secondary points of deposition. Thus amber with typically "Baltic" spectra could have come either from the original or near-original deposits on the east Baltic and Jutland shores, or from the secondary deposits distributed far and wide from eastern England to the northern Ukraine. In order to have any hope of resolving this matter we have to turn to purely archaeological methods of investigation. For instance, we may consider the evidence of amber distribution in southern Europe, by types and periods, and with reference to sources. We may also see what light the study of bead types and functions sheds on the matter.

Amber in southern Europe

We have looked at the distribution of natural amber sources in Europe (Fig. 12) and of archaeological amber finds in early Mycenaean Greece (Fig. 13). The next step is to consider the spread of amber south of the Alps at approximately the same time. Figure 16.1 shows the distribution of amber finds in Italy and Jugoslavia, down to the Peschiera period (see Appendix 1, p. 307). Since the chronology of many of the sites in question is very imprecise, it is difficult to be sure that some of the finds shown as Late Bronze or Early Iron Age are not in fact earlier. It is also hard to identify which finds are contemporary with the early Mycenaean period; probably very few.

A substantial quantity of amber reached northern Italy (down to the Po valley) in the earlier Bronze Age, being found on Polada-type sites and more especially in *terremare*. The latter are not easily datable for they contain bronzes characteristic of the south German phases B, C and D, a majority being of the last-named.

On the other hand, amber in central and southern Italy and in Sicily during the Shaft Grave period is infrequent. Most of the finds claimed to be of this date[5] are either unsupported by firm associational evidence, or unpublished (the Salina find is an exception). Even in Sicily during times datable by middle Mycenaean ceramics (Plemmyrion) the quantity is very small.

The situation in Jugoslavia is no different: a mere three sites of the Early and Middle Bronze Age have, to my knowledge, produced amber (Bela Crkva, Belotić and Karavlaške kuće); of these, the first two could pre-date, the latter post-date, the Shaft Grave period, and none is near the coast.

The combined evidence of amber distributions in Italy and Jugoslavia in the Early and Middle Bronze Age thus provides little or no support for the idea of a derivation of early Mycenaean amber from, or via, those areas. It would be

FIG. 15 ☐ Amber necklace from Kakovatos, tholos A. (Photograph by the author.)

dangerous, however, to use this *argumentum ex silentio* to argue that the amber trade to Greece made no use of the Adriatic. One of the areas in Greece where amber is most densely concentrated is the west coast of the Peloponnese, and the Adriatic is, after all, the shortest route from there to those areas of central Europe where we know amber to have been in common circulation. Amber may well have been brought down it in the Shaft Grave period, but this cannot be demonstrated even by circumstantial evidence. In any case, as we shall see, there is another line of argument which produces very different results.

Shapes and function

As we have seen, the great majority of the amber beads are of simple shapes for stringing onto a necklace, though a few are different. We have to ask next whether the bead typology tells us anything about where they were made. For the great majority of pieces there are no clear indications. Mrs Hughes-Brock and I suggested that the lop-sidedness of many of the beads made Mycenaean manufacture—usually meticulous—unlikely. Amber typically requires very little working: it is often found in the form of water-rolled and worn pebbles, and would require little more than smoothing and perforating. Such skills were of course within the capabilities of the craftsmen of "barbarian" Europe. On the other hand, none of the most characteristic forms of the amber-producing area of Jutland, at any rate, are found in Greece apart from the undiagnostic flattened spherical shape;[6] similarly, there are certain pieces, like the "seals", which must have been of Mycenaean manufacture. So far, then, there is evidence for both importation as ready-made beads and for modification on the spot—the latter perhaps not being very common.

The pieces which clinch the argument are the so-called spacer-plates, whose function was to separate the strands of a multiple-thread necklace or related ornament. These much-studied objects have long occupied a key place in the study of early Mycenaean foreign connections, and a few words about the current situation are necessary. It fell to Merhart[7] to notice that amber spacer-plates of the general form found in the Shaft Graves also occur in central Europe and in the Wessex culture. Hachmann[8] provided a list of finds and—most important—demonstrated that the Greek and British pieces were worn in a different way from the German. Sandars[9] introduced the terms "basic pattern" and "complex-bored" to describe the particular types of perforation found on these pieces, and Gerloff[10] brought Hachmann's lists up to date and examined the dating of the central European pieces. Since then, further finds have been published (these are listed in Appendix 2 (p. 309)). There are now over 70 finds known, half of them in Germany (Fig. 17).

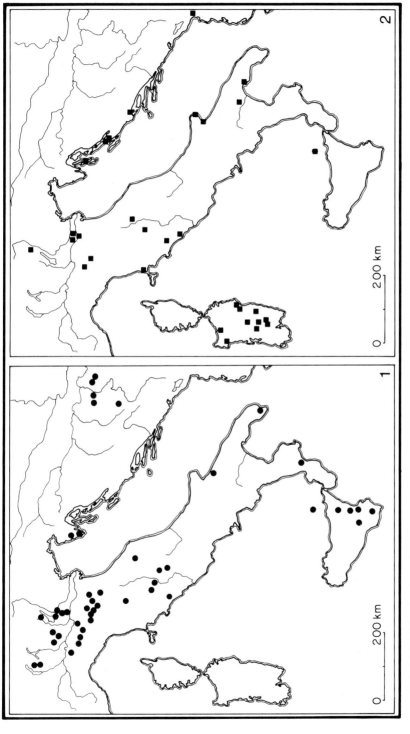

FIG. 16 ☐ Distribution of Bronze Age amber finds in Italy and Jugoslavia. (1) Earlier period (down to Peschiera phase, Br D); (2) later period (Protovillanovan, Ha A-B).

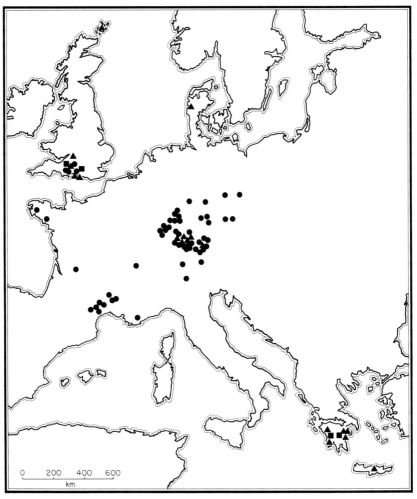

FIG. 17 ☐ Distribution of amber spacer-plates (after Gerloff). ▲, complex-bored with V-perforations; ■, end pieces with converging perforations; ●, all other types.

Spacer-plates are especially important because of their unusual and diag-nostic form. Beads in other materials in early Mycenaean Greece can have double or multiple perforations, but not commonly until LH IIIA; in any case, no piece is known that can be compared in detail with the amber spacer-plates. Spacers in other materials do occur, but in this precise form they are alien to the early Mycenaean world, though their function would have been well-enough understood.

The question of which spacer-plates outside Greece are nearest to the Greek examples was solved over 20 years ago by Hachmann,[11] who demonstrated convincingly, on the basis of the position of finds in Tumulus Culture graves and the likely reconstruction of the Wessex finds, that the former came from a pendant or "collier"-type necklace, the latter from a crescentic necklace not unlike a lunula in appearance (Fig. 18). Thirty-eight finds of spacers from central Europe were listed by Gerloff[12] and a further seven from France; of these only seven are of the complex-bored type "of basic pattern" (with V-borings between the main perforations), and therefore typologically comparable. Furthermore, of those seven, several are of different shapes and sizes (mainly smaller) from the "standard" British and Greek pieces. Shape, section, size and quality of work also set apart the remainder of the continental pieces.

If the Greek spacer-plates are not, then, similar to the central European, how similar are they to the British? Measurement of both showed that they are indistinguishable,[13] and can most plausibly be seen as having a common origin: whether one chooses to interpret this as meaning the same workshop or even craftsman, or as the general area in which such ornaments were worn, is a matter of personal taste. The evidence is, I believe, good enough to support even the former notion.

Even if the continental spacer-plates are somewhat different in detail and in function, however, it would be unrealistic to suppose that they are completely unconnected with the Graeco-British series. Indeed, the position of the finds in southern France, like the Grotte du Collier, Lastours (Aude) or the Grotte du Hasard (Gard) are suggestively placed when one considers *how* amber reached the Mediterranean lands (Fig. 17). In specific details, however, these pieces differ significantly from the complex-bored plates of basic pattern, and whatever else may be said about them, cannot have come from the same workshop or craftsman as the Graeco-British pieces, nor indeed do they reflect at all the same fashion in jewellery.

There can be little doubt that the fashion of wearing necklaces and breast ornaments in which spacer plates of amber were an important part was quite widespread during the Middle Bronze Age of southern Germany and south-eastern France, and that local craftsmen in several different areas worked at producing these pieces. It is hard to imagine that the man who produced the spacers from Upflamör-Lautrieb, tumulus 11, burial 5 was not aware of the similarity of his work to that of the craftsman responsible for the Wessex pieces; at the same time, he was not necessarily trying to produce the same effect. It seems reasonable, therefore, to think in terms of a general milieu where such amber ornaments were produced, and within it various local groupings where they were, in time, adapted to specific local fashions. Examination of the dating of the Tumulus Culture finds[14] has shown, further-more, that the complex-bored beads "in basic pattern" fall earlier in the

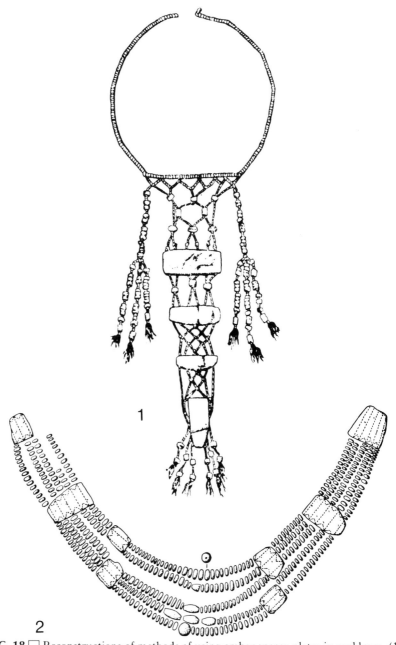

FIG. 18 ☐ Reconstructions of methods of using amber spacer-plates in necklaces. (1) Pendant type (Asenkofen grave E); (2) Collier type (Upton Lovell G.2e). (After Hachmann, 1957b; Annable and Simpson, 1964.)

period (Br B) than the rest of the complex-bored pieces, which date Br C2-D. Simple-bored pieces are more widely-spread in time, and in one case (Mutterstadt) were part of a crescentic necklace. This suggests that the various types should not be separated too rigidly from each other.

A brief word must be added about the celebrated gold-bound amber disc from the tomb of the Double Axes at Isopata near Knossos.[15] There are specific differences, but also specific similarities, between this piece and those from the Wessex barrows of Wilsford G. 8 and Preshute G. 1a (the Manton barrow), where they appear in pairs (Fig. 19). Being isolated, I do not feel that the Isopata piece can help the argument either way, though the balance of probability still lies in favour of a British origin.[16]

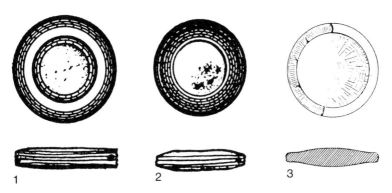

FIG. 19 □ Gold-bound amber discs from Wessex and Crete. (1) Wilsford G.8; (2) Manton (Preshute G. 1a); (3) Knossos, Tomb of the Double Axes. (After Annable and Simpson, 1964; Evans, 1914.)

The early Mycenaean amber trade

We have seen that of the large numbers of beads found in early Mycenaean Greece very few tell us anything specific about their origin. Some must have been fashioned locally, though equally, the specific technique of boring of others makes a local origin most unlikely. And, as has been stressed, the amber must have been imported from somewhere.

The crucial pieces are the amber spacer-plates. It seems hard to see these as anything but objects fashioned in north-west Europe and by one means or another transported to Greece. How this happened is what we must now consider.

The shortest and easiest route to Greece from the richest amber-producing areas of Europe is by way of the great rivers of the north European plain into central Europe, by the tributaries of the Danube to the Alps, over the Brenner

Pass to the head of the Adriatic, and then by sea to Greece. This is essentially the scheme which almost all authors have followed, with variations, since Navarro's classic article of 1925.[17] We cannot, of course, say that this is not what happened, but we can point to the possibility of a different scenario. As we have seen, typological analysis links the Greek spacers with the British, and not—except in a general way—with the German. There are no intermediate finds in Italy or the Balkans which would help us. A direct line from Britain to Greece would take one through France, over the Alps and down through Italy. A more reasonable and easier route would be to follow the Rhône valley to the Mediterranean and travel from there by sea around the foot of Italy. For this latter route we *could* point to the group of spacers, and of course the sizeable distribution of ordinary amber beads, in the Languedoc—except that the spacers are not of the required form and the dating is too late. The alleged Mycenaean connection of the "engraved" bead from Lastours[18] is most implausible. These pieces cannot, then, by themselves be used to support such a link. The fact that Breton elements are also involved in the general connection between the Wessex culture and Mycenaean Greece does not assist the argument one way or the other.[19] We are in fact powerless to specify more closely how the amber travelled, and it would seem to me no less likely that it came all the way from Britain by sea than that it travelled across France to the Mediterranean. On this matter the evidence does not permit anything more than speculation. I think, though, that there is enough at our disposal to amount to a reasonable hypothesis that the trade was highly directional and not carried on by numerous "middlemen" across Europe.

Gerloff has argued[20] that Wessex had craftsmen who were specialists in the working of amber (amber cups, pommels, etc.), and that the fineness of the work on the spacer-plates is a characteristic hallmark of their products. This naturally reinforces what I have argued here. On the other hand, most of the ordinary beads in Mycenaean Greece were not so worked, and there are no particular grounds for preferring one point of origin to another for them. It is merely economy of hypotheses that makes one prefer a similar origin for all the early Mycenaean amber, rather than imagine it being gathered in from various different sources. Some of the Mycenaean beads are quite large, but not larger than can be found in any of the naturally occurring deposits we have listed, including the east coast of England. One should bear in mind, too, the scale of the supposed trade we are talking about. Amber is light, and hundreds or even thousands of beads can easily be carried by one man. All the amber in early Mycenaean Greece could have been carried in a single journey—though no doubt more than one did in fact occur. In this connection it is worth speculating on how much amber may once have been buried in relation to what now survives. Naturally we cannot know what the earth still holds in store for us, or what has already been destroyed. It is highly unlikely, however, that another Mycenae remains to be found, or has ever been found. By far the largest amount of amber came from Mycenae; elsewhere one has odd beads or, at most, tens of beads. There are numerous finds of all periods where amber has *not* occurred, even allowing for poor recovery rates (the large cemetery of Tanagra in Boeotia, for example, where there are many beads of other materials, but not a single piece of amber). It is most unlikely that amber was ever common as an ornament of any Mycenaeans except the first—and then principally those of Mycenae and the west Peloponnese. I therefore consider it unlikely that regular boatloads of amber were arriving on Greek shores at any stage of the Bronze Age. The idea of regular exchange of amber for faience or any other commodities[21] seems implausible. This supposed contact has been used to support the idea of a regular tin trade to the north-west.[22] Tin is a different matter; the amber trade must not be exaggerated.

If the above is accepted, the implications for chronology are clear. The period of deposition of spacer-plates in Greece is LH I–IIA, i.e. *c.* 1550–1440 B.C. If one wishes to include the gold-bound disc from Isopata of LM III A1, the bracket can be extended to *c.* 1375 B.C. The end-point does not in any case assist us as much as the starting-point. If the Shaft Grave spacers are of British manufacture, the amber craftsmen of Wessex must have been at work by 1550 B.C., and we should probably envisage them having produced such objects over at least a century, although it is just possible that the Kakovatos pieces are heirlooms.

Spacer-plates occur in graves both of Gerloff's Wilsford series and of her Aldbourne series, so that the associations of spacers in Wessex are somewhat miscellaneous—probably the most regular association is with faience beads. This makes a span of a century or even two, as the Greek parallels suggest, not unreasonable for the lifetime of the form.

As far as the continental pieces are concerned, we have seen that the basic-pattern examples are present already in Br B. I can see nothing to exclude a general synchronization of that and even part of the succeeding period with LH I and IIA in Greece. Put in a loose way, 1500 B.C. is likely to represent a point in the Tumulus period, as it is also in the Wessex culture.

In the early Mycenaean period we see a very limited distribution of amber in Greece: relatively large amounts on few sites, as compared with the small amounts on large numbers of sites found later on. One appears, therefore, to be dealing here with a highly centralized system in which wealth was concentrated in small areas and, no doubt, small numbers of people. Redistribution was an almost negligible factor, unless one imagines that the finds of the next period are redistributed from this.

Renfrew has suggested[23] that the amber trade is an example of the "prestige chain" model of exchange, by which a commodity is utilized mainly in exchanges between notable persons and neither used in daily life nor kept in a single owner's possession for an indefinite period. I do not believe that the available facts fit this interpretation. In the first place, I have argued that the amber trade in the early period was a highly directional one: as such it should be typical rather of Renfrew's "directional commercial trade" where the quantities fall off steeply from the source or supply zone but are present in abnormally large quantities for the shape of the curve at a relatively distant point or points. This model seems more apt for amber than Renfrew's subsequent one for directional trade[24] which depends on the effect of redistribution within central places, and produces an unevenly decreasing curve with marked "bumps" in it.

On the other hand, once within the early Mycenaean sphere the idea of a prestige chain exchange is highly plausible. Early amber normally occurs in "rich" contexts, that is in well-equipped tombs, and this is especially so in the Shaft Grave period. Such movement out from the main centres as did take place is best explained as having been between notables or those who had established gift-exchange links. There was clearly no general access to the amber supply in this period.

The later period (LH III)

Amber was used as a material for ornaments in middle and late Mycenaean Greece, but its spread and occurrences were of a rather different nature from that in LH I–II.

The maps in Figs 20 and 21 shows clearly two main things: (1) the quantity of amber in LH III is much less than in LH I–II, and (2) the distribution is much greater. In LH IIIA amber still occurs in some quantity at and around Mycenae, and there are a few finds near Pylos; it also occurs in Kos, Crete, Cyprus and Syria in the east, and Zakynthos, Sicily and Salina in the west, with finds reaching north to Thessaly. In LH IIIB amber appears in northwest Greece for the first time, and disappears altogether at Pylos, perhaps because few grave-groups are attributable to the period; in LH IIIC and "Submycenaean" there are more finds from the north and west, as well as the east (Rhodes, Alalakh, Cyprus)—generally amber was more widely distributed in LH IIIC than at any other time.

The range of bead types is more restricted in the later than the earlier Mycenaean period. Really the only unusual type to appear with any regularity is the so-called "Tiryns shape", described as "a stubby, roughly cylindrical or concave biconical bead with a central swelling and sometimes a 'collar' at each end" (Fig. 14, 6–7). Its most famous appearance is on the Tiryns wheels (Fig. 22), but the type occurs elsewhere in Greece and also up the Adriatic on both sides (Fig. 23). The only datable pieces in Greece are LH IIIC or

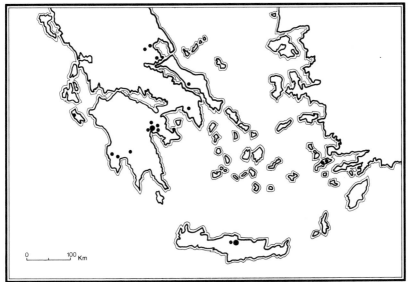

FIG. 20 ☐ Distribution of amber finds in Greece in LH IIIA. Size of dot proportional to number of separate finds at each find-spot.

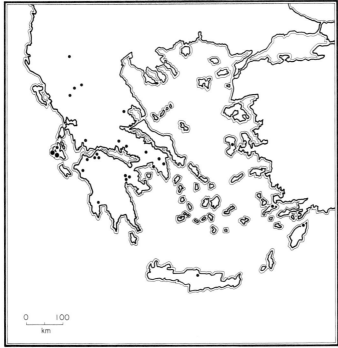

FIG. 21 ☐ Distribution of amber finds in Greece in LH IIIB–C.

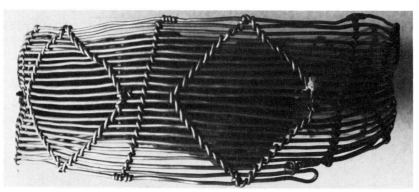

"Submycenaean", i.e. twelfth to eleventh centuries; in Italy they occur in Protovillanovan contexts. Since the dating of the Italian finds depends on the Greek it is not possible to suggest a point of origin for the type, which must be seen in the wider picture of amber dissemination in the Late Mycenaean period. The specific nature of the Tiryns wheels must also be taken into account.

Amber was a good deal more common in Late Bronze Age Italy than in earlier periods, both on northern sites (*terremare*) and in central and southern Italy. Of the latter finds, those from Plemmyrion and Salina date to the middle Mycenaean period and are presumably to be seen as part of the same process that brought Mycenaean pottery to the area. Those from Lipari and Torre Castelluccia are probably twelfth century in date; the Lipari pieces, of Tiryns type and in a pithos burial of Ausonian II date, are part of an assemblage seen by its excavator as wholly intrusive.[25] In this connection, the finds from the Po valley site of Frattesina must be mentioned.[26] Little has so far been published about this site, but the material recovered is of the highest importance. Imported material includes a late Mycenaean sherd, ivory pieces for working and ostrich-eggs: there was also evidence of glass- and metal-working on site. The amber finds are varied: the most characteristic are ribbed conical beads and beads of Tiryns type, though in addition there are globular, biconical, lentoid and annular pieces. No information seems to be available on the find circumstances of these pieces, though I venture to suggest, however, that Frattesina is one place where amber could have been worked. Dr Bietti Sestieri has not found positive evidence of such working, but it is arguable whether it would survive in any case. Arts and crafts, particularly ornament manufacture, were certainly being carried out on a sizeable scale, and amber, which appears on the site in forms little known from elsewhere, like the ribbed conical shape, could well have been among the materials worked. Might the Tiryns shape have originated there?

In Jugoslavia and Albania I know of only seven finds that are likely to be contemporary with late Mycenaean Greece, though many more appear in the earliest Iron Age (Fig. 16.2). Of these, the beads from Barç (which I have not seen) go with very late Mycenaean pottery and are probably to be seen in connection with the north-west Greek finds of late LH IIIB or early IIIC.[27] Several of the Jugoslav and some of the Albanian finds (perhaps early Iron Age in date) are of the Tiryns type, while the fluted beads known from Frattesina recur at Privlaka in Bosnia. The greatest quantities of amber come from Istria—an important situation at the head of the Adriatic—though few of them certainly date to the period in question rather than HaB or later.

FIG. 22 ☐ "Wheel" of woven and wound gold wire, with bronze spokes and amber beads of "Tiryns type", from the Tiryns Treasure. (Photographs by the author.)

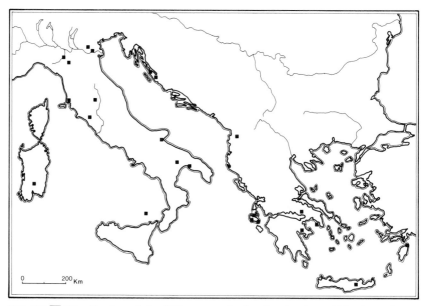

FIG. 23 ☐ Distribution of the "Tiryns type" of amber bead, twelfth–eleventh centuries B.C.

The evidence of late Mycenaean amber is far from conclusive, but points in a very different direction from that of the early period. The one type that is diagnostic is found most notably up the Adriatic, and on a site (Frattesina) where production of jewellery is known to have taken place. The largest finds of amber in Greece come from the west (Kephallenia), and several areas in the west and north-west received amber for the first time (Achaea, Epirus, Aetolia). Amber is well known along the Adriatic in the Iron Age, and some finds from there date to the Late Bronze Age. It seems most reasonable, therefore, to see the amber trade as having been conducted along the Adriatic from at least 1200 B.C. on. How the amber reached the Adriatic is another matter. I have already touched on the geographical possibilities (p. 79); it remains to add here that at least some of this late amber in Greece is "Baltic", including the Tiryns wheels beads.

The type of trade that accounts for the observed distribution of later Mycenaean amber is different from that postulated for the earlier period. The route by which it got to Greece was different, and its dissemination within Greece was far more widespread. Here it is much more plausible than it was in the early period to think in terms of a "prestige chain" exchange.[28] According to the general formulation of the model the quantities should fall off only gradually from the supply zone. With amber we have a zone of abundance over central Europe down to the Alps, and a markedly smaller quantity south of the Alps. Perhaps the best adaptation of the model is to evisage all of central Europe as constituting the "supply zone" which the Alps then restrict; thereafter the gradual decrease is a clear feature. Furthermore, within Greece it is evident that amber was rather more widely available than hitherto, in that it found its way into the hands of considerably more people. It is possible that once within Greece the exchange of amber in this period was not so much a prestige affair as before, and more related to the activities of entrepreneurs.

Amber thus serves a crucial role in the definition of trade to and from Mycenaean Greece, since its origin as a raw material can be shown to lie outside Greece. The places where it was fashioned into beads are harder to distinguish, but some definite answers are obtainable. The situation with other materials is much more complicated, especially those involving specialized technological knowledge such as glass and faience. Since several authors have considered that beads of faience were used as the direct exchange medium for amber, we must now turn to a consideration of glass and faience as traded commodities in Bronze Age Europe.

Faience

Few topics have caused so much confusion and controversy in Bronze Age studies as the study of the material usually called "faience". Faience properly so-called is the glazed majolica emanating originally from Faenza (French: *Faience*) in Emilia-Romagna. It is characterized by its white core and its glaze, which was applied after the firing of the core. The term was taken over by Egyptologists to describe various kinds of vitreous material known from ancient Egypt, and was also widely used in Near Eastern studies, where comparable materials occurred from an early date. Beads of a silica-based compound similar to Egyptian faience occur in central Europe, Malta, Britain and elsewhere, in varying contexts of second millennium B.C. date. All authorities accept that the technology originated in the Near East; what is in question is the place of manufacture of these beads.

The story of the "faience bead connection" goes back to the last century.[29] Sir Arthur Evans, among others, remarked on the similarity of British to Egyptian eighteenth dynasty beads.[30] The classic study by H. C. Beck and J. F. S. Stone in 1936 came down in favour of a foreign origin for the British beads, and V. G. Childe spotted a number of similar beads in the museums of central and eastern Europe.[31] Stone and Thomas provided an enlarged catalogue in 1956, in an article which also gave the first results of scientific analysis, conducted by the technique of emission spectrography. Their conclusions were again that a foreign—probably Egyptian—origin was the most likely for all European Bronze Age faience, though they admitted that their analytical results were inconclusive. In 1965, the traditional view reached its most complete and developed form. Gimbutas pointed to the hitherto unnoticed or unpublished beads in the southern USSR and in other parts of central and eastern Europe, particularly Slovakia, and, on the assumption that they were imported, claimed a broad contemporaneity for all of them; this is one of the mainstays of her Bronze Age chronology. In much of Europe this remains the position: publications of beads emanating from Czechoslovakia and Poland, where the most recent finds have been made, are firm in their belief that the beads were imported from the eastern Mediterranean.[32] The first serious attempt to argue that local production was possible came in 1970, when Newton and Renfrew reworked the analytical figures produced by Thomas in 1956, and showed that discrete groupings could be discerned. In 1971 I also argued for local production, on the basis of the clearly separable bead types in central Europe, and the early 1970s saw a sudden flurry of activity in the analysis of faience beads, by neutron activation and by X-ray fluorescence. Unfortunately, the two main studies[33] produced diametrically opposite results, which has made archaeologists working on the problem of Mycenaean contacts tend to concentrate on typological rather than analytical procedures. In fact, little work has been done on the problem since 1973, so that the time is ripe for a fresh consideration, especially as continental scholars continue, almost without exception, to speak of an Egyptian origin without further comment.

Terminology

Many different kinds of composite glassy material, utilizing the same basic components, are known from the fourth millennium B.C. onwards. The main building block of all of them is silica. The differences between "glass", "faience", "glass-paste" and the like are in fact chemical. According to Brill,[34] in "glass" the chemical reactions go furthest towards completion, there is more alkali than in faience, and the temperature of firing is higher; under the microscope glass appears as a vitrified mass, with the occasional bubble and "stone" (piece of unfused quartz). In "glassy faience", there is less crystalline quartz than in faience and a more homogeneous spread of the colour (which penetrates throughout) and the glassy matrix; under the microscope one can see, embedded in this matrix, bubbles and small lumps of quartz, and also quartz crystals. Chemically defined, it is not homogeneous like glass. Finally, "faience" has, as a finished product, two parts—body and glaze. The body contains 95–98% SiO_2 and 2–5% CaO and/or Na_2O; it appears snow-white, and the silica grains have an "alpha quartz crystal structure", indicating firing to less than 870°C; they are connected by some glassy "cement", and the whole is surrounded by an encircling "tissue". There are also void spaces among the quartz crystals. A layer of fluid glass forms around the crystals during firing, cooling to become the glassy cement seen under the microscope. The glaze is a true glass, as described above, and is usually blue in colour (if copper oxide has been the colouring agent). It contains, in addition to SiO_2, 15–20% alkali, 5–10% CaO and 2–4% CuO.

Mycenaean glass-pastes, as well as most of the European beads, may represent a fourth stage, where the basic mixture would be similar but contain less alkali. This would produce a glass in which the quartz crystals fused enough to be impacted together, but not enough to produce any real vitrification on the surface. The amount of vitrification would in any case depend on the heat at which the beads were fired; this would probably be rather less than for faience.

Materials and manufacture

The question of how Bronze Age faience was made is controversial. Because faience is a silica-based substance, the necessary raw materials could be obtained from a number of sources: crushed quartz, flint, feldspar, or (most likely of all) sand, which would be mixed with an alkali (to bind the grains together), a colouring agent, and a lime to reduce the temperature at which fusion takes place. So far, so good; what is more difficult to understand is how the characteristic appearance of faience—whitish core and coloured glaze— was achieved. There are basically two schools of thought: the traditional view, that the core was made first, coated with a slip and then fired again; and the view, or views, that faience is "self-glazing", the glaze layer occurring by "wicking out" or some similar process. The former has been held to imply a rather complex technology which would not easily be repeated outside the main manufacturing areas; this argument is the main prop for the theory of exportation from the Near East. The latter view, on the other hand, would, if shown to be possible, imply that many areas of the Bronze Age with a knowledge of pyrotechnology to pottery-firing level would have been technically capable of producing faience for themselves.

The standard view, as given by Beck, Lucas and others,[35] has it that faience is

> a composite material comprising a pre-fired core and a blue surface glaze . . ..
> The core, usually consisting of finely ground sand mixed with a small amount of alkali, is shaped and fired. The alkali reacts with the sand, effectively holding the grains together. A prepared blue glaze, essentially a low-melting point soda-lime

glass, is then applied to the core surface and the whole refired under oxidizing conditions to yield the final product.[36]

According to Stone and Thomas, the glaze would be applied to the core in powdered form as a slip.[37]

This was undoubtedly one possible method of achieving the results that Egyptian faience-makers did, but was it the only one? One crucial objection to this process is that Egyptian faience objects are glazed over their entire surface, without any trace of the way the object was supported during firing. This objection has led some authors to suppose that the objects must have been enveloped by a protective substance which protected the unfired surface while promoting the necessary chemical reactions.[38]

Two sets of laboratory experiments which sought to reproduce the methods of faience manufacture have claimed to have found the solution. Noble[39] gives three recipes, for standard faience, semi-glass, and blue faience glass; these are variations on recipes produced by Rhodes.[40] The assembled powders must be mixed into a paste, either with water (which tends to give too little adhesion to the mixture), with gum (as in modern Iran),[41] or with clay, which reduces the vitreosity obtainable. Complicated shapes are said to be impossible because of the fragility of the material—yet the wealth of vases and other elaborate objects from the Near East, Egypt and Crete contradict this. An obvious point which is, however, not remarked on in the literature (and for which I thank Mr Stanley Warren), is that better forming properties are obtained from very fine quartz grains—indeed, with them reasonable cohesion can be obtained even using water.

Noble's methods take no account of the fact that the objects were not supported in the kiln, however, and it is the second set of experiments, those by Kiefer and Allibert, which seem able to overcome these difficulties most convincingly.[42] They, like Noble, gave good reasons for believing that faience was self-glazing: not only does the glaze cover the entire body, but the detail on it is very fine; it is very resistant to scratching, and is very thin. Chemical analysis, too, suggests that the glaze layer does not result from the normal process of covering a paste body with a glaze layer. Experimentation with firing temperatures showed that the range employed was 870–920°C. Two recipes are given, one containing copper oxide and soluble alkaline salts such as natron, the other containing "frit", that is, a material such as a slag resulting from copper refining. The crucial difference in the method adopted by Kiefer and Allibert lies in the use of an enveloping material to achieve a uniform glaze over the whole body. The best substances were found to be calcite-based, with the addition of talc or bauxite, niter and calcined oxides with a strong concentration of copper. Alternatively the use of soluble salts like natron or alum could produce efflorescence on the surface of the paste, and the enveloping material could be dry, just being heaped up round the objects.

Good results were obtained by several of these methods, and there seems little reason to doubt that Egyptian and related faiences were made in ways similar to these.

Not only must the right recipe be found, but the resulting paste must be formed into shapes. Beads might be formed in various ways: by moulds, by hand, by using two pieces of wood like butter-pats, by using a box like a cake-icer, or by a simple ring device for extracting a tube of the mixture from its parent mass. To make discoid beads, one could either follow these methods or cut off slices from a tube of material. Star-shaped and other more complex types would be made by hand. For the segmented beads Beck and Stone favoured the butter-pat method, and in experiments produced some remarkably good imitations.[43] The use of the mould is attested for Mycenaean jewellery, but not for European beads.

The central perforation could have been made either by pushing a thin rod of wood or metal through the bead, or by firing the bead with an organic object, such as a straw, in the centre. The bead could most easily have been made by dipping a straw into a paste, and cutting off pieces of the required length.

How far does the technology of Egyptian faience bear upon the faience objects (mainly beads) of "barbarian" Europe in the Bronze Age? It is obvious that the materials used must have been similar, if not identical. Most faience beads that I have examined (in Britain and in central Europe) are barely, if at all, vitreous: the presence of a glazed layer is not obvious. The beads are opaque and the colour ranges from whitish to light blue and green: weathering is known to affect the surface of the faience. Under the microscope the material can be seen to be extremely unhomogeneous, with small cavities, impurities, and individual crystals readily discernible. The colouring and surface texture are the same over the whole area of the bead, however, which suggests that an enveloping material of the type suggested by Kiefer and Allibert was used. The lack of vitrification could be due either to the recipe used (e.g. insufficient alkali) or to the firing temperature being too low. Whatever the reason, it seems quite clear that most of the beads of Bronze Age Europe are technically inferior to those of Egypt and the Near East. The technology involved is quite within the capacity of Bronze Age pottery-firing skills. Technically, therefore, there is no reason to believe that local manufacture of faience beads could not have been taking place throughout Europe. Whether it *was* in fact taking place must be decided by two lines of argument: archaeological, that is typological and contextual, and analytical, that is based on the results of constituent analysis.

Distribution and types of Early Bronze Age faience[44]

The distribution of Early Bronze Age faience beads covers a wide geographical area, but occurs in clusters. It is by no means clear that all of these are even approximately contemporary. The faience bead "horizon", if it is accurate to use such a term, occurs in central Europe during the earlier part of the Early Bronze Age, which might be dated before 2000 b.c. if calibrated radiocarbon dates are any guide (cf. p. 278). Most of the beads from the graves of Early Bronze Age Wessex, on the other hand, can hardly date before 1500 B.C., but the beads recently found at Shaugh Moor on Dartmoor with a radiocarbon date of 1480 ± 90 b.c. could be earlier. The occurrence of small blue glass beads in north European graves of periods II and III, and in France, demonstrates that wide divergences of type, technology, date and area have often in the past been glossed over. In order to understand how and when faience manufacture originated and spread, we must first carry out a survey of each area where it occurs.

The production of glass pastes had been in progress since the fifth millennium in the Near East; in Egypt it became a major industry in the third millennium, while the first finds in Crete occur in EM II (it is uncertain whether these are locally made or imported, and if the latter, from where). On the Greek mainland a bead came from the Macedonian mound of Ayios Mamas, allegedly dating to the Early Bronze Age,[45] but I have seen this piece and am doubtful that it is of glass paste. Glass paste beads were found in a number of MH contexts on the mainland.[46] Faience production got under way during the Old Palace period on Crete, with the Vat Room deposit at Knossos and certain seals in Mesara tombs providing the earliest certain evidence for local production. On the mainland, production did not start until the Mycenaean period, probably not before 1500 B.C. since the faience objects in the Shaft Graves are certainly imports. There is no question of any close connection between the Aegean and Europe before 1500 as far as faience is concerned, because the types produced in Middle Minoan Crete are quite distinct from anything found to the north and west. Even after that, possible connections seem few and far between, with quite different types involved: Mycenaean faience and glass was used for elaborate plaques and highly ornamented beads, as well as for a variety of simple bead shapes. Yet the segmented type was rare, only occurring on a few sites near Mycenae and at, for instance, Nichoria in Messenia.[47] Star beads—of an individual form—are known from a few sites, but the four-pointed bead seems to be entirely absent.

The faience and glass industries of southern Italy, Sicily and Malta (Fig. 24) in the earlier part of the Bronze Age are almost certainly connected with those of the East Mediterranean; in most cases it is likely that the beads are actual imports, so close do the forms appear. Beads of glass paste have been reported from Early Bronze Age Castelluccio contexts,[48] and certainly occur in the Sicilian Middle Bronze Age, both in domestic contexts, as in a hut on Salina (Aeolian Islands),[49] and in funerary contexts, as at Thapsos and Plemmyrion.[50] There are also finds from later contexts, such as those from

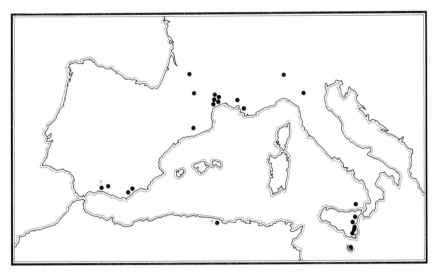

FIG. 24 ☐ Distribution of faience and glass-paste in the western Mediterranean, earlier Bronze Age.

Torre Castelluccia, of bright blue translucent glass, in the form of a necklace of annular and discoid beads with bone terminal spacers.[51] Several hundred beads come from this site, which other material connects intimately to the west of Greece (e.g. amber beads, bronze types). The beads from Malta were noted by Stone and Thomas: they consist of very small disc beads and some segmented specimens.[52] Coming as they do from the Tarxien Cemetery, they belong to the local Early Bronze Age which is, however, a rather hazy concept: at least part of the Tarxien Cemetery period must run parallel to the Thapsos period in Sicily, according to ceramic evidence, which would place them in the same time bracket as the pieces from Sicily. A similar origin for both groups of beads would seem likely.

Elsewhere in Italy a group of faience objects have been noted from *terremare* and related sites: the main occupation of these is of Middle Bronze Age date, though there is also Early Bronze Age material. The objects of faience include both buttons and beads (Fig. 25.10) and the former are unique—local manufacture thus seems assured.[53] Possibly of Early Bronze Age date, on the other hand, are the biconical beads from Lucone di Polpenazze on the western shore of Lake Garda. This site might provide a link with the finds from the Bleiche at Arbon on Lake Constance, where a star and a quoit bead were found.[54] It is possible that if more lake-side settlements had occupation spanning this period, more such finds would have been made. At present though, the number of finds of faience from Italy is not large.

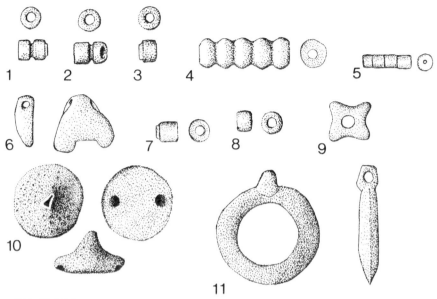

FIG. 25 ☐ Some types of faience bead from various parts of Europe, earlier Bronze Age. (1–3) Segmented beads, Poland; (4) segmented, Britain; (5) segmented, Slovakia; (6) pendant, Poland; (7–8) cylindrical, Slovakia; (9) four-pointed, Hungary; (10) button, Italy; (11) ring pendant, Britain.

Also of interest are the small group of faience beads in Spain, more numerous than hitherto believed to be the case. As well as beads from Fuente Alamo, Almeria, which were known to Beck and Stone in 1936, other finds or possible finds come from El Argar, Monachil (Granada) and Velez Malaga (Malaga) (the contexts are apparently Argaric Early Bronze Age),[55] and from La Roca del Frare (Barcelona), a cave without good contextual information.[56] Continuing north-eastwards up and along the Gulf of Lions one comes to a group of rather varied finds from the south of France, from settlement caves and from dolmens. These amount only to some seven finds, however, which is hardly the massive evidence for use of the Rhône valley as a trade route which some authorities would wish us to envisage. It is worthy of note that an amber bead was found with the faience in the Roca del Frare cave, though as far as I am aware, this association does not recur in any of the numerous southern French sites containing amber (cf. p. 80).[57]

Stone noted a reference to faience beads and a "bead factory" on the Pic des Singes, Béjaia, Algeria, which would, if confirmed, be an interesting addition to the map.[58] On the whole, though, it has to be admitted that the evidence for faience distribution in the central and western Mediterranean is not extensive (Fig. 24), and for production negligible.

Faience was being produced in Mesopotamia by the Ubaid period and possibly even earlier, so that it comes as no surprise to find objects of some glass-paste substance in southern Russia, the Ukraine, and the Caucasus. Unfortunately, many of the sites where such finds have been made were dug long ago, and some of the finds are now lost. I have not been able to see any of the reported faience from the Soviet Union, and as the forms in any case are distinct from those current elsewhere in the European Early Bronze Age, their relevance to the task in hand is questionable. Beads of "glass" or "faience" come from two chronological contexts: Usatovo and Catacomb Grave (a single find, of 43 beads, was made in a barrow in Galicia, with material of the Mierzanowice group). The Usatovo group is a late variant of Tripolje, and though some have argued[59] that it should run parallel with an advanced stage of the Bronze Age, a third millennium date is preferable both from radiocarbon determinations and from typological analogies. What remains uncertain is the precise nature of the "glass" objects found, and the exact context in which they occurred: Usatovo barrows often continue in use right through the Bronze Age. At the type-site itself two beads came from Kurgan 2, grave 1: one was dark and ribbed, the other whitish and irregular piriform. They came from quite different levels, though they are both thought to have belonged to primary burials.[60] At Sofijivka cremation cemetery biconical, spherical and ribbed beads occur, but apparently from stray contexts; at Parkany near Odessa a single "glass" bead was found in Kurgan 51, grave 1, with a bone disc, copper pin, and pot.[61] This find should perhaps be seen in relation to the "dark blue glass bead" from the Werteba Cave (Bil'če Zolote, Boršćiv, near Černivci) in Podolia, said to be associated with a dagger of Early Bronze Age date.[62] Other pieces said to be of glass appear to fall in the Middle Bronze Age, occurring in graves of Komarov type (as at Komarov itself, or Selence near Terebovlja).[63]

The finds of Catacomb Grave associations are also miscellaneous in character. Most remarkable is the group from the habitation site of Babino near Cherson on the Lower Dnieper, where yellow beads were found, including "rounded" examples and others "shaped like a bird's head".[64] The only piece that has been illustrated shows a very strange shape indeed, but most of the other finds are of simple annular or tubular beads. A single find has been attributed to a Pit Grave context, that from Perejezdnaja Kurgan 1, grave 4, but from the available accounts a much later date would seem equally possible.[65] Finally we may mention an intriguing find made in 1891 at Vorobjovka near Kursk in a Timber Grave (and therefore considerably later than those dealt with hitherto): six small faience beads were said to have been found together with an Egyptian scarab.[66] Unfortunately no confirmation of this find is available.

The Caucasian area was prolific in glassy objects during the second millennium, and two finds have been quoted from the third millennium.[67] In view of the proximity of this area to Iran and Mesopotamia this is not surprising, and I do not propose to consider the finds made in the Caucasus or Transcaucasia further except to remark that the area could well have served as a point of origin for the technology used for glass manufacture in the Ukraine. Early glass in the Soviet Union, then, gives hints of a wide diffusion at an early date, but because of the lack of detailed analysis no definite statements can be made. Only those finds from the western border republics bear any relation to the finds from central Europe.

In Romania few finds have been made. From Brailiţa grave 20 came 156 beads, mostly annular but three in the form of a flat oval pendant, in a cemetery of the Usatovo group.[68] A single segmented bead from Almaş (Braşov) is much quoted; more numerous were the finds in cemeteries 2 and 4 at Monteoru, not yet published.[69] A biconical bead from Poiana is also often quoted in the literature, but examination of this piece showed that it is probably not of faience but clay.[70]

We now come to the very numerous finds of faience beads made in central Europe, notably Hungary, Czechoslovakia and Poland. Well over 50 finds are involved, and the find associations are remarkably homogeneous. By far the majority come from contexts early in the Early Bronze Age: Pecica and related groups, Nagyrév, Kisapostag, Nitra, Mierzanowice, Košt'any, Strzyżów, early Únětice and related. A much smaller number of finds date to later Early Bronze Age contexts: Vatya, Otomani, perhaps Mad'arovce, and later Únětice. The map in Fig. 26 shows the main concentrations of find-spots. By and large this is also the area of the groups mentioned: the beads are not distributed continuously, but then neither are the sites as a whole. The most interesting thing about the central European faience is that particular areas specialized in particular shapes, a fact which is of considerable significance when we come to consider the production area of the beads. Thus the four-pointed bead is common in Hungary, the short cylindrical, long, thin segmented, wedge-shaped and others occur in the Košice area (and nowhere else), the facetted annular are especially common in west Slovakia, and segmented and annular are the Moravian types.

I have examined many of these groups of beads, mostly through a magnifying glass though a few only through the museum case. The groups are very homogeneous between sites, and, in my opinion, definitely all came from the same workshop or source (after all, this may have been no more than a single craftsman turning out large numbers of beads over a short period). The case of the Košice beads shows that individual forms were characteristic of individual areas, but also that the source for that area was capable of producing several different types of beads simultaneously. In the east the colour is a deep blue, very opaque, while in west Slovakia it is very bright. The Moravian and Polish beads vary in colour from pale blue and green to almost colourless. There is no

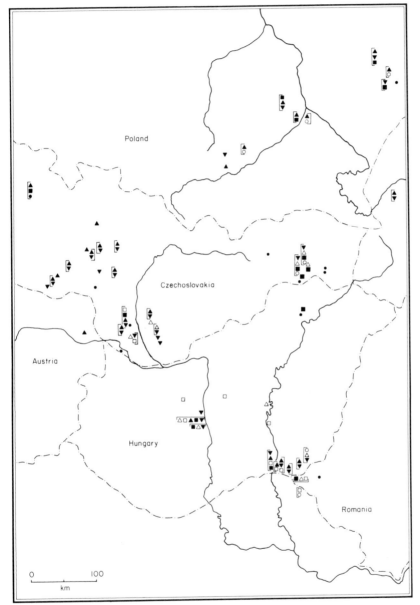

FIG. 26 ☐ Distribution of faience beads in central Europe, showing marked clustering in particular areas of Hungary and Czechoslovakia. Key to bead types: ○, discoid; ▲, segmented; △, facetted annular; ■, cylindrical; ▼, annular; ☐, four-pointed; ●, other or unknown. The brackets indicate multiple types from a single site.

sign of surface glaze, though a few crystals on the surface have become vitrified in a few cases.

In other areas of central Europe the situation is much less clear. An early Únĕtice cemetery at Polepy in Bohemia produced 22 annular beads, quite different from those in Moravia; a segmented bead came from Horní Přím, along with two cylindrical dark green beads. In Austria a single segmented bead comes from the Leopoldsdorf cemetery; all the other finds from Austria and Germany are of glass and later in date. On the other hand, the well known star and quoit beads from the Bleiche at Arbon on Lake Constance fall absolutely in line with the faience from other parts of Europe—its date is the later part of the Early Bronze Age.

In Britain the position is unusual in that there are many finds, but rather a small total quantity of beads. Practically the whole of Britain is covered (Fig. 27), with clusters in Wessex (mainly segmented beads) and south-west Scotland (mainly star beads), and secondary groups in the South-East, East Anglia, the Peak district, Ayrshire, Morayshire, N. Ireland and elsewhere. The segmented beads closely resemble the Moravian examples, though they are usually compared to Egyptian finds. A four-pointed bead from Stainsby (Lincs.) has been compared to Hungarian examples, but is much larger.

With two exceptions (Rillaton and Figheldean) all the Wessex beads come from female burials, and do not occur in dagger-graves. Only one (Amesbury G. 44) accompanied Wilsford-series grave-goods.[71] Almost half, according to Gerloff, occur in or with cinerary urns, which are either collared and often cord-decorated, or else of the cordoned biconical type. The female grave-goods of the Aldbourne series include ornaments of gold, amber and shale, and miniature vessels such as grape and incense cups.

In Denmark and northern Germany only the Fjallerslev segmented bead fits into the Early Bronze Age pattern as seen elsewhere; graves of Montelius II and III were furnished with small blue glass beads which seem, from the description of them as "*bunte funkelnde Glas*", to have been truly vitreous and translucent. It is argued below that this represents a more developed stage in the process of manufacture, and should thus represent a later date: these beads are not therefore of importance to the present discussion.

Local groupings and production centres

It is apparent from this survey that distinct local groups can be defined. In the Soviet Union and Romania there is too little material for groupings to be distinguished, but in Hungary and Czechoslovakia several types occur which are restricted to those areas (Fig. 26). The four-pointed bead, small and irregular, may be taken to define one area: it occurs at Mokrin in the Banat, at

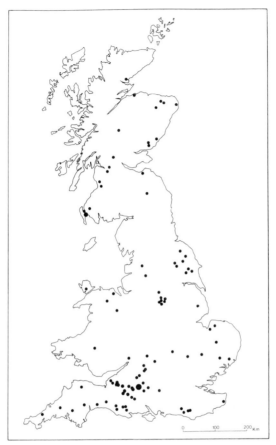

FIG. 27 ☐ Distribution of faience beads in Britain (all types). Data kindly provided by P. Peek and S. E. Warren (University of Bradford).

Deszk, Óbeba, Oszentiván, Pitváros and Szöreg on the lower Tisza, at Dunaújváros, Pákozdvár and Vatya in central Hungary, and apparently at Majcichov and elsewhere in south-west Slovakia. All known examples are very similar to one another, and a local distribution centre on the middle Danube must be postulated—this type is not known in Egypt and the Levant. Similarly, the sites around Košice in eastern Slovakia have a variety of types not found elsewhere—"wedge-shaped" beads, tiny long thin segmented beads, short cylinders, and others. In south-west Slovakia the "facetted annular" bead is commonly found—at Nitra, Čierny Brod, Branč, and elsewhere. In all these cases, there is no reasonable alternative to regarding them as the product of a local workshop.

With the segmented beads of Moravia, one cannot automatically claim local production. They do constitute a group, being similar in size and shape and concentrated within fairly close geographical bounds, and this, on the analogy of the Slovakian and Hungarian beads, would be sufficient evidence for local production. Yet the peculiar nature of the overall segmented bead distribution necessitates the introduction of additional evidence, which scientific analysis must provide.

Much the same considerations apply when one turns to the British group. For the Scottish beads, a local origin has been argued[72] on the grounds that the unusual star beads are not paralleled, or are very rare, in the East Mediterranean; clearly the situation is similar to that in Slovakia. In the case of the Wessex group, on the other hand, this argument does not apply. There are certain morphological differences between the Wessex and some Egyptian beads, e.g. the size of the perforation, the nature of the segmentation; but close analogies are available from Egypt and the Levant, and one must remember that only a minute proportion of the thousands of faience beads once produced have been available for study or analysis. Close parallels can certainly be found; did they then emanate from the same source?

In the case of the Wessex group, the balance of archaeological evidence is very finely poised. On the one hand amber spacer-plates almost certainly show a connection with the Aegean (though not with Egypt), while on the other the scattered and varied collection of British beads taken *as a whole* probably indicates local production in at least some areas, especially as some types are not known or are very rare in the East Mediterranean (star and quoit). Other evidence—for instance glass slag at the Culbin Sands[73]—tends to support this idea.

In the last resort, however, it is only scientific analysis that can provide an answer to the problem, and to this possible solution we now turn.

Scientific analysis

At least three different techniques—emission spectrography, neutron activation and X-ray fluorescence—have been used to examine the composition of the faience beads, and because their procedures and results are so different in type results cannot be compared directly. The analyses by Thomas in 1956 were not considered by him to favour one origin rather than another, but Newton and Renfrew reworked these statistics to demonstrate that at any rate the Scottish beads could be separated analytically from the rest.[74] In 1972 Aspinall and his co-workers, using neutron activation analysis, pointed to the differences in tin content between British and other groups of beads, and the following year Harding and Warren were able to distinguish four separate groups among the beads of Czechoslovakia, and others among those from Hungary—a conclusion which agreed well with the archaeological considerations outlined above.[75] In other papers Warren discussed further analyses, which, along with stylistic considerations, tended also to favour the idea that local manufacture of the British beads is involved—though he has always been careful to point out that importation cannot be disproved, nor local manufacture proved in the absence of actual workshop sites.[76] In summary, the bulk of analytical work suggests that faience beads found in central Europe and Britain had different composition patterns from those found in Egypt, and were therefore most likely to have been produced locally, not imported.

Studies by McKerrell,[77] on the other hand, purport to show that the faience beads of Europe (and especially of Britain) are in fact of East Mediterranean origin. Crucial to McKerrell's argument is the hypothesis that "the metallic composition of copper and bronze artefacts produced in a particular locality should be reflected in the analysis of the blue glaze of faience made in that same area".[78] This is on the assumption that "the possible sources for the blue colourant are limited to a copper ore, metal, corrosion product, or smelting/melting waste of some kind". The possibility that cobalt might have been used is not considered, presumably because McKerrell did not detect it analytically (his analyses remain unpublished). Even assuming that copper products were those invariably used for colouring the faience, it is by no means obvious that the analytical properties of the faience glaze should relate to those of metal artefacts, particularly as it is not known in what form the copper would have been used. In any case, the elements which allegedly demonstrate that British bronzes and faience have different composition patterns can equally be used to argue that British and Egyptian faience can be separated by this means.[79]

Although a good deal of work on the analytical side has been done since 1973, notably at Bradford, very little has been published, and the overall picture remains much as it was in the early 1970s. In particular, no further work has been done on the faience beads of southern Europe, some of which might reasonably be expected to be of Aegean or Egyptian origin (for instance in Sicily or Malta). Nevertheless, the balance of opinion (in Britain, at least) has swung decisively towards the idea of a local origin, and I have no doubt that the archaeological configuration, taken together with the more ambiguous indications of composition patterns, combine to demonstrate at least some local production both in western and in central Europe. This certainly does not rule out the possibility that some beads may be imported, but it makes it less likely.

Early and Middle Bronze Age glass

A repeated theme evident from the foregoing description and discussion is that some of the finds generally considered under the heading of faience are in fact of fully translucent, or opaque but glassy, material that can legitimately be called glass. In a paper delivered in 1973 to a conference on "Wessex, Mycenae and the Early Bronze Age" Stanley Warren concluded with a question: "Is there any evidence for glass in the Early/Middle Bronze Age in Britain?" At that time the answer was not sure; today it seems certain that such glass does exist. Mrs Guido has, in her most valuable survey of the glass beads of the British Isles,[80] listed those pieces which appear to be possibly of Bronze Age date—some of them Late Bronze Age, but others apparently Early or Middle Bronze Age. In Knackyboy Cairn, Isles of Scilly, for instance, an irregular greenish-blue semi-translucent bead and a large globular glass bead were apparently found with a faience star bead as the grave-goods of a cremation burial with urns.[81] A small opaque blue glass bead is reported as having come from a cist in a cairn at Chewton Mendip, Somerset, together with grape cup, amber beads and bronze knife-dagger. Other finds, made long ago and therefore poorly documented, may well bear out this picture of genuine glass beads in Wessex Culture contexts. In particular, the recent recognition by Mrs Guido of a large plum red bead from a Wessex barrow at Wilsford (G. 42) puts it beyond reasonable doubt that glass beads were in circulation during the Early Bronze Age in Britain.[82]

Glass beads have been reported in Early Bronze Age contexts in central Europe, but the finds in general are rather old and the reports not absolutely to be relied upon. The find from Melk in Lower Austria, for example, has been attributed to an Early Bronze Age grave, though Dr Haevernick assures me that this is not the case.[83] Píč reported nineteenth-century finds from Bohemia as being of glass in Únětice graves.[84] Reinecke, similarly, reported glass beads from Early Bronze Age graves at Hochstadt and Pörndorf in Bavaria.[85] These finds remain unsubstantiated, but by the Tumulus period the matter can hardly be doubted: for instance, from Huglfing–Uffing, tumulus 2 came a flattened spherical blue bead of translucent glass, found with the earliest burial in the tumulus, which can be assigned to Br A2–B1.[86] From Roggendorf in Lower Austria came a ring-shaped bead of dark glass attributed to Br B; a number of finds of Tumulus Bronze Age date were reported from Bohemia.[87] Similarly in northern Germany a number of graves of periods II and III contained glass beads.[88] In Slovakia graves of the Piliny culture contained bluish beads, as did the contemporary hoard of Žehra-Dreveník II.[89] Undoubtedly there are many more finds, but they have never been assembled and comprehensively studied.

In the Urnfield period, glass beads became very common, especially in the Lausitz and Velatice groups. So many and so varied are the finds that anything other than local or at any rate localized production is unthinkable, and analyses of Ha A beads from grave 340 at Volders, south Tirol, and elsewhere in Austria, bears this out: the copper used for colouring resembled local coppers of known character.[90]

This, however, leaves unanswered whether or not the MBA glass beads could have been imported. Undoubtedly they *could* have been; they are mostly simple annular beads of translucent blue glass, and such pieces were very common in the East Mediterranean. But local production of faience seems assured in at least some areas of central Europe during the Early Bronze Age, thereby suggesting local production of glass during the Middle Bronze Age is a natural step. There are no concentrations such as characterized the earlier distribution, but the evidence has yet to be systematically assembled, and analytical work has barely begun.

Conclusions

The principal conclusion of this discussion is that the majority of faience or glass-paste beads of the European Early Bronze Age, and probably of later periods, were locally made and not imported from the rich centres of the south-east. The following points support this hypothesis.

(1) The forms that can be considered really typical of the central and western European area appear rarely, if it all, in the south-east: segmented beads are a rarity in Greece, though they are common enough in Egypt and elsewhere. The four-pointed shape is not found outside Europe.

(2) The area between the Near East and central Europe has very little glass, a fact which militates against its being considered a bridge area.

(3) The distribution of faience beads in Europe is dense and falls into a number of distinct local groups.

(4) Localized bead-types can be distinguished.

(5) Constituent analysis indicates that local groupings can be identified.

On the chronological question, it has been shown that the calibrated radio-carbon chronology of the European Early Bronze Age places the faience in central Europe earlier than large-scale production of the material in the Aegean area.[91] But do the beads in any one area provide a reason for assuming their contemporaneity in that area? Does each group represent a short horizon of production, or did production continue over a period of decades or even centuries? Most of the finds in each group come with a homogeneous assemblage, which supports the idea of a short period of production. A short vogue for the form, when every self-respecting chieftain's wife was buried with some of the currently fashionable jewellery, seems the most likely hypothesis. Whether one can go further and relate all finds of faience in a given area to a uniform time-bracket is more questionable. For the faience of central Europe this might seem a reasonable procedure; in the case of Wessex and other groups the consequences might be more drastic.

Other prestige items

Luxury goods did not stop at jewellery and objects of exotic materials like amber or *lapis lazuli*. A whole range of material can be seen to be of "foreign" provenance, mostly "one-off" pieces that have few, if any, parallels in Greece. This is especially true in the Shaft Graves. There are also various categories of material which may well have been exchanged but are archaeologically invisible. These include foodstuffs, liquids like wine, oil or perfumes, textiles, wooden furniture and other objects, as well as the raw materials for making such pieces—wood, wool, flax, stones and other substances for inlay or whole objects, glass and faience, and so on. They also include animals and human beings, who may have been "exchanged" either as foreign princesses in marriage links or as slaves and captives.

I have already argued that the exchange of foodstuffs over long distances is inherently unlikely. But this is not to rule out the possibility that trade in special foodstuffs may have taken place. In the Athens markets today you will find ten or twenty different varieties of olive or fig on sale, the most expensive up to twice the price of the cheapest. Delicacies of one kind or another—red mullet, roasted pistachios, Malmsey wine—were no doubt moved about in the Bronze Age as in later times. Certain vessels were no doubt intended for specific liquids or foodstuffs: notably for the export of spices and perfumes. The lists of herbs and spices on the Linear B tablets of Mycenae and Tiryns[92] provide eloquent testimony of the production of such commodities. Why, after all, are there hundreds of Mycenaean vases in the Near East and Egypt, especially when so many of them are closed shapes like stirrup-jars and alabastra? And a group of tall-necked Cypriot vessels have been seen as evidence of a trade in opium,[93] but if this is so, it was a commodity that Greece did not import—not, at any rate, in these characteristic containers.

Similar difficulties attend the examination of any possible trade in fine textiles, furniture, or other perishable commodities, which were no doubt exchanged but which remain archaeologically invisible. Much has been made of the folding stools found in a score of Nordic graves of Period II,[94] for depictions of folding stools are also to be seen in the fresco art of Crete—notably the "Campstool fresco"—and places further east. The folding stools of the two areas do indeed show close similarities, but it must be remembered that the form is a simple one and was most likely widely distributed. In my view a direct connection between Scandinavia and the East Mediterranean is a very far-fetched explanation of this phenomenon.

Individual objects

Individual prestige objects that were moved from one area to another form a large part of the total evidence for connections between Greece and other countries during the Bronze Age. Almost any genuine Mycenaean object found in reliable contexts in the west or north, however mundane or common-place in Greece, might have assumed prestige proportions in the "barbarian" world. All such objects are considered separately in other parts of this book. The importation of isolated prestige objects into Greece relates mainly to items of southern or eastern origin: sealstones and gems, stone vases, faience objects and other such material. The Shaft Graves have their fair share of these pieces, though tying down their points of origin is a major problem: for example, the silver and lead stag rhyton (assumed to be Anatolian), a faience vase from grave II of Cretan or Egyptian origin, glass and faience plaques and beads (e.g. from graves Ξ and Y), and vases of Egyptian alabaster. Other such pieces occur sporadically in early contexts.[95] Their significance has to be judged in the special context of the Shaft Grave phenomenon and does not necessarily relate at all closely to the situation at other periods.

A number of glass objects found in early Mycenaean contexts (Mycenae, Kakovatos, Thorikos) are also probably imports from the east,[96] and the possibility that blue glass ingots might have been imported has been referred to in Chapter 3.

Levantine cylinder-seals have been found on a number of sites in Greece,[97] notably Thebes, where a hoard of 36 was found in 1963, 32 of them Oriental.[98] A cylinder-seal was also found in the Cape Gelidonya ship excavation. Con-siderable argument surrounds the place of origin of many of these pieces;[99] but of those for which some agreement is possible it appears that around half are suggested as of northern Syrian origin, and half as local imitations. That these were scarce and treasured possessions in the Aegean is shown by the length of time they stayed in circulation: that from the Cape Gelidonya ship, which sank some time near 1200 B.C., had been made probably in the eighteenth century, while the collection from Thebes, found in a LH IIIA2 context, ranged in date from the time of Ur I to the mid-second millennium B.C. They usually occur singly, as the personal seals of individuals; it is stated that "every Eastern merchant had his own seal",[100] ready to be got out to stamp commodities bought and sold, to sign and seal transactions. The form was in origin entirely Eastern; that it was imitated in the Aegean demonstrates both the force of fashion and the prestige attached to the objects. The popularity of this trend is shown by the fact that more than 100 have been found in the Aegean. That the Thebes group should be so large and miscellaneous is of exceptional interest, though it sheds little light on the nature of the connection.

Also of undisputed external manufacture are the various Egyptian objects found in Greece.[101] These are not numerous, and usually occur singly, but they have been put to extensive use as dating tools for the Aegean sequence.[102] In this they can be more or less helpful—their original context as evidence of international contact had in most cases been long since forgotten. As an example of this we may take the four faience plaques bearing the cartouche and names of Amenophis III found at Mycenae, and taken by Hankey to be possible relics of an official Egyptian visit to Mycenae in the time of Amenophis III.[103] I choose these not only because I was privileged personally to find the only complete one, that from Citadel House, but also because they exemplify the way in which objects—even prestige objects deriving from specific sources or specific events—can become totally divorced from those sources or events. The context of the Citadel House piece is good: it was in a crushed lead vessel on the floor of the Room of the Fresco in the House of the Idols. This house was destroyed in a conflagration that was well-dated to LH IIIB2, i.e. around 1200 B.C.; the dates for Amenophis III are given by Hornung as 1405/2–1367/3.[104] For comparison, one may quote the LM III A1 tomb at Sellopoulo,[105] where a scarab of Amenophis III was found—in this case, presumably, virtually contemporary with the other contents of the tomb. The other plaques were fragmentary and probably redeposited. Whatever the precise means by which these semi-official objects originally came to Mycenae, they were presumably treated as valuable souvenirs, being carefully kept and stored (in one instance) until the destruction of the house they were in some 200 years later. Most of these Egyptian objects were clearly isolated instances of importation and bespeak political rather than commercial contact. Much the same may be true of the Keftian "tribute" depicted in Egyptian tomb reliefs: whatever light Egyptians may have wished to see them in, they are today best interpreted as the products of the exchange of gifts between rulers or of trade missions.[106]

Metal vessels

Vases and other containers of bronze, silver and gold were among the choicest products of the early Mycenaean metalsmith's repertory. A few metal vases also appear in the "barbarian" world before the Urnfield period. If, as has been claimed, this is evidence of export, whether of ideas or of actual objects, the implications would be considerable, even though any such export of these fine objects must have been on a restricted scale.

Sheet metal vessels had been produced in the Aegean Early Bronze Age though not in Middle Helladic until the very end. Grave Beta, one of the earlier tombs in Shaft Grave Circle B at Mycenae, had an electrum armband,

while graves Gamma, Iota, Nu and Delta had cups; several others have gold
clothing ornaments. In Continental Europe, on the other hand, vessels in
sheet metal are rare until the developed Bronze Age, even though small objects
in sheet gold and bronze were made there earlier than in the Aegean. The
shape of the few Early Bronze Age vessels we have has been compared to
Mycenaean models, while the decoration of Late Bronze Age vessels is
attributed by some authors to an Aegean origin.

For the vessels of the Carpathian area, the work of Amalia Mozsolics[107]
remains basic. Four cups from the former Bihar county, one from Biia (Mag-
yarbenye), and two fragments of a bronze vessel from Şmig (Somogyom) are
all that is known. None of these pieces is Mycenaean; the only question is
whether some of them imitate, consciously or unconsciously, Mycenaean
types and techniques. Mozsolics has listed Mycenaean parallels, especially for
such details as handle types, but they are all general and need not indicate any
more than a widespread goldworking tradition. The decorative motifs, as on
cup 4 from Kom. Bihar, are discussed in Chapter 7. These cups underline the
independence and wealth of the Transylvanian goldworking school; to suggest
that that school was dependent on Aegean forerunners for inspiration is to
detract from the technical and artistic excellence which it represents.

The fragment of a bronze cup from Vel'ka Lomnica in Slovakia[108] cannot
be used, as it sometimes has been, to prove the existence of Mycenaean
importation into central Europe. It has no find circumstances and came from a
locality rich in remains of several periods. The tube-like rim, decorated with
oblique ribbings, is certainly similar to that on Mycenaean bronze cups[109] but
the presence of traces of iron on the inside of the Vel'ka Lomnica rim seems an
awkward problem, even though there is the well known iron dagger from
Ganovce to support the idea that Early Bronze Age iron is acceptable.[110]
Nevertheless, to claim as a Mycenaean import of the Shaft Grave period an
object bearing traces of iron seems less than reasonable. Pottery cups with
fluted rim do occur for instance at Blučina,[111] and foliate designs are found on
pottery cups at Suciu de Sus,[112] but in no case is the parallel any more than
general.

The famous treasure from V'lči-Tr'n has been seen by some authors as
Mycenaean in inspiration, if not in date,[113] but the most convincing analyses
refer it to the advanced Early Iron Age even if, like the Thracian tombs of the
same period, it contains memories of Mycenaean days long past. Piggott
thinks it could "fit in an ultimately Mycenaean context"; Bouzek agrees that
shape, decoration and handle-types are paralleled on Shaft Grave vessels, but
thinks that Macedonian Early Iron Age kantharoi are closer, while the lids may
be paralleled by Greek Geometric examples.[114] The use of inlays has been
thought to be crucial by some, a technique found at the time of the Shaft
Graves and not again until Classical times; though Sandars points out that in

Anatolia inlaying goes back to Alaca Hüyük and is seen again in the inlaid furniture of the King's Tomb at Gordion.[115] On balance, direct importation from Greece seems most unlikely at any period; the most that one could say about the vessels of this hoard is that the general conception recalls Mycenaean types.

A well known group of metal cups in western Europe has attracted much attention, some of them at least being regarded by all authors as Mycenaean-inspired, if not actual imports. Of these, the cup from Dohnsen (Celle, Lower Saxony) must surely rank as an Aegean product:[116] the form of the handle, the general shape with spout, and the decorative motif (a version of the foliate band, FM 64) mark it as unmistakable Aegean work. In a recent study, Matthäus has argued strongly for Cretan manufacture on the basis of parallels for the decoration, but distinguishing Cretan from mainland products in Late Bronze I is a tricky business, especially if—as Matthäus allows—Cretan artisans were active in mainland workshops. It was allegedly found by children playing, and lay on the surface of a spur between two sand pits. There was no trace of any prehistoric activity in the vicinity, nor did investigation reveal anyone in the village with the opportunity to have brought such an object back from the Aegean in recent times. On balance, it seems unwise to accept the Dohnsen cup as evidence for prehistoric trade without clearer indications of its history.

Three gold cups, with a possible fourth, are much less convincing as Aegean products though they did undoubtedly come from local contexts. The Rillaton[117] and Fritzdorf[118] cups (Fig. 28.1, 7) are related not only by general form and handle-type, but also by their use of rhomboidal rivet-washers—a detail which alone argues strongly for local, non-Aegean, production. With the Fritzdorf cup one may take the fragment from Ploumilliau (Fig. 28.3),[119] with which it is related by the decoration of dots around the rim. Gerloff[120] has devoted a long discussion to these pieces, and compares biconical cups, with concave neck and spherical base, that are very common in pottery in the Breton, Adlerberg, Rhodanian and Únětice groups. One may further compare the cups of amber and shale which are known in some numbers from southern Britain (Fig. 28.2). In fact the biconical cup form was common throughout the Early Bronze Age of western Europe; and I owe to Dr Joan Taylor the observation that in looking for parallels for goldwork, one should not look at other gold pieces—which are and were rare, and often *hapax legomena*—but at similar objects in other materials. Several authors have pointed out that the true analogies for the shape of the Rillaton cup lie not in Aegean vessels but in British Beaker pottery. Two other features of this cup have been compared to Aegean prototypes—the shape of the handle, and the fluted walls. For the former, the Fritzdorf cup is a good parallel, and this shape is also seen on the amber and shale cups already mentioned; it is quite true that the handle design of certain Mycenaean vessels was very similar, and chronologically a general

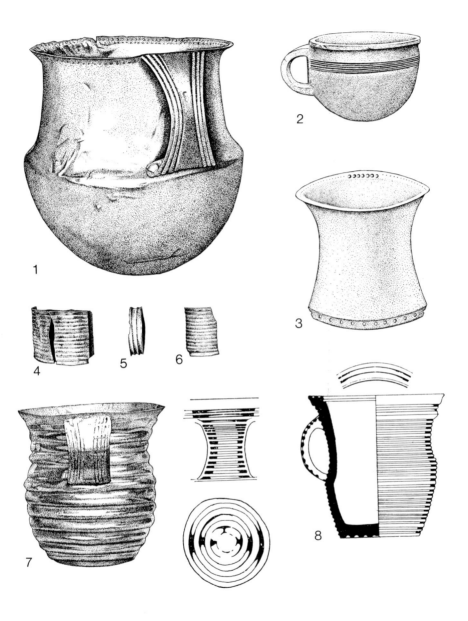

FIG. 28 ☐ Gold cups and related material from western Europe. (1) Fritzdorf cup; (2) Hove amber cup; (3) Ploumilliau cup neck; (4–6) Little Cressingham box fragments; (7) Rillaton cup; (8) Food Vessel from Balmuick, Perths. (After von Uslar, 1955; Briard, 1965; Clarke, 1970; Taylor, 1980; Curwen, 1954.)

connection cannot be ruled out, but the existence of a local group of this type makes outside influence unnecessary. It would in fact be a natural development of the handles of non-metallic cups.

For the fluted walls, analogies are plentiful. Several examples of fluting on goldwork are known—e.g. the Little Cressingham boxes (Fig. 28.4–6), the Mountfield and Cuxwold armlets, and the Scottish hilt bands.[121] Clarke has also compared a "hybrid" Beaker-Food Vessel from Perthshire (Fig. 28.8), and there are also very good parallels on Late Neolithic pots from south-west Germany.[122] There is no need to see any direct influence on the Rillaton cup—or on any other piece of Wessex goldwork—from Mycenaean Greece; all the necessary analogies to explain it can be found west and north of Brittany.

A word must also be said about beaten bronze vessels of the European Late Bronze Age and their decorative techniques. Childe and Hawkes[123] saw the shape of the Friedrichsruhe-type cup, which appeared in central Europe in Br D, as Aegean in origin (Furumark shape 213), and its relatively sudden appearance there, after the Aegean had been producing rather similar vessels for several centuries, raises the question of whether the introduction of the type may not have been due to direct Mycenaean influence. It was at this time, too, that so many other bronze types became common to the two areas, and a connection in bronze production is assured for many classes of evidence. But Aegean vessel types do not include any close parallel for the Friedrichsruhe shape,[124] and in any case the great majority of Aegean bronze vessels, especially those with a general resemblance to the northern type, are early in the Late Bronze Age. For these reasons a direct connection is impossible. But what of the ornamentation of these vessels? Childe[125] compared the bossed decoration on a silver cup from Byblos with the central European systems as described by Merhart;[126] the goldwork of the Shaft Graves was also richly decorated with bosses, both large and small. In neither case, however, do these strictly resemble the rigid *Gleich-Buckel* and *Punkt-Buckel* systems, the earliest continental decorative forms, except by virtue of being bossed; there is in any case a time difference of 400 years and more. On early Mycenaean sheet metalwork, the bosses were often extremely large, and usually variable in size on any one piece. In the European *Buckel* systems, on the other hand, one or two sizes of boss and dot were chosen and then formed into patterns. Though it is not impossible that the introduction of bossed bronze work into Europe was a result of contact with Greece in the thirteenth to twelfth centuries B.C. (it does in fact represent a technological more than an artistic advance), there is nothing to suggest that the Mycenaeans exported their techniques wholesale. In this connection the bowl from Pylos Chamber Tomb K-2, decorated in embossed dots, is of great interest, especially as the bird motifs on it are more nearly paralleled on Protovillanovan pottery (see p. 205).

Pottery imitations of metal vessels *(Fig. 29)*

As well as the vessels of gold and bronze in central and western Europe, a number of instances of alleged imitation of Aegean metal vessels in clay have been cited. The most famous of these is an extraordinary cup from Nienhagen (Halberstadt, Saxony) which, while basically conical in shape, has a pillar handle that has been seen by many authorities as derived from the handle on Vapheio cups.[127] It is usually stated to have come from an Únětice context, but in fact the cemetery from which it emanated contains graves dating from the Neolithic to the Migration Period, and no other grave-goods occurred in the grave in question.[128] Even if an Únětice date could be regarded as certain, a connection between a crude and unique pottery vessel in Saxony and a group of elaborate metal vessels in Greece seems to me to be most unlikely. Another pottery vessel from Germany, that from a megalithic tomb at Oldendorf (Lüneburg, Lower Saxony), has also been positively appraised as evidence for contact by some writers:[129] the carinated cup has a high ribbon handle and what appears to be the imitation of a rivet with washer at the junction of handle and rim. Parallels for the handle can be quoted in Minyan or early Mycenaean pottery or on metal cups, but it is obvious to the merest apprentice that this is no Aegean work: the profile of the vessel shows it to be a typical local product, though the omphalos base and the handle do indeed mark it out as something special. One suggestion[130] has been to see a connection with certain Baden culture vessels, but here again the nature of any such contact remains mysterious.

An other oft-quoted pot is the cup from the Ledro lakeside settlement, in a Polada culture context:[131] this vessel has straightish concave sides and a high-swung handle. Given the range of one-handled straight-sided cups in the Polada repertoire, any connection with Vapheio cups in the Aegean seems remote in the extreme, especially as radiocarbon dating rules such a connection out.[132]

An extraordinary lid from a Věteřov context in Olomouc appears similar, by virtue of its handle form, to Aegean stirrup-jars, but this appears to be another instance of the confusing nature of coincidence.[133]

Finally, we may recall the quatrefoil-mouthed pottery vessels from Pecica Level XIII that Childe[134] saw as related to silver vessels from MM II–III Crete, to the alabaster vase from Shaft Grave IV,[135] and to certain Anatolian vessels. Although a connection is not impossible chronologically, any relationship must be so general as to be almost valueless in terms of culture contact.

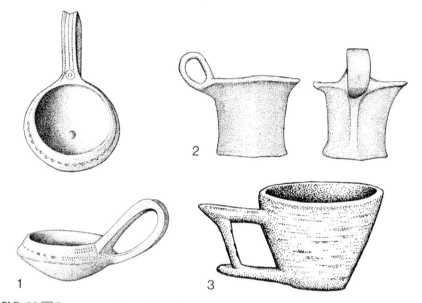

FIG. 29 ☐ Pottery vessels, perhaps imitating metal forms, allegedly of Aegean inspiration. (1) Oldendorf, Lower Saxony; (2) Ledro, north Italy; (3) Nienhagen, Saxony. (After Sprockhoff, 1952; Barfield, 1966; Gimbutas, 1965.)

Other objects

Ornaments in gold, notably ear-rings, have also been said to show connections between Greece and the barbarian world in the Bronze Age. The similarity between the ornamented gold ear-rings from Shaft Grave III at Mycenae[136] and a piece from Tufalău has often been noted (Fig. 30).[137] The classification of the ear-rings from Romania[138] bears out that the Tufalău pieces do not all correspond to the normal run of Transylvanian ear-rings; but their nearest analogies in fact do lie in Romania, in certain pieces from Sărata-Monteoru (where "lock-rings" were especially prolific). A common origin for the Tufalău and Mycenae pieces might be postulated, perhaps in Anatolia, where comparable ornaments occur in Troy II and III. The decoration on the surface of the Mycenae ring, its rhomboidal section and circular shape make identical production centres unlikely, but the general form certainly allies it with the Lower Danube area, though spirally-terminating ornaments have a long tradition in Greece. On the other hand, such boat-shaped ear-rings in gold as occur in Greece[139] invariably take the form of a crescentic ring with hollow expanded surface at the bottom *opposite* the terminals, as opposed to being *at* the terminals on the Romanian types.

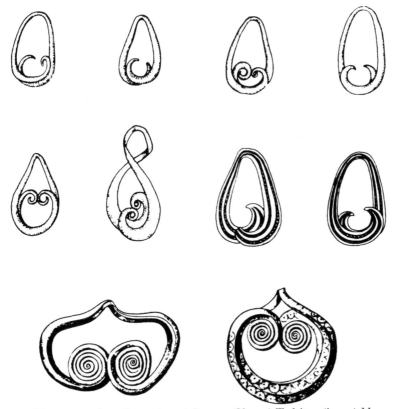

FIG. 30 ☐ Ear-rings from Romania and Greece. (Upper) Tufalău; (lower) Mycenae, Shaft Grave III. (After Hachmann, 1957a; Schmidt, 1904.)

Another type of ear-ring that occurs both in Greece (specifically Crete) and in Europe is the crescentic or tapering penannular ring. In the Ashmolean Museum in Oxford are two gold crescentic ear-rings, stated when bought to have come from Dover and Folkestone. This provenance cannot be verified; certainly the form is not a British one. These two pieces, along with the tapering penannular object from Normanton barrow 155, have been claimed to be Aegean imports.[140] In the case of the Normanton piece, the materials—gold on a bronze core—have been taken as indicating also a technological connection with the Aegean. Such a diagnosis requires special pleading for the two pieces "from Kent"; and it takes no account of the fact that the bronze core of the Normanton pendant (for that is what it must be) was cast with the two ends projecting outwards, and so cannot have been an ear-ring: it is not a question of damage.[141] More important is the fact that the tapering penannular ring has a wide currency in Europe during the Bronze Age, mainly in bracelet form but also as ear- or finger-rings. They occur especially in eastern Europe at the start of the Late Bronze Age (being known in both bronze and gold), but are found too in central Europe.[142] This is not a western form. How the Normanton pendant is best explained is hard to say: the combination of materials is a typical Wessex feature, as is gold plating; in this piece, as in several others (halberd pendants, gold-bound amber discs, pins with crutch head or with perforated spherical head), Wessex craftsmen apparently adapted to their own purposes forms whose main currency was on the continent.

This discussion of Wessex crafts leads us to consider another famous but "difficult" object—the zig-zag bone mounts from Bush Barrow (Fig. 31.1). Here again the comparanda are so few that certainty about use, function or origin is quite impossible. We may recall that there are two end-pieces and three middle pieces; the diameter is up to c. 2·6 cm.[143] The importance of these strange objects increased enormously when the Greek excavators of Shaft Grave Circle B discovered similar objects in Grave Iota, which dates to Dickinson's "middle phase", late Middle Helladic, about 1550 B.C.[144] Here too there are two end-pieces and fragments of three middle pieces; they are described in the published report as being of ivory (Fig. 31.4). The two sets are not identical, even if the materials are similar: the diameter of the Iota pieces is 4–5 cm, and at least one of them is very thick. They further differ from the Bush Barrow pieces in being genuinely zig-zag in shape, whereas the latter are really notched bands. These objections, however, can hardly lessen the impact of such very specialized objects appearing in the two widely separated contexts. It is not widely appreciated that in neither area is the general form unique. In the west, for instance, there is an intriguing find of four small gold "crowns" from the Kerlagat dolmen in the Carnac region of the Morbihan (Fig. 31.3).[145] It has also been pointed out on several occasions that zig-zag decoration, especially of the notched band variety, is a typical British Early Bronze Age ornament, notably on Beakers (Fig. 31.2) but also on lunulae and other pieces of goldwork. There would be no particular reason to suggest external influence (save possibly from Brittany) on the Bush Barrow mounts were it not for the existence of the Mycenae pieces.

Equally, one may point to the existence in Greece of other bone or ivory objects cut in the same zig-zag fashion, though admittedly all are later in date (Fig. 31.5). Two are from the Mycenae Acropolis and appear to have no recorded context.[146] One (NM 1028) is similar to the Iota pieces but much larger and thicker; the other (NM 2670) is elliptical. In 1978 the German excavators at Tiryns found another example, and other similar pieces, not all hollow cylinders but usually interpreted as furniture fittings, are known from Menidi, Thebes and houses at Mycenae.[147] Given the relative rarity with which ivory survives, the existence of three objects with much the same technique of decoration must warn against a too facile assumption of external influence. Tempting

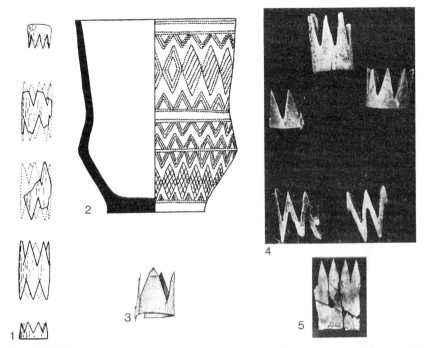

FIG. 31 ☐ Zig-zag mounts and their comparanda in Britain, France and Greece. (1) Bush Barrow, Amesbury, Wilts; (2) Beaker, Calne Without G.2(c); (3) gold object, Kerlagat dolmen, Carnac; (4) ivory mounts, Shaft Grave Iota, Mycenae; (5) "comb", Mycenae. (After Annable and Simpson, 1964; Taylor, 1980; Poursat, 1977; no. 4 courtesy of the National Archaeological Museum, Athens.)

though it may be to imagine a direct correspondence between Mycenae and Wessex to account for these extraordinary objects, other explanations are possible.

I leave till last a still more extraordinary group of objects that again provide enigmatic indications of contact between widely separated areas, though this time in the Late Bronze Age, at the very end of the Mycenaean period. The two "wheels" from Tiryns (Fig. 22)[148] not only include amber beads of the ribbed, "Tiryns" type, they also have an intriguing arrangement of gold wire forming the "hub". This gold wire is worked in a technique described by Beck as unique; a long piece of the wire was doubled over and coiled into circles, and other pieces of wire are wound diagonally across these circles. The technique of a group of gold figure-of-eight ornaments from Hradec Králové in Bohemia is identical, a fact which most commentators have explained in terms of trade contact.[149] The technological and cultural context in which these two strange sets of objects were produced is, because both are *hapax legomena*, quite unknown to us and, therefore, caution in seeking "explanations" is necessary. At the very least it is appropriate that we should look at the ancestry of the technique of making ornaments from double-folded wire. In Greece this goes back to the Shaft Graves, where gold bracelets with spiral terminals were produced; admittedly a very different end-product, but one that demonstrates familiarity with the technique of making and working wire.[150] Most of the other examples one can cite belong to the Submycenaean period, as at Salamis and the Kerameikos;[151] this date conflicts neither with that assumed for the Tiryns hoard or with that for comparable ornaments from Italy, for which a Protovillanovan context seems assured.[152] The general technique of folding wire double and coiling it into rings has a longer ancestry in central and eastern Europe, however: it goes back to the *Noppenringe* of the Early Bronze Age but can be seen also in the ornaments of the Late Bronze Age.[153]

Nothing can "explain" the Tiryns wheels in any satisfactory way, but it does seem likely that they exhibit techniques and forms, both in amber and in gold, which were current in the eleventh century world and which owed their existence to a long technical development stretching back to the Early Bronze Age. Direct contact between Greece and central Europe cannot be ruled out.

Conclusions

The Bronze Age trade in luxury items could encompass great distances, but (almost by definition) did not involve large quantities of material. The cases of amber and *lapis lazuli*, where very distant sources are assumed, but the weight of imported material was relatively slight, are instructive. In such cases it is necessary to question the relationship between exchange and regular production in the economy. Those benefitting from the importation of prestige goods can have been only very few. The population of the Pylian kingdom has been variously estimated at 40 000, 50 000 or 100 000 at the time of the Linear B archives:[154] imported prestige items can have had little impact on most of that population. Furthermore, the great majority of the items that can be shown to have been imported belong to the early Mycenaean period, and only rather few to the middle and late periods. This serves to confirm the general impression of selectivity, even scarcity, as far as the bulk of the population was concerned, though it must be remembered that intact rich graves also cluster in the early period.

The impact of the importation of Aegean luxury goods into "barbarian" Europe must also be considered. This question is the more complicated in that any Aegean import may have been liable to be considered as a prestige, if not a luxury item. Double-axes, for example, which are considered in the next chapter, were ordinary carpentry tools in Greece, but in Europe (if their presence could be proved) they may well have assumed a more special significance. In fact, proven exports from Greece are extremely few—some would doubt their existence at all except in the countries immediately bordering Greece. The impact on the economy of those or more distant countries can be considered minimal.

What remains important about the few proven cases of prestige-goods import and export is the ability of Bronze Age populations to create, if not maintain, the exchange mechanisms involved. Especially in the case of amber, the raw material was (in all likelihood) brought over great distances to take up its position as the hallmark of wealth in the Aegean world. This importation may not have been regular or frequent, but it was certainly long-lived, and at least two phases of importation into Mycenaean Greece seem likely, possibly more. Whatever the precise nature of the mechanism of exchange involved, it achieved its end of putting exotic materials in the hands of a few people at a great distance from source. The case of faience is more difficult, and I have indicated my belief that no more than the export of the necessary technology need be involved, at least for the beads of central and western Europe. For most of the other items, the isolated nature of any possible exchange makes an assessment of their significance impossible, but it is hard to see it as having been very great, or impinging on more than a very few people. In Europe, dynasties of chieftains who manifested their dominant status by display of exotica from the Mediterranean represent one of the unlikelier canvasses that one could paint with the available materials.

Notes

1. Catling (1956, p. 116); M. Burchardt, *Z. für ägyptol. Sprache und Altertumskunde* **50,** 1912, 61–63, pl. V. Cf. the sword from Ras Shamra-Ugarit bearing the cartouche of Mereneptah: C. F. A. Schaeffer, *Antiquity* **29,** 1955, 226–229; *Ugaritica* **III,** 169–178, pl. VIII (a *Griffangelschwert*, but not of normal European type).

2. Harding and Hughes-Brock (1974), with full references to matters not referenced here.

3. Mylonas (1972, pp. 188-189, 206, 350–352, pl. 186).

4. Blegen *et al.* (1973, pp. 137, 143, 151, 162, figs 227, 231, 232).

5. N. Negroni Catacchio, *Sibrium* **10,** 1970, 278.

6. C. J. Becker, *Acta Archaeologica* **25,** 1954, 241ff.

7. G. von Merhart, *Germania* **24,** 1940, 99–102.

8. Hachmann (1957b).

9. Sandars (1959).

10. Gerloff (1975, pp. 261–263).

11. Hachmann (1957b).

12. Gerloff (1975, pp. 261–263).

13. Harding and Hughes-Brock (1974, p. 157).

14. Gerloff (1975, p. 220).

15. A. Evans, *Archaeologia* **65**, 1914, 42, fig. 56.

16. Professor Stuart Piggott has pointed out to me that Stukeley referred to "clay" discs that could have been amber: *Stonehenge* 1740 (London, Innys and Manby), 44f., pl. XXXII. Cf. J. J. Taylor, *Bronze Age Goldwork of the British Isles*, 1980 (Cambridge, Cambridge University Press), p. 47. Muhly (1973, p. 250) states incorrectly that such a disc was found at the Knowes of Trotty. Gold discs and amber beads (including a spacer) were found there, but not a gold-bound amber disc.

17. J. M. de Navarro, *Geographical Journal* **67**, 1925, 481–504.

18. Guilaine (1972, pp. 162, 207).

19. Gerloff (1975, p. 218).

20. Gerloff (1975, p. 219).

21. J. G. D. Clark, *Prehistoric Europe: the Economic Basis*, 1952 (London, Methuen), pp. 266ff.

22. Muhly (1973, pp. 271ff., 349).

23. Renfrew (1972, p. 467f.).

24. Renfrew (1977, p. 85f.).

25. L. Bernabò Brea and M. Cavalier, *Meligunìs-Lipára* I, 1960 (Palermo, Flaccovio), pp. 153ff.

26. A. M. Bietti Sestieri, *Padusa* **11**, 1975, 1–14. Mus. Rovigo.

27. Z. Andrea, *Studime Historike* **26**(9), 1972, part 4, 82 ("rruazat prej qelibari").

28. Renfrew (1972, p. 467).

29. Beck and Stone (1936) quote the case of the Rev. J. Skinner in 1826 who appears first to have "vaguely recognized" the connection.

30. A. Evans, *Proc. Soc. Antiquaries* **22**, 1907–8, 123; *Palace of Minos* I, 1921 (London, Macmillan), pp. 490ff.

31. For example, Childe (1929, p. 269).

32. For example, E. Lehečková, *Annales du 5ᵉ Congrès de l'Association Internationale pour l'Histoire du Verre* (Prague 1970), 1972, p. 32; A. Krauss, *Materiały Archeologiczne* **9**, 1968, 164. J. Vladár, on the other hand, one of the firmest believers in direct contact between Mycenaean Greece and central Europe, has accepted a local origin for these beads, as in *Pohrebiska zo staršej doby bronzovej v Brančì*, 1973 (Bratislava, Slovak Academy of Sciences), pp. 152–153, 220 esp. n. 157.

33. McKerrell (1972); Aspinall *et al.* (1972).

34. R. H. Brill, *Scientific American* **209**, November 1963, 120–130, and personal communication.

35. Beck and Stone (1936, p. 207); Lucas and Harris (1962, pp. 156ff.).

36. McKerrell (1972, p. 286).

37. Stone and Thomas (1956, p. 38).

38. Kiefer and Allibert (1971).

39. Noble (1969).

40. D. Rhodes, *Clay and Glazes for the Potter*, 1957 (London, Pitman).

41. H. C. Wulff, H. S. Wulff and L. Koch, *Archaeology* **21**, 1968, 98–107. Lucas (1962, p. 176) discounted the use of gums.

42. Kiefer and Allibert (1971).

43. Beck and Stone (1936, p. 210, pl. LXVI, fig. 3).

44. Stone and Thomas (1956); Foster (1979, pp. 22ff.).

45. W. A. Heurtley and C. A. R. Radford, *BSA* **29**, 1928, 149–150, fig. 29; Heurtley (1939, p. 202).

46. Mostly listed in E. C. Banks, *The Early and Middle Helladic Small Objects from Lerna*, 1967 (Ann Arbor, Univ. Microfilms), pp. 673–684; add: Ch. Tsountas, *Hai proistorikai akropoleis Diminiou kai Sesklou*, 1908 (Athens, Greek Arch. Soc.), pp. 136ff., pl. 5, 9–12; V. Milojčić, *Germania* **37**, 1959, 77 (Sesklo T.25, T.43); Orchomenos T.43 (reference from O. Dickinson).

47. N. Wilkie, *Hesperia* **44**, 1975, 78.

48. P. Orsi, *BPI* **28**, 1902, 114, 117, pl.2, 33; 187, pl.6, 6 (Valsavoia and Cava Cana Barbara).

49. Bernabò Brea and Cavalier (1968, p. 167, pl. LXXXV).

50. P. Orsi, *Monumenti Antichi.* **6**, 1895, 133–134, fig. 49; *BPI* **17**, 1892, 127; *Not. Scavi* 1899, 31–32; G. A. Colini, *BPI* **30**, 1904, 253, figs 54–56; Stone and Thomas (1956, p. 84). In the new tombs at Thapsos (excavated in 1970) were found a good number of paste and glass-paste beads: *Voza* 1973, 40, 44.

51. Mus. Taranto. C. Drago, *BPI* **8/5**, 1953, 158; cf. Peroni (1959, p. 166, tav. XIX, 10).

52. Stone and Thomas (1956, pp. 57, 81, 84); Evans (1971, p. 163).

53. L. Barfield, *Antiquity* **52**, 1978, 150–153.

54. Lucone: Barfield, *op. cit.*, with refs; Barfield (1971, pl. 35). Arbon-Bleiche: F. Fischer, *Die frühbronzezeitliche Ansiedlung in der Bleiche bei Arbon TG*, 1971 (Basel, Schweiz. Ges. für Ur- und Frühgeschichte), pp. 13, 34, Taf. 5, 35–36.

55. Information kindly provided by Dr Martin Almagro Gorbea, Museo Arquelogico Nacional, Madrid.

56. R. J. Harrison, R. M. Jusmet and P. Giro, *Madrider Mitteilungen* **15**, 1974, 95ff.

57. Roudil and Soulier (1976).

58. Stone and Thomas (1956, p. 57).

59. Sulimirski (1970, pp. 183f.)

60. V. U. Selinov and E. F. Lagodovskaja, *Sov. Arch.* **5**, 1940, 248; Gimbutas (1965, p. 45).

61. Gimbutas (1965, pp. 45, 52, with refs to earlier publications).

62. T. Sulimirski, *Proc. Prehist. Soc.* **30**, 1964, 59, 62; 1970, 174, 188.

63. Sulimirski (1968, pp. 111, 205 etc.).

64. A. V. Dobrovolskij, *Kratkie soobščenija instituta archeologii* (Kiev) **7**, 1957, 40–45, fig. 2. Cf. E. V. Machno and S. N. Bratčenko, *Archeologija* (Kiev) **24**, 1977, 53–60 on "Babino-type" beads from a Catacomb Grave burial at Kompanijciv.

65. Tallgren (1926, p. 113); Sulimirski (1966–8, pp. 3–27).

66. Gimbutas (1965, p. 46 with refs).

67. M. A. Besborodov and J. A. Zadneprovsky, *Slavia Antiqua* **12**, 1965, 127–142.

68. I. T. Dragomir, *Materiale şi cercetări archeologice* **5**, 1959, 685.

69. Almaş: first noted by Childe in *Essays in Aegean Archaeology presented to Sir Arthur Evans*, ed. S. Casson, 1927 (Oxford University Press), p. 2; stated by Beck and Stone (1936, p. 229, n. 4) to be in Braşov Museum (presumably after Childe); I did not see it there on a visit in 1974.

70. E. Dunăreanu-Vulpe, *Dacia* **5–6**, 1935–6, 162. Bucharest, Institute of Archaeology, inv. no. II. 6460; I examined this piece in 1970.

71. Gerloff (1975, pp. 204–206).

72. Newton and Renfrew (1970).

73. Newton and Renfrew (1970, p. 203).

74. Stone and Thomas (1956, pp. 68ff.); Newton and Renfrew (1970).

75. Aspinall *et al.* (1972); Harding and Warren (1973).

76. A. Aspinall and S. E. Warren, "The problems of faience beads", paper presented at the Conference on "Wessex, Mycenae and the Early Bronze Age", Newcastle upon Tyne, 1973 (circulated privately). Cf. Aspinall and Warren (1976).

77. McKerrell (1972).

78. McKerrell (1972, p. 287).

79. McKerrell used lead, tin and silver as the basis for the claim that British bronzes and faience are separable analytically in copper type. His data are drawn from a variety of sources: those for silver are based on analyses by neutron activation carried out in Bradford and are either already published (Aspinall *et al.*, 1972) or available on request from the Bradford team. McKerrell's own analyses by XRF have never been published: it is not even known what objects he worked on to produce his range of values for Egyptian faience, and it seems likely that some of the analyses were carried out on objects other than beads.

McKerrell (1972, 1976a) used lead, tin and silver to demonstrate that Egyptian and British faience were similar in composition, and the copper content of the faience beads different from the copper in contemporary bronzes. His results for tin (1972, pp. 288ff., fig. 1) clearly show no such thing; the tin levels of Egyptian and British faience are distinct, and were used by Newton and Renfrew as the basis for their 1970 paper. McKerrell suggests the use of a tin opacifier to explain the high levels of tin in British beads (sometimes 100% or more of the copper level, i.e. 100 parts of tin to 100 parts of copper). This technique is essentially Near Eastern, certainly not western European (McKerrell, 1976a, p. 305). The possibility that the archaeological evidence demonstrates otherwise did not, apparently, occur to McKerrell. The recipe was, no doubt, Near Eastern in origin, like the technique of faience-making in general; yet the analytical evidence clearly demonstrates that it was used for British beads but not, generally, for Egyptian ones. And to argue, as McKerrell does (1976a, p. 308), that because the original Egyptian bead population was so high, practically every value of bead content found in Britain was being produced in large numbers in Egypt, seems a curious approach to the interpretation of the existing analyses.

On the question of lead content, I thank Mr S. E. Warren for the observation that lead is a good glass-forming element in its own right, and could well go into solution readily as compared with copper or tin. Much here would depend on what precisely was being used and how, neither of which is known. The complexity of the issue is demonstrated by the fact that one of the North Molton biconical beads has a copper-coloured lead glaze.

It is interesting that McKerrell (1976a, pp. 300, 315; 1976b, p. 123) accepts that faience beads in central Europe were in all probability locally produced. He reaches this conclusion on two grounds: that the radiocarbon dates indicate a date for Br A1 earlier than Eighteenth Dynasty Egypt, so "there is thus a far less plausible background to an importation thesis from the Near East"; and "the metal involved in their manufacture can fairly closely be tied in many cases to the Singen or *Ösenring* metal". These vague statements suppress the chronological and geographical range over which faience occurs in central Europe.

In another recent publication on the subject of faience (1976b, pp. 125–126) McKerrell shifted his position on the British beads: "the XRF analyses . . . are not consistent with the known local metal compositions but . . . some do resemble New Kingdom Egyptian metal (and faience). Additionally, the North British beads, in particular, also parallel the analytical composition, shape and fabric of many of the later central European examples . . . . . A pointer perhaps to two distinct points of origin." A very different conclusion to that of 1972: "It would seem that the British faience beads are very likely to be of Eastern rather than local origin with at least a fair probability that they derive from Eighteenth Dynasty Egypt."

I thank S. E. Warren and R. A. P. Peek for their generous help over many years with the problems of faience beads.

80. Guido (1978).

81. Dr Julian Henderson, University of Bradford, kindly advises me that although the turquoise and blue glass beads from Knackyboy were not altogether firmly associated, they are likely from their compositions to be of Bronze Age date.

82. I thank Mrs C. M. Guido for kindly supplying information on this bead. Dr Henderson's analysis of the bead has revealed a composition pattern markedly different from those of locally produced Iron Age beads.

83. Dr Haevernick writes (letter of 5 August 1973): "The bead from Melk is neither Bronze Age nor does it really belong to the grave, as indicated. I was on the spot and have made a careful examination. It must absolutely be struck off the list."

84. Píč (1899, pp. 193, 199).

85. P. Reinecke, *Germania* **17**, 1933, 12ff.

86. J. Naue, *Die Bronzezeit in Oberbayern*, 1894 (Munich, Piloty and Löhle), p. 130. Munich, Prähistorische Staatssammlung, inv. no. 90. 189.

87. K. Willvonseder, *Forschungen und Fortschritte* **13**, 1937, 4; Píč (1900, pp. 142, 146, 150, 155).

88. V. Furmánek, *Slovenská Archeológia* **25/2**, 1977, 315–316.

89. *Pace* E. Lehečková, *op. cit.* p. 32 (n. 34).

90. H. Neuninger and R. Pittioni, *Archaeologia Austriaca* **16**, 1959, 52–66. The procedure used (semi-quantitative spectrographic analysis) would today hardly be considered adequate, and one may certainly question the assumption that all the Austrian beads emanated from the same source—at least on the basis of the evidence provided.

91. For example, Renfrew (1968).

92. Ventris and Chadwick (1973, pp. 221–231, 441–442); Chadwick (1976, pp. 119–121).

93. R. S. Merrillees, *Antiquity* **36**, 1962, 287–292; V. Karageorghis, *Antiquity* **50**, 1976, 125–129.

94. Camp-stool freso: A. Evans, *Palace of Minos at Knossos* IV, 1935 (London, Macmillan), pp. 379ff., esp. p. 387, figs 321–323, pl. XXXI, and fig. 329 (Tiryns signet, folding stool with back). Northern camp-stools synthesized by O. Wanscher,

Nordische Klappstühle aus der Bronzezeit, 1940, and W. Wegewitz, *Die Gräber der Stein- und Bronzezeit im Gebiet der Niederelbe*, 1949 (Hildesheim, Lax), pp. 172ff., with refs. The complete example from Guldhøj depicted in, for example, J. Brøndsted, *Nordische Vorzeit* II, 1962 (Neumünster, Wachholtz), pp. 59–60, 288 with refs. Cf. Randsborg (1968, p. 22). Recent synthesis: O. Wanscher, *Sella Curulis. The Folding Stool, an Ancient symbol of Dignity*, 1980 (Copenhagen, Rosenkilde and Bagger), pp. 9ff. (Egypt), 75ff. (Nordic Bronze Age), 83ff. (Creto-Mycenaean).

95. Dickinson (1977, pp. 77, 81 etc.).

96. B. Craig, quoted in D. Barag, Mesopotamian Core-formed Glass Vessels (1500–500 B.C.), in A. L. Oppenheim *et al.*, *Glass and Glassmaking in Ancient Mesopotamia*, 1970 (Corning, Museum of Glass), pp. 189ff.

97. Catalogue by Buchholz in Bass (1967, pp. 152ff.). Cf. F. Schachermeyr, *Ägäis und Orient*, 1967 (Graz/Köln, Böhlau), pp. 54ff. Buchholz lists 107 pieces, but of these more than a dozen are of Iron Age date and some 17 are not closely (or at all) provenanced.

98. N. Platon, *Illustrated London News* 28 November 1964, pp. 859–861; full bibliography in Buchholz, *op. cit.* E. Porada, *Cyprus and Crete*, pp. 111ff.

99. Most recently I. Pini in *Cyprus and Crete*, pp. 121ff.

100. Bass (1967, p. 164) quoting G. R. Driver, *Semitic Writing from Pictograph to Alphabet*, rev. ed. 1976 (Oxford, University Press), pp. 15, 63.

101. J. D. S. Pendlebury, *Aegyptiaca*, 1930 (Cambridge, University Press); R. B. Brown, *A Provisional Catalogue of and Commentary on Egyptian and Egyptianizing Artifacts found on Greek Sites*, 1982 (Ann Arbor, Univ. Microfilms). Many of the objects listed here are faience and glass; excluding beads of these materials, some 82 objects are listed.

102. For example, most recently by Hankey and Warren (1974; forthcoming).

103. V. Hankey, *J. Mediterranean Anthropology and Archaeology* 1, 1981, 45.

104. Quoted in Hankey and Warren (1974, p. 400).

105. M. R. Popham, E. A. Catling and H. W. Catling, *BSA* **69**, 1974, 203, 211, 216–217, fig. 14F, pl. 38, g-i.

106. R. S. Merrillees in *Eastern Mediterranean*, p. 183.

107. Mozsolics (1965–6). This author's lumping together of all gold hoards which do not seem to fit in any other Bronze Age context into the Hajdúsámson horizon (e.g. Borodino, V'lčitr'n) is naturally open to criticism, and not acceptable to me personally.

108. M. Novotná, *Sborník československé společnosti archeologické* **3**, 1963, 137–140.

109. For example, Karo (1930a, Taf. CXXXVI, nos 786–787); Matthäus (1980a, pp. 218–219, Taf. 41, no. 342 etc.).

110. Vladár (1973, pp. 293f.).

111. J. Dezort, *Obzor Prehistorický* **13**, 1946, 62.

112. P. Reinecke, *Wiener Prähistorische Zeitschrift* **29**, 1942, 103; on Suciu de Sus generally, Coles and Harding (1979, p. 404 with refs).

113. From the extensive literature: V. Mikov, *Zlatnoto s'krovišče ot V'lčitr'n*, 1958 (Sofia, Bulgarian Academy of Sciences); Mozsolics assigns the hoard, without comment, to her Hajdúsámson horizon, and therefore contemporary with the Shaft Graves, on the basis of such details as form of handles and decorative motifs. M. V. Garašanin,

Studia in honorem Veselini Beševliev, 1978, 284–287, asserts that the hoard is "aus dem Rahmen des thrako-kimmerischen Kreises mit Sicherheit auszuschalten", and favours instead the Late Bronze–Early Iron Age (Br D–Ha A1) on the basis of the similarity of some of the decorative motifs to those on Dubovac-Žuto Brdo and related pottery, and metalwork of the Uriu-Domăneşti and Cincu-Suseni phases. Review of the literature over the years: A. G. Bonev, *Archeologija* **19/4**, 1977, 11–19.

114. Piggott (1966, p. 125, n. 56); Bouzek (1968, pp. 27f.).

115. N. Sandars, *Prehistoric Art in Europe*, 1968 (Harmandsworth, Penguin Books), pp. 213, 319 n. 38.

116. E. Sprockhoff, *Germania* **39**, 1961, 11–22; Matthäus (1977–8) with full list of parallels for form, shape and decoration, and discussion of find circumstances; Matthäus (1980a, pp. 224ff.) (type 35, "rundbodige Tassen mit seitlichem Ausguss"; closest parallel is a cup from Thera-Akrotiri, area △3).

117. S. Piggott, *Ancient Europe*, 1965 (Edinburgh, University Press), p. 134, pl. 17b; Gerloff (1975, pp. 107, 190, pl. 50 A1).

118. R. von Uslar, *Germania* **33**, 1955, 319–323.

119. Briard (1965, pp. 76–77).

120. Gerloff (1975, pp. 190ff.).

121. Gerloff (1975, p. 190); Taylor (1980, Nf 14–16 (pl. 26c); Lc 7; Sx 13; El 2; Bt 2; Fi 1; CoFm 21 (pl. 28a-f)); J. M. Coles, *Proc. Soc. Antiqs Scotland* **101**, 1968–9, 49, figs 35.2, 36.1, 37.1.

122. D. L. Clarke, *Beaker Pottery of Great Britain and Ireland*, 1970 (Cambridge University Press), Vol. 2, frontispiece and fig. 1081; C. Köster, *Prähistorische Z.* **43–4**, 1965–6, 40, Taf. 16, 2, 4.

123. Childe (1948, pp. 188–189); C. F. C. Hawkes, *Proc. Prehist. Soc.* **14**, 1948, 203–204.

124. Matthäus (1980a).

125. Childe (1948, p. 181, fig. 7).

126. v. Merhart (1952, pp. 38ff. [= 1969, pp. 335ff.]).

127. Illustrated, for instance, in M. Ebert (ed.), *Reallexikon der Vorgeschichte* I, 1924 (Berlin, de Gruyter), pl. 53a, and Gimbutas (1965, fig. 22.1).

128. A point made by Matthäus (1977–8, pp. 60–61), but hitherto ignored. On the cemetery and cup, Th. Voges, *Jahresschrift für die Vorgeschichte der sächsisch-thür-ingischen Länder* (Halle) **7**, 1908, 17ff.; H. Mötefindt, *Jahresschrift . . .* (Halle) **10**, 1911, 77f., Taf. X.5, and *Arch. Anzeiger* 1912, 99–103.

129. Notably by Gerloff (1975, pp. 194–195). See E. Sprockhoff, *Germania* **30**, 1952, 164ff., Abb. 4, Taf. 4.1.

130. V. Milojčić, *Germania* **31**, 1953, 10f.

131. L. Barfield, *Antiquity* **40**, 1966, 48f., pl. 8b; J. Rageth, *BRGK* **55**, 1974, 133f., Taf. 34.15.

132. O.T.P.K. Dickinson and A. F. Harding, *Antiquity* **46**, 1972, 316–317.

133. K. Reichertová, *Arch. Rozhledy* **1**, 1949, 61–62, fig. 30.

134. V. G. Childe, *The Dawn of European Civilisation*, 6th ed., 1957 (London, Kegan Paul), pp. 33, 132.

135. Karo (1930a, no. 389, Taf. CXXXVIII).

136. Karo (1930a, pp. 51–52, Taf. XX, 53–55).

137. H. Schmidt, *Z. für Ethnographie* **36**, 1904, 615–624; A. Evans, *The Shaft Graves and Bee-hive Tombs of Mycenae*, 1929 (London, Macmillan), pp. 47–48; Bouzek (1966, p. 254, fig. 8).

138. Zaharia (1959, pp. 103–134); Schmidt, *op. cit*; the distribution extends up into central Europe: I. Hasek, *Acta Universitatis Carolinae, Philosophica et Historica* **3**, 1959, 105–112; Vladár (1973, pp. 263ff.).

139. Levkas: W. Dörpfeld, *Alt-Ithaka*, 1927 (Munich/Gräfelfing, Uhde), pp. 288–289, pl. 60.4.

140. Hawkes (1961) for the original discussion; Branigan (1970, pp. 95–97) for the claim of an Aegean derivation.

141. I thank Dr Joan Taylor for this observation.

142. Jugoslavia: Benac-Čović (1956, p. 52, pl. 17.9 (Ha A)); Niš Catalogue (1971, pp. 74, 256, plate) (MBA; pendant with central knot or button). Romania: many examples in Petrescu-Dîmboviţa (1977), of MBA (Tufa), Uriu-Domăneşti (Batarci, Domăneşti, Guruslău, Uriu) and Cincu-Suseni (several examples) date.

143. Annable and Simpson (1964, pp. 45, 99, no. 174).

144. Mylonas (1972, p. 121, no. 514); Dickinson (1977, p. 43).

145. Z. le Rouzic, *Revue des Musées, Fouilles et Découvertes Archéologiques* **30**, 1930, 169ff., figs 2.3, 3.2, 4.6–7; Taylor (1980, p. 45, pl. 25f.).

146. Poursat (1977, pp. 11, 177, no. 13/1028, pl. II (described as "peigne de coiffure"); p. 79, no. 268/2407, pl. XXIII). NM 2670 is not included in Poursat.

147. Kilian (1981, p. 180, fig. 33a). The conical toothed pieces ("hoofs") from the House of Shields at Mycenae are comparable to the Mycenae Acropolis pieces: A. J. B. Wace, *BSA* **49**, 1954, 242, pl. 36d; Poursat (1977, p. 40, no. 128/7393, 7480, pl. XI). The pieces from Menidi, Thebes and the House of Sphinxes at Mycenae, on the other hand, have narrow slits cut down into the ivory and are comparable neither in form nor execution: all these, and the other pieces, are usually interpreted as furniture legs or other attachments; Poursat (1977, p. 151, no. 441/1982, pl. XLVI); Symeonoglou (1973, pp. 56–57, fig. 245); A. J. B. Wace, *BSA* **49**, 1954, pl. 39b.

148. Karo (1930b, pp. 127–128, Beil. XXX–XXXII); Beck *et al.* (1968).

149. Marinatos (1960, pp. 151–157).

150. Karo (1930a, p. 53, Taf. XXI nos 65–66).

151. S. Wide, *Athenische Mitt.* **35**, 1910, 29f., Abb. 25, 26, 28; Müller-Karpe (1962, p. 84, Abb. 2, 8).

152. Gualdo Tadino: R. Peroni, *Inv. Arch. (Italia)* fasc. 3, I.6, 5-(3), 14–15; Fontanella di Casalromano (Mantova): Müller-Karpe (1959, p. 262, Taf. 86, 8).

153. Zaharia (1959, pp. 107, 113, Abb. 1); V. Podborský, *Mähren in der Spätbronzezeit*, 1970 (Brno, Universita J. E. Purkyně), Abb. 5–7.

154. W. A. McDonald and G. R. Rapp, *The Minnesota Messenia Expedition: Reconstructing a Bronze Age Regional Environment*, 1972 (Minneapolis, University of Minnesota Press), pp. 111–113, 128, 141, 254–256; Chadwick (1976, pp. 67–68); cf. Renfrew (1972, pp. 232ff.); J. Carothers and W. A. McDonald, *J. Field Arch.* **6**, 1979, 433–454.

□ 5
Trade in everyday items

The treasures of the Shaft Graves, of Peristeria, or of Vapheio were, no doubt, important to the people who owned them. Their significance for the economy as a whole is much harder to estimate. Indeed, a case can be made that trade and exchange affecting the few who were buried in these splendid tombs were of little importance to the economy as a whole. The regional economy, in the terms I have set out in Chapter 2 above, depended on agricultural and industrial production. The factors regulating the lives of most people living in the kingdom of Pylos, as much as in the environs of Stonehenge, were those pertaining to the agricultural year and the availability (or otherwise) of materials for making tools to carry on that work, or, in the case of artisans, for making the various objects which the Mycenaean world required. It follows that most materials and products will have moved around on a district or regional level, and that more distant exchange of daily commodities is unlikely to have taken place. These were not the days of bulk grain carriers plying the Atlantic, and where such transport can be proven—as with metal ores—its significance is correspondingly greater.

But here the problems of demonstrating that such trade existed are also greater. Such items as pottery seem to have been very little moved, and where they were their provenance is all the harder to pin down. Grain, if it survives, cannot be provenanced. Metal ores present their own problems. It is mainly the form of artefact types—especially bronzes—which enables detailed attribution to specific sources and workshops. In this chapter we shall be looking at some of these everyday items to see which—if any—indicate connections with the European world.

Pottery

Pottery is, by its very nature, less likely to be moved about on a regular or large-scale basis than are the individual objects—especially prestige

125

objects—considered above. Apart from a few especially elaborate wares which may have been transported for their own sakes (e.g. Kamares ware in Egypt) one assumes that it was the contents of the vases which were important, rather than the vases themselves. Pottery imports to Greece are in any case very few. They fall into two main categories: imported amphorae from the Near East, and hand-made burnished ware found on a variety of sites in the twelfth century.

Since Mycenaean pottery is so common in the Near East and Cyprus, one might expect that the reverse would also be true—but not a bit of it. The only vessels imported from the Near East were "Canaanite" amphorae, and even then not on a large scale: the classic study lists only nine of Bronze Age date, all from the mainland.[1] So small a number, even allowing for the addition of more recent finds, leads to a presumption that their value was more to do with exotic tastes in wine than inherent desirability.

Strangely, Cypriot pottery seems to have had little or no popularity in the Aegean area in the Late Bronze Age. Only a few pieces are known, almost none from the mainland.[2] That Cypriot pottery could, and did, travel westwards as well as southwards and eastwards is shown by the finds from Thapsos (p. 247, Fig. 56).

The "barbarian" ware found on Greek sites in the twelfth century represents a special problem which is considered below (p. 216). It is unlikely to have been the result of importation, at least as far as the majority of it is concerned, and therefore need not detain us here. Undoubtedly the result of export, on the other hand, was the Mycenaean pottery to the east, west and (in very small quantities) north. This is considered more fully in Chapter 9; the quantities north of Greece are so small as to be insignificant, while the nature of the finds in Italy and Sicily, which are considerable in number, suggests that both commodities (but not only, or mainly, oil or spices as in the east) and fine pots in their own right were traded.

The limits of this exchange of Mycenaean pottery were Sardinia and the Po Valley in the west, Albania, Macedonia and Thrace in the north, the Euphrates in the east, and Nubia in the south—a wide spread indeed. But many of the find-spots to the west and north have produced no more than the odd sherd of Mycenaean pottery, and cannot possibly be construed as part of a regular exchange network on this basis alone. At the same time Mycenaean pottery (when unambiguously identified) is absolutely unequivocal in its indication of contact, however remote. The evidence of other classes of material, notably bronze, is much harder to assess, for the same types could be, and demonstrably were, made by different smiths in different areas. Only detailed consideration of each type of object can hope to decide whether the evidence for contact is credible.

Tools and implements

Tools and implements, mainly of bronze, represent everyday objects *par excellence*. These are the objects with which the hewers of wood hew, the tillers till, and the butchers slay. We are concerned with all sorts of implement except those used for personal adornment, and those used in warfare.

A detailed study of these pieces[3] showed how scanty the evidence is for any sort of trade involving tools. Agricultural tools show no connections whatever between Aegean and European series. With carpentry tools, matters are a little more complex. Many types (e.g. saws, awls, drills, gouges, chisels, adzes, flat axes) occur in one form or another in both general areas, but without any likelihood of a connection since the types are basic and widespread. The case of socketed axes makes the point well, for this was an absolutely typical European Late Bronze Age form, found in their thousands throughout Europe. There is no certain example known from Greece. There is a mould for one at Troy and an actual piece from elsewhere in the Troad;[4] there are a good many from Bulgaria and a few from Albania.[5] Yet Greece remains totally distinct as far as this common bronze form is concerned, preferring other types of splitting tool—notably the double-axe.

Double-axes were a special tool type in the Aegean, especially in Crete where they occur in some profusion from a relatively early date.[6] On the mainland, too, where the shaft-hole was generally oval in contrast to the round hole of the Cretan axes, the form became popular and in the north-west two specific variants were created ("Hermones–Kierion" and "Kilindir–Begunci" types) (Fig. 32). Two aspects of the double-axes are of particular concern to us here: the finding, or alleged finding, of various double-axes of Mycenaean type in the Ukraine and in central and north-west Europe, and the geographical extent of double-axe distribution in the Balkans (Fig. 54).

Double-axes of clearly Mycenaean type are found in Albania and Bulgaria, but also in the Ukraine. Two hoards there contain such axes, and three other single examples are known.[7] The finds are old ones, but there is no reason to doubt their validity; the axes themselves are indistinguishable metrically from Mycenaean axes found in Greece. A Mycenaean presence in the Black Sea region, further supported by the recent finding of ingots in Bulgaria (p. 49), is not unimaginable though it does remain rather speculative. By what means and for what purpose these 11 pieces reached their distant destination remains far from clear. Local smiths were turning out socketed axes by the dozen, and are not known—here or anywhere else in barbarian Europe—to have been casting double-axes.

The case of the double-axes of Switzerland, France and the British Isles is very different. Not one of these has a satisfactory context or provenance, and detailed examination of the recent history of some of them has demonstrated

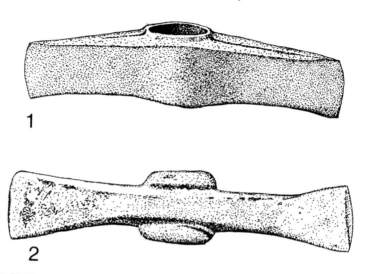

FIG. 32 ☐ Two specialized forms of double-axe found in the south Balkan area. (1) Hermones or Kierion type; (2) Kilindir or Begunci type; both from Niš region. (After Niš Catalogue, 1971.)

that modern purchasing and collecting are involved. Opinion has tended very much in recent years to disregard these pieces as evidence of trade from Greece to northern Europe, though the matter is unproven.

The specialized double-axe forms known as the Hermones–Kierion and Kilindir–Begunci types (Fig. 32) are distributed through the Balkans in such a way as to suggest that their centre of production lay in the Greek border area (Fig. 33). They seem to indicate that tool types could be adapted differentially in different cultural zones, perhaps on functional grounds.

Another well known object is the mould for a winged axe found in the House of the Oil Merchant at Mycenae.[8] Winged axes are absolutely not an Aegean type, being found rather in central and western Europe and in Italy. The specific axe in question has been shown to be characteristic of the type known in Italy as the Ortucchio class:[9] another was found in the Surbo hoard.[10] An axe of the Poggio Berni class is in the British Museum, allegedly found in Greece,[11] not a context that one can place any confidence in on its own. The axe-mould may be important for chronological reasons, but here we have to ask rather what it was doing at Mycenae. It was apparently not put to use, for no examples of finished axes of this type have ever been found in Greece. Childe remarked: "The mould must surely have belonged to a smith from the Apennine Peninsula who had crossed the sea to work for a rich patron at Mycenae".[12] One might have more confidence in this interpretation if we knew a little more about how smithing operated in the Bronze Age world.

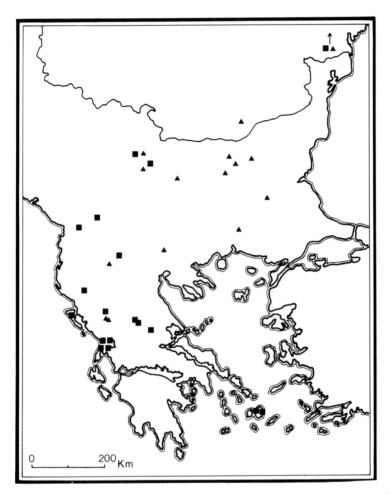

FIG. 33 ☐ Distribution of Hermones-Kierion (■) and Kilindir-Begunci (▲) double-axes. (After Bouzek, pers. comm.; Buchholz, 1983.)

There is no other indication of the actual manufacture of Italian bronzes on Greek sites in this or any other period of the Bronze Age,[13] but a considerable number of objects (mainly of bronze) of Italian affinities, if not actual manufacture, have been found in Greece in LH IIIB-C contexts. Violin-bow fibulae, of which several have been found at Mycenae itself, are a case in point; Peschiera daggers are another. Should one see this as evidence for resident smiths? It is perhaps safer simply to remark on the community of bronze-working methods and forms in Italy and Greece from around 1200 B.C.

A couple of other axe types deserve mention. Single-bladed shaft-hole axes were not a Mycenaean type, though they do occur in Epirus and in Albania; it has been demonstrated that they were an Adriatic form, and are found on both sides of that sea during the later part of the Bronze Age.[14] In this connection an extraordinary piece from Dodona, without context, must be mentioned: it looks like a version of a disc-butted axe of Hungarian type (*Nackenscheibenaxt*).[15] It is not, however, a true representative of that class of object, nor are other pieces of this form known in the region. If it has any significance at all, it must be of the most general kind. On the other hand, trunnion axes do show undoubted connections between Greece and other areas.[16] The form has a long history in the Near East and Anatolia, and has been connected with particular metallurgical techniques, especially sheet metal working. Only a handful of examples occur in Greece: one from Asine is in a level dated to LH IIIC, another occurred in the Anthedon (Boeotia) hoard which contains a tripod fragment and is therefore presumably later than 1200 B.C. A mould for a trunnion axe was found at Troy, without definite context, but presumed to come from the Seventh City. On the other hand, quite a few trunnion axes are known from Italy; where datable they are from Protovillanovan contexts. This may then be another type that links the bronzeworking traditions of Greece with those of Italy in the twelfth century and later.

Metalworking tools are an important class of object in the Late Bronze Age world.[17] However, because they were used to carry out essentially similar operations, it is not unexpected that close similarities between tool forms in different areas occur. Hammers and anvils are a case in point. An object described as an anvil was found on the Cape Gelidonya ship,[18] but such pieces were not otherwise known in the Bronze Age Aegean (by contrast to the situation in western Europe, for instance).[19] Hammer-heads of similar form occur from the Greek world and from Italy and Sardinia, but too much significance should not be read into this. On the other hand, the recent finding of a beautiful pair of tongs of Syro-Palestinian or Cypriot type at Siniscola, Sardinia, is probably of greater significance, as no other pieces of this kind are known in the west.[20]

Quite distinct from the tools of industrial production that we have been considering hitherto are the various types of personal objects, whether for personal adornment (like rings and pins) or for some other basic function in everyday life (like knives). Since many of these classes must be related directly to fashion and to individual whim rather than to efficiency, it might be expected that there would be more variation between pieces than was the case with the objects of industrial production, but this does not seem to be the case: clearly established forms were followed almost everywhere. In general, connections between Greece and the north and west are sparse in the early Mycenaean period, but become much closer after 1200 B.C.

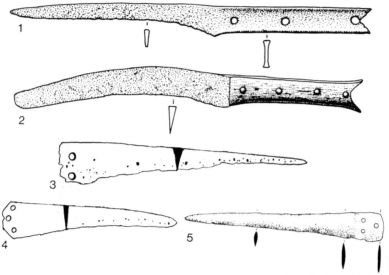

FIG. 34 ☐ Knives of Mycenaean and related type from Italy, Jugoslavia and Albania. (1) Pertosa; (2) Scoglio del Tonno; (3) Vajzë; (4) Midhë; (5) Iglarevo. (After Bianco Peroni, 1976; Prendi, 1977–8; Kilian, 1976.)

This statement can, for instance, be borne out by a study of the knife types (Fig. 34).[21] The great majority of Mycenaean knives are one-edged, straight-backed objects with organic handles.[22] A few such pieces have been found in Italy: a possible example at Santa Sabina in Apulia, in a tomb together with two LH IIIB vases, one, possibly two, at Scoglio del Tonno, and at the Pertosa cave in Campania.[23] A variant form is seen on a flanged knife from a grave at Iglarevo in Metohije;[24] this is not a local type and seems to be an import, though it is uncommon in Greece (Fig. 34.5). From the same grave came a modified type A rapier (p. 153) and a dagger, perhaps originally a knife, with three rivet-holes arranged in triangular fashion: this makes it akin to a large group of such pieces found in north-west Greece and Albania (at least one other is known from Jugoslavia). There is a variety of local forms of knife in the north-west of Greece as in other types, e.g. two curved knives from Elaphotopos and Kalbaki;[25] the finding at Assiros of a mould to cast curved knives is therefore of considerable importance.[26] Generally, local workshops seem to have been quite capable of turning out their own bronzes without the need for importation from the south.

A small group of one-edged knives with straight backs is also known in the Balkans, where they occur in the second phase of Late Bronze Age hoards. At first sight some of these seem very close to Mycenaean types, but it must be remembered that the form is a very simple one and exhibits few specific features. Besides, the late date of the Balkan pieces appears to rule out any direct connection.[27]

These isolated occurrences of rather unspecific types of knife give way after 1200 B.C. to the export (or dual production) of much more specific types (Fig. 35). Of these, by far the best evidence comes from the group of knives with a defined end to the organic hilt ("stop-ridge"), a type that is at home in the Urnfield world, especially in Italy and the Alps, where they have been named the Matrei type and Mühlau variant.[28] At least four examples of this general class are now known from the Aegean: three are from Crete, while one is alleged to come from Corfu (Fig. 35.2). This last is a particularly interesting piece as it is decorated with dot and circle designs in an irregular group near the stop-ridge: dots and circles also appear on Italian examples,[29] but it is perhaps the appear-

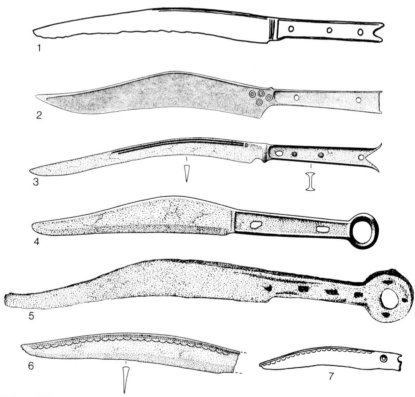

FIG. 35 ☐ Late knife types in Greece and Italy. (1 and 7) Dictaean Cave; (2) "Corfu"; (3) Celano; (4) Peschiera; (5) Ialysos, Moschou Vounara tomb XV; (6) Pertosa. (After Boardman, 1961; Bianco Peroni, 1976; Maiuri, 1923–4.)

ance of a squid ("nautilus") on a knife from Phaestos, apparently also executed in this technique, that is most remarkable.[30] The chronological context
of these pieces is shown by the recent discovery of a knife of this sort at
Knossos, where the LM IIIC date was undeniable,[31] and, less certainly, by an
example from the Dictaean Cave.[32] The distinctively Cretan decoration on the
Phaestos piece might be taken as evidence of local manufacture, but it could
equally well have been added later to suit local taste. There can be little doubt
that the form is an Italian and Urnfield one,[33] and it is more likely than not that
these pieces are imports.

There are other examples of knives from the Aegean of twelfth century date
which find their best parallels in Italy.[34] Two small pieces from the Dictaean
Cave, for instance, have a decoration of pendent semicircles along a curved
back (Fig. 35.7).[35] A close parallel for this came from the Pertosa Cave (Fig.
35.6),[36] but the decoration is widespread in Italy and similar to that known on
central European knives; it is not Aegean, and an Italian manufacture for these
Cretan knives would be perfectly possible on typological grounds. The story is
not quite so simple with a knife with zoomorphic handle found in the great LH
IIIC cemetery of Perati in Attica.[37] Parallels can certainly be quoted for the
general form and conception, and it is hard to imagine that the maker of this
knife was not well aware of the widespread currency of bird symbols in
Urnfield art; but it is a unique piece, and in any case there are several other
examples of the use of similar bird symbols in late Mycenaean craftwork (on
the rim of the Tiryns hoard vessel or the Pylos strainer, for example);[38] some
authorities favour an East Mediterranean derivation for the conception.[38a]

The case of knives with ring-end, an example of which has long been known
from Ialysos, Moschou Vounara T. XV,[39] is more difficult to assess because
nothing is known about the normal method of termination of the organic
handle (Fig. 35.5). A solid-handled piece from Mycenae Chamber Tomb
103[40] has a button termination, and the well known knife from the Mycenae
"Tsountas Hoard"[41] has a T-shaped termination, also known on certain
classes of sword.[42] These instances might imply that a disc or roundel was the
usual form of the end of these knives. On the other hand, ring-ended knives are
known from the early Mycenaean period, even if not in the precise form of the
Ialysos piece; this was clearly another option for the termination of the hilt.
The ring would serve as a means of suspension, for instance from a belt, just as
pen-knives today have a loop for attachment. On the Ialysos knife, the flanges
go right round the ring end, and there are even rivets through the ring; the
organic hilt thus continued round it (Fig. 35.5). It is quite possible that a
ring-end was also used on some of the standard Mycenaean knives whose hilt
termination is not preserved, and that the ring-end was therefore not unusual.
Parallels in the Urnfield world[43] are instructive and, indeed, close, but do not
have to be invoked until more is known about the finished appearance of

normal Mycenaean knives. The absence of a stop-ridge on the Ialysos knife[44] and the marked step between blade and handle makes a connection with the Italian knives of Montegiorgio type more likely, but even here the correspondence is not precise (Fig. 35.4).[45] The status of certain razors found in Greece is similarly uncertain, but two examples, from Tylissos and from Lakkithra, seem conceivable as Italian products.[45a]

Personal items

Turning now to smaller objects for use with clothing, or as personal ornaments, virtually all the evidence for contact with lands to the west and north of Greece comes from the later period.

Pins

Pins of various kinds had been known before the Late Bronze Age[46] and continued in use through it. Often they were of bone and have therefore received less attention than they deserve.[47] Already in the Shaft Graves pins were present: these included the type with simple shank surmounted by a large head of different material (ivory, rock-crystal) which occurs in Graves Alpha, Omicron, Upsilon and III and at other sites.[48] Much the same type, in different materials (glass-paste on iron) recurs at Perati tomb 108,[49] and at a late tomb at Knossos.[50] Other pin forms are those with conical or biconical head (Fig. 36.1), with disc head ("seal pins"), or with crook-like shank.[51] Such forms were common in Italy in the *Terremare* and northern lake-sites in the Middle and early Late Bronze Age,[52] but the types are widespread and no particular significance can be attached to this.[53] In any case, the popularity of bone pins,[54] which must frequently not have survived, or survived in an adequate state of preservation, shows that conclusions about dress or fashion, let alone ethnic affinities, on the basis of Mycenaean bronze pins would be premature and unwarranted (Fig. 36.6).

In the twelfth century new types of pin appear.[55] These are characterized not only by their novel forms of head but also by their length. Since the time of the Shaft Graves, pins had not surpassed a length of 20 cm. By contrast, the pins from the Deiras cemetery at Argos (Fig. 37.1–2) are up to 35 cm in length; those from the Gypsadhes cemetery at Knossos (Fig. 36.7–9) up to 26 cm; those from Submycenaean tombs at Athens 47 cm. Perhaps more unusual are the shank and head forms: the shank is swollen (Fig. 36.2–4),[56] either biconical or globular,[57] the head may be disc-like ("seal-headed"). On

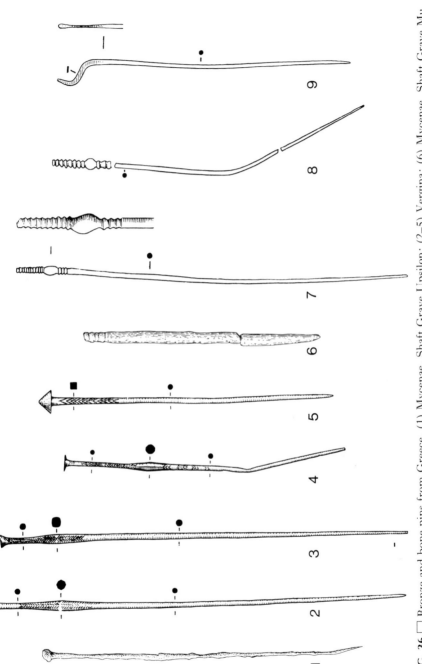

FIG. 36 ☐ Bronze and bone pins from Greece. (1) Mycenae, Shaft Grave Upsilon; (2–5) Vergina; (6) Mycenae, Shaft Grave Mu (bone); (7–9) Knossos, Upper Gypsadhes tomb VII. (After Mylonas, 1972; Andronikos, 1969; Hood, Huxley and Sandars, 1958–9.)

one form the upper part of the shank is ribbed or moulded (Fig. 36.7–8). A further variant form has a smooth undecorated head and shank bent into an S-shape, not unlike Early Iron Age "swan's-neck" pins (Fig. 36.9).

Any assessment of the likely origin or affinities of these pieces is bedevilled by the small quantity of material available and the attendant chronological difficulties. Each main type appears only on a dozen or less sites, often ranging in date from LH IIIC to Protogeometric, perhaps 200 years or more. Some pin forms, moreover, were of such simplicity or enduring attraction that detailed correspondences simply cannot be demonstrated: such is the case with the pins with flattened rolled-over top, which occur in later Mycenaean and Submycenaean contexts in Cyprus and mainland Greece.[58] Analogies to this type can be quoted from the Near East on the one hand, but from Italy and central Europe on the other.[59] In reality it seems unnecessary to invoke either as the immediate source for the type in Greece: the type was widespread in time and space.

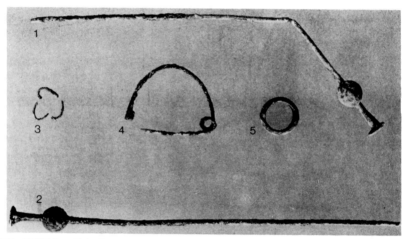

FIG. 37 ☐ Small finds from the Deiras cemetery at Argos. (1 and 2) Long pins with globular swelling on shank; (3 and 5) finger-rings; (4) arc fibula. (After Deshayes, 1966.)

Hardly more precise in its analogies is the "vase-headed pin" (i.e. with spherical swelling on the shank and disc head). The type is known in Anatolia (Boğazköy and Troy VIIb),[60] the Balkans, Italy, and central and eastern Europe.[61] A characteristic feature of the Greek pins (seen, for instance, at the Kerameikos and Argos) is that the globular swelling is well down the shank (Fig. 37.1–2), and though Italian parallels of Protovillanovan context are known they are not otherwise very close.[62] On present evidence this group of Greek pins seems likely to be of local production, even if the inspiration for the form came from outside; but the early Mycenaean composite type with globe on the shank should not be forgotten.

A pin from a LH IIIC tomb at Diakata on Kephallenia with moulded shank, otherwise unprofiled, has no obvious parallels until Villanovan examples in Italy.[63] This same moulding or fluting also occurs on some of the pins with swollen shank,[64] either above or below the swelling, or both. The pin with swollen shank is widely known in Bronze Age Europe from the Middle Bronze Age on, but usually with a perforated swelling, after the manner of a toggle pin—which, indeed, some of them may be.[65] It has been pointed out that the burials of the Tumulus Culture in central Europe provide a good general parallel for the form and deposition pattern of the latest Bronze Age pins of Greece, though the dating is much earlier and the forms are not identical.[66] The discovery of pins with swollen shank in Albania[67] and Macedonia[68] may relate to the Greek examples but does little to help date the origin of the type. It is undoubtedly true that the form appeared in Greece in the twelfth century after centuries of being at home in central Europe, but what conclusions should be drawn from this are far from clear.

The single late example of a double-spiral-head pin from Mazarakata on Kephallenia[69] may well relate to Italian pieces of comparable date. The form is a long-lived one, recurring in many places of the Old World;[70] it was present already in the Aegean during the Early Bronze Age.[71] The position of Kephallenia, however, and the presence of such pins in Late Bronze Age Italy[72] makes a connection, or even importation, possible.

Summarizing the evidence to be derived from pins, it is clear that this group of evidence did not play any very important part in the trade and exchange patterns of the eastern Mediterranean during the Late Bronze Age. The types distinguished in the main part of the Mycenaean period were by no means peculiar to Greece, but cannot be taken as evidence of contact in view of their frequency in many parts of Europe. Only in the twelfth century does the arrival of new types suggest that exotic forms were copied within Greece, and a few pieces, like that with double-spiral-head from Kephallenia, could be actual imports. Whether or not the fashion for long dress pins at the end of and after the Mycenaean period indicates, as some authors have suggested, a change of fashion in clothing—itself possibly even to be connected with a change of climate and/or a change of population—remains in the realm of interesting speculation, and hardly seems susceptible of proof by archaeological means.

Fibulae

The case of safety-pins (fibulae) presents us with one of the classic problems of European prehistory. Safety-pins with parallel pin and bow, the so-called "violin-bow fibulae", appear with some frequency in Greece in the twelfth century; by the eleventh they had been replaced by the D-shaped form with arched bow. The same types make their debut in Italy, the Balkans and central Europe at much the same time. Since the type is patently not a mainstream Aegean one, a derivation from outside has been sought; the "arrival" of the fibula in Greece, together with—or at least at the same time as—other "foreign" forms has been seen as evidence of the arrival of new elements in the population, even as signs of the "Dorian invasion".[73] The problem with such a theory is, as we shall see, that there is little evidence for the chronological priority of the type in the northern and western areas.

The systematic study of early fibulae is fairly well advanced in the main areas in which they occurred.[74] At a future date a complete comparative study will be necessary, a task that cannot be undertaken here. Following Sundwall's typology, over 30 varieties of violin-bow fibulae may be distinguished, several hundred pieces between the Alps and the Mediterranean. It is abundantly clear that several of these types were equally at home in Greece or Italy, and some appear in Jugoslavia as well (Fig. 38).[75] Detailed analysis, however, does not suggest a Greek–Jugoslav production *koine*; nor is the Hungarian sequence at all closely related.[76] Central European pieces with leaf-shaped bow are also of a different type; the simplest forms of fibula were exceptional north of the Alps.[77] On the other hand almost all of the types common in Greece appear at Peschiera or on other sites in northern Italy, a fact which may well suggest specific connections with that area.

The earliest dated finds in Greece belong to LH IIIB,[78] probably—to judge from the associated pottery and the context of the rest—the end of LH IIIB, around 1200 B.C., though simple forms occurred in a number of tombs at Mycenae which could date well back in LH IIIB. The earliest finds in Italy are in the Peschiera horizon and late *terremare*, equivalent to Br D north of the Alps. In Jugoslavia some finds may be Br D but more are Ha A1 and 2. It is certain that there is nothing earlier than Br D on the European side, and since Br D is dated precisely by correspondences with LH IIIB the circle of reasoning is complete! In Müller–Karpe's scheme of chronology Br D is placed in the thirteenth century, but there is no compelling reason why it should not continue considerably after 1200 B.C. The problem is thus not soluble by normal archaeological dating methods.

Much of the same story may be told for the earliest arc fibulae, which first appear at the very end of the Bronze Age in Greece, and thus barely concern us here.[79] The Greek series is very much less like the Italian than was the case with the violin-bow type, and the Jugoslav series[80] corresponds to that in Italy rather than that in Greece. None the less, the simple early types, like those with plain or twisted bow and simple catch, do appear in all areas and must bespeak common production traditions, even perhaps common styles of

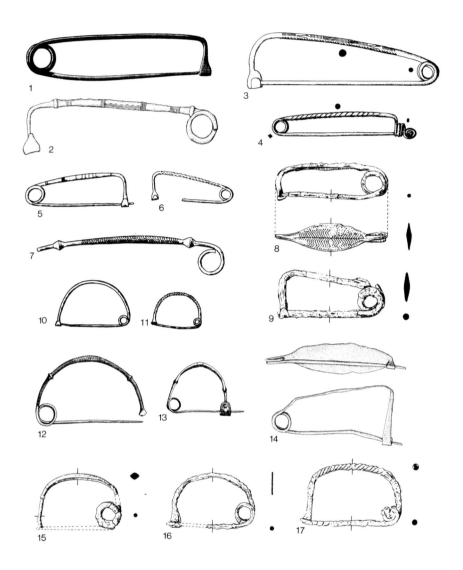

FIG. 38 ☐ Violin-bow and arc fibulae from Greece, Italy and Jugoslavia. (1) Mycenae; (2) Marathon; (3) Split region; (4) Podumci (Unešić); (5–7, 10–11) Peschiera; (8–9, 15–17) Perati; (12–13) Vergina; (14) Vardino. (After Montelius, 1924; Vinski-Gasparini, 1974; Müller-Karpe, 1959; Iakovides, 1970; Andronikos, 1969.)

clothing.[81] One early arc fibula was even found by Schliemann at Troy and is further evidence that Troy was experiencing the same innovations in bronze techniques as the rest of south-eastern Europe.

Arc fibulae formed part of Milojčić's "zweite Welle" of northern influence in Greece. By 1100 B.C. both Italians and Greeks, as well as the peoples around them, were using them. Is there any means of telling who invented the new form? On the face of it, it could have originated in any of the Adriatic lands, especially as there is no independent dating evidence for the Italian and Jugo-slav series. Here the finds from Perati may be significant: the arc fibulae from tombs 336 and 74 (Fig. 38.15, 17), which are dated by Desborough to late in LH IIIC, are "transitional" in shape, being much too tall for a violin-bow, but having a flattened top to the arc, which is never found on Italian examples. No other find can definitely be dated earlier than this; these pieces may be a step in the process that led to the formation of the fully arched fibula.

If this idea is correct, Milojčić must have been wrong in supposing a north-ern origin for the type in Greece, though close connections with Italy during the twelfth century must have been an important factor in the development of specific fibula forms. The consequences of this hypothesis would not be very drastic since it is clear from other classes of evidence that Italy and Greece, especially Crete, were in close contact as regards bronze technology during and after the twelfth century; but it would alter the picture, as known at present, of an "influx" of northern elements at the time of the Mycenaean collapse.

By the eleventh century, other types of fibula, such as the form with stilted bow, were becoming common in both Greece and Italy, but these lie outside our chronological range.[82]

The evidence from fibulae indicates clear connections between Greece, Italy and the Balkans, which at the very least bespeak common smithing production in the various areas. Although the types were certainly non-Mycenaean in the sense that they do not appear prior to 1200 B.C., it is by no means certain that they are therefore of northern origin or inspiration. The problem of where these types originated may best be considered when we come to look at the whole question of bronze production in the late Mycenaean period.

Rings

The finger-ring was a well-known, though never very common, ornament in the Mycenaean world. Most early rings were of gold, and therefore count as prestige objects; they include the fine signet rings of the Shaft Graves and elsewhere. A group of gold rings from Sicilian cemeteries (Pantalica, Caltagirone)[83] decorated with spiraliform decoration have been considered to be Mycenaean-inspired, but they are plainly not Greek productions (Fig. 39.1).

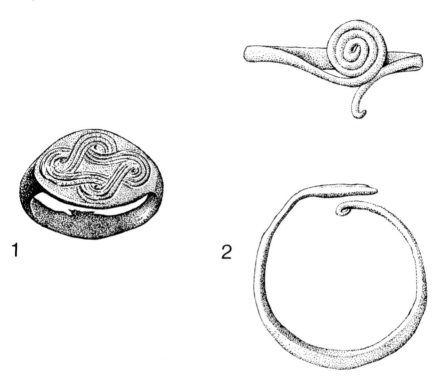

1   2

FIG. 39 ☐ Rings from Sicily and north-west Greece. (1) Pantalica; (2) Romanò. (After Tinè and Vagnetti, 1967; Andreou, 1978.)

By contrast, rings and bracelets of various kinds were common in many parts of "barbarian" Europe from an early stage of the Bronze Age. There is thus little cause to see connections between the two traditions until the twelfth century, when a couple of specific ring types make their debut in Greece.

Rings and bracelets with antithetic spiral terminals (Fig. 39.2) appeared in Greece during the latest Mycenaean period.[84] Parallels and predecessors were noted long ago by Childe[85] and more recently by Desborough and Kilian–Dirlmeier.[86] The northern origin, or at least priority, cannot be doubted on present evidence; the form was at home in central Europe in the Tumulus period, while no Greek example is certainly earlier than LH IIIC. The Attic and other pieces date to late LH IIIC-Submycenaean and later; the form continued in popularity down to the seventh century.[87] Were the early examples of this type in Greece made there or imported?

The earliest finds of this type date to the Early Bronze Age and come from central Europe.[88] It was especially common in the Tumulus Bronze Age of Bavaria, Bohemia and Moravia[89] where it survived into the Late Bronze Age, though in reduced numbers. The multiple-twisted variant was quite common in Jugoslavia;[90] two of these came from Serbia and Macedonia, which makes it at least possible that the Epirote examples were imported. Several were found at Vergina, where a rarer type, that made from two pieces of metal, was found; it is also known at Perati. In general, though, too few examples have been found for large-scale hypotheses to be built around them, even if the date and general form are suggestive.

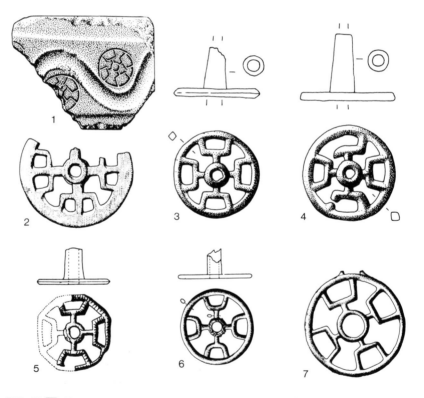

FIG. 40 ☐ "Wheels" and wheel-impressions from Greece and Italy. (1) Relief pithos, Tiryns; (2) ivory, Mycenae, chamber tomb; (3) bronze, Argos, Deiras tomb XXII; (4) bronze, Tiryns; (5) lead, Porto Perone; (6) bronze, Borgo Panigale; (7) bronze pendant, Tolfa. (After Kilian-Dirlmeier, 1979; Woytowitsch, 1978.)

"Wheels" (Fig. 40)

One of the most intriguing and enigmatic groups of material, yet one clearly indicating connections with neighbouring lands, is the group of "wheels" represented by half-a-dozen examples in Greece.[91] The function of these pieces is unknown; they consist of a hollow shank or axle and openwork wheel-disc, and have often been considered to be pin-heads. They might equally well serve as an item of ornament in a number of other ways, for instance on clothing or hair.[92] Another possibility is that they were stamps for pottery, and relief-pithoi at Tiryns do bear ornament of this sort (Fig. 40.1).[93]

The examples known from Greece are in bronze, lead and ivory or bone; they use either simple spokes or the very individual branching spoke. Dated examples come from LH IIIC contexts.[94]

General analogies for the form are plentiful throughout Italy, especially in the north and centre of Italy from *terramara* times on.[95] But the precise form of these pieces is harder to parallel. In particular, the Argos wheels (Fig. 40.3), with the characteristic "branching" spokes, have very precise Italian parallels at Leporano, Grotta di Polla and Borgo Panigale (Fig. 40.5–6)—in the first two cases accompanied by Mycenaean pottery.[96] The same formation, though on a pendant like that from Mycenae, is seen at Fontanella and Tolfa (Coste del Marano) (Fig. 40.7).[97] The more usual type has six plain spokes and goes back to the Middle Bronze Age.[98] Both forms are known as pendants north of the Alps.[99] Wheel-like pendants with a cross or four spokes have been found at Lipari in late levels and at Mycenae in a LH IIIB–C context.[99a]

The form is thus clearly a western one, but—like several other bronze types—seems to have been adopted by Greek smiths in the twelfth century. In this connection the finding of a mould for casting just this type of object in Macedonia is of great interest. The value for dating is more dubious, however; in Italy the general type extended from the *terremare* to Protovillanovan and later, and the context of these pieces in the local sequence is not altogether clear. The origins of the type with forked branches, however, seem to be firmly in the twelfth century.

Tweezers

Catling[100] discusses the Aegean types of tweezers, which were quite common at all times. The same is true for most other areas, and detailed comparisons are not possible. It is possible, however, that the pinched-spring type is connected with certain of the Italian finds.[101]

The Mycenaeans and Europe

Conclusions

The bulk of the evidence from objects of daily use for contact between the Aegean and the barbarian world comes from bronzework, not from pottery. With the exception of one disputed group of material no pottery was imported into Greece from the west or north, while pottery exports were restricted to the northern border area, to southern Italy and the Tyrrhenian Sea province, which is the only area where contacts of any regularity can be assumed. The evidence of bronzework suggests that prior to 1200 B.C. contact was slight and sporadic. After 1200 B.C., a variety of tool and ornament forms became current throughout southern Europe, and some of them may represent actual exports; cumulatively, it is likely that smithing production in the various areas converged, leading to the turning out of identical types in widely separated regions. The conclusions that may be drawn give chronological information of some precision, but are rather more ambiguous as far as economic and social contact is concerned.

Notes

1. V. Grace, "The Canaanite Jar", in S. S. Weinberg (ed.), *The Aegean and the Near East*, Studies presented to Hetty Goldman on the Occasion of her 75th birthday, 1956 (Locust Valley, Augustin), pp. 80–109, list (of those figured) pp. 101ff. Analysis of a Canaanite jar from Athens, Tomb 1: P. Åström and R. E. Jones, *Opuscula Atheniensia* **14/1**, 1982, 7–9.
2. G. Cadogan, *Proc. First Cyprological Congress*, Nicosia 1972, pp. 5–13; R. S. Merrillees, *Trade and Transcendence in the Bronze Age Levant* (SIMA 39), 1974 (Göteborg, Åström), pp. 5–11. A "Mycenaean jug of Base-Ring fabric" is reported from a tomb in Athens by R. S. Merrillees, *Report Dept of Antiqs Cyprus* 1979, p. 128, quoting *Proc. First Cyprological Congress*, Nicosia 1972, pp. 1ff. The first authenticated finds of Cypriot pottery on the mainland now from Tiryns: Kilian (1981, p. 170, Abb. 40, 5) (LH IIIB2 context).
3. Harding (1975).
4. Schmidt (1902, p. 267, no. 6769); *Arch. Anzeiger* 1940, 580, fig. 10. An example from "North Greece" is in the Kanellopoulos collection, and J. Deshayes (*Les outils de bronze*, 1960, II, 64f., nos 1236–7) mentions pieces "from Crete" (these references from J. Bouzek).
5. Černych (1978, pp. 185ff.); Prendi (1977–8, p. 56, Tab. XI, 6–9).
6. H.-G. Buchholz, *Zur Herkunft der kretischen Doppelaxt*, 1959 (Munich, Kiefhaber and Elbl); *Prähistorische Z.* **38**, 1960, 39–71.
7. Harding (1975, pp. 190ff. with refs).
8. A. J. B. Wace, *BSA* **48**, 1953, p. 15, pl. 9b; F. H. Stubbings, *BSA* **49**, 1954, 297–298.
9. Bietti Sestieri (1973, pp. 396ff.).
10. Macnamara (1970).

11. Bietti Sestieri (1973, pp. 393, 399, pl. XLI, 2).

12. V. G. Childe, in *Civiltà del Ferro*. Documenti e Studi **6**, 1960, pp. 575ff.

13. Except perhaps for "wheels" in view of the findings from Kastanas, Macedonia.

14. Harding (1975, pp. 188ff. with refs).

15. C. Carapanos, *Dodone et ses ruines*, 1878 (Paris, Hachette), p. 97, pl. 53, 4. NM Athens 278.

16. Harding (1975, pp. 184ff. with refs).

17. Harding (1975, pp. 194ff. with refs).

18. Bass (1967, p. 102, figs 112–113, B135).

19. M. Ehrenberg, *Antiq. J.* **61/1**, 1981, 14–28.

20. F. Lo Schiavo, *Sardegna Centro-Orientale*, 1978 (Sassari, Dessi), pp. 86–87, tav. XXVII, 2.

21. Harding (1975, pp. 195ff. with refs).

22. Sandars (1955).

23. Bianco Peroni (1976, nos 16, 17, 21, 71, 74). The Santa Sabina knife is broken and corroded and what is illustrated by Bianco Peroni as a rivet did not appear to me to be one when I inspected this piece. For reasons unclear to me Bianco Peroni treats one of the Scoglio del Tonno knives as an import (no. 71), the other not. Her "Scoglio del Tonno type" does not seem to me to be homogeneous. The dogmatic assertions of Matthäus (1980b, p. 130) are unhelpful; the Pertosa knife I compared with examples from the Dictaean Cave and this comparison stands (1975, p. 196); the piece from Fucino (Bianco Peroni no. 241) may be correctly compared with the "Ortucchio Type", but such an attribution is of little help and an affinity to Mycenaean knives remains possible. It is also worth recording that Matthäus writes with the benefit of Mrs Bianco Peroni's Corpus of Italian knives at hand, which was not the case when I wrote my 1975 article.

24. Kilian (1976, pp. 112ff., Abb. 1).

25. Dakaris (1956, pp. 115–116, fig. 2, 3); Vokotopoulou (1969, pp. 184ff., fig. 2.).

26. *Arch. Reports for 1980–81*, 31, fig. 53.

27. Seen in hoards from Jugoslavia, e.g. Vojilovo: J. Todorović, *Starinar* **7–8**, 1956–7, 276, fig. 2, 4; Romania, e.g. Tăut, Uioara de Sus, Petrescu-Dimbovița (1978, Taf. 159. 5, 191–2, nos 758ff.).

28. Müller-Karpe (1950, pp. 318ff., Abb. 4–5); Bianco Peroni (1976, nos 23–37).

29. On both Matrei and (especially) Fontanella types (Bianco Peroni, *op. cit.*).

30. Milojčić (1955, pp. 155ff., Abb. 1, 13). Milojčić saw the design as "corresponding" to the "Wasservogelprotomen" of central Europe.

31. *Arch. Reports for 1979–80*, 48; *Arch. Reports for 1982–3*, 71, figs. 50–51. Professor P. M. Warren has kindly made a drawing available to me.

32. Boardman (1961, pp. 18–22, fig. 6B).

33. Bianco Peroni (1976); Říhovský (1972), types Malhostovice, Pustiměř. *Contra*: Matthäus (1980b, p. 131).

34. Harding (1975) for fuller details.

35. Boardman (1961, pp. 19–20, no. 69, fig. 4, pl. X); Milojčić (1955, p. 156, Abb. 1, 7).

36. Bianco Peroni (1976, no. 20).

37. Iakovides (1970, B344, fig. 149 (M53), pl. 95); Bouzek (1969, pp. 26–27, Abb. 9); J. Sakellarakis, *Arch. Eph.* 1971, 188–233.

38. Karo (1930b, pp. 130ff., pl. 33f.); Blegen *et al.* (1973, pp. 230–232, fig. 291: 1a-e).

38a. Matthäus (1980b, p. 133), and H. Müller-Karpe, *Jahresbericht des Inst. f. Vorgeschichte der Univ. Frankfurt* 1975, 21. In my 1975 article I did not speculate on the origins of the concept beyond remarking that zoomorphic knives in Greece, Italy and central Europe of roughly the same date would seem to have been connected in some way: a view which still seems to me reasonable. It is interesting to speculate on why Matthäus finds it worthwhile to attack Bouzek and myself on this issue, but not Müller-Karpe whom we were following (*Germania* **41**, 1963, 9ff.). In any case, citing zoomorphic parallels for the Perati knife would seem to lack just that sort of methodological rigour which Matthäus elsewhere finds so desirable.

39. Maiuri, *Annuario* 1923–4, 174–175, fig. 101, n. 26. The similarity to Urnfield types was first noted by Milojčić (1948), but Sandars (1955, pp. 181, 185, 193) places the knife in her class Ib.

40. Sandars (1955, p. 194, fig. 3.1).

41. Sandars (1955, p. 194, fig. 3, 4); Spyropoulos (1972, p. 15, fig. 13, pl. 7 a–b). Another example, with further refs (total of *c.* 6 examples) from Gypsadhes T.I: N. Sandars, *BSA* **53–4**, 1958–9, 232f., fig. 32.

42. Sandars (1963), classes Eii, F, Dii, G.

43. Notably the Baierdorf and Dašice types: defined originally by Müller-Karpe (1950, pp. 320ff., Abb. 5, 1–2; 1954, pp. 116ff., Abb. 2); Říhovský (1972) and Bianco Peroni (1976) give lists, subdivisions and variants (e.g. Malhostovice, Montegiorgio) for East Austria/Moravia and Italy respectively. In Jugoslavia a good parallel may be cited from the hoard of Trlić: D. Garašanin, *Starinar* **11**, 1960, 81, fig. 21 right (wrongly correlated in text as fig. 21 left).

44. *Pace* Sandars (1955, p. 181). I have not seen this piece and the published illustration is poor.

45. Bianco Peroni (1976, nos 1–6).

45a. Matthäus (1980b, pp. 113ff., Abb. 1, 5).

46. Branigan (1974, pp. 34ff., pl. 17–19).

47. For example, Wace (1932, p. 212) (Mycenae, tombs 519, 521, 524, 532); Blegen (1937, pp. 185–186 (Prosymna—eight tombs)). Survey in Hood and Coldstream (1968, pp. 214ff.).

48. Mylonas (1972, pls 20a, 182d, 208γ); Karo (1930a, p. 57, pl. XXXI, nos 102–105). Cf. examples from Thebes (palace) in rock-crystal (Mus. Thebes), Volimidia Angelopoulou T.7 (Mus. Chora).

49. Iakovidis (1970, B288ff., pl. 116a, no. D142).

50. Hood and Coldstream (1968, p. 212, fig. 4, B5).

51. *Conical or biconical head*: Mycenae, T.61 (2 examples). NM Athens, no. 2892.

Eutresis: Goldman (1931, pp. 218–219, fig. 289).

Pylos, Gouvalari Tum. 2 T. 1. Mus. Pylos.

Pylos, Papoulia tholos 5 and Kokkevis tombs. Mus. Chora.

Disc head: Mycenae. NM Athens 4546. Deeply ribbed shank.

Pylos, Vayenas tholos. Mus. Chora.

Thebes, Kolonaki T. 17. Mus. Thebes.

Mallia, House Z. Deshayes and Dessenne (1959, p. 72, pl. XX, 4, XXIX, B5).

Crook shank : Mycenae, Shaft Grave III. Karo (1930a, Taf. XXX, no. 75).
Crete. Fitzwilliam Mus.
52. Säflund (1939, tav. 59, 11); Carancini (1975, nos 1687ff).
53. Cf. Austria: Willvonseder (1937, p. 248, pls 4, 55); Hungary: Patek (1968, pl. X, 6; II, 7).
54. Bone pins occurred quite commonly at Citadel House, Mycenae; cf. recent finds from Tiryns: Kilian (1981, pp. 179–180, Abb. 33b); Poursat (1977, pp. 16f., nos 34, 35, 39 pl. 3). Present too in the Shaft Graves: Mylonas (1972, pl. 136b).
55. Discussion in Hood and Coldstream (1968, pp. 214ff.); Snodgrass (1971, pp. 226ff., fig. 81); Desborough (1972, pp. 295ff.); Deshayes (1966, pp. 204–207).
56. Standard type: Mycenae. Desborough (1965, pl. 23d–e; 1972, p.71, pl. 10).
Kerameikos: Müller-Karpe (1962, p. 86, figs 4, 11 etc. (graves 16, 41, 52, 70)).
Lefkandi: Desborough (1972, p. 189, pl. 39).
Vergina. Andronikos (1969, pp. 234–235, fig. 74).
Elis, gr. 4. V. Leon, *Jahreshefte des österr. arch. Inst. in Wien* **46**, 1961–3, Beiblatt, 49f., fig. 25a (reference from J. Bouzek).
Mouliana tomb A. *Arch. Eph.* 1904, 31, fig. 7.
North Peloponnese. *Corpus Vasorum Antiquorum* Mainz I, 12, figs 1–2 (cited by J. Bouzek).
Knossos, Ag. Ioannis. S. Hood, *BSA* **63**, 1968, 214, fig. 4, B4.
Karphi. J. D. S. Pendlebury, *BSA* **38**, 1937–8, 106, pl. 28.
Vrokastro. Hall (1914, p. 147, fig. 87k).
Diakata. See n. 63.
57. Ithaca, Pherai, Athens and Ialysos: Jacobsthal (1956, p. 3).
Argos, Deiras T. XXXIII, XXIX. Deshayes (1966, p.205, pl. 24, 2, 2; 87, 6; 92, 4).
Athens, Kerameikos tombs 20, 46, 27, 2, 24, 42. Müller-Karpe (1962, p. 60, Abb. 1, 3; 3, 1; 1, 7–8; 2, 16; 3, 12–13).
Salamis. S. Wide, *Athenische Mitt.* **35**, 1910, 29, Abb. 11, 14).
Kaloriziki T. 26. Catling (1964, p. 239, pl. 41j).
Lefkandi. Desborough (1972, p. 190).
Rion, Achaea. *Arch. Eph.* 1973, Chron. 15ff., fig. 1, pl. 10f. (quoted Schachermeyr, 1980, p. 258).
Elis. *Arch. Deltion* **17**, 1962, Taf. 146e (quoted Schachermeyr, 1980, p. 241).
Elis, gr. 13A, V. Leon, *Jahreshefte d. österr. arch. Inst. in Wien* **46**, 1961–3, Beiblatt, 55, fig. 256.
58. Athens (Kerameikos). Müller-Karpe (1962, p. 87, fig. 5, 1).
Diakata, Kephallenia. *Arch. Deltion* 1919, fig. 32, 1.
Salamis (two). S. Wide, *Athenische Mitt.* **35**, 1910, 29–30, fig. 13.
Episkopi, Enkomi and ?Nicosia. Catling (1964, p. 238, figs 22, 22–24).
Kirrha, L. Dor *et al.*, *Kirrha, Etude de préhistoire phocidienne*, 1960 (Paris, Boccard), p. 142, pl. LX, no. 13.
59. Carancini 1975 (*Rollennadeln, spilloni a rotolo*); J. Říhovský, *Die Nadeln in Mähren und im Ostalpengebiet* (PBF xiii, 5, Munich, Beck) (*Rollenkopfnadeln*); Snodgrass (1971, p. 227 for a Near Eastern origin).
60. Boğazköy: Childe (1948, p. 182, pl. 15, 2). Troy VIIb: Dörpfeld (1902, p. 355, fig. 292a).

61. Jacobsthal (1956, pp. 160–163); J. Alexander, *Proc. Prehist. Soc.* **30**, 1964, 167–168; Andrea (1972, p. 82, 93 right).

62. Carancini (1975, nos 1862–1864).

63. *Arch. Delt.* 1919, fig. 32; Carancini 1975 (*spilloni con capocchia a noduli serrati*).

64. Type with ring mouldings:
Argos, Deiras tomb 14, 18. Deshayes (1966, p. 206, pl. 100–1, pl. 24, 3–4).
Knossos, Upper Gypsadhes tomb VII. S. Hood *et al.*, *BSA* **53–4**, 1958–9, fig. 34, pl. 60a.
Boubousti. Heurtley (1939, fig. 104z).
Vrokastro. Hall (1914, p. 144, fig. 85).

65. On toggle pins, C. F. A. Schaeffer, *Ugaritica* **II**, 1949, 49–120; P. Charvát, *Památky Arch.* **67/2**, 1976, 341–358.

66. Hood and Coldstream (1968, pp. 215ff.).

67. Examples from Vajzë and Barç in Tirana Museum; cf. Hammond (1967, pp. 359f., fig. 25B); Andrea (1972, pp. 82, 93).

68. Vergina, see n. 64 above.

69. P. Kavvadias, *Hi proistoriki archaiologia*, 1909, 1914 (Athens), 369, fig. 463.

70. Jacobsthal (1956, pp. 126ff.); J. L. Huot, *Syria* **46**, 1969, 57–98.

71. Branigan (1974, p. 181, Type XI, pl. 19).

72. Carancini (1975, pp. 11ff., 128ff.).

73. So Milojčić (1948).

74. The main older publications for Greece and Italy, Blinkenberg (1926) and Sundwall (1943), are being superceded by *Prähistorische Bronzefunde* volumes. At the time of writing (1982) Crete, the Greek Islands and Thessaly have been covered (Kilian, 1975; Sapouna-Sakellarakis, 1978), and two volumes for Italy are promised. For other areas there are systematic studies for Jugoslavia (most recently Vinski-Gasparini, 1974) and South Germany, Austria and Switzerland (Betzler, 1974). Cf. now J. Alexander and S. Hopkins, *Proc. Prehist. Soc.* **48**, 1982, 401–416, where the problems of dating are barely touched upon.

75. For example, Sundwall's type AIIa: (1943, pp. 67–68), = Blinkenberg's (1926, p. 47), 12 a-d.

76. L. Marton, *Archaeologiai Értesítö* **31**, 1911, 329–352. Most of the figure-of-eight bow fibulae are clearly unrelated and of a different, distinctively local type, while the form is anyway exceptional in Greece. Several authors, from Blinkenberg to Bouzek, have mentioned that this type was especially at home in Hungary, also appearing in Bosnia, Croatia, Moravia, Bohemia and Bavaria. Thus the distribution map in Bouzek (1969, Abb. 11), shows a number of pieces which should not strictly belong there: the Grünwald group, for instance. Nor are the simple types so widely distributed as Bouzek implies.

77. Betzler (1974, nos 1–7).

78. Kos, Langada tomb 20 (LH IIIB-C transition): Morricone (1965–6, p. 134, fig. 119); Metaxata tomb B2, S. Marinatos, *Arch. Eph.* 1933, 92–93, fig. 42; Tiryns, *Arch. Reports for 1978–9*, 16; Kilian (1981, p. 176). Kallithea, *Praktika* 1977, 184ff.; 1980, 106–110.

79. Desborough (1964, p. 58); Bouzek (1968, pp. 155–158); Desborough (1972, pp. 300ff.).

80. Batović (1959). Albanian arc fibulae fit into the classes there distinguished.

81. The following arc fibulae can be attributed to a Bronze Age context:
Argos, Deiras tomb 29. Deshayes (1966, pp. 207–208,pl. 87, 6).
Perati, tomb 36. Iakovidis (1970, A274f., fig. 122, pl. 80a).
Perati, tomb 19. Iakovidis (1970, A330, B274–6, fig. 233, pl. 101b).
Perati, tomb 74. Iakovidis (1970, A85, B274–6, fig. 122, pl. 27).
Mouliana tomb A. *Arch. Eph.* 1904, 30, fig. 7.
Salamis. S. Wide, *Athenische Mitt.* **35,** 1910, 29, fig. 15.
Kerameikos. Kraiker and Kubler (1939, pp. 82–85); Müller-Karpe (1962, p. 60).
Fragments from graves 41 and 52; whole examples from graves 24, 27, 42, 46, 47, 108, 2, 20, 43, 44, 70 and 33. A total of 33 fibulae published there, belonging to Blinkenberg's types II.1 or 2, II.3, II.7, II.16, II.19 and II.20.
Assarlik, Caria. Blinkenberg (1926, p. 67, II.10a).
Troy. Dörpfeld (1902, p. 414, fig. 431).
Atsipades, Pezoulos (Ay. Vasilios, Rethymnon). K. Mavrigiannaki, *Arch. Eph.* 1975, 46, pl. 20 zeta. Cremation cemetery of LM IIIB-Subminoan date.

In addition to the pieces listed here, many of the Cretan arc fibulae are assigned to "Subminoan", but whether this should be included as Bronze Age is, of course, open to question.

82. Bouzek (1968, pp. 158f.) compares Blinkenberg type I.12a (from Kydonia) with Italian type DIIa, and with two Bosnian pieces. The two-piece fibula from Kavousi (Blinkenberg I.14a) also has Italian counterparts; but the most important type of this general group was the "Jadran" (Adriatic) type as defined by R. Drechsler-Bizić, *Arheološki Radove i Razprave* **2,** 1962, 295–312; pieces have been identified at Karphi (Pendlebury, *BSA* **38,** 1937–8, 115, pl. 28, 1, no. 171) and the Dictaean Cave (Boardman (1961, pp. 36–73, pl. 13, fig. 6, no. 162)).

83. Tinè and Vagnetti (1967, tav. xxv, nos 121–122).

84. I. Kilian-Dirlmeier, *JbRGZM* **27,** 1980, 249–269.
Additional finds not listed by Kilian-Dirlmeier:
Saraj, Brod. P. Mačkić, D. Simoska and V. Trbuhović, *Starinar* **11,** 1960, 202, fig. 16; in an adjacent grave was found a leaf-bow violin-bow fibula (fig. 21).
North Albania. Prendi (1958, no. 30).
Manaccora. Baumgartel (1953, p. 20, pl. 10, 2).

85. Childe (1948, p. 185, pl. 19).

86. Desborough (1965, pp. 224, 228); I. Kilian-Dirlmeier, *op. cit.*

87. Bouzek (1968, p. 179); Kilian-Dirlmeier, *op. cit.*

88. For example, Baldegg LU, C. Strahm in *Archäologie der Schweiz* **III,** 1971, 13, Abb. 9, 16.

89. Many examples in, e.g. E. Čujanová-Jílková, *Mittelbronzezeitliche Hügelgräberfelder in Westböhmen*, 1970 (Prague, Archaeological Institute).

90. Glasinac: Benac and Čović (1956), many examples.
Kostolac: Garašanin (1954, p. 24, Taf. XII).
Bingula-Divoš (hoard): Holste (1951, Taf. 12, 22).
Pudarci: T. Todorović, *Starinar* **13–14,** 1962–3, 185–186, figs 1, 3).

91. Kilian-Dirlmeier (1979, p. 31, Taf. 110, 4–5); Kilian (1981, p. 157, fig. 10) (developed LH IIIC). The forking spokes are to be seen on Kilian-Dirlmeier's

"Stempelanhänger", nos 155–157, of Geometric date; these probably were used for impressing pots in the way described. Distribution map: Matthäus (1980b, p. 121, Abb. 10).

92. Used as a hair fastener on the nape of the neck on face-urns in Italy: Carancini (1975, pp. 379f.); Matthäus (1980b, p. 121), quoting Montelius (1904, Taf. 221, 15 (Chiusi)).

93. Kilian (1981, pp. 157–158, fig. 10).

94. Argos, Deiras tomb XXII. Deshayes (1966, p. 203, pl. XXIV, 8; LX, 5, no. DB11).

Mycenae, Acropolis. Schliemann (1878, p. 74, no. 120); NM Athens 1412–3. Lead.

Mycenae, chamber tombs. Poursat (1977, p. 79, no. 262, pl. XXIII).

NM Athens 2646. Bone or ivory.

Teichos Dymaeon. Mus. Patras. Six-spoked, lead. Surfaces slightly ribbed. With axle, and similar to the Argos piece in size.

Tiryns. Kilian-Dirlmeier (1979, pp. 31, 267, Taf. 110, 8).

Tiryns, grave 3/1974. Kilian-Dirlmeier (1979, pp. 31, 267, Taf. 110, 9). Lead.

Kastanas. Mould. Final publication under the direction of B. Hänsel, in preparation.

95. Carancini (1975, pp. 323ff. (spilloni a rotella), nos 2635ff.); Woytowitsch (1978, pp. 111ff., Taf. 50–1).

96. Leporano: Lo Porto (1963, p. 301, fig. 24). Polla cave: B. d'Agostino, *Dialoghi di Archeologia* **6/1**, 1972, 5–10. Borgo Panigale: R. Scarani, in *Preistoria dell'Emilia e Romagna* **I**, 1962, tav. 50, 77.

97. Woytowitsch (1978, nos 38–39).

98. Müller-Karpe (1959, Taf. 103, 29).

99. Kossack (1954, pp. 85ff., Taf. 16, esp. no. 19) (mould known from Rötha-Geschwitz, Kr. Borna, Saxony).

99a. Matthäus (1980b, pp. 128–129); L. Vagnetti, in *Temesa e il suo Territorio*, Atti del Colloquio di Perugia e Trevi (1981), 1982, 170ff., fig. 1, with refs.

100. Catling (1964, pp. 227–229).

101. Gualdo Tadino: *Inv. Arch. Italia*, fasc. 3, I.6, 5 – (3), 26; Garda and Castellaro di Gottolengo: *BPI* **35**, 1910, 145, pl. 13, 6; 195, fig. 5.1.

Warfare, weapons and armour

The nature of warfare in the Bronze Age world

Weapons relate to the style of warfare in use at the time they were made. The assumption, or demonstration, of the movement of weapons between different areas therefore makes assumptions about the comparability of styles of warfare in those areas: a weapon in a grave outside its normal area of distribution was presumably used there, though whether by or against the inhabitants of that area we cannot know. The export of Mycenaean swords and spearheads to "barbarian" lands, or the adoption of European types in Greece, must bespeak broadly comparable styles of warfare.

The information of artistic depictions, as well as the greater frequency and richness of weapons in graves, means that our information on methods of fighting is much more complete in the Mycenaean than the barbarian world.[1] The most immediate difference is in the use of the light chariot, probably, as in Homer, to transport the warrior to the scene of battle rather than for use as a genuine war chariot.[1a] Wheeled vehicles were present in Bronze Age Europe, but they seem to have been heavy four-wheelers, used no doubt for bringing the hay in and the manure out. The Mycenaean warrior started early wearing protective clothing (notably the helmet, but by 1400 the whole panoply of armour), and carried shield ("tower" or figure-of-eight type), sword, spear or javelin, and dagger; in some cases also bow and arrow. Much depends on the interpretation of the spear, often depicted as well as frequently occurring as actual spearheads on archaeological sites; the important question is whether spears were thrown or thrust.[2] Probably both types were used: a decision must depend on the width and weighting of the blade and the length and weight of the shaft (seldom known). The spear was clearly the first line of attack (or defence), no doubt supplemented by the bow and arrow; when this was exhausted, hand-to-hand fighting with sword and dagger would ensue. That people went to considerable lengths to avoid fighting at all is one interpretation of the scale of defensive fortifications erected at several centres in the late Mycenaean period.

Since there are few depictions of fighting in the rest of Bronze Age Europe, and those only where rock art is involved, we are in a poor position to enumerate detailed comparisons. As in Greece, by the Middle Bronze Age the spear and sword were known, while the bow and arrow continued from earlier times. In the European Late Bronze Age, most of which falls later than the Mycenaean period, one has the impression that the spear had gained in popularity to judge from the numbers of spearheads found in hoards;[3] the sword was also well represented, as it had been in the late Middle Bronze Age, and was often elaborately decorated where the details of the hilt are preserved to us. Especially in the Nordic area the sword seems to have been the main weapon of war (such encounters no doubt being preceded by archery engagements), and some weapons are heavily used.[4] The advent of body armour and shields lagged hardly, if at all, behind their first appearance in Greece, though information on them is much scarcer.

If the main weapons of war can thus be seen to be broadly comparable throughout Europe after c. 1500 B.C., the role of warfare in society must surely have been different. Certainly by the time of the Pylos tablets, and probably also at Knossos too, military equipment was centrally controlled and—if the tablets are correctly interpreted—a complex hierarchy existed to conduct and control military operations. Such operations were presumably at a regional level, though if the Trojan War has any historical reality at all it must demonstrate the conducting of such operations on a higher level.

In the barbarian world considerable effort could be, and was, directed to the creation of fortified sites, but only at certain times and places and not commonly prior to the latest part of the Bronze Age. The overriding impression of small socio-economic units brings with it the implication of small-scale conflicts, frequently, no doubt, resolved by individual combat, in which the preserved archaeological weaponry would play its part. In such cases the possession of prestige goods, including or especially goods from far-off lands, may have lent moral support, if not technical superiority, to the combatants.

Against this background we may turn to examine the several classes of arms and armour of the Bronze Age world, starting with offensive weapons and proceeding to defensive equipment.

Swords

The sword, at the time of the Shaft Graves, was a new invention. The earliest Aegean sword, as opposed to dagger, dates to MM III, while in central Europe

the evolution of the early (Sauerbrunn-Boiu) type was complete by Br B2-C.
Between 1600 and 1100 b.c. the sword underwent constant development and
improvement; the invention or introduction of superior equipment or techniques in matters of war usually results in their rapid dispersal and widespread
adoption, so that sword-smithery can be considered a sensitive indicator of
production contacts and military history.

Prior to 1200 b.c. the Aegean series of swords was richer and more varied
than the European, the two traditions being independent and distinct, except
where a few cases of import or imitation were concerned. Towards 1200 b.c.,
however, the European flange-hilted type was introduced into Greece and
widely, though not universally, adopted there. Our examination of swords
thus falls into two parts: the influence of the Aegean series on the European
between 1600 and 1200 b.c., and the affinities of the Aegean flange-hilted
swords after 1200 b.c.

Aegean swords

The first swords in Greece and Crete were long thin thrusting weapons that
have been termed rapiers (Fig. 41.1). They begin in Crete in the Middle
Bronze Age and continue through the early Mycenaean period, giving a life-
span for the type of perhaps 400 years.[5] These weapons attain a length of a
metre or more and are characterized by their high stepped midrib, rounded
shoulders, small tang, and (where it survives) elaborate decoration of the hilt.

Clearly of Aegean manufacture is a typical class A sword from Vajzë in the
Vlorë district of Albania (Fig. 41.2).[6] Its precise associations are unknown; it
remains the only true early Mycenaean weapon from the north. A weapon from
a grave at Iglarevo (Metohije), recently published,[7] seems also originally to
have been a class A rapier, decorated with kidney-shaped sheet metal attachments in the manner of Shaft Grave weapons. This piece was subsequently
altered, twice, by the welding on of a hand-guard and a flanged hilt, making it
resemble a type D sword in its final form (Fig. 41.3).

Long thrusting swords occur throughout Middle Bronze Age Europe, but it
has often been claimed that a direct connection exists between a group of such
pieces in Transylvania and the Aegean series. J. D. Cowen wrote in 1966:

> Of none of these can it be said with confidence that they were actually imported
> from the Mycenaean area; but they are so clearly related to the long rapiers of
> Karo's type A that a Mycenaean influence of some kind seems assured.[8]

Rapiers are not restricted to Transylvania, however, and it is necessary to
consider the Transylvanian pieces in their wider setting before coming to any
conclusion.

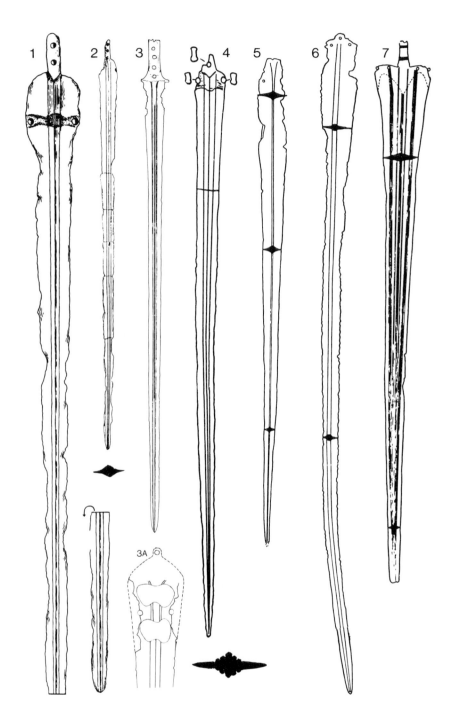

There are three main types of Romanian rapier (Fig. 41.5–7).[9] The first, represented by three pieces, has a long narrow blade, rather wider heel, and— most characteristic—a rhomboidal blade section. The second has a more or less pronounced midrib which is rounded or angular (five examples in Romania, one in Bulgaria). Finally, a sword from Roşiori de Vede that was reworked in antiquity has no close parallels. A further example of unknown type (now lost) came from Tavaličevo (Kjustendil) in Bulgaria,[10] and two swords apparently from the Bratislava area are said to belong to this general type.[11]

Large numbers of thrusting swords were produced in central Europe in the Middle Bronze Age. Most of these are *Griffplattenschwerter* of one form or another and quite distinct from this Romanian group. Typically these rapiers were rivetted with two or more rivets in a rounded or trapezoidal grip-plate, while with the later, Rixheim pieces the blade tapers both downwards and up towards the hilt. But there are a few pieces that do not fit a pattern of this sort. In particular, Schauer's[12] Ober-Illau type shows long narrow blades, rhomboidal blade-sections with a hint of a midrib on some pieces, and broken— hence inefficient—heels. This is a Swiss type,[13] dated by Schauer to Br D, and the hoard from Ober-Illau itself, with its 25 fragments, makes it likely that working took place locally. There are at least two other anomalous pieces in the Upper Danubian area: those from Burtenbach and from Wels-Rosenau.[14] The rhomboidal blade-section of the first makes it a better parallel than the second to the Romanian rapiers. The Wels sword is very damaged, has a flange-hilt and a lenticular blade-section, and only its length (721 mm) and apparent absence of rivets mark it out as in any way similar to the Romanian rapier series, as has been alleged.

Rapiers were also used in Italy and Sicily. In the north the types are central European-related. There are no swords of any description from southern Italy until the flange-hilted series begins, but rapiers occur in Sicily in tombs of Thapsos date (locally Middle Bronze Age = LH IIIA).[15] Some have seen these as Aegean-inspired, even as Mycenaean products, but it is clear that the latter cannot be true and the dating makes the former a little unlikely.[16]

Finally, we come to two tanged thrusting swords from Albania of a type which some have seen as being of Mycenaean type, from Pazhok and from Midhë in the Mati valley (Fig. 41.4). These have a rhomboid or ribbed cross-section and a trapezoidal heel or broad tang, with three rivets, two in the shoulders and one in the tang or heel. These two pieces do not look like true

FIG. 41 ☐ Rapiers from Crete, Albania, Jugoslavia and Romania. (1) Mallia; (2) Vajzë; (3) Iglarevo (3A reconstruction of original form of heel); (4) Midhë; (5) Alma; (6) Dumbrăvioara; (7) Roşiori de Vede. (After Sandars, 1961; Prendi, 1977–8; Kilian, 1976; Kurti, 1977–8; Alexandrescu, 1966.)

Mycenaean products; in fact their nearest analogies are the Sicilian swords just discussed. The Pazhok sword was found in a secondary burial together with a knife, flint arrowhead, gold ornaments and an imported Vapheio cup probably of LH IIA.[17] The Midhë sword came from a tumulus, but its associations are unknown to me.[18] Most of the material from the Pazhok tumuli is of very late Bronze Age or Iron Age date, and the finding of a pot of fifteenth century date there certainly does not mean that is the date of the burial. On balance a later date is preferable, but all that can be said is that the LH IIA pot provides a *terminus post quem*.

The demonstration of a wide distribution of tanged or rivetted thrusting swords, both short and long, makes specific connections with the Aegean series less likely than has been assumed to be the case. Detailed comparison of Aegean, Albanian and Romanian swords makes it clear that such similarities as exist are by virtue of their being the same sort of weapon. Only in overall length is any close similarity discernible.

On none of these pieces is the original form of the hilt attachment or heel preserved, but in most cases it is clear that whatever its precise form it cannot have been that of Aegean type A swords. The midribs, moreover, are usually different, leading to a rhomboidal blade section as opposed to the normal Aegean stepped variety. The number of such weapons in the Danubian province suggests that they were being turned out locally; it certainly makes importation unlikely.

Consideration of the chronological situation does not resolve the matter, but it provides suggestive pointers. Only two of the Romanian series have associations: in the Drajna de Jos hoard (Br D) is a blade fragment which is either a rapier or a spearhead.[19] Its section is like the Romanian examples with midrib, though it must have been much shorter than the rest. The other associated piece is that from the hoard from Sokol (Silistra), Bulgaria[20], also dated to Br D. Both these are admittedly fragments in founders' hoards, but their late dating by comparison with the time-span of Mycenaean type A swords is not encouraging for proponents of close contact.

Several thrusting swords of the later horned (C) and cruciform (D) varieties have been found north of Greece. The most splendid is the fine Ci sword from Tetovo near Skopje (Fig. 42), nearly a metre in length, though no details are available on its find circumstances.[21] Two complete type C swords have recently been found in tumuli in Albania: at Komsi in the Mati valley (Fig. 43.1) and at Gërmenj near Lushnjë.[22] Another, sharpened so much that the blade edges are worn right away, came to light by chance at Galatin near Vraca in north-west

FIG. 42 ☐ (Upper) Mycenaean bronze sword from Tetovo, Jugoslav Macedonia (detail of hilt); (lower) copper ingot of ox-hide form bearing Cypro-Minoan signs from Serra Ilixi, Sardinia. (Photographs by the author.)

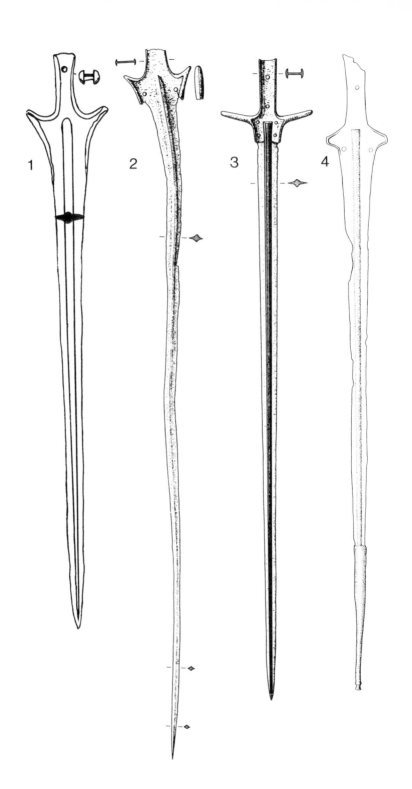

1   2   3   4

Bulgaria (Fig. 43.2).[23] No less than four type D swords have been found in various parts of Albania (Fig. 43.4).[24]

The well-known group of horned swords from Bulgaria (Fig. 43.3) and Romania[25] (to which a vaguely comparable fifth example from Albania may be added)[26] may well owe their existence to the imitation of Mycenaean class C swords, but one must remember that the provision of a hand-guard would be a universal need for which the local smith would anyway have had to provide. These swords (with the exception of the Albanian example) are locally homogeneous, and comparison of their metrical characteristics with Aegean type C swords confirms that the two groups relate only generally to each other. The same is true of an apparently "horned" sword reputedly from Adliswil (Zürich), now lost; its proportions differ markedly from those of the Cii swords and it should be dropped from consideration.[27] A piece found in 1854 in "the Quarentine" or "bed of the Sâone" at Lyons, on the other hand, looks like a genuine Di sword, but the provenance must be regarded as questionable.[28]

The extraordinary solid gold weapon, badly damaged, from the Perşinari (Dîmbovița) hoard has with some justification been seen as resembling certain classes of Aegean sword, particularly in its angular shoulders.[29] These never appear on the usual local swords and daggers, but are seen on Karo type B weapons and on the hilts of some type A swords.[30] On the other hand, the technique of casting hilt and blade together is never found in Greece, being an entirely "European" practice. Like the Borodino weapons, this piece is so extraordinary in almost every respect that extraordinary explanations do not seem out of place: more than any number of gold vessels, this piece could with some justification be taken as being related in some rather vague way to Aegean types.

Randsborg has made a case for seeing the influence of Type Di swords on a weapon from Jutland.[31] The piece in question is in fact plainly a member of the local (Ib) class of swords and has absolutely nothing to do with Aegean swords: this statement is supported by detailed arguments in Appendix 4 (Fig. 44.1).

So far we have been concerned with Mycenaean swords in the border areas of Greece where there was no existing local sword-making tradition. We come now to the vexed topic of the swords (and daggers) with T-shaped hilt (better described as having integral pommels) in central and northern Europe, where a firmly established tradition of sword-smithing existed from the Middle Bronze Age. The discussion revolves mainly around the two swords from

FIG. 43 ☐ Mycenaean and related swords from Albania and Bulgaria. (1) Komsi; (2) Galatin; (3) Dolno Levski; (4) Rrethe Bazjë. (After Kurti, 1977–78; Hänsel, 1973; Prendi, 1977–78.)

Hammer in Bavaria and Dollerup in Jutland (Fig. 44.5), but includes also a group of daggers of similar form.[32] Both swords, which are very similar though not identical, are typical Ib swords with the exception of the added cast pommel and in the case of Hammer the flanges continuing round the shoulder. Analysis of the metrical characteristics of Aegean and European swords bears this out: the Hammer sword differs in almost every particular from the Aegean swords with integral pommel, but it falls within the requisite range for most features of Ib swords.

Why are only two swords with integral pommel known from central and northern Europe? The standard answer has been that this is the result of direct Mycenaean influence, the copying of later Mycenaean types (Sandars types Dii, Eii, F and G) by European craftsmen. This must remain a possibility—it cannot, indeed, be absolutely disproved. More plausible hypotheses do, however, exist. In the first place, consideration of their function shows that virtually all swords had a pommel (Fig. 44.4, 6). There is nothing unusual about Hammer or Dollerup in this respect. What they do exhibit is an unusual way of dealing with the problem of fastening the pommel. But *how* unusual a way was this? A considerable number of daggers solved the problem in this way, from Italy to Hungary;[33] further, we must ask how many swords may once have had an integral pommel that does not survive. If we take the early flange-hilted swords in southern Germany, Switzerland and Austria studied by Schauer,[34] we find that of 54 pieces the form of the hilt end can be determined with certainty in only 23 cases (including Hammer). It is quite possible that other pieces, particularly of Schauer's Mining and Nitzing types, also had integral pommels. Similar considerations apply to the Dollerup sword in its Nordic milieu.

Sandars[35] has further pointed out that Aegean integral pommels do not have rivet-holes in them, as both the Hammer and Dollerup pieces do (the Hammer sword had additional rivet-holes added during a subsequent repair).[36] This point further demonstrates that the memory of true Aegean swords, if any, is very faint.

At first sight it is strange, in view of the considerable evidence for the movement of Mycenaean weapons beyond Greece in the early period, to find when we turn to the late period that such movement of swords practically ceased. The fragment of a type Fii sword in a hoard from Surbo, Apulia, clearly relates to the sizeable group of such weapons known from north-west Greece of LH IIIB-C date;[37] neither its geographical position nor its context need occasion any surprise. The sword fragment from Pelynt, Cornwall, on the other hand, cannot but occasion considerable surprise, if not scepticism.[38] Though its find circumstances are unknown and its attribution to Pelynt dubious, cogent reasons have been put forward why the piece should not be dismissed as a collector's stray.[39] In the first place, it hardly seems like a

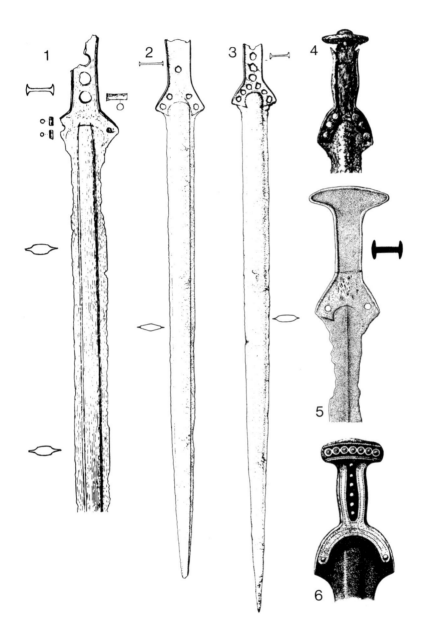

FIG. 44 ☐ Swords of types Ia and Ib from central and northern Europe. (1) Ørskov-hede; (2) "Mantlach"; (3) "Upper Bavaria"; (4) Torup, Ribe; (5) Dollerup; (6) Muldbjerg. (After Randsborg, 1967; Schauer, 1971; Sprockhoff, 1931.)

collector's piece, being battered and broken—though of course some collectors do collect extraordinary things. It was first recorded in the Truro Museum in 1871. All authorities are agreed that it is in fact an object of Aegean manufacture, and it has been assigned to Sandars Class F, for which a date of LH IIIB in Greece would be acceptable.

Nice though it would be to welcome the Pelynt hilt into the fold, and impossible though it is to be sure one way or the other, on balance the evidence weighs against this being a Bronze Age import. Dr Macnamara has set out the available facts. The sword-hilt was not known to Jonathan Couch, who originally (between 1835 and 1845) presented Truro Museum with both sketches and finds from barrows in Pelynt parish. Yet W. C. Borlase saw it in 1871 and labelled his sketch of it as being a "brazen spear-head presented by Jonathan Couch", from Pelynt. Now Borlase may well have known something we do not; equally, confusion may have crept in, as anyone who has worked with provenances in museums will appreciate. The "Pelynt sword-hilt" is thus hardly the rock on which to build up an edifice of trading contact.

Why are there no more later Mycenaean swords in the barbarian world? We have enumerated ten examples of types A to D, which between them cover LH I-IIIA, in the northern border area; but not one of the later types F-H, which typically occur in LH IIIB-C, has been found in that region, though type F does occur in Epirus. To some extent this may be due to chance, especially in view of the Surbo find, but a more likely explanation is that by LH IIIB the processes which led to the widespread adoption of "European" forms had got under way; the "type II sword" was becoming known and, since it proved itself technically superior, was preferred to Mycenaean types. If, as has been suggested, metal was scarce in the late Mycenaean world anyway, there would be all the more reason to keep the stock at home and restrict its movement out of the home market.

Northern swords in Mycenaean Greece

Mycenaean swords down to LH IIIB were overwhelmingly narrow, tapering, pointed weapons with high midrib, suitable for delivering thrusting blows. The development of shorter, wider swords with blade of gently lenticular section was presumably related to changes in the tactics of hand-to-hand fighting: types E, F and G are mostly long daggers or very short swords which would serve only at the closest range, whereas the thrusting weapons, often of considerable length, used hitherto must have been used more like fencing foils. It was presumably because of the inadequacy of the later Aegean sword types that a change was initiated to the widely used longer and stouter "European" type of sword. The hilt arrangement of these weapons was the same as on Aegean swords, that is, organic hilt-plates were rivetted together between raised flanges (except that the Europeans often cast on metal hilts, something the Bronze Age Greeks never did); but the blades rendered these swords capable of a much more versatile application, for they could be used to deliver both cutting and thrusting blows: hence the commonly-used name "cut-and-thrust sword". Since the catalogue created in the early years of this century by J. Naue these have been known as "Type II swords", a class also worked on by E. Sprockhoff and many others, but I shall refer to them here simply as "European swords" or "flange-hilted swords".

The early history of the "European sword", as traced by J. D. Cowen,[40] shows beyond doubt that the general type existed in central Europe long before it appeared in Greece. Forerunners of the form were present already in Br B, and the fully-fledged flange-hilted sword was present before the end of Br C. In Greece, the earliest pieces appear in (probably near the end of) LH IIIB, perhaps around 1200 B.C., and they continue in unbroken line down into the Iron Age, when the form was taken over in iron. From LH IIIB down to Protogeometric there are some 40 bronze swords of this type in Greece, Crete and Cyprus, and a few more in the Near East (notably Ugarit). This figure should be contrasted with over 70 (of the appropriate types) from continental Italy, and 130 or more in Jugoslavia. In addition there are a half a dozen each from Albania and Bulgaria.

The standard work on these swords in Greece[41] classified them according to the central European scheme of things, which was at the time the best known. Since then, however, the corpus of Italian swords has appeared[42] and that for Jugoslavia is in preparation,[43] so that a better framework for the understanding of the Greek series is at hand. Detailed comparisons will not be attempted here, but some indication of the context and affinities of the Greek swords will be given.

The sword was a functional object, and in considering how best to divide them pride of place should be given to how the weapons were intended to be used. The prime considerations are thus manoeuvrability and effectiveness at their task, and the main variables affecting these are weight, length, strength or stoutness, ease of gripping, protection of the hand, and durability of both blade and handle (especially, with the latter, of the method of attachment of hilt-plates and pommel). Within these major divisions will come typological niceties such as the number of rivets—assuming it is not a functional feature. Cowen realized these points and his divisions reflect them. Schauer, who has reworked the same material, is much more concerned with the typological niceties, though his work, being a *Prähistorische Bronzefunde* volume, is much easier to use than Cowen's because all the objects are illustrated.

The crucial difference between the earliest Urnfield swords and the later ones lies in the latter's stouter, leaf-shaped blades, and better designed hilts.

The straight-sided blade probably proved inadequate for delivering a heavy cutting blow. The presence or absence of a pommel tang by comparison is a relatively minor factor, as all swords would have terminated in a pommel anyway—Mycenaean, Nenzingen, and Erbenheim types—as preserved pieces or metal-hilted swords show. In these respects the existing classification of Aegean European swords leaves something to be desired, especially as none of them has a significantly leaf-shaped blade. Exactly the same is true of the Italian series of swords, with the minor—though admittedly interesting—exception of the northern rod-tang swords and of three moulds for Erbenheim swords from Piverone (Turin). In these, and in some other respects, the Italian series of swords is a good place to start from in one's search for analogies.

In a detailed classification of all Balkan and Italian swords of standard "European type", based on such characteristics as presence of a pommel-tang, form of the grip, and angularity of the shoulder, I found that the Greek swords were represented in some 13 main groups or sub-groups: of these, seven were closely similar to or near relatives of Italian pieces, five included Albanian swords, four Jugoslav, and two Bulgarian—figures which bring out the importance of the Italian series for understanding the Greek. These included not only the standard "European" form of sword, but also more idiosyncratic features such as the long pommel-tang. As far as the Balkans were concerned certain swords did show close similarity but they are mostly rare or untypical of Greece.[44]

For the makers and users of European flange-hilted swords, the Mycenaean boundary was meaningless as a cultural barrier after 1200 B.C. This enforces consideration of the significance of the distribution of the swords. Catling suggested they were originally introduced by "barbarian mercenaries, enlisted by hard-pressed Mycenaean princes at a time of great disturbance".[45] The spur or tang of his Group II, however, evolved locally, or was fitted on to the new type of sword as it had been to the old (e.g. Sandars C or D). Group III he then took to be "a second northern influx introducing a northern modification of Group II, with the size reduced, the blood-channels restored, and the blade profile developed to the characteristic leaf-shape".

Of the original northern inspiration of the type II sword there can be no doubt. Whether or not the pommel-tang was first added to these swords in Greece is debatable: one group is distributed predominantly in central and northern Greece and the borders, while the rest of the Aegean swords with pommel-tangs are related to the Italian series. Neither Greek nor Italian is connected, except in the most general way, to the Erbenheim or Letten types. The German pommel-tang, in existence by late Br D, shows few similarities to Greek examples, though functionally little difference can be discerned. Our continuing ignorance about how pommels were fixed on to swords of any description makes a judgement difficult.

What the connections imply in human terms is hard to say. Rather than "barbarian mercenaries" or invaders one can envisage a change in weaponry owing to the rise of new techniques of combat. The presence of these swords in graves with Mycenaean pottery suggests that Mycenaean Greeks themselves wielded these weapons, though such arguments involving material culture must be used with extreme care. Whatever the human explanation, Italy seems to have played an important part in the production and diffusion of the Greek weapons.

Swords: conclusions

Some Mycenaean swords were made in and carried to neighbouring lands—southern Italy, Albania, Macedonia and Bulgaria. All other finds of "Mycenaean" swords in Europe, with the possible exception of the Pelynt and Lyons hilts, can be discounted as Mycenaean products: if there was Mycenaean influence on some of them, it was of a most general nature.

The type II series in Greece is more complex than had been assumed, and when divided into appropriate types, can be seen to show the influence of Italian traditions, though a few were distinctive as local products and some are of the "Paneuropean" type. The earliest finds are in LH IIIB, while the latest in Greece are very similar to early iron IIa swords, which suggests a late (1000 B.C. or later) date. The identity of the details of some of these pieces provides further evidence for direct and frequent contact, whether by peaceful trading or by war.

Spearheads

Aegean Late Bronze Age spearheads fall into a number of well-defined categories.[46] It would be tedious to enumerate these in detail and besides, we are here principally interested in those cases where Aegean types occur outside the Aegean and vice versa. Such instances are not numerous.

Aegean spearheads prior to the Late Bronze Age were hafted by tangs or rivets, not sockets. In two instances, Aegean types are paralleled in Albania, notably with the strange "shoe-shaft" type, known from Middle Bronze Age contexts on both Crete, the mainland and from Vajzë.[47] Only a handful of socketed spearheads come from contexts said to date before the Late Bronze Age,[48] and the start of the form around 1600 B.C. must be the result of new ideas taking root at that time, as the Shaft Graves show; the slit socket on these pieces has no European ancestry but had been used in Anatolia and the Near East in the early second millennium.[49] It is not, of course, a cast socket such as is found on the European series; it is hammered round and was sometimes fastened with a ring at the base. It remained the standard Mycenaean hafting form, although cast sockets were also present from quite an early date.

As well as this basically technological development, the form of spearheads varies considerably: the blade may be wide and leaf-shaped or narrow and bayonet-like, and the socket may be long or short and extend up through the blade or not—considerations that must depend at least in part on function, i.e. whether they were to be used for throwing (lance) or thrusting (spear).[50] More idiosyncratic developments, such as the "fiddle-shaped" blade or facetted socket, are mostly late and seem likely to represent the influence of external traditions.

Four main traditions are discernible in Aegean Late Bronze Age spearheads. There is a common type with smooth profile, where the blade and socket merge smoothly: this form is that most popular in Crete from the time of the "Warrior Graves", but also widely known elsewhere.[51] A second main group has a clear separation of blade and socket: this type starts in the Shaft Graves and occurs in various forms throughout the Late Bronze Age, albeit in modest numbers.[52] A third group has a leaf-shaped blade;[53] and finally there are spearheads with concave-sided blades.[54]

Several examples of the first group have been found to the north of Greece: two in Albania, seven or more in Bulgaria (Fig. 45.1), and one alleged to come from Italy. The Albanian pieces come from burials, though unfortunately without good contexts; one of the Bulgarian weapons comes from a grave (together with a horned sword, above), one from a hoard, and the rest are chance finds.[55] About the piece from "Italy", which is in Vienna, nothing can be said; certainly no reliance can be placed in this provenance.[55a] The second group is not represented in the north, though a comparable example was found at Troy.[56] With the third group, the leaf-shaped spearheads, a considerable quantity of material is available for comparison between the Greek and the Balkan forms; generally speaking, this was not a standard Mycenaean or Minoan type and only appears in Greece in and after the thirteenth century— examples occur in, for instance, the Mycenae Acropolis Hoard, the Enkomi Weapon Hoard, the graves at Mouliana, and at Langada T.21 on Kos, datable to the LH IIIB-C transition.[56a] There are also later pieces of this type, as at the Kerameikos, Kition and Corinth.

One basic problem met with here is that the form is a simple one and occurs widely. Nevertheless, it is clear that most variants of the basic type are late in date and northern in distribution, as far as Bronze Age Greece is concerned. The true javelin-head, for instance, a short weapon with evenly tapering socket, occurs in a couple of examples on Crete, and in later contexts at Athens, Corinth and Delphi, but is otherwise found in northern Greece (Fig. 45.4), with many comparable pieces known from Albania, Bulgaria and

Jugoslavia. Two other groups of wide-bladed short spearhead are distributed almost entirely in north-west Greece and neighbouring Albania: these were highly localized types, which most of Late Bronze Age Greece did not share in.

Much the same is true for the concave-sided spearheads which, however, appear in much smaller numbers and do not allow very firm statements about distribution or origins. It has often been pointed out[57] that the general form is at home in the Danubian province, but specific parallels are more restricted. The bulk of these pieces again comes from the north-west of Greece and Albania, though the odd piece found its way south, such as the fiddle-shaped spearhead from Kangadhi in Achaea (cf. Fig. 45.3),[58] very probably a product of the Albano-Epirote workshops. A piece from Konitsa in Epirus, on the other hand, relates closely to a type known in the Croatian lowlands and may itself be imported.[59] Whether the concave-sided spearhead originated on the Danube, however, is a much more difficult question, since the dating of the one area depends on that of the other. In Italy the flame shape did become popular, but not until considerably later, e.g. Terni phase II, Tarquinia;[60] here the evidence for an eastern priority of the form is unequivocal.

The technique of facetting the sockets (Fig. 45.2, 6), on the other hand, as seen on some "fiddle-shaped" spearheads, as well as some others, is widely known in Early Iron Age contexts in Italy. One example that I have examined closely, that from Peshkepia (Fig. 45.6), shows signs of grinding—many slight parallel scratches—which was apparently the means of finishing this rather complex shape after initial hammering. There is no means of knowing where this technique was invented; the earliest datable piece is that from Kangadhi (LH IIIC). In spite of the heavy preponderance of Italian examples, a Greek origin is quite possible; the spears of this type from Epirus were possibly all the work of one man, and some were perhaps from the same mould; Greek production is thus assured. No Italian example is known to date as early as LH IIIC.

We come lastly to two isolated spearheads which are clearly imports into Greece, both from central or northern Greece. An example from Agrilia, grave Q, has a rib or fold on the socket, which marks it out as a member of a group found through Serbia and Croatia.[61] Finally, a spearhead from Diakata on Kephallenia with rounded leaf-shaped blade and squared-off base is paralleled at Vajzë in Albania and again in the Danube-Sava province.[62]

In the early period there was very little exchange of ideas involving spearheads between the various areas. Where late types can be seen to have been imported into Greece their area of production was to the north in the Balkan peninsula; and many of the so-called intrusive types in Greece during the latest Bronze Age were in fact of local origin or at least production. There are two clear cases of Jugoslav spearheads occurring in Greece, both of them far to

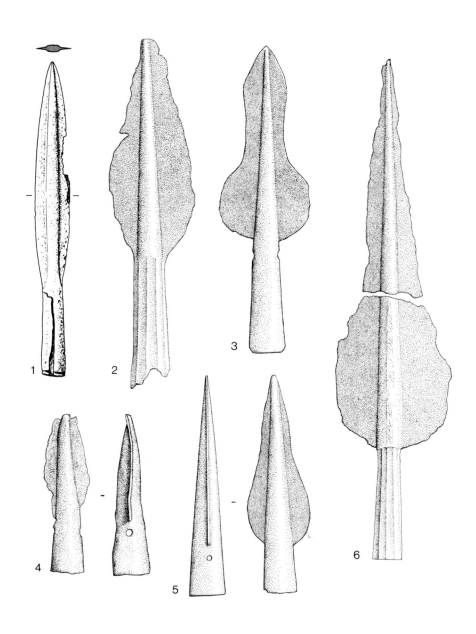

FIG. 45 ☐ Spearheads from Bulgaria, Albania and Greece. (1) Peruštica (after Hänsel, 1970); (2) Maliq; (3) "Thebes area"; (4) Vardino; (5) Proptishti; (6) Peshkepia.

the north; there is none, surprisingly, that can be attributed to an Italian source. There is little convincing evidence for suggesting a northern origin for the flame-shaped spearheads that have been made to play such an important part in the reconstruction of the events of the Late Bronze Age in the Aegean. Their first occurrence in Greece dates to LH IIIB-C, around 1200 B.C., and they certainly cannot be put much before that in the rest of Europe. The "fiddle" shape is in fact restricted to northern Greece and not found at all in Jugoslavia; and pieces of the Metaxata classes are distinctively different from their Jugoslav relatives. While a generic relationship is possible, the interpretation of these spearheads as evidence for large-scale population movements seems implausible.

From this it is apparent that spearhead types characteristic of one area found their way into other areas, though not in large numbers and not usually over any great distance. In the main Mycenaean period a few mainstream Greek weapons passed to the northern border area; in the twelfth century a few Balkan types occurred in Greece, but by far the majority of these were distinctively Albano-Epirote and have little to do with developments on a wider scale. Instead they bear out that this area was one of distinctive local production during the final Bronze Age and Early Iron Age.

Arrowheads[63]

Bow-and-arrow was a regular part of the armoury of the Bronze Age in both Greece and Europe but most of the forms are generalized and unspecific. General parallels to Mycenaean forms may be found in Italy,[64] but no significance can be attached to this. A case made by Randsborg[65] for regarding an arrowhead from Ørskovhede as Aegean in derivation is quite unconvincing: the Aegean types quoted are neither particularly close to the Ørskovhede piece nor are they common, and in any case the miserable fragment which survives, even allowing for the excavator's drawing, is hardly enough from which to build up detailed typological comparisons.

There is no sign that arrowheads of "northern" type appeared in the Late Mycenaean world.

Daggers

Objects as small and portable as daggers, which were commonly carried in much of the Bronze Age world, might be expected to have travelled widely beyond their place of manufacture, but with a few exceptions this appears not to have been the case. To some extent this was no doubt the result of different traditions of warfare in Greece and in the barbarian world: after the time of the

Shaft Graves daggers are uncommon in Greece anyway. Early Mycenaean daggers either have horned or angular shoulders, as in the Shaft Graves; later, triangular concave-sided affairs with a row of rivets set across the heel become the norm.[66]

A group of Albanian daggers or short swords with triangular heels and three large rivets bears a superficial resemblance to the latter group, especially in the size of the rivet heads (Fig. 46.5).[67] They correspond to a short sword type current in central and southern Italy at an advanced stage of the Bronze Age, known especially from finds at the Pertosa and Manaccora caves.[68] It is possible that the type was ultimately influenced by the Mycenaean form, but the details differ—notably the triangular heel—and the dating is far too late for a close correspondence to be possible. Closer analogies are present in Early and Middle Bronze Age metalwork,[69] but even here the triangular heel is unusual and the large conical rivets are, as far as I know, unparalleled. In fact the presence of several daggers of this type at Pazhok and Kukësi indicates a late date with some certainty.

The dagger from Vodhinë grave 16 is more problematical, as it genuinely does bear a strong resemblance to Middle Minoan pieces of Branigan's type IIIb.[70] Its stratigraphic position in the Vodhinë tumulus was, apparently, clear: grave 16 overlay grave 17, in which was found a fiddle-shaped spearhead of the type discussed above (p. 167). There is no question but that this last is a late Mycenaean type, LH IIIC wherever there are any good indications or parallels. Thus, although Hammond had tried to argue that the type could be much earlier,[71] we are left with the fact that a dagger of EM-MM type was buried in an Albanian tumulus not earlier than the twelfth century. This actually tells us little about the nature of contacts between the two areas; if the dagger really was not less than 500 years old when buried it hardly bespeaks a lively exchange of ideas but rather the treasuring of a prized possession through centuries. It also puts in doubt the chronological significance of the Vapheio cup found at Pazhok (p. 239).

There is one probably imported Mycenaean dagger in Albania, from Pazhok tumulus 3 (Fig. 46.4); it has three rivets, perhaps of silver, in a horizontal row across the heel, and this belongs to the standard Greek type.[72] Its context has never been published, but to judge from other objects from Pazhok it could be late. That the occupants of Albanian tumuli sought objects from far afield is also demonstrated by the finding at Vajzë grave A14 of a hiltless *Vollgriffdolch*, probably of Uenze's Italian type.[73] If this indicates close contact with Italy, or at any rate an exchange mechanism by which a dagger made in Italy found its way to a grave in Albania, other correspondences with Italy are harder to spot:[74] though there are some Epirote daggers with Italian parallels, in general the Greek and Italian sequences do not converge.

Other daggers

Branigan claims a dagger from Winterbourne Basset Down as Cypriot.[75] It is quite true that comparison of the outline shapes reveals a close similarity, but the edges of the British dagger are strongly corroded, so that the original formation is quite uncertain. In any case, were one to look for parallels abroad, there are some to be found nearer home than Cyprus; for instance in Jugoslavia, Italy or Denmark.[76]

The perennial problem of "Cypriot daggers" can be dealt with very briefly, since they are not Mycenaean but Cypriot, and because Gerloff and Watkins have given them a very full discussion.[77] They have to be taken into account, however, since they are potentially an integral part of East Mediterranean–European contact. Gerloff's list includes four from Hungary, one from Austria, one from Switzerland, 20 from France and one from Britain. Catling[78] has pronounced them genuine Cypriot work, some at least of them attributable to LC 1. He considers the entire Plouguerneau find, including seven daggers, two flat axes and two flesh-hooks, of Cypriot origin. The only question therefore is the date at which they reached France. On the other hand, Watkins stresses that several of the pieces alleged to be Cypriot are nothing of the sort. For the remainder the find circumstances are unknown or suspect; some are certainly collectors' items, and must be left out of consideration. Knowledge of the external relations of the British Bronze Age, for instance, is hardly furthered by the inclusion of the Egton Moor dagger, which was brought into Whitby museum many years ago with the information that it had been "found on the moor".

Recent finds in Sardinia, on the other hand, have produced exciting proof that Cypriot dagger forms did find echoes, if not direct importation, in distant lands. A group of ten tanged daggers, a lance-head, and a socketed object form a hoard believed to have been found in the region of Ottana (Nuoro) (Fig. 46.1–3). Two of the daggers have hook-tangs in the Cypriot manner; the rest resemble Arreton Down tanged daggers,[79] but in neither case is the similarity so exact as to suppose Cyprus or Britain was the place of manufacture. At the same time the forms are certainly not local ones, and though the British connection should not be overstated (since the form is essentially quite a simple one) the Cypriot link seems undeniable.

Whether this influences the situation with the French hook-tang weapons is a matter of opinion. It certainly suggests that East Mediterranean influences could reach so far west back in the Bronze Age, and lends some support to the view that the distribution of hook-tang weapons is too widespread to be fortuitous, but it cannot validate the claims of all dubious French finds.

A variety of miscellaneous pieces have been claimed to be of Mycenaean inspiration, such as dagger representations on pottery in Hungary and on the

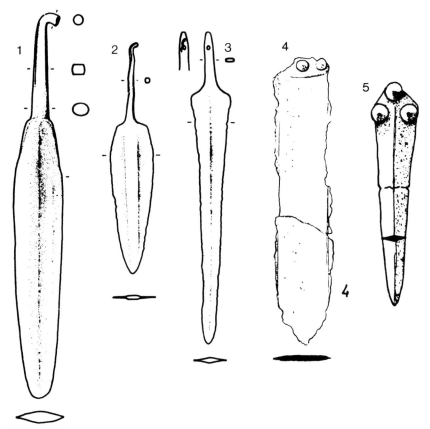

FIG. 46 ☐ Daggers from Sardinia and Albania. (1–3) Ottana; (4) Pazhok; (5) Vajzë. (After Lo Schiavo, 1980; Prendi, 1977–78.)

Stonehenge great trilithon, and a mould for a strange wide object with midrib from Spišský Štvrtok, Slovakia; but in all cases the eye of faith is needed to descry any real resemblance to Mycenaean pieces and they do not, in my opinion, merit detailed consideration.[80]

Peschiera daggers

As well as the flange-hilted European sword, the flange-hilted dagger made its first appearance in Greece around 1200 B.C. These implements, which are rather like miniature swords, are usually known as Peschiera daggers after the station of Imboccatura del Mincio (Peschiera) on Lake Garda where the type was especially frequent in contexts equivalent to Br D and later.[81] This dagger form appears throughout early Urnfield Europe in a number of characteristic types, which have been enumerated by R. Peroni.[82]

Thirteen daggers of this type are known from Greece.[83] Peroni assigned all those known to him to his "Psychro class", after the Dictaean Cave where no less than five Peschiera daggers have been found, and the new finds are of more or less the same type. A date of LH (LM) IIIB-C was assumed, though without any firm evidence; there are still no good published associations, but an LH IIIC date is indicated.

The Psychro type was, for Peroni, found in Italy only at Scoglio del Tonno and Peschiera. It is characterized by its long, slightly stepped grip with a single rivet, and gently outcurved blade. It is now clear that there are many more Italian examples of this general class than used to be thought the case, and that fine subdivision will be possible, when adequate *corpora* of both these and the Greek pieces are available. At present it seems unlikely that the Greek Island weapons can be ascribed to an Italian source, nor that they relate very clearly to the mainland pieces. The rhomboid section of the Dodona dagger makes it look rather more Italian than the rest, while the flattish section of the Teichos Dymaeon weapon recalls that at Scoglio del Tonno. But certainty is at present impossible.

The appearance of this "European" type in Greece, and the fact that the island group appears to be a self-contained, non-Italian, unit suggests that wider influences, though not necessarily actual imported goods, were reaching Greece. If local production can be assumed, the adoption of common bronze forms by smiths in widely separated areas is presumed. Yet there can be little doubt that Italy in general, and Peschiera in particular, was the immediate source of these new ideas, for the Balkan types are generally different.

Peschiera daggers form an important part of the evidence for contact between Italy and Hungary during the Late Bronze Age.[84] Though these pieces and others in Hungary bear a general resemblance to those from Greece, they cannot have any direct connection with the Aegean; rather, they must be seen as part of a wider bronzeworking tradition embracing both areas.

Two flange-hilted daggers in Albania should be mentioned here,[85] though they are not "Peschiera" daggers but very short type II swords. One is from Barç and has wide pommel-ears on a straight-sided hilt and rhomboid sectioned blade; the other is from Vajzë and is broken, but ridges outline the blade. These pieces emphasize the fact of local production of weaponry in this area.

Armour

If offensive weapons are in use by both sides, defensive armour is a natural result. It is therefore surprising that archaeological finds of armour (body-armour and shields) are extremely rare, though depictions of warriors wearing it are well known in Greece and do occur in the barbarian world. One reason for this scarcity is the materials used, which must normally have been organic. This was not because it was more difficult to make a bronze shield: but because, as experimental reconstructions have shown, sheet bronze on its own provides little protection, and can readily be cut by a blow from a sword or penetrated by a thrust from a spearhead. In the west, shields were of wood or leather, and in Greece too the detachable nature of, for instance, the Tiryns helmet makes it clear that a leather basis was required. This is undoubtedly the reason why so few finds of armour occur, and one must beware of believing that the bronze examples we have were necessarily typical of armour in general at that period.

Nevertheless, in spite of these difficulties and the relative paucity of material, we do have a good idea of the main elements of defensive armour in both Greece and Europe in the Late Bronze Age. We may conveniently divide the discussion into the main constituents of the Bronze Age warrior's panoply: cuirass, greaves, helmet and shield.

The cuirass[86]

The Dendra find (Fig. 47),[87] dated to LH IIIA1, has reversed (temporarily, at least!) von Merhart's theory of a Danubian origin for body-armour.[88] It has further drawn attention to a number of similar pieces from the Aegean (e.g. Dendra T.8, LH IIB, Thebes, LH IIIA2) which had not been recognized for what they were.[89] It is quite possible that even these are not the earliest cuirasses in Greece: that "breastplates" were used in earlier times may be shown by the gold finds from the Shaft Graves, and an early Mycenaean tomb with sheet armour would come as no great surprise.[90]

Evidence derived from representations is notoriously untrustworthy, and the only decisive piece is the appearance in the Linear B tablets of a design, similar to the actual finds, signifying "corslet". In the later Mycenaean period the fashion changed: the Warrior Vase and other depictions show a short-skirted garment, probably of leather, covered with (? bronze) bosses and ornaments, and the "accessories" (o-pa-wo-ta) on the Linear B tablets have been assumed to be the composite parts of something similar. This is the function ascribed to the Kallithea bronze edgings[91] which must have been attached to a leather backing; other similar finds come from Kephallenia,[92] and they may have been applied in the same way to a leather backing.

Paulík and Snodgrass have provided a detailed discussion of the central European body-armour, in particular the cuirasses from Čaka, Čierná nad Tisou and Ducové.[93] The cuirass from St. Germain du Plain is now seen as an

FIG. 47 ☐ The Dendra warrior (reconstruction drawing by K. McBarron).

import from the Carpathian basin, the reverse of von Merhart's conclusion. All these pieces are different in detail from the Dendra cuirass—which is not even a "bell-cuirass"—yet, in view of their chronological posteriority, must owe something to the Dendra piece and its hypothetical contemporaries. At a later date, a connection between the bossed edgings from Kallithea and the west European pieces decorated in *Perl-Buckel-Technik* is also likely, while the Greek Geometric cuirasses must be linked to the East Alpine/Hallstatt group as represented by the Kleinklein and related pieces from Slovenia.[94]

The date of the Čaka burial is Br D, and the other Slovakian finds follow soon after; in the west, the cuirass from Grenoble cannot be much later.[95] Br D corresponds at least in part to LH IIIB (thirteenth century), which still leaves a gap of 200 years or more from which no finds are known. Our understanding of the elegant bell-cuirasses of both Greece and central Europe after 1200 B.C. would undoubtedly be better if we were able to fill in the blank that the two centuries before that date represent.

The clear chronological priority of the Greek finds shows that the idea, if it *was* transmitted, originated in the south. Given that leather or linen armour must already have existed, and that sheet bronze technology was developing at just this time, however, it would require little more than one bronze-clad warrior making an appearance among "barbarians", or vice versa, for the notion to catch on. The cuirass does not count as evidence of regular contact across Europe, rather the taking-up in one area of an idea invented in another.

Shields[96]

Early Mycenaean shields, which do not survive *in corpore*, were either of the figure-of-eight or the tower variety. In the late Mycenaean period the majority of depictions appear to show round or nearly round shields, with the exception of the depictions on a sherd from Iolkos of shields with incurved edges, and on a fresco fragment from Tiryns.[97] Round shields are known from Egyptian depictions of the Sea Peoples, from Cypriot figurines and ivories, and from a few representations in the Mycenaean province, notably on painted vases and a stele from Mycenae and Tiryns. They are mostly small and genuinely round. The shields on one side of the "Warrior Vase", on the other hand, are larger, and both these and the smaller examples on the other side have a broad notch or cut-out in the bottom, perhaps to rest on the knee when in the half-kneeling position. The fragments of a piece of armour interpreted as a shield from Kaloriziki in Cyprus, dating to the threshold of the Iron Age, have been reconstructed with a comparable notch, though some authorities have expressed doubt about the overall form of this reconstruction.[98] The Kaloriziki shield did, however, have a large central boss, examples of which are known from other sites towards and after the end of the Bronze Age.

Though argument has raged for years over whether these are genuinely parts of shields, the facts are indisputable in at least some instances.[99]

The earliest European find reported to have been a shield was the fragmentary wooden object intermixed with bronze rivets found by Colt Hoare in Bush Barrow near Stonehenge, a grave of the earlier part of the "Wessex culture".[100] This identification is naturally quite uncertain, but there is nothing that absolutely rules it out. European Bronze Age shields are generally of the "Herzsprung" or "Nipperwiese" type, round and ribbed with a V- or U-shaped notch interrupting the ribbing. Most of these pieces are much too late to need consideration here (Ha B or equivalent); but the shield of this type from Plzeň-Jíkalka in west Bohemia was allegedly found with a hoard of Br D date. Controversy has surrounded this "association",[101] but it is possible to take a more positive view of it since the recognition of shield fragments in Hungarian hoards of Ha A1 (or even Br D), though admittedly these are of a simple round type decorated with bosses.[102] Other early shields may have been of wood or leather decorated with studs.[103]

Although it is impossible, because of the scarcity of finds, to trace the steps in the process in detail, it seems inconceivable that such idiosyncratic features as the V-notch would appear in both Greece and central Europe without connection. The nature of that connection must, however, be traced from other classes of material.

Helmets[104]

The well known "boar's-tusk" type of helmet, which occurs from late Middle Helladic[105] to the very end of the Bronze Age, is known from numerous depictions and from the actual finding of boars'-tusk plates in graves. The question of where in the Aegean this type originated does not concern us here, but the finding of boars'-tusk plates at Mariupol on the Sea of Azov has been taken as supporting a northern origin.[106] These finds belong to the "North Pontic culture" and have been assigned to the second half of the third millennium B.C.

Perhaps of a similar date is a vase-lid from Gumelniţa layers in the Ruse (Bulgaria) tell,[107] with its decoration of bands of alternating crescents identical in conception and composition to the boars'-tusk helmet; similar motifs are found on other vessels.[108] Whether or not this has anything to do with boars'-tusk helmets is doubtful, but a generic connection seems just possible. In any event there is no evidence for the currency of this type of helmet in the barbarian world; if helmets were worn, they were presumably of leather until sheet bronze started to be used. It is possible that sheet bronze plaques and roundels could have been used as attachments for helmets or other items of defensive armour.

Certain other early types of helmet are known from depictions in the Aegean area,[109] but it is only when we come to consider conical bronze helmets that questions of contact with the north arise. The earliest certain example is from Knossos, Hospital Site Grave V, dating to LM II;[110] the conical shape with perforated knob on top makes it practically identical to a group of helmets from central Europe which appear to start in Br D (Oranienburg).[111] A helmet from Beitzsch in the Lausitz was allegedly associated with an Early Bronze Age hoard, but this association has usually been viewed with scepticism.[112] The Knossos helmet also provided the earliest *in corpore* cheek-pieces, though depictions show they were used already with boars'-tusk helmets. The first known European examples (Pass Lueg, Weissig)[113] are of early Urnfield date.

By LH IIIC the variety of possible helmets available to the Mycenaean warrior was greater, though few examples survive.[114] Some of these were simple cap helmets, apparently with a crest; they do not resemble, except in date, early cap helmets from Europe,[115] though we do not know what leather versions of these would have looked like. The elaborate helmet of Submycenaean date from Tiryns bears a decoration of bosses and openwork triangles, in Merhart's *Punkt-Buckel* technique, which appears in very similar form on the crest helmet from Pass Lueg near Salzburg.[116] The Tiryns helmet is unique in Greece, both in form and in ornament, and cannot serve as an indicator of regular external influence; but in view of the decorative techniques used on it, European connections are likely. Considerable discussion has centred on the horned helmets from the Mycenae Warrior Vase, but horns (or something very similar) were known already on boars'-tusk helmets[117] and need occasion no surprise; the use of horned helmets by the Enkomi figurines, the Shardana or the Peleset need not indicate any particularly close connection, and Scandinavian examples are much later. Sandars has shown convincingly how long an ancestry the horned helmet has in the Near East; any connection with Sardinia should be later in date than here concerns us.[118]

The evidence from helmets is thus too ambiguous and too poorly dated for firm conclusions about cross-cultural connections, but if the Beitzsch helmet really can be dissociated from its Early Bronze Age "associations", a priority of the form in Greece is likely. Only with the Tiryns helmet does the possibility of a European contribution to the series become likely, at a time when sheet metal helmets were in any case becoming widely diffused.

Greaves[119]

Although actual finds of bronze greaves are very few, there are numerous illustrations of them on painted vases, and it is quite clear that greaves were a standard part of the equipment of the Late Mycenaean warrior.

Much the earliest *in corpore* example (LH IIIA1) is again the piece (a single greave) from the Dendra Panoply Tomb[120] which is fastened on apparently only by its inherent springiness. The next examples are those from Kallithea and Enkomi,[121] dating to LH IIIB and C: these are of the looped type for a cord fastening ("*geschnürte*"). Another find that should be mentioned here is the pair of greaves found in 1960 on the southern slopes of the Acropolis in Athens, with two bronze knives (one very long), a pair of bronze tweezers, and an amphoriskos whose date is quite uncertain.[122] It was originally thought to be Geometric. Penny Mountjoy has recently made a fresh study of this group and favours a Mycenaean date: there is no Geometric (or any other!) analogy for the vase, and the bronzes seem Mycenaean. In view of the repoussé technique used on the greaves (small and large bosses) a late date in the Mycenaean period would be indicated. This dating for the Athens greaves, while difficult to prove in view of the uniqueness of the accompanying pot, is perfectly acceptable in terms of the general development of Mycenaean armour as known at present.

The European greaves are similarly scarce and though often hard to date, appear to start at about the same time as the late Mycenaean examples. The classic study by Merhart in 1958 showed that early greaves date to the early Urnfield period, for the single greave from Rinyaszentkiraly (Somogy), found in the last century, was part of a hoard containing end-winged axes with nicked end, flame-shaped spearheads, a *Dreiwulstschwert* and other early forms—thus attributable to the *ältere Urnenfelderzeit*, i.e. before 1100 B.C.[123] Von Brunn assigns the hoard to his phase 2, which is roughly equivalent to German Ha A1. All the other datable pieces known to Merhart were of Early Iron Age date. But since his study appeared, several new finds have been made. Hoard 2 from Cannes-Ecluse (Montereau, Seine-et-Marne),[124] containing a fragmentary greave, is unfortunately not by itself closely datable, but appears to contain forms (median-winged axes) that indicate its contemporaneity with nearby hoard 1. This latter is, by virtue of the axes, Rixheim-type sword and bracelets, attributable to early Bronze Final, i.e. Br D in German terms. The publication of the hoards of north Croatia[125] produced two more datable greave associations: Poljanci, hoard 1 (Slavonski Brod), which contained a violin-bow fibula, flame-shaped spearheads, and socketed axe with V-shaped mouldings, and is attributable to Vinski Gasparini phase II (Br D-HaA1 in German terms); and Kloštar Ivanić (Kutar), where a pair of greaves occurred in a scrap hoard the other contents of which are not very informative but which, taken as a whole, suggest a date in the local phase III (Ha A2). Other possible fragments occur in the huge hoard of Brodski Varoš (Slavonski Brod)[126] and Veliko Nabrde (Osijek), both of Phase II. Another recent find, also in Jugoslavia, was from a tumulus at Dabrica (Stolac) in Hercegovina, unfortunately unassociated.[127]

Italian greaves are all later than this. The earliest pair known is that recently found at Malpensa (Lombardy), attributable to "Protogolasecca II" (tenth century, Ha B1);[128] the two pairs hitherto the earliest known, from Pergine (Valsugana, Trento) are attributed to the ninth century, Ha B2.[129] As far as Italy is concerned, then, the available evidence suggests a rather later adoption of this, as of other pieces of body-armour, but the scarcity of finds warns against an over-facile assumption that developments in Italy lagged significantly behind those elsewhere in Europe.

Conclusion: the role of arms and armour in Bronze Age Europe

Arms and armour were undoubtedly objects of great concern to certain members of Bronze Age society. Not only were they functional, they also served to highlight status through the elaborateness of their construction and decoration, or through their technical superiority. The very existence of weaponry points to inter-group interaction; the difficult thing is to decide on the scale of that interaction, particularly when it was over some distance.

Some Mycenaean weapons found their way to lands bordering on Greece, where their context appears to be "local", that is, part of a local assemblage. A very few weapons may be claimed as of northern origin and transported to Greece, mainly to areas away from the main centres. The study of Graeco-barbarian contacts in weaponry is dominated, however, by the appearance around 1200 B.C. of European swords, daggers and (possibly) spearheads. Detailed examination of these objects suggests that Italy played a major role in disseminating the types—even that some objects were exported from Italy—but that in general it is likely that local production of the European forms took place in Greece.

Around 1200 B.C. similarities may also be seen in the defensive armour in use in each area, but here the evidence for a priority in Greece cannot be gainsaid. In view of the notorious ineffectiveness of sheet bronze for defensive purposes, however, the adoption of such objects in Europe may have had more to do with display and social function than with technical considerations, and it cannot be concluded that there was no defensive armour in Europe prior to 1200 B.C. What is certain, and seems likely to remain true, is that there was no armour of Dendra type elsewhere in Europe. In view of the weight and restricting nature of the Dendra panoply for fighting, however, that may have been a blessing rather than a privation.

Notes

1. H.-G. Buchholz (ed.), *Kriegswesen*, Teil 1, 1977, Teil 2, 1980, *Archaeologia Homerica*, Kapitel E. (Göttingen, Vandenhoeck and Ruprecht); Sandars (1983, pp. 44ff.).

1a. Crouwel (1981).

2. Höckmann (1980) and *Arch. Korrespondenzblatt* **11**, 1981, 205–208.

3. For example, Tenja: Vinski-Gasparini (1973, pls 31–32); Şpălnaca: Petrescu-Dîmboviţa (1977, pls 201–202).

4. K. Kristiansen, *Arch. Baltica* **2**, 1977, 77–91.

5. Sandars (1961, p. 26). The latest example, from Routsi tholos 2, dates to LH IIIA1.

6. Korkuti (1970, tab. III.7).

7. Kilian (1976).

8. Cowen (1966, p. 310).

9. Alexandrescu (1966, pp. 119–120).

10. Cowen (1966, p. 310).

11. One is now lost but is said to have come from the Danube at Bratislava (M. Novotná, *Die Bronzehortfunde in der Slowakei*, 1970 (Bratislava, Slovak Academy of Sciences), **14**); the other, whose label bears the inscription "Poszony-Szentgyörgy", is in Budapest and is assumed to have been found at Sväty Jur near Bratislava. Bouzek (1968, p. 39, n.18) has, however, pointed out that the name "Pozsony" (= Bratislava) was added to the label at a later date, so that the original "Szentgyörgy" could refer to one of the many Hungarian (especially Transylvanian) villages of that name. The patina and casting are different from those usual on Hungarian bronzes, however, and the general form is reasonably similar to that of Aegean pieces: Mozsolics (1967, pp. 58, 155, Taf. 45; 2).

12. Schauer (1971, pp. 80–81, pls 38–39).

13. The fragment from Val di Non, Bolzano, could belong to it: Bianco Peroni (1970, p. 19, no. 27).

14. Schauer (1971, nos 72 and 328).

15. Tinè and Vagnetti (1967, pp. 19ff., tav. XV, nos 61–63); Voza (1973, pp. 31, 40, tav. VI, no. 116). Cf. also Sandars (1961, pp. 26f., no. 75 with refs). L. Vagnetti, *Studi Micenei ed Egeo-Anatolici* **7**, 1968, 132f., n.33, 39, suggests the same. Monte Dessueri: *Monumenti Antichi* **21**, 1912–13, 349ff.; Bernabò Brea (1966, p. 131).

16. Bianco Peroni (1970, pp. 22ff., nos 38–46) attributes these Sicilian swords to her Pertosa type, but their tangs as opposed to triangular heels makes this impossible. Cf. p. 170 for Albanian examples of the short sword of Pertosa type.

17. Korkuti (1970, p. 46, pl. III, 6); LH IIA according to Dickinson (1977, pp. 95, 104).

18. D. Kurti, *Iliria* **7–8**, 1977–8, 312, pl. II, 2.

19. Cowen (1966, p. 311); Petrescu-Dîmboviţa (1977, p. 78, pl. 92, 3).

20. Hänsel (1973).

21. Mikulčić (1966, pl. 2, fig. 1d).

22. D. Kurti, *Iliria* **7–8**, 1977–8, 312, pl. II, 1; Prendi (1977–8, p. 37, pl. XIII, 1).

23. Hänsel (1970, pp. 28–29, Abb. 1).

24. Gërmenj (Lushnjë), Bruç (Mat), Rrethe Bazje (Mat), and Nënshat (Shkodër): Prendi (1977–8, Tab. XIII).

25. Sandars (1963, pp. 121, 146); Hänsel (1970); M. Irimia, *Dacia* **14**, 1970, 389–395.

26. Prendi (1977–8, p. 37, pl. XIII, 6).

27. Sandars (1963, p. 146 with refs).

28. Ibid., pp. 125, 148; Randsborg (1967, p. 11, fig. 7a), citing E. Chantre, *Etudes Paléoethnologiques dans de Bassin du Rhone*, Album I, 1875 (Paris, J. Baudry), p. 124, no. 237, III, 84, pl. XV bis, 3.

29. Gimbutas (1965, pp. 55–56, pl. 8b, 1).

30. Mylonas (1972, pl. 67 beta, 69 alpha).

31. Randsborg (1967).

32. Schauer (1971, pp. 113–114, pl. 50, no. 346).

33. For example, Vel'ka Lehota, okr. Prievidza: Hampel (1892, Taf. 137: 25). Mould in NHM Wien: Hampel (1887, Taf. II, 5); Szentgál (Veszprém), Ajak (Szabolcs-Szatmár): Moszolics (1971, pp. 60–61, fig. 4, 1); Bakonyszucs-Szazhalom: E. Patek, *Acta Arch. Hung.* **22,** 1970, 43, Taf. III, 3; Piliny: Ashmolean Museum, no. 1927.1457. Cf. Mozsolics (1971, p. 62) and Peroni's Villa Capella type of Peschiera dagger (1956, pp. 71, 86, Taf. 1, 4).

34. Schauer (1971, nos 324–378).

35. Sandars (1963, p. 143).

36. H. Müller-Karpe, *Germania* **40,** 1962, 264; Schauer (1971, p. 113).

37. Macnamara (1970, pp. 241ff.); Wardle (1977, pp. 191ff.); Papadopoulos (1976, pp. 307ff., pl. 16).

38. Sandars (1963, p. 152 with refs); Branigan (1970, pp. 93–95, fig. 3, 4).

39. Notably by E. Macnamara, *Cornish Arch.* **12,** 1973, 19–23.

40. Cowen (1955, 1966).

41. Catling (1956, 1961).

42. Bianco Peroni (1970).

43. By A. F. Harding on the basis of the numerous notes left by the late J. D. Cowen.

44. The classification by Catling (1956, 1961) follows that of Cowen (1955) who in turn based himself on Sprockhoff (1931). All the Greek pieces correspond to Sprockhoff's type IIa ("das gewöhnliche Typ"), which Cowen had divided into Nenzingen, Erbenheim, Letten and Hemigkofen types and the Ennsdorf variant. Catling's Group I corresponds to the Nenzingen type and consists of swords of classic "European" formation: it is found in all parts of the Urnfield world and not just in central Europe. Very close to Catling no. 1 (Mycenae), for instance, is Bianco Peroni's no. 135 (Cetona) or a sword from the Sviloš (Beočin) hoard (Holste, 1951, Taf. 16:40); it also recalls a sword from Donja Brnjica in Kosovo. In view of the wide currency of the general form, however, no special significance should be attached to these parallels.

Within Catling's Groups II (= Erbenheim) and III (= Letten) closer relationships may be discerned. The two swords from Graditsa (nos 12–13) form part of a compact group in central and northern Greece and adjacent areas, and also resemble closely Italian swords of type Allerona (Bianco Peroni, 1970, nos 153–163), especially that from Allerona itself (no. 153). Characteristic of the type are the long pommel tangs, slightly convex grip and hand-guard, blade-ridges curving out to the point of the shoulder. Four other examples of the Allerona type are known: Krklino (Bitolj, Štip Museum Catalogue, 1971, 82, no. 216), Vajzë Tumulus B (Hammond, 1967, p. 320, fig. 20J), Schiste Odos (*pace* Catling who assigns it his Group III), and Visoj (Hammond, 1972, fig. 10j).

Rather different is a group of swords with straight-sided grip and long rounded guard, with medium-sized pommel tang. The sword from Anthea, Patras (Catling no. 6) resembles very closely indeed an example from S. Benedetto in Perillis (Bianco Peroni no. 156); rather less closely others from Italy within the Allerona class and a sword from Padua.

Within Catling's Group IV it is worth mentioning a sword allegedly from Lake Trasimene (but undoubtedly a collector's piece without good provenance, Bianco Peroni no. 172) which falls very close to this otherwise East Mediterranean group. (Four swords of this type were also found in the House of the High Priest at Ugarit: *Ugaritica* III, 1956, 256–259, fig. 223 left.)

45. Catling (1961, p. 121).

46. Hitherto there has been no systematic and thorough study of Late Bronze Age spearheads. Snodgrass (1964, pp. 115ff.) dealt with Late Mycenaean types in his study of "Early Greek" armour and weapons; otherwise it has been left to site publications (e.g. Karo, 1930a, pp. 206f.) to distinguish the main varieties. O. Höckmann (1980, published 1982) has now produced a systematic study. Cf. also Höckmann in H.-G. Buchholz (ed.), *Kriegswesen*, Teil 2 (*Arch. Homerica* Kapitel E), 275–319, and *Arch. Korrespondenzblatt* **11/3**, 1981, 205–208.

47. Branigan (1974, pp. 18, 162–3, types II and V); Höckmann (1980, Group B).

48. Branigan (1974, pp. 19, 163, type XI (Malthi and Ayia Photia)); also Mochlos grave XX, R. B. Seager, *Explorations in the Island of Mochlos*, 1912 (Boston and New York, American School of Classical Studies at Athens), plate fig. 45.

49. A. de Maigret, *Studi Semitici* **47**, 1976, 95ff., fig. 23. Höckmann (1980).

50. Cf. Höckmann (1980).

51. Equivalent to Höckmann's Groups D, E, and H.

52. Equivalent to Höckmann's Groups C, F and G.

53. Equivalent to Höckmann's Group K.

54. Snodgrass (1964) Type B; Milojčić (1948), "geflammte" type.

55. Vajzë, tumulus A, "from the soil": Hammond (1967, pp. 229, 337, fig. 23D) (poorly illustrated in the original publication and not seen by me); Pazhok (Mus. Tirana, context unknown to me). Peruštica (Plovdiv): Sandars (1963, pl. 22:8); Černych (1978, pp. 228ff., pl.61:4). Lesura (Vraca): B. Nikolov, *Archeologija* **8/3**, 1966, 48ff.; Hänsel (1976, p. 38); Černych (1978, pl. 61:5). Kričim (Plovdiv), Krasno Gradište (Kalakastrovo), Dolno Levski (Pazardžik): Černych (1978, pl. 61:1, 2, 3); examples with cast socket, Sokol (Nova Zagora). Vardyn: Černych (1978, pl. 60: 2, 62:3). A spearhead of this type was seen by me in Plovdiv Museum in 1971.

55a. G. Jacob-Friesen, *Bronzezeitliche Lanzenspitzen Norddeutschlands und Skandinaviens*, 1967 (Hildesheim, Lax), 386, no. 1848, Taf. 187, 9.

56. Dörpfeld (1902, p. 395, fig. 380).

56a. Sandars (1983, p.53) makes a case for regarding the Langada 21 spearhead as unique, a direct copy of a Balkan form. Given the corpus now provided by Höckmann (1980, pp. 67ff., 147ff., Abb. 15), there seem in fact to be a number of comparable pieces in Greece, and importation is less likely.

57. For example, by Snodgrass (1964, p. 119).

58. Papadopoulos (1979, pp. 164, 227, fig. 317(c)). Other spearheads with concave-sided blade: 1. *Fiddle-shaped blade*. "Thebes" (Ashmolean Museum): Desborough

(1964, p. 67, pl. 22d). Vodhinë, gr. 17: Hammond (1967, p. 338, fig. 24, 3); Prendi and Budina (1970, Tab. II). Pazhok: Unpublished, Tirana Museum. Long example: Cepunë: Prendi and Budina (1970, p. 64, Tab. II, 4). 2. *Flame-shaped blade, tapering evenly below the main contraction.* Gribiani: Dakaris (1956, p. 131, fig. 8); Papadopoulos (1976, no. 117, pl. 20 centre). Siatista area: Unpublished, Thessaloniki Museum. Metaxata, gr.A7: S. Marinatos, *Arch. Eph.* 1933, 92, fig. 41 right. Ithaca, Polis: S. Benton, *BSA* **35**, 1934–5, 72, fig. 20, 16. Kiperi-Parga: Vokotopoulou (1969, pp. 197f., no. 1, fig. 8b, pl. 28); Papadopoulos (1976, no. 118, pl. 20 bottom right); Wardle (1977, fig. 14, no. 1071). Mazaraki: Vokotopoulou (1969, p. 196, fig. 6c, pl. 27b, g); Wardle (1977, fig. 14, no. 1066); Papadopoulos (1976, p. 134, pl. 20 top). Kalbaki, tomb A: Dakaris (1956, p. 115, fig. 1); Papadopoulos (1976, no. 166, pl. 20). Metaxata, gr. A9: S. Marinatos, *Arch. Eph.* 1933, 92, fig. 41 left. Agrilia, gr. Z: Volos Museum no. M2651. Pazhok: Unpublished, Tirana Museum; very long piece. Maliq: Prendi (1966, p. 266, Tab. XX). *Related group with concavity near tip of blade*: Mouliana tomb B: *Arch. Eph.* 1904, 48, fig. 11 upper. "Crete" (Ashmolean Museum): Catling (1968, pp. 93–94, fig. 2, 8). Cf. examples from Italy and Jugoslavia: Gornji Log, Müller-Karpe (1959, Taf. 125, A1).

59. Vokotopoulou (1969, p. 197, fig. 7a, pl. 28a). Papadopoulos (1976, no. 127, pl. 20 bottom left). Tenja hoard: Holste (1951, Taf. 14, 6); Vinski-Gasparini (1973, Tab. 31, 10).

60. Müller-Karpe (1959, pp. 197ff., Abb. 33, Taf. 39–41).

61. Agrilia, gr. Q: Volos Museum no. 2647. Jugoslav examples: Otok-Privlaka, Maly Žam and Bersaska: Holste (1951, Taf. 6, 4 (Vinski-Gasparini 1973, Tab. 27, 25), 21, 28–9; 21, 2). Pričac, Budinšćina and Lisine: Vinski-Gasparini (1973, Tab. 72, 5, 77, 24, 97, 11). Čermožišče. Müller-Karpe (1959, Taf. 134, 17–19). "Serbia": Garašanin (1954, pp. 60–61, Taf. 38). Brza Palenka: D. Srejović, *Starinar* **11**, 1960–1, 57–59, fig. 20 (decorated). Cf. too Hungarian hoards: Lovasbereny, Zsujta etc.

62. Diakata: *Arch. Delt.* 1919, 119, fig. 36, 3. Vajzë: Museum Tirana. Rudnik, Bingula-Divoš, Pocrkavlje i Brod, Donja Bebrina: Holste (1951, Taf. 20, 5, 10, 15 (Vinski-Gasparini 1973, Tab. 87, 5), 7, 32, 15, 2 (Vinski-Gasparini 1973, Tab. 94, 6)). Rudnik: Garašanin (1954, p. 29, Taf. 16). Miljana: Vinski-Gasparini (1973, Tab. 112, 3–4).

The type with parallel-sided leaf-shaped blade and rectangular base has been listed and discussed by Harding (*British Museum Quarterly* **37**/**3–4**, 1973, 140ff.) and by Kilian (1976, p. 128, Abb. 7). In 1973 I attributed a spearhead from Koukousos to this group, on the basis of a poor sketch in Hammond (1967, fig. 23J). It is clear from the photograph, however (Hammond, 1967, pl. XXI), that this attribution was erroneous, and the type is found only in Italy and Albania. Papadopoulos (1976, no. 124) gives the place-name of this find as Kakousioi.

63. Greek arrowheads have been classified by H.-G. Buchholz, *Jb. deutschen arch. Inst.* **77**, 1962, 1–58; the central European sequence is discussed by R. Mercer, *Proc. Prehist. Soc.* **36**, 1970, 171–213.

64. For example, Säflund (1939, tav. 55, 7–9, 63, 1–10).

65. Randsborg (1967, pp. 12ff.).

66. Blegen (1937, pp. 330ff.).

67. Vajzë, Tumulus A, "from the soil": Hammond (1967, p. 330, fig. 21E); Prendi

(1977–8, pl. XIII, 13). Pazhok, 3 examples: Museum Tirana. Çinamak, near Kukësi: *Buletin Arkeologjik* 1969, 48, pl. i; N. G. L. Hammond, *BSA* **69**, 1974, 141, fig. 4c. Grojnice, Mostar: V. Ćurčić, *Wissenschaftliche Mitt. aus Bosnien und der Hercegowina* **11**, 1909, 95, Taf. XVIII, 4.

68. Bianco Peroni (1970, pp. 22ff., nos 38–46 (type Pertosa)). Lengths vary from *c*. 30 to 50 cm. Bianco Peroni dates the type to LH IIIA on the assumption that the Sicilian tanged swords belong to this type. This is not the case, and a later date is likely: some examples, e.g. Çinamak, are probably Iron Age.

69. Thus Branigan (1974, no. 307, pl. 8), who attributes it to his type XIIIa without comment; the drawing, after Hammond (1967, fig. 21E), is highly misleading. Hammond (1967, p. 330) assumes an MM date.

70. Hammond (1967, p. 330, fig. 21F); Branigan (1974, no. 179, pl. 4), and *BSA* **62**, 1967, 214–216, fig. 1, 3.

71. N. G. L. Hammond, *BSA* **66**, 1971, 231ff.

72. Prendi (1977–8, p. 32, pl. VII, 4).

73. Hammond (1967, pp. 329f., fig. 21D2); O. Uenze, *Die frühbronzezeitlichen triangulären Vollgriffdolche*, 1938 (Berlin, de Gruyter), 21–29, Taf. 9–20.

74. Bianco Peroni's forthcoming work for the PBF series will provide a definitive classification. Such contact as there is, is restricted to Epirus, as with a triangular dagger from Dodona with three horizontally-placed rivets in a curved heel, which is best paralleled by simple Italian types as at Peschiera (Müller-Karpe, 1959, Taf. 105, 22); or the straight-sided piece from Mazaraki (Vokotopoulou, 1969, p. 194, fig. 5a, pl. 27b) which has parallels in the small tanged daggers from North Italy (Müller-Karpe, 1959, Taf. 106, 8) and in a variety of southern and Sicilian pieces: P. Orsi, *Monumenti Antichi* **9**, 1899, tav. VII, 6.

75. Branigan (1970, pp. 93f.).

76. Müller-Karpe (1959, Taf. 89, 32); Vinski-Gasparini (1973, pl. 21, 1); Aner and Kersten (1971, Taf. 1, 6; 15, 90; 1976, Taf. 110, 1265).

77. Gerloff (1975, pp. 149ff., 255ff., pl. 64); T. Watkins, in *To illustrate the Monuments, Essays on Archaeology presented to Stuart Piggott*, 1976 (London, Thames and Hudson), pp. 136–143.

78. H. W. Catling, quoted in Gerloff (1975, pp. 150–151).

79. F. Lo Schiavo, *Sardegna Centro-Orientale*, 1978 (Sassari, Dessi), pp. 75–79, tav. XXIII-XXIV; *Atti della XXII Riunione Scientifica* (1978), 1980, pp. 341–358; Gerloff (1975, pp. 128ff., 252ff., pls 49–51).

80. J. Makkay, *Acta Arch. Hung.* **23**, 1971, 19–28; T. Kovacs, *Folia Arch.* **24**, 1973, 7–31; J. Vladár, *Arch. Rozhledy* **24**, 1972, 23, 25, 104, Taf. 4, 1, and *Die Dolche in der Slowakei* (PBF VI, 3, Munich, Beck), 1974, 40, Taf. 4, no. 95.

81. Cf. Müller-Karpe (1959, Taf. 107).

82. Peroni (1956).

83. Matthäus (1980b, pp. 122–123, Abb. 11).

84. Mozsolics (1971, pp. 64ff.).

85. Andrea (1972, p. 93, 1. (Barç)); the Vajzë piece is apparently unpublished (Mus. Tirana).

86. Most recently Catling (1977a); Snodgrass (1971).

87. Åström (1977).

88. G. von Merhart, *Origines* 1954, 33–61 (Reprinted in *Hallstatt und Italien*, 1969 (Mainz, Römisch-Germanisches Zentralmuseum), pp. 149–171.)

89. Catling (1977a, pp. 98f. with refs). The datings given here are Dickinson's (pers. comm.), for which I express my thanks.

90. Cf. Catling (1977a, E84–5) on various pieces from Shaft Graves IV and V, and E87 for his conclusion.

91. Yalouris (1960).

92. S. Marinatos, *Eph. Arch.* 1932, pl. 16.

93. Paulík (1968); Snodgrass (1971); Čaka: A. Točík and J. Paulík, *Slov. Arch.* **8**, 1960, 59–124; B. Novotný, *Sborník Filozofickej Fakulty Univerzity Komenského* **17**(6), 1966, 27–34 (Čierná nad Tisou).

94. G. von Merhart, *op. cit.*; J. Kastelić and S. Gabrovec, *Situla* **1**, 1960, 3–80.

95. W. Déonna, *Préhistoire* **3**, 1934, 93–134; H. Müller-Karpe, *Germania* **40**, 1962, 279.

96. Most recently H. Borchhardt (1977); P. Schauer, *Jb. RGZM* **27**, 1980, 196–248 (review article). Cf. Z. Bukowski, *Archeologia* **22**, 1971, 42–76; Coles (1962).

97. G. Daux, *BCH* **85**, 1961, 769f., fig. 20; G. Rodenwaldt, *Tiryns* **II**, 1912 (Athens, Eleutheroudakis and Barth), p. 16, Taf. 2, 3.

98. Catling (1964, pp. 142ff.); H. Borchhardt (1977, p. 34).

99. Snodgrass (1964, pp. 38ff.); the arguments reviewed by him in *Hamburger Beiträge zur Arch.* **3**/1, 1973, 41–50.

100. Sir R. Colt Hoare. *The Ancient History of Wiltshire* **I**, 1812 (London, Miller), p. 203; J. M. Coles (1962, p. 172) remarks: "There seems no possible way in which these objects could be arranged to form a shield".

101. H. Hencken, *AJA* **54**, 1950, 307ff.; Coles (1962, p. 162 and *Germania* **45**, 1967, 151ff.); O. Kytlicová, *Arch. Rozhledy* **16**, 1964, 517ff.; J. Bouzek, *Germania* **46**, 1968, 313–316.

102. P. Patay, *Germania* **46**, 1968, 241–248: shield fragments from the hoards of Nyirtura (Br D-Ha Al), Bodrogkeresztúr (Ha A1-2), Keszöhidegkút (Ha A2), Otok-Privlaka (Ha A1). The identification as shield bosses of certain discs in hoards such as Zvolen-Pustý hrad by Paulík is also of note (*Studijní Zvesti AÚ SAV* **15**, 1965, 17ff.).

103. Coles (1962, 171f.); P. Stary, in *Vorzeit zwischen Main und Donau, Neue archäologische Forschungen und Funde aus Franken und Altbayern* (ed. K. Spindler), 1980, 51f. (Universitätsbibliothek Erlangen-Nürnberg).

104. Hencken (1971); Borchhardt (1972, 1977).

105. Eutresis: H. Goldman, *Excavations at Eutresis in Boeotia*, 1931, p. 220, fig. 290; positively assessed by Hencken (1971, p. 18); negatively by Borchhardt (1972, p. 20, n. 103). Late finds: Kallithea (Yalouris, 1960, p. 44, Beil. 41, 4); Knossos (information from Dr O. Dickinson).

106. Borchhardt (1972, pp. 20, 28ff., Taf. 1:3, 5, Abb. 2a; 1977, E62); Makarenko, *Eurasia Septentrionalis Antiqua* **9**, 1934/6, 135–153, figs 11–15.

107. G. Georgiev and N. Angelov, *Izvestija Arch. Institut* **18**, 1952, 149f., fig. 129, 4.

108. G. Georgiev and N. Angelov, *Izvestija Arch. Institut* **21**, 1957, 72, fig. 33, 1; 80, fig. 42, 2.

109. Borchhardt (1972, 1977).

110. S. Hood and P. de Jong, *BSA* **47**, 1952, 256ff.

111. Hencken (1971, p. 37, fig. 13e).

112. H. Hencken, *Proc. Prehist. Soc.* **18**, 1952, 36–46.

113. Hencken (1971, pp. 179ff.); cf. his advocacy of a low date for a homogeneous hoard find in *Proc. Prehist. Soc.* **18**, 1952, 36ff. The controversy is reviewed by Borchhardt (1972, pp. 55ff.).

114. Borchhardt (1972, pp. 37ff.; 1977, E66ff.).

115. Hencken (1971, pp. 155ff.).

116. G. Daux, *BCH* **82**, 1958, 706–707, fig. 26; Hencken (1971, pp. 23ff., fig. 8; 58f., fig. 31).

117. Borchhardt (1972, p. 23, Taf. 4.2).

118. Sandars (1978, pp. 106–107, 160–161).

119. Catling (1977b); P. Schauer, *JbRGZM* **29**, 1982, 100–155.

120. Åström (1977, pp. 35ff.).

121. Yalouris (1960, pp. 45ff.); Catling (1964, pp. 140ff.).

122. N. Platon, *Arch. Delt.* **20**, 1965, Bl, 30–32; **21**, 1966, Bl, 36–38, figs 1, 2, pl. 60; P. Mountjoy, "A case for a LH IIIC date for the bronze greaves from the south slope of the Acropolis at Athens", unpublished article kindly lent to me prior to publication.

123. G. von Merhart, *BRGK* **37–8**, 1956–7 (1958), 91–147.

124. G. Gaucher and Y. Robert, *Gallia préhistoire* **10**, 1967, 169ff., 205ff., figs 46–48.

125. Vinski-Gasparini (1973, pp. 181, 183, Tab. 48, 19, 96, 2–3).

126. Vinski-Gasparini (1973, Tab. 57, 9).

127. B. Čović, *Glasnik Zemalskog Muzea Sarajevo* **29**, 1974, 19–32.

128. A. Miro Bonomi, *Atti della XXI Riunione Scientifica*, 1977 (1979), 123ff., figs 1–2.

129. G. von Merhart, *BRGK* **37–8**, 1956–7 (1958), 103; G. Fogolari, *Not. Scavi* 1943, 4ff.; *Wiener Prähistorische Zeitschrift* **30**, 1943, 73ff.

□ 7
Artistic motifs and symbolism

No topic in the field of Mycenaean relations with the north has been so controversial as has the study of motifs said to be of Mycenaean inspiration. Such motifs appear on a variety of objects, most of them patently not (and not claimed to be) of Mycenaean origin, at various stages of the Bronze Age, but overwhelmingly of the later Early Bronze Age (Br A2 and equivalent). Their appearance, as well as that of later motifs and symbols, has been used in the current debate both for socio-economic and for chronological inferences: extreme views[1] even see parts of central Europe as developing wholly under the influence of East Mediterranean civilization.

The trouble with this whole discussion is that it is almost totally unsusceptible to objective analysis. Since the matter under study is "art", rigid categorization is neither possible nor meaningful, for the artist must be allowed his licence: one man's similarity is another's identity, and yet another's coincidence. This basic and inherent difficulty has been propounded by the habit of mind which sees the more or less simultaneous appearance of comparable objects or designs as inevitably being related, and related in an unequal way, one being dependent on the other. While this is no doubt sometimes the case, there is no good reason to elevate an empirical observation to the status of a law which states that all contemporaneous, or near-contemporaneous, appearances of a design must be connected.

But what would such a connection, if it could be proved, demonstrate? This is quite uncertain. Most authors have spoken of "influence" and "imitation", interpreting this when pressed to mean that the craftsmen of one area had seen the products of another area, found them attractive, and set about copying them. This implies that the existing repertory of designs and forms in the receptor area was flexible enough, one might even say poor enough, to be able easily to accommodate the ideas transmitted. The fact that such a notion of "transport" or "diffusion" is less than flattering to the skills of craftsmen and artists in the receptor area seems rarely to have been appreciated. In fact scholars in those very areas today have been among the foremost in supposing that their Bronze Age forefathers' artistic repertoire was essentially derivative, taken second-hand from those zones of "civilization" which have so much influenced the later course of European culture.

One can trace this trend back to Åberg and Montelius, but since the last war it has mainly been kept alive by central European scholars, from Germany to Hungary. Influential books on the chronology of the European Bronze Age depend on the notion of contact with Mycenaean Greece.[2] Few voices have been raised in protest, save the odd iconoclast, and only recently have detailed analyses presented arguments at variance with the traditional trend.[3]

This is not the place for a piece-by-piece analysis of all the relevant material: this has often been done before, and it cannot, in my view, lead to any more certain a picture than has ever been the case. Instead, after a brief presentation of the material, an attempt will be made to set it in its cultural context, for only in this way can any meaningful appreciation of its significance be attained.

Spiraliform designs in the Carpathian Basin

Pride of place has traditionally been ascribed to a group of bone, antler and metal objects with spiral-related designs in and around the Carpathian basin. These much-discussed pieces consist of cylinders, discs and harness-pieces in bone or antler, discs and vessels in gold, and of swords and axes in bronze.

Seven principal motifs occur on these objects (Fig. 48):

(1) The pulley motif (*Wellenband*), composed of a curvilinear maeander, usually around small compass-drawn circles. This is the most frequent design on the bone and antler objects, occurring for instance on the cheek-pieces from Malé Kosihy, Nitriansky Hrádok, and Veselé, or the cylinders from Blučina (Fig. 48.1).

(2) The flat maeander, as on cheek-pieces from Vattina or the cylinder from Tiszafüred (Fig. 48.2).

(3) Running spirals, as on the Ţufalău discs, Wietenberg hearth and pottery, and Early Bronze Age bronze axes and swords (Fig. 48.3, 4).

(4) Designs based on groups of incomplete concentric circles touching tangentially (*Spiralhaken*), seen on the Surčin disc and other pieces (Fig. 48.5).

(5) Dot-and-circle decoration, as on the cylinders from Věteřov (Fig. 48.7).

(6) The "arcaded maeander", on a cylinder from Vattina and a knob from Tószeg (Fig. 48.6).

FIG. 48 ☐ Spiral and related designs in the Carpathian Basin. (1) Malé Kosihy; (2) Tiszafüred; (3–4) Ţufalău; (5) Surčin; (6) Vattina; (7) Velký Žernosek; (8) Hajdúsámson; (9–17) designs on Wietenberg pottery. (After Hüttel, 1981; Hachmann, 1957a; Horedt, 1960.)

(7) Scroll-like designs, typically U- and V-shaped motifs with curling terminals: Ostrovul Mare discs, Wietenberg and Cîrna pottery.

Other motifs include zig-zags, crosses and related designs.

The first four of these have numerous parallels in the Aegean, as has often been pointed out. The running spiral was especially common in Minoan-Mycenaean art, but analogies here are more generalized and greater significance attaches to the more precise nature of the other three forms. All of these have numerous parallels in the Shaft Graves.[4]

Discs

Eight discs are decorated with maeanders or with *Spiralhaken*. Unfortunately, very little is known of undecorated discs of bone and antler—either none have been found, or else excavators have not thought them worth publishing.[5] But there are finds which urge caution in this respect: at Zagreb, for instance, is a thin disc of wood bearing a faint decoration that seems to include concentric bands. With the material from Vattina on view at Novi Sad is a bone disc, thick enough for a hole to be pierced in the side, with a decoration of dot-and-rings round the outside and round the central perforation. These two objects suggest that discs of bone and other organic materials were probably quite common, and only those with spiraliform decoration have attracted attention in the publications.

This view is further confirmed by examination of the metalwork. The obvious candidates for consideration are disc-butted axes: indeed, when one considers the function of the bone discs, a possible use such as this must loom large. The Surčin disc (Fig. 48.5), which I have been able to examine closely, has in its underside one large central hole and five smaller holes set at equal intervals round the edge, sloping diagonally inwards. Some of the other discs have no visible means of attachment and may have been glued onto whatever they were part of, while others have a central hole and in the case of Sepsé, a hole at the edge as well. The discs are of a size comparable to that of the disc butts, and the decoration is, in general, close. The Füzesabony disc, with its five spirals running anti-clockwise, is similar to the axes like those from Apa, and the Věteřov disc is related to the Szeghalom and Someşeni axes.[6] The axes in question come from hoards of Mozsolics' Hajdúsámson horizon (B IIIa) and are synchronous with the bone objects since the latter came (in Hungary) from Füzesabony levels (B III). The technique is admittedly somewhat different—the axes, like all the decorated bronzework of the Hajdúsámson horizon, are ornamented with spirals formed by several thin concentric curves, and are off-set by small dots along their outer edges. The spirals are apparently drawn by hand. A further parallel worthy of mention is between the Tiszafüred disc and the base of cup no. 4 from the former County Bihar.[7] A note of caution must be sounded: the *Spiralhaken* motif is found on Iron Age fibulae from Jugoslavia, so that at best the value of the motif as evidence of cross-contact is lowered, while at worst the Surčin disc could be of Iron Age date.[8]

Cylinders

When we turn to the cylinders—of which some eight are decorated with maeanders or spirallic motifs—we must first mention the five similar pieces which are not so decorated. Some of these have dot-and-circle decoration, while others have no decoration at all. The former appear on the cylinders from Věteřov, Mojžíř, Velké Žernoseky and Malé Čičovice, while a related theme is on the Vattina piece. The bottom of the Füzesabony cylinder is almost identical to that on horse cheek-pieces from Mezöcsat and Köröstarcsa.[9] The other cylinders are undecorated.

The pulley motif as seen on three cylinders (and on 8+ cheek-pieces) is a typical theme in metalwork of the same period. The *Spiralhaken* of the Haj-dúsámson and Apa hoards (notably the swords), on the broad sides of disc-butted axes, are basically spiral pulley motifs done in a different material by hand, with some elaboration and in groups of parallel lines. Other important occurrences of this motif are on the Pipe and Kárász collection armbands where it is almost identical to that on the cylinders and cheek-pieces. Simi-larly, the arcading on the cylinders from Vattina and Tószeg is exactly paral-leled by that on the shoulder of cup no. 4 from Kom. Bihar.[10]

The fact that there are other, differently decorated bone cylinders in the central European area clearly affects the value of the spirally decorated cylin-ders as evidence of contact or influence.

Cheek-pieces

Spiral and maeander motifs are known on ten antler cheek-pieces in the Carpathian Basin, mostly in the form of pulley motifs (Fig. 48.1). Others have decoration of a different sort or none at all. We enter here a large and complicated field which is beyond our present scope: the origin and diffusion of horse-riding and harness in barbarian Europe.[11] The pieces in question are assigned by Mozsolics to the periods B III–IV, the majority to B III, equivalent to Br A2. The very earliest such objects in Hungary are believed to date only to B II,[12] though horses were present there since at least Baden culture times.[13] A group of German Copper Age antler bars have been seen as cheek-pieces, but this is disputed.[14]

Most authors have looked to the Russian steppe for the origins of horse-riding, perhaps because safety seemed to lie in the unknown. In fact the main studies on horse-harness in the Ukraine have shown how late is the date at which cheek-pieces are attested, though in fact the main dating aid has been cross-connection with Greece.[15] The evidence for harnessed animals in the Near East goes back into the fourth millennium B.C., but horses are not unequivocally present before 2000 B.C., and the earliest harness is somewhat later. This is not long before the Shaft Graves, where horse-drawn chariots are clearly depicted, and a pair of mysterious objects in bone have been interpreted as horse bits.[16] But then horse bones were present already in Troy VI and in Middle Helladic contexts in Greece, presumably domesticated, but whether ridden or not we do not know.[17] Horses and harness were thus present throughout central and eastern Europe and the Near East by the middle of the second millennium B.C.; the difficulty is to specify precisely where the technology was first developed, and in which direction it spread. This problem is the more difficult because cross-dating with Mycenaean Greece has been the main means of determining the chronological position of the European pieces.

My concern here, however, is with the fact and form of decoration of the cheek-pieces: general considerations of how and when the practice of horse-riding reached Europe must be left to more qualified authorities than me.

Antler cheek-pieces of bar form are found widely in Europe in the Bronze Age: in addition to central and eastern Europe we may specifically mention Italy[18] and Britain.[19] The great majority are either not decorated or have only dot-and-circle decoration. The pieces decorated with "Mycenaean" motifs thus represent only a small section of the whole.

Goldwork

"Dass die Scheiben von Cófalva mit mykenischen Erzeugnissen zusammenhängen, ist kaum zu bestreiten."[20] "In Ungarn, ja im ganzen Karpatenbecken kein Gegenstand als sicheres Importstück aus der Ägäis bezeichnet werden kann (auch die Scheiben von Cófalva nicht)."[21]

Of the metal objects that are said to reflect Mycenaean influence, only the roundels from Țufalău and Ostrovul Mare[22] could conceivably be candidates for consideration as imports or even imitations. The rest of the discs, while clearly interrelated and of the same general type, are decorated in a different way or not at all.

The Țufalău (Cófalva) treasure consists of five gold axes of "Caucasian" type, one with a discoid decoration on its flat side, eight gold "lock-rings", a gold twisted armring with spiral ends and the fragment of another, an "ingot" of gold, a "perforated ball", and a series of phalerae—nine small convex discs with boss decoration and four gold discs with spiral decoration in the form of spirals running anticlockwise around a central circle (Fig. 48.3, 4). The Ostrovul Mare treasure consists of three bracelets, ten lock-rings, and three large and 30 small convex phalerae, all in gold. All the phalerae have a decoration based on spiral designs, which correspond to those listed above.

Parallels for the running spiral round the edge of a phalera are of course numerous. It is striking, though, that the Shaft Graves do not provide any pieces identical in form and decoration to the Romanian phalerae.[23] Though a close relationship has been assumed, there cannot be any question of importation. Furthermore, spiral decoration had a good local ancestry and numerous local parallels.

The Ţufalău and Ostrovul Mare discs are part of a larger group of (mainly gold) decorated discs, found principally in Transylvania, which were used for dress ornamentation. They date to the Early and Middle Bronze Age (Wietenberg and Gîrla Mare). Decorative motifs vary from those based on spiral designs (Sacheihid 1, Graniceri 1, Vărşand) through floral and foliate designs (Graniceri 2) to maeanders and even stylized animal figures (Sacheihid 2, Graniceri 1). The decoration is usually executed in lines of repoussé dots. In this respect, the group seems to be a continuation of earlier traditions: gold was worked regularly in the Chalcolithic in Transylvania and pendants in flat sheet gold were common with or without repoussé decoration,[24] and sometimes with spiral terminals. Hungary and Transylvania continued to be a local centre of the sheet goldworking industry into the Hallstatt period, as is shown by the Velem-Szentvid and related finds.[25]

The variety in the precise form of decoration on the Ostrovul Mare discs is to be attributed, in my view, to careless workmanship. The craftsman did not plan his decoration with sufficient care, with the result that sometimes the spirals joined up, at others they did not and were either left unjoined or connected up at the expense of even spacing. This betrays an amateurishness that would be unthinkable in Mycenaean goldwork, which was usually carefully planned and immaculately executed.

Some of these designs also occur on gold vessels and ornaments: most notably on gold cups from Bihar County (now western Romania) and bracelets from Pipe (Braşov) and an unknown locality in Transylvania (Kárász collection).[26] These pieces are carefully decorated, using compass-drawn circles as the basis for the designs, and correspond more closely to the bone and antler objects than to any other metalwork. At all events they show that spiral and maeander designs based on compass-drawn arcs or circles were used on a rather wider range of materials than the artists' preference for bone implies.

Bronzework

Much of the metalwork of the Early Bronze Age in the Carpathian Basin is decorated with motifs based on spirals (Fig. 48.8).[27] This can be seen especially clearly on disc-butted axes and on swords, but related designs occur too on daggers, on shaft-hole axes, and some other forms. Typically the ornament consists of swirling motifs composed of multiple parallel lines edged with dots: they look like, but are not, spirals. Bordering these curvilinear designs are frequently found arcade motifs, hatched pendent triangles, and groups of dots or lines. In addition, spiral-ended rings show the presence of genuine spiral motifs. These designs on metalwork correspond to the swirling designs found on pottery of the same period, on sites of the Füzesabony and Vărşand groups. Metalwork is much less frequent in the Wietenberg culture area, but finds of similar axes suggest that their decoration corresponds also to that on Wietenberg pottery.

These designs are *sui generis* and, as any neophyte can see, bear no real resemblance to those found in Mycenaean Greece. As far as I am aware, the only author who seriously claims that they do, and that they are actually derived from Mycenaean ornament, is Vladár.[28] It need only be remarked that he was unable, indeed made no attempt, to produce a single analogy—let alone a convincing analogy—for either the designs or the technique of drawing them on Carpathian Basin bronzework.

Pottery and other objects

The question of the affinities of these Transylvanian gold discs cannot be seen out of their local context. On pottery of the Wietenberg culture, which is itself a candidate for inspiration from Mycenaean Greece, the spiral is commonly found, and is repeated on the famous hearth.[29] The repertoire of designs on Wietenberg pottery is very large (Fig. 48.9–17): spiral and related designs are only one element in a rich fund of ornament on which Wietenberg artists drew.[30] Much the same can be said for pottery of the Cîrna—Gîrla Mare group of the next phase of the Bronze Age. Designs there are predominantly curvilinear, and based on varieties of spiral and scroll design. In them presumably resided a symbolism of which we are totally unaware: the motifs are usually small-scale and self-contained, and recur on the well-known cult figurines of this group. It is naturally quite beyond the scope of the evidence to suppose, as some have done, that these symbols meant the same thing on the Danube as they did in the Aegean.

Carpathian Basin: summary

Spiraliform and related designs occur widely in and around the Carpathian Basin in that part of the Early Bronze Age normally designated the Apa-Hajdúsámson horizon (B IIIa) or, in cultural terms, the Füzesabony–Oto-mani–Wietenberg groups, and, rather later, the Vattina–Gîrla Mare group. There is a rich repertoire of designs shown on pottery and metalwork in all these areas, many (but not all) based on curvilinear, typically spiraliform, motifs. As we have seen, the general notion of spiral- and maeander-based designs was widespread in space and in the mediums used; while a small group of objects use very specific designs based on compass-drawn arcs and circles. It is these latter which have been alleged to be derived directly from Mycenaean art. In order to assess the problem satisfactorily we must consider both the feasibility of such derivation (both chronologically and in human terms) and other possibilities for explaining their appearance.

We will consider chronological aspects in more detail in Chapter 10, but it must be remarked here that whatever one thinks of the likelihood of a Mycenaean derivation for spiral decoration, there are difficulties in the way of accepting it on chronological grounds. The first of these is a general one, made previously by several writers:[31] spiral ornament in the Aegean had a long life, at least 500 years in its developed Late Bronze Age form, with numerous appearances back to the Neolithic before that. It is often unclear which phase of spiral decoration the Carpathian Basin analogies are supposed to refer to: most analogies, for instance, are drawn from the Shaft Graves (LH I), but the Wietenberg hearth is usually compared to those in late Mycenaean palaces (LH IIIB), a difference of up to 350 years.

Most authors plump for a synchronism between the Shaft Graves, or LH I (sixteenth century), and the "ornament horizon" of the Carpathian Basin. This is the part of the Mycenaean period when there is least evidence for overseas enterprise, in the form of exported pottery. Quite why it should have been then that the decorative influences were felt, and why they were felt in an area so remote from Greece, has never been satisfactorily explained. In any case, radiocarbon dating indicates quite clearly that the Br A2–Apa–Hajdúsámson horizon must fall earlier than the sixteenth century (cf. p. 279).

But quite apart from the arguments based on radiocarbon dating, which central European scholars will dismiss out of hand, an appeal to reason, and a look at the commonness of spiral decoration, should lead to the realization that there is nothing Mycenaean about the Carpathian Basin group. We may mention first of all the prevalence of the designs on bone and antler: apart from two well-known objects from Alalakh none of the Mediterranean parallels is in these materials, nor are the designs on objects of comparable function (where this is known). We have not a shred of evidence for direct contact between Greece and the Carpathian Basin in the early Mycenaean period: not a sherd of pottery north of Albania, not a bronze north of Macedonia—and most of these are not of the Shaft Grave period—in fact nothing. Why, then, apart from the fun of letting the imagination run riot, pretend that these objects are something they plainly are not?

I have already stressed the prevalence and long history of spiral decoration, which goes back to the Neolithic in many parts of south-east Europe. If one is looking for an ancestry for spiral designs on Wietenberg pottery, better to start with the numerous instances of such design on late Neolithic and Chalcolithic pottery in Romania: Boian, Vădastra, Cucuteni-Petreşti, not to mention the elaborate curvilinear designs of Gumelniţa—Salcuţa—Tripolje. Why, for that matter, look to Greece? Why not Anatolia? True spirals were used on pottery there from Hacılar I times, and running spirals as early as the mid-fourth millennium. Related designs are to be found in EB II Alaca Hüyük (c. 2300 B.C.), and spirally terminating gold ornaments in Troy II. Spirals also occur on Hittite cylinder seals, and Mellaart claims parallels for the Carpathian Basin bonework in Beycesultan IVa—II (1500–1200 B.C.).[32] Numerous other cases could be cited.

There are obvious differences, moreover, between Wietenberg and Mycenaean spirals. The former are usually "stabbed", stamped, incised, channelled or in relief—rarely painted. They are usually formed in bands or by one or two incised lines. It is clear that running spirals were but part of a large repertory of related designs that included spiral and swastika-like maeanders, leaf-designs, a variety of geometric ornaments based on the triangle, flame patterns, and the Wietenberg "cross".[33] These others are in no way similar to Aegean decorative motifs, yet they are clearly related to the spiral designs they accompany.

The specific aspect of the Carpathian Basin bonework—and, apart from the gold vessels and bracelets, only the bonework—which makes one hesitate in dismissing it from consideration is the fact that these designs are very specific; and they are specific because they are drawn by using compasses. The pits where the point of the compasses rested can frequently be seen, which is seldom the case on Mycenaean examples of such designs. Use of the compasses for drawing designs on bonework was common throughout the Bronze Age, and most of the designs produced were not of the "Mycenaean" variety. Much the most common was the common-or-garden dot and circle, which is seen on bonework of all periods of the Bronze Age in many different areas: it is quite unspecific and cannot be used for dating purposes. At the same time, once dot-and-circle decoration was being used for decorating bonework, it was a natural step to start using arcs to create curvilinear patterns. Dezort showed long ago the stages in which the ornament is built up on the more complex designs (Fig. 49);[34] it is also possible theoretically to see a typological sequence in these designs from simple to more developed. We might thus start with simple dots and rings, often multiple (Malé Kosihy cylinder), move on to intersecting rings (as on the disc cheek-piece from Tószeg) or to the use of a line joining two rings diagonally (disc cheek-piece from Cîrlomaneşti); next might come the joining of a small ring to a large one (Tószeg); the creating of more flowing designs by using joined antithetically-placed semicircles (Vattina); and finally the fully fledged maeander band weaving its way round the outside of the dots and circles. Here all the steps of the process can be clearly seen, including pieces that went wrong (cheek-piece from Spišský Štvrtok); no such demonstration of the experimental process is visible on Mycenaean artwork. One might, indeed, more logically suggest that Mycenaean art motifs came from the Carpathian Basin, since they appear to arrive fully-developed.

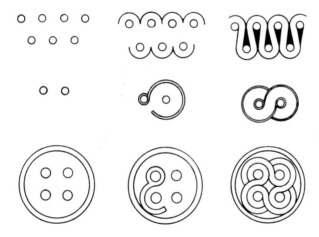

FIG. 49 ☐ Stages by which compass-drawn motifs were built up. (After Dezort, 1946.)

In conclusion, I see no compelling reason for seeing any connection what-soever, in time or conception, between artistic motifs on bone, antler, gold, bronze or clay in the Carpathian Basin and those in Mycenaean Greece. The widespread recurrence of spiraliform designs encourages the belief that these similarities are coincidental, and radiocarbon dating supports the divorcing of the two traditions by placing Br A2 and its relatives earlier than the six-teenth century. Even if this were not the case the archaeological arguments can stand up by themselves, and the cause of Bronze Age research is done no good by some of the wild suggestions which have emanated from central Europe in recent years.

The Borodino hoard (Fig. 50.1–5)

The Borodino hoard was found in 1912 by a German settler during agricultural work near Borodino in Bessarabia (today Odessa region), which lies about 100 km from the Black Sea and 120 km north of the Danube. The 17 objects included two silver spearheads, four axes in semi-precious stone and the fragment of a fifth, three stone perforated "mace-heads", a silver dagger inlaid with gold plate, a silver pin, and several fragmentary objects. Controversy has raged ever since over whether the hoard (which was found in a pot) is homogeneous and if so, what is its date. The controversy revolves around the affinities of the forms of the objects on the one hand and their decoration on the other, and scholarly opinion has been divided into those who favour an early date, contemporary with the Shaft Graves,[35] and those who would place the hoard much later.[36] All authorities agree that the forms are not Mycenaean: it is the decoration which has been supposed, understandably, to derive from Mycenaean prototypes.

There are four basic patterns: spectacle spirals or a derivative (both sides of the pin-head); zig-zags with a variety of infilling motifs (ends of the pin-head, base of spearhead sockets); running spirals (spearhead sockets); and s- and crook-motifs (inlay on dagger blade). The first of these, the spectacle spiral motif (Fig. 50.3), is one of wide distribution in a variety of forms, of which the most obvious is the copper or bronze spiral pendant itself. Plausible analogies are to be found on pottery from Cîrna and Craiova, of the Vattina-Gîrla Mare culture.[37] There is a very striking Mycenaean example of the motif, on the well-known rhomboid beads or plates from Shaft Graves IV and V;[38] but its reappearance on a ring from Praisos about 500 years later urges caution.[39] The technique of adding small dots along each line of the motif on the Borodino pin is paralleled on, among other things, disc-butted axes of Mozsolics types A and B, where, however, the motifs are rather different.

The running spiral on the base of the broken spearhead (Fig. 50.5) certainly resembles Aegean spirals, though this precise form is not the standard Mycenaean one. It goes back to the Early Bronze Age on Crete on stone vases and sealings. In the Middle Bronze Age it is found in Crete, and elaborate versions of the design are present in the Shaft Graves. It does not seem to occur after the early Mycenaean period.[40] The second spearhead has a decoration of zig-zags and rhombs (Fig. 50.1) and though rhomboid buttons occur in the Shaft Graves this certainly could be merely fortuitous. All the motifs

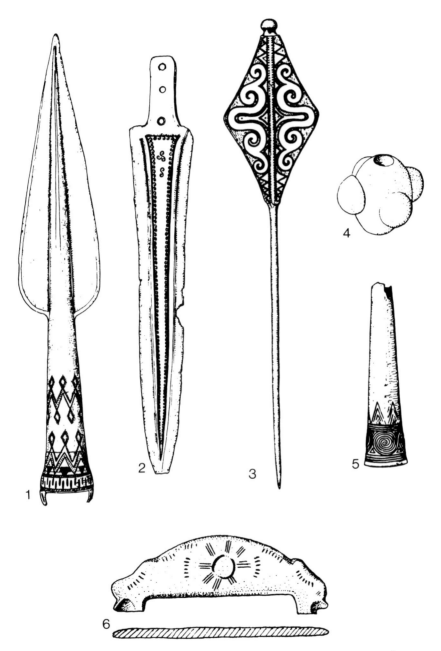

FIG. 50 □ Objects from the Borodino hoard (1–5); bronze object from Spišský Štvrtok (6). (After Hachmann, 1957a; Vladár, 1973.)

occur on pottery in Romania, at dates ranging from Wietenberg through Cîrna to Balta Verde, which leaves one a long time-span (Early to Late Bronze Age) to choose from.[41]

The stone objects in the Borodino hoard are also difficult. The mace-heads with protrusions (Fig. 50.4) can be paralleled in Wietenberg material and by the pommel of the Apa sword, but this form is widely distributed in time and space.[42] The stone battle-axes clearly stem from the Troy II tradition but the best parallels seem to be Caucasian, dating to the Koban phase.

The metalwork itself is no more helpful. The pin and dagger are almost unparalleled; for the former one must quote the rhomboid-headed pin from Medgidia,[43] a bare 125 km from Borodino, but on this piece the ornamental system is quite different, as it is too on the pins from Smel, Komarov and Băleni. The dagger (Fig. 50.2) is unique. If the inlay technique of the Shaft Grave daggers is a significant parallel, a date as early as LH I is again possible. The only dagger at all similar is from a Koban context, dated eleventh to ninth century by Safronov.[44] The spearheads have more numerous parallels, at any rate in shape—the closest piece comes from Ivance, Hungary[45] and is decorated with zig-zags round the socket base. Unfortunately it has no context; nor can a spearhead of rather similar shape from Podlaza apparently of Ha A be said to provide reliable evidence for date. Gimbutas, Safronov and other authors have pursued the line that spearheads of the Seima complex are similar, and tried to date them by this means; but the extremely complicated and hugely scattered finds simply do not allow a close dating, even if the general similarity to the Seima complex seems assured.[46]

Until more comparanda for Borodino come to light, the dating and significance will remain disputed. Certainly it has little to do with metalwork of the north Pontic region as known at present.[47] It includes motifs that would be at home in Mycenaean Greece, but not in a form that a Mycenaean craftsman would produce. Contemporaneity with the Shaft Graves cannot be ruled out, and whatever its date it might fit ultimately in a context of contact with the south; but equally chance and the tendency of motifs to recur have to be borne in mind. Preferred parallels for the forms are late. Whatever the truth, it is unlikely that the Borodino hoard indicates direct or regular contact with Shaft Grave Greece, and therefore cannot serve as a building-block for elaborate theories of Mycenaean princesses in far-off lands.

Sulimirski has drawn attention to certain other decorated objects in metal and stone from the North Pontic area.[48] The daggers from Voloskoe and Dnepropetrovsk provinces decorated with rows of hatched triangles may relate to the triangle decoration on the Borodino spearheads, but certainly have nothing to do with Mycenaean daggers, and the same is true of two stone battle-axes from barrows at Popovka, Horoženo and Bešovo. A socketed spearhead with crude or derivative versions of antithetic spirals on the socket, and a derivative pulley motif on the base, from Cjurupinsk near Cherson, is more interesting. It is certainly not a Mycenaean product, nor can one say its decoration is strictly "in the Mycenaean style": morphologically and syntactically the spearhead and its decoration are quite different. It is even doubtful if compasses were used to draw the patterns. It appears to offer the kind of parallel which can only be attributed to coincidence or to the breadth of decorative traditions, and cannot be explained as the result of direct or even indirect contact.

Late Bronze Age metalwork in central Europe

Spirally coiled terminals on leg- and arm-bands, fibulae, rings and other objects were a very common feature of the Middle and Late Bronze Age in central Europe, and spiral ornament appeared frequently on objects of sheet bronze, such as belt-plates.[49] One class of material that bears spiral designs particularly close to Mycenaean examples are the solid-hilted swords, which start as early as Br B1.[50] On the earliest type, Spatzenhausen, there appear only series of concentric circles, evenly spaced round the upper part of the grip, while the imitation rivets are surrounded by similar rings. On the "Transitional sword" (B2) from Göggenhofen, the separate rings are already joined up into a running spiral (anticlockwise), while other swords of this type still have separate rings. On the Hüttenkofen variant there are on the grip multiple parallel lines in wavy decoration like the pulley motif. On swords with eight-sided grip, the most common decoration is that of isolated rings of concentric circles, arranged in rows (usually four) but on some of these the circles are joined up into running spirals.[51] This type is dated to Br C. By the time of Riegsee swords (Br D), more elaborate designs were being used. Spirallic and whorl-like decoration was laid vertically along the grip, which, being smooth all round, presented no constructional constraint on the syntax. Thus the sword from Gablingen bears a decoration of vertical running spirals in the form of closely interlocking backward S's, in ten rows with eight columns on each side.[52] Other Riegsee swords tend to have a related, though less obviously spiral-based, decoration.

   In the Urnfield period, it is striking that most classes of *Dreiwulstschwert* (swords with three ribs on the grip) bear on their shoulder a genuine pulley motif with compass-drawn dot-and-circle at the pulley-point. It appears on swords of Müller-Karpe's types Erlach, Schwaig, Illertissen, Liptau var. II, also in rather sketchy form on Högl and Aldrans, and continues to be found on some *Schalenknaufschwerter* (swords with bowl-like pommel). This covers the period Ha A to early B. Also on the *Dreiwulstschwerter* are a variety of running spirals set between all or some of the three ridges. They are particularly common on the Erlach, Illertissen (very rich decoration) and Aldrans types, but appear on all the rest except Högl. In the eastern area of Europe, there was a distinct preference for other, non-spirallic decoration, particularly on the shoulder and pommel; in the west, swords were left undecorated rather than use ornament not based on spirals. With the *Schalenknaufschwerter* the isolated ring of concentric circles came back into vogue, though running spirals are found as well.

Swords of Boiu type should also be mentioned: these have a spectacle motif, usually a double-spiral, on the hilt. Werner argued that this might be derived from the Mycenaean practice of putting spiral designs on the upper blade of long swords, but Cowen has shown that all the elements of the Boiu sword are derivable from local sources.[53] In this case, as in that of the *Vollgriffschwerter*, it is the inspiration of the original design that must be investigated, since local development will account for subsequent embellishments. As we have seen, spiraliform decoration was popular in eastern Europe from Br A2 into Br B, and solid-hilted swords belong with the general expansion of spirally decorated bronzework.

The period covered by these swords stretches from Br B to Ha B1, which means that they must be synchronous with the Mycenaean period over the lifetime of the earlier types. Why no one has chosen to derive their decoration from Mycenaean prototypes, as they have with the Carpathian basin bonework, is beyond me.

Foliate bands and ivy-leaf designs

Childe first drew attention to the possibility that foliate designs in Minoan and Mycenaean art—the "sacral ivy-leaf" in particular—might be copied *in corpore* by the bronze openwork pendants of the central European Early and Middle Bronze Age (e.g. Kisapostag).[54] We have already mentioned (p. 107) the case of the Vel'ka Lomnica bronze cup fragment, with its oblique ribbing on the rim, and the foliate designs seen on Suciu de Sus pottery. It seems clear to the dispassionate observer that the similarities are of the most general kind and cannot legitimately be used to support the notion of close connection between the two culture areas.

Symbols and symbolism

Many of the motifs considered above as elements of the artistic conception of potters and painters in the Bronze Age world must have possessed a significance over and above the purely artistic: that is, they operated, and were

perceived, as symbols. We enter here a field of enquiry which is hardly susceptible to objective analysis and will not therefore detain us long. The world of
symbols at the present day is a difficult enough field of investigation: the
Bronze Age world of symbols is next to unknowable.

To a large extent the amount of faith which one puts in the significance of
symbols as cross-cultural contacts is a direct result of personal choice, of what
sort of explanation each individual scholar finds satisfying, for it is impossible
to prove one way or the other whether or not the symbols of one area were
considered efficacious in another. I must declare at once that my own stance in
this matter is essentially negative, and I propose to do little more than list those
symbols and motifs which have been alleged to link Greece and the barbarian
world.

Birds and animals

The use of birds and bird-motifs is one of the main cases where a connection between barbarian and Greek worlds is credible, even likely. Birds or
bird motifs occur on a number of late Mycenaean objects: notably on the
cup and tripod cauldron of the Tiryns treasure, on the handle of a knife
from Perati, on LH IIIC pottery from Ialysos and—most interesting—on
the rim of a bowl from a LH IIIC chamber tomb at Pylos (Fig. 51.1).[55]
There are a few examples of birds in Mycenaean art, including one on a
bronze vessel, and it is possible to interpret some motifs in earlier
Mycenaean ornament as bird-related,[56] but in general one can say that this
was not a Mycenaean motif. In the Urnfield world, on the other hand, it
was extremely common, especially on bronzework.[57] In this connection the
motif on the rim of the Pylos bowl merits special attention. It is formed of a
diagonal line connecting two antithetic birds' heads, and is executed in
pointillé technique. Numerous general analogies may be quoted, but there
are also quite specific ones: namely those on Protovillanovan pottery, as
from Pianello (Fig. 51.2, 4), and metalwork, as on the Tolfa fibulae (Fig.
51.5).[58] In view of the numerous other connections with Italy in the twelfth
century this highly specific parallel comes as no surprise. The value of this
link for chronological purposes has not perhaps been fully appreciated:
Müller-Karpe[59] dated the Tolfa hoard to the tenth century, which is manifestly wrong; Bietti Sestieri, on the basis of this and other parallels in bronzework, suggested the eleventh century. This view is obviously right; one
might go further and say that the hoard is likely to be earlier rather than
later in that century.

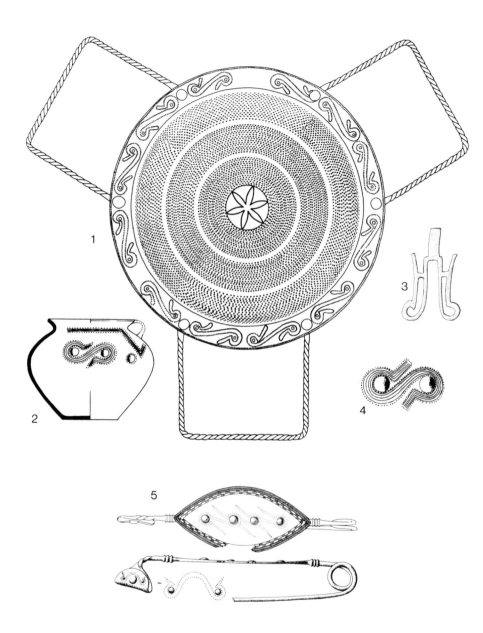

FIG. 51 ☐ Pottery and bronzes from Greece and Italy decorated with antithetically opposed birds' heads. (1) Pylos, chamber tomb K2; (2 and 4) Pianello di Genga; (3) Pigorini Museum, Rome; (5) Coste del Marano (Tolfa). (After Matthäus, 1980a; Müller-Karpe, 1959; Bietti Sestieri, 1973.)

Much the same considerations apply to a pair of bronze vessel-handles from Mouliana tholos tomb A (LH IIIC) which terminate in bull's heads. In this case, though, there are plenty of local (Aegean) parallels for miniature bulls, including at least one vessel with bulls' heads on the handles.[60] None of these parallels is in bronze, however. The Tolfa hoard again contains the best parallel in bronze, with its two cups with bull's-head handles, but the form of the modelling and the technique of attachment are different. It is hard, especially in view of the Pylos bowl, to believe that the recurrence of the motif is mere coincidence; I return to the significance of Tolfa and other Protovillanovan finds below (p. 260).

Bouzek has compared the use of bull-like "rhyta", allegedly used in the "sanctuary" at Uherský Brod, with bull rhyta and figurines in MM Crete.[61] He has also claimed parallels between the actual form of the sanctuary and the finding of bovine skeletons, but it seems clear from the fragmentary nature of the remains at Uherský Brod that this was a reading based more on faith than reason. Much the same may be said for the "hornlike protrusions" on hearths and house-urns, which bear only the faintest resemblance to Cretan horns of consecration. Nor is it enough, to my mind, to cite instances of animal or snake figurines in the Mediterranean zone as support for a comparable "animal cult" in central Europe.[62]

A small bronze plaque from Spišský Štvrtok, convex on one edge and straight on the other and bearing in its centre a plausible sun-symbol, has been seen by its excavator as terminating in two stylized lions' heads (Fig. 50.6), enabling far-flung—not to say far-fetched—parallels from the East Mediterranean to be quoted.[63] The contents of this book will not be to the taste of those who find such arguments convincing.

Other motifs

The double-axe has often been seen as a symbol connecting the Aegean world, where it was undoubtedly important, with central Europe. Double-axes were certainly depicted already in the Neolithic, and appear as ingots in the Early Bronze Age; a series of pendants of hour-glass shape and the hour-glass motifs on Late Bronze Age fibulae have been alleged to relate either to double-axes or to Aegean altar symbols.[64] The absence of votive, or even functional, double-axes north and west of Bulgaria (where they certainly are present) renders this connection less than convincing.

Sun and moon symbols (if that is really what they are!) occur frequently in the central and north European Bronze Age.[65] Sun and moon were, of course, important in Egyptian religion and certainly appear in scenes of Minoan–Mycenaean cult; those who find such parallelism impressive can undoubtedly unearth more of it. This leads us on, however, to consider the wheel, or depictions of it, which are sometimes hard to distinguish from (?) depictions of the sun or moon. It is an undoubted fact that model spoked wheels (if that is what *they* are!) appear in central Europe in the later Early Bronze Age, that is at a time not far removed from their first appearance in Greece, on the stelae of the Shaft Graves. Vladár considers them to have been the wheels of cult vehicles: they might just as easily have been toys. Either way they imply the existence of full-size vehicles with four-spoked wheels. In this instance, where we are concerned with a basic technological invention, a much more positive view can be taken: it is likely that the spoked wheel was widely adopted in Europe and the Near East soon after its invention. This does not, of course, imply synchroneity or any other direct connection between any two appearances of the form.

A variety of motifs connected with cult apparatus—altars, hearths, columns etc.—have also been alleged to show parallelism between Greece and central Europe.[66] Of these much the most interesting and plausible is the hearth from Wietenberg near Sighişoara in Transylvania. This elaborate clay construction was decorated with concentric bands of running spirals and zig-zags, and although these can perfectly well be paralleled on local pottery, a connection with the famous painted plaster hearth of Pylos is usually quoted.[67] Here it is rather the fact than the form of the decoration which is important, and the world is divided into those who believe this to be significant, and those who do not. In view of the ease with which the Wietenberg hearth fits into the local artistic milieu, and the sheer unlikelihood of specific contact with a Mediterranean site 1000 km to the south, I feel I need make little explanation or apology for falling in the second category.

I leave till last an intriguing group of finds from central Europe which do undoubtedly bear similarities to objects in far-off places: the so-called "loaf-of-bread idols", oblong or oval clay objects with circular hollows and connected channels excised out of the surface.[68] These mysterious objects (tallies? moulds for seals? cult objects?) appear in Hungary and Slovakia in Mad'-arovce and Otomani contexts, in Jugoslavia in Vattina contexts, and on lake-sites of the north Italian Early Bronze Age, and though they thus do not affect Mycenaean Greece directly, they have been used to demonstrate "the intensity of European culture contacts with the Mediterranean area with the high point at the beginning of the Middle Bronze Age".[69] In fact Aegean and Near Eastern analogies have also been quoted: Early to Middle Minoan seals with "cup-and-ring" decoration are known, and a few comparable examples are known further east, extending back even as far as Tell Halaf.[70] It has even been suggested—nay, stated in dogmatic terms—that these clay objects were used in the amber trade with northern Europe.[71] These problems are not soluble without further evidence; it is not inconceivable that the same functions may have motivated the production of comparable objects in far removed lands. Direct connections (which detailed analysis of the objects effectively rules out) seem most unlikely, and the chronological spread is in any case wide.

Decorative motifs—conclusions

No definite answer can be given to the question of the true affinities of Transylvanian and other spirallic art, but some general observations may be made which may serve to illustrate the extent of the popularity of spiral motifs in prehistoric Europe. Bone- and antler-work decorated with compass-drawn circular patterns have been shown to fall into their local milieu as far as both their form and their decoration are concerned. Chronologically speaking, a connection with Mycenaean Greece is possible, especially in view of the C14 date for Nitriansky Hrádok; but though some of the designs are extremely close to those in Greece, it is perhaps more likely that they were already part of the local artist's consciousness and not directly copied: a common origin for the designs, embracing both Greece and Eastern Europe, may be suggested. Similar conclusions may be reached for the metal objects, which fall rather more clearly into local groups. Later occurrences of these designs probably reflect an awareness of a European tradition rather than direct inspiration from Mycenaean art. In the last resort, however, the question must be kept open, since all these considerations are subjective; the most that can be said is that the archaeological evidence does not rule out the possibility of some connection, direct or indirect, between Greece and eastern Europe during the sixteenth century B.C. and later.

Notes

1. For example, Vladár (1973).
2. For example, Hachmann (1957a), Hänsel (1968).
3. In greatest detail Schickler (1974: review of Hänsel, 1968); P. Šalkovský, *Slov. Arch.* **28/2**, 1980, 287–312; Goldmann (1981).
4. Parallels for these designs are as follows: No. 1. A variety of objects in the Shaft Graves, e.g. gold button no. 683 (Karo, 1930a, Taf. LXII); on pottery, Furumark (1941) motif no. 53 (wavy line); a group of ivory objects from Alalakh. No. 2. Many pieces from the Shaft Graves, e.g. gold buttons no. 685 (Karo, 1930a, Taf. LXII), grave stelae (Taf. X), and buttons no. 320 (Taf. LX). No. 6. This design is not exactly

paralleled in Mycenaean Greece, but is rather similar to that on grave stelae 1430–1 (Karo, 1930a, Taf. VIII). No. 4. Very common on gold buttons from the Shaft Graves, especially V; particularly close parallels are between the Surčin disc and Mycenae disc 316 (Karo, 1930a, Taf. LX); the Věteřov disc and Mycenae discs 678 (Karo, 1930a, Taf. LXII); the Füzesabony disc and Mycenae discs 319 (Karo, 1930a, Taf. LX). An identical example occurs on an Iron Age fibula from Slovenia: V. Radimsky, *Die prähistorische Fundstätten, ihre Erforschung und Behandlung*, Sarajevo 1891. Another possible parallel is between the Vattina disc and Mycenae discs like no. 708 (Karo, 1930a, Taf. LXV).

    5. Točík (1959) mentions none, for example.

    6. Mozsolics (1967, Taf. 12; 13).

    7. Mozsolics (1964, Abb. 4).

    8. The fibula in question (see n. 4) is an infilled version of a spectacle fibula.

    9. Mozsolics (1953, pp. 79f., figs 14–15); Hüttel (1981, p. 70, nos 52–53, Taf. 6).

    10. Disc-butted axes: Mozsolics (1967, passim). Armbands: Mozsolics (1965/6, Taf. 23, 1). Bihar cups: Mozsolics (1964, Abb. 4).

    11. Basic synthesis: Hüttel (1981). Pioneering works from the earlier literature: Mozsolics (1953, 1960); Potratz (1966).

    12. Hüttel (1981, pp. 70f.).

    13. Hüttel (1981, pp. 113ff.).

    14. J. Lichardus, *Germania* **58**, 1980, 1–24; Hüttel (1981, pp. 16ff., 22ff.).

    15. K. F. Smirnov, *Sov. Arch.* **34**, 1961/1, 46–72; Hüttel (1981, pp. 28ff., 39ff., etc.).

    16. Karo (1930a, p. 113, Taf. LXX, nos 532–535). Full summary of the arguments in Hüttel (1981, pp. 40ff.).

    17. Hüttel (1981, p. 40, n. 11); J. Wiesner, *Arch. Hom.* IF 35 n. 111. Crouwel (1981, pp. 32ff.) discusses the slight evidence for an earlier (EH) appearance.

    18. Säflund (1939, pp. 183ff., tav. 5b); Hüttel (1981, pp. 182ff.); Woytowitsch (1978, pp. 117–119, Taf. 52–54).

    19. W. B. Britnell, *Antiq. J.* **56**, 1976, 24–34.

    20. Mozsolics (1950, p. 21).

    21. Mozsolics (1965/6, p. 44).

    22. Ţufalău: Hachmann (1957a, pp. 173, 221, Taf. 66). Ostrovul Mare: G. Severeanu, *Bucureşti* **1–2**, 1937, 7–11.

    23. Cf. Hachmann (1957a, pp. 173f.).

    24. H. Dumitrescu, *Dacia* **5**, 1961, 69ff.

    25. Mozsolics (1950).

    26. Mozsolics (1964, 1965/6).

    27. Mozsolics (1967).

    28. Vladár (1973, pp. 312ff.).

    29. Horedt (1960, pp. 116ff., Abb. 9; Abb. 3).

    30. Horedt (1960).

    31. For example, S. Piggott, *Antiquity* **34**, 1960, 287.

    32. J. Mellaart, *Anatolian Studies* **18**, 1968, 194.

    33. Horedt (1960, p. 117, Abb. 5–9).

    34. J. Dezort, *Obzor Prehistorický* **13**, 1946, 57–63.

35. For example, Hachmann (1957a, pp. 171f.); followed (by implication) by Hänsel (1968).

36. For example, Safronov (1968) (thirteenth century B.C.); Schickler (1974); M. Gimbutas, *Proc. Prehist. Soc.* **22**, 1956, 143–172 (around 1400 B.C.); O. A. Krivcova-Grakova, *Bessarabskii Klad*, 1949 (Moscow, State Historical Museum), p. 28, gives 1200 B.C. Bočkarev (1968) and Gimbutas (1965): fifteenth–fourteenth centuries. Goldmann (1981) appears to take the view that Borodino is contemporary with the Shaft Graves but not with Apa-Hajdúsámson. A spectacle-spiral motif on a Tumulus period "diadem" from Pitten, Lower Austria, said to resemble that on the Borodino pinhead, is said to suggest that the developed Tumulus Culture runs parallel with the Shaft Graves.

37. Safronov (1968, p. 123, fig. 7, XII–XIII).

38. Karo (1930a, Taf. LXI, LXVI, nos 341–349, 668–673).

39. N. Platon, *Crete* (1966, London, Muller), fig. 113 (quoted Safronov, 1968, p. 121).

40. P. Warren, *Minoan Stone Vases*, 1969 (Cambridge University Press), p. 61, P323, P452–5; Renfrew (1972, pl. 23, 1); A. Evans, *Palace of Minos at Knossos* **II**, 1928 (London, Macmillan), fig. 411B; **III**, 1930, 20–1, fig. 10; Mylonas (1972, pl. 121 beta).

41. Cîrna: Dumitrescu (1961); Wietenberg: Horedt (1960); the various motifs drawn out by Safronov (1968, fig. 7, X etc.).

42. Horedt (1960, p. 130, Abb. 14); Hachmann (1957a, p. 172, Taf. 63, 3); Safronov (1968, pp. 90–91).

43. I. Nestor, *Marburger Studien*, 1938, 175–189.

44. Safronov (1968, p. 119, fig. 8, 8) (Tlijiska Mogila).

45. Hampel (1890, Taf. 27).

46. M. Gimbutas, *Proc. Prehist. Soc.* **22**, 1956, 145, 151ff.; Safronov (1968, pp. 127–128).

47. For example, A. M. Leskov, *Jung- und spätbronzezeitliche Depotfunde im nördlichen Schwarzmeergebiet* I (PBF XX, 5), 1982 (Munich, Beck).

48. Sulimirski (1971, pp. 711–712, 719, figs 2, 5).

49. I. Kilian-Dirlmeier, *Gürtelhaken, Gürtelbleche und Blechgürtel der Bronzezeit in Mitteleuropa* (PBF XII, 2) 1975 (Munich, Beck).

50. As classified by Holste (1953) and Müller-Karpe (1961).

51. Holste (1953, Taf. 9: 2, 4, 5).

52. Holste (1953, Taf. 14: 3).

53. Werner (1952, p. 294, Abb. 1); Cowen (1966, pp. 292–295).

54. Childe (1927, pp. 2–3, fig. 3).

55. J. Bouzek, *Eirene* **6**, 1967, 133; **8**, 1969; Bouzek (1969, p. 60, fig. 23); Matthäus (1980a, pp. 254f.). Tiryns: Karo (1930b, pp. 131f., Beil. 31, 4); Matthäus (1980a, p. 252, Taf. 42, no. 360). Perati: Iakovides (1970, II, pp. 344f., fig. 149). Ialysos: G. Iacopi, *Annuario* **13–14**, 1930–31, 294, fig. 38; 314–315, figs 61–62; Pylos: Blegen *et al.* (1973, pp. 230ff., fig. 291, 1a–e); Matthäus (1980a, pp. 292ff., Taf. 51 no. 446).

56. Matthäus (1980a, p. 253, 196f., Taf. 35, no. 296); E. A. and H. W. Catling, *BSA* **69**, 1974, 236, no. 28, fig. 23, 28, pl. 41a–d (Knossos, Sellopoulo T. 4, LM IIIA1).

57. Kossack (1954); A. Jockenhövel, *PBF* **XX**, 1, 1974, 85, n. 3.

58. Müller-Karpe (1959, Taf. 53, 1, 54, 9, 55, 1); Bietti Sestieri (1973, fig. 21, 4–5).

59. Müller-Karpe (1959, pp. 49ff., Abb. 64).

60. Matthäus (1980a, pp. 274ff., Taf. 49, nos 412–412A; 276, n. 37).

61. Bouzek (1966, pp. 262f., fig. 15); V. Hrubý, *Památky Arch.* **49**, 1958, 48ff., fig. 7, 4–7.

62. Bouzek (1966, p. 268); e.g. Vladár (1973, p. 343, fig. 92).

63. Vladár (1973, pp. 311, 318ff., fig. 64, 1, 67).

64. Bouzek (1966, pp. 264–265); Z. Fiedler, *Památky Arch.* **55**, 1954, 329–336.

65. Coles and Harding (1979, pp. 314, 368, 408 with refs). Vladár (1973, pp. 319, 343).

66. Bouzek (1966, pp. 261ff.).

67. K. Horedt and C. Seraphin, *Die prähistorische Ansiedlung auf dem Wietenberg bei Sighişoara-Schässburg*, 1971 (Bonn, Habelt), pp. 74f.; C. Blegen *et al.*, *The Palace of Nestor at Pylos* I, 1966 (Princeton, University Press), pp. 85ff., figs 65–66, 73. Cf. Coles and Harding (1979, pp. 149f.).

68. G. Bandi, *Preistoria Alpina* **10**, 1974, 237–252; Coles and Harding (1979, pp. 183, 206, n. 60 for further refs).

69. Vladár (1973, p. 323).

70. G. Bandi, *op. cit.*, 247, figs 16–17; quoting *Corpus der Minoischen und Mykenischen Siegel* II/1, 1969, nos 117, 193; **VII**, 1967, nos 13, 217; **II/5**, 1970, nos 26, 16, 48 etc.

71. G. Bandi, *op. cit.*, 249ff.

8
The northern contribution to the Mycenaean world

Whatever the extent of the Mycenaeans' knowledge of the northern and western world, the preceding chapters have endeavoured to make clear that materials reached them from it, in small quantities or large, as finished products or raw materials, by means of corporate effort or individual enterprise. The inflow varied in quantity and over time, but seems to have been perceptible throughout the Late Bronze Age. In most instances little attempt seems to have been made to supply a proven market, and importation was haphazard. On the other hand, the existence of resident aliens has been suggested for the late period (late LH IIIB–early LH IIIC) on the basis of the presence of "non-Mycenaean" pottery on Mycenaean sites. In this chapter an assessment of the scope and scale of the "barbarian" input into Mycenaean Greece will be attempted.

It is abundantly clear that with the exception of the pottery alluded to imports generally consisted of raw materials; the few proven instances of finished objects of northern or western type found in Greece strike one the more forcibly by their isolation. Much the easiest to study is amber, because of its restricted natural occurrence and—although the "doctors disagree"—analytical characterization. Assuming, as is most reasonable to do, that the bulk of the amber is "Baltic", phases of deposition and probably, therefore, importation can be discerned, with by far the most prolific occurring in the sixteenth century B.C. Thereafter the quantities deposited in graves are much smaller, though it does occur on many more sites.

It has already been stressed that amber, being light in weight and not required in great volume, would have been easy to transport physically. The extent to which the supply of amber was related to demand, and, if so, who ensured its continuance, are questions whose solution is quite beyond us. I

have given my reasons for believing that an exchange route through central
Europe is less likely than one linking Greece more or less directly with south-
central England. Yet it cannot be denied that great difficulties lie in the way of
this interpretation, not least the chronological objection that the evidence for
Mycenaean interest even in the Central Mediterranean in LH I is thin, and
arguably for MH non-existent; whereas amber was present in quantity at
Mycenae by the start of LH I. Such difficulties can be multiplied, but they
should not be overplayed: for the manifest fact is that the amber *did* reach
Greece, most probably from one of the "Baltic" sources. The explanation of
this fact is one part of the explanation of the Shaft Grave phenomenon as a
whole: how were any of the objects of foreign origin acquired? Unlikely
though the amber or *lapis lazuli* routes may seem, the materials *were* transported and *did* adorn Mycenaeans. In the case of amber, it adorned
Mycenaeans but not Bronze Age Illyrians—in complete contrast to the Iron
Age situation where plenty was reaching present-day Jugoslavia and Albania.
In Italy, too, the quantities of Bronze Age amber are small by comparison with
those in the Iron Age. These facts strongly suggest that the supply routes and
mechanisms bringing amber to early Mycenaean Greece were quite specific
and different from those in the late Mycenaean period or in the Iron Age.

It would be hard to reconstruct this situation as anything remotely
approaching one of regular supply and demand. Demand there no doubt was,
but the supply was visibly erratic except to Mycenae and the west Peloponnese
in LH I–IIA. If the Bronze Age world was a non-market-oriented one, the
methods of procurement are unlikely to have been dependent on market
factors such as competition. Whether or not a "prestige-chain" linked Greece
with Europe, it is evident that the movement was highly directional and not
brought about by a filtering of goods "down the line".

The case for believing that metal entered the Mycenaean world from the
north and west must, I have suggested, be modified somewhat. Gold sources
are quite widespread, and there is no reason to suppose that the central
European and Balkan ones would have supplied Greece rather than those of
the East Mediterranean area. I have described the evidence for East Mediterranean tin sources and believe exploitation of these alluvial deposits, or others,
not yet identified, to be much more plausible than export from Cornwall,
Brittany or the Erzgebirge. Etruria and Sardinia might have been a source of
tin for Greece, especially if copper was also being moved from the West.

The arguments for seeing an export of copper ingots to Greece from Italy
are less clear-cut than one might wish, but on balance the distribution of
ox-hide ingots seems likely to indicate an exchange pattern of this sort. It is
impossible to estimate the scale on which such an exchange took place, but
very circumstantial evidence suggests that each consignment of ingots on
board ship might have been destined for an individual centre (e.g. Pylos) and

have been intended to last some time, perhaps a matter of months. The lack of metallurgical evidence from Greece makes an assessment of smithing capacities and requirements doubly difficult. With the ox-hide ingots the problem is complicated by the clear indication that they were also used locally on Sardinia, where fragments occur in founders' hoards. In view of the presence of substantial copper deposits on Sardinia it would be a case of coals to Newcastle to suggest a westward export from the Aegean, and the balance of probability must favour export from the west, though it cannot yet be proved analytically.

This leaves us with the other items of trade to consider—individual pieces, invisibles and the like. It is immediately apparent that imported objects from the barbarian world other than amber and metals were extremely few. Nothing in the Shaft Graves other than amber can be put definitely in this category: not the ivory zig-zag mounts, nor the gold ear-rings of "Transylvanian" type, certainly not the "halberd" from Grave VI with its asymmetric outline and massive conical silver/gold rivets.[1] In fact there are no objects (other than amber) in the entire early Mycenaean period that clearly emanate from the northern or western world. Even invisibles such as wool and textiles, slaves and hunting-dogs seem extraneous to the main theme of life in the early Mycenaean period, though their presence cannot be disproved.

In the later period a few items of northern or western origin did find their way into Greece. There is a fragmentary bone horse-snaffle from an "early LH IIIC" context at Tiryns.[1a] The winged-axe mould from Mycenae is the most celebrated and obvious case. Certain spearheads are of northern types, and various bronze forms linked north and north-west Greece with adjacent areas. A bone pin from an early LH IIIC context at Kastanas has been seen as being of a Noua type,[2] though in Macedonia and Bulgaria there are surely many surprises in store because of the relative lack of research: it remains to be seen how isolated a case the pin from Kastanas is. In the meantime, theories of transhumant pastoralists coming seasonally down to the Aegean from the Carpathians are perhaps best left to one side.[3] In general, though, most of the bronzes that appear to link Greece with European lands in the late (post-1200 B.C.) period belong to the family of such pieces that covered much of Europe at this time, and cannot be used to demonstrate specific points of origin for specific types. The "European" swords are a case in point: a non-Greek origin for the general form of the flanged-hilt sword is not in doubt, but that does not make the actual pieces found in Greece non-Greek; rather it suggests a community of smithing practices over a much wider area than hitherto. The same sorts of argument, though with a less clear-cut chronological background, apply with Peschiera daggers, violin-bow fibulae, certain types of spearhead, techniques of sheet metal-working and other forms. The implications of this technical and psychological convergence are considerable, and will be explored below.

In the earlier Mycenaean period generally distinct and distinctive forms of bronze artefact were produced in Greece and, to a lesser extent, in Europe. A smith in Greece, when required to produce a sword, turned out one of two or three types that were current throughout the land at the time: the different types may have related to personal preference (on the part of smith or user) or, more likely, to functional differences in the methods of warfare being practised. Swords in the barbarian world, where present, were quite different. After 1200 b.c. the two series became indistinguishable: the concept "sword" generally meant the same thing to a Greek as to a European. The extent to which this can be called a northern contribution to the Mycenaean world is a matter for debate. Here problems of chronology are paramount, as will become more evident in Chapter 10. The case of the flanged-grip sword is relatively straightforward; with violin-bow fibulae, Peschiera daggers and other forms in this group, questions of priority are almost impossible to resolve without independent dating evidence. Certainly it appears that most of the bronzes in question (I except sheet armour from this generalization) are non-Aegean in ancestry and to that extent can be accepted as part of a series of innovations in material culture that appear around 1200 b.c. It would be unwise to see in these innovations the arrival of "foreigners" in Greece, whether as smiths, mercenaries or invaders, for reasons elaborated in Chapter 2; equally it would be incorrect to imagine that Greece could be seen in isolation from its European neighbours in this period.

It is easy enough to conceive of bronzes and jewellery as arriving in Greece from abroad without the need for the immigration of people to bring the objects. The case of pottery, however, is different, especially where coarse pottery is concerned, for it is hard to believe that heavy crude cooking and storage vessels can have been moved beyond the confines of the settlement where they were made. The appearance of such wares, when a non-indigenous origin can be demonstrated, might be a powerful pointer in the direction of immigrant potters. For present purposes, such a pottery appears in one period only, in LH IIIC and the end of LH IIIB, where a distinctively "non-Mycenaean" hand-made ware is now recognized as appearing on a number of sites that preserve levels of this date, mainly in central and southern Greece, but also on Crete. The pottery, whose existence was recognized only relatively recently, is variously known as "Barbarian Ware", "North-West Greek Ware" and "Hand-made Burnished Ware" (HMB).[4]

The evidence that this pottery as a separate entity belongs to LH IIIC was recognized by Dr E. French in the mid-1960s, during work on material from the recent Mycenae excavations. Only brief mentions of it were made in print, however, until Rutter published a small group of it from his examination of the LH IIIC material from Korakou; in this article he sought parallels outside Greece, concluding that certain wares in the east Balkans (specifically the Coslogeni group of south-east Romania) provided very close analogies.[5]

Within a few years the existence of the pottery was reported on a string of sites—notably Lefkandi, Aigeira on the north coast of the Peloponnese, Tiryns, Sparta (the Menelaion), Kalapodhi in Phocis, Pellana, Delphi, Teichos Dymaeon (Achaea), Perati, Athens, and other sites.[6] Interestingly enough, it has apparently also been found at Kommos and Chania in west Crete.[7] It is certainly more widely distributed than so far appears the case, for being coarse and hand-made it attracts little attention where fine Mycenaean fabrics are present, and must frequently have been regarded simply as Neolithic or Middle Bronze Age, if not actually thrown out without a further thought. Its context is usually the early phase or phases of LH IIIC, and with few certain exceptions does not appear before then.

The pottery (Fig. 52) is not all identical, either in fabric, surface treatment, or shapes, but certain recurring features may be mentioned. The pottery is invariably made by hand. The fabric is usually described as coarse, with large grits; micaceous and sandy fabrics are also found. The surface treatment is widely comparable, that of burnishing; colour is very variable but always dark. The use of plastic decoration, especially finger-impressed cordons, ledges and rims, is widespread, and includes specific types such as horseshoe ledges. Reconstructable shapes include predominantly wide-mouthed jars, with some open bowls, cups and mugs. Further common features will no doubt become available as more material is published.

In considering the status of the LH IIIC hand-made burnished wares, whether imported, intrusive or indigenous, reliance must be placed on the statements of those specialists who have been studying it: I am not one of them. The interpretation of the facts established by the specialists is quite another matter, and must go hand in hand with other classes of evidence. Crucial to this assessment is the question of foreign analogies to the Greek hand-made ware, something which has been one of the main stumbling blocks, for few people are competent to assess both ends of the material.

The following facts have to be established:

(1) Is "barbarian ware" genuinely a novelty?
(2) What are the precise stratigraphic situations and associations of the pottery?
(3) Was it locally made or imported to the sites where it occurs? If imported, was such importation local, regional or international?
(4) Where do its closest analogies lie?
(5) What possible mechanisms could account for the appearance of the ware on Greek sites?

To the question "Is the hand-made pottery new in LH IIIC?" (LH IIIB at Tiryns), the answer is emphatically yes. In spite of the fact that sherds on some sites may not have been recognized for what they are and classified as residual

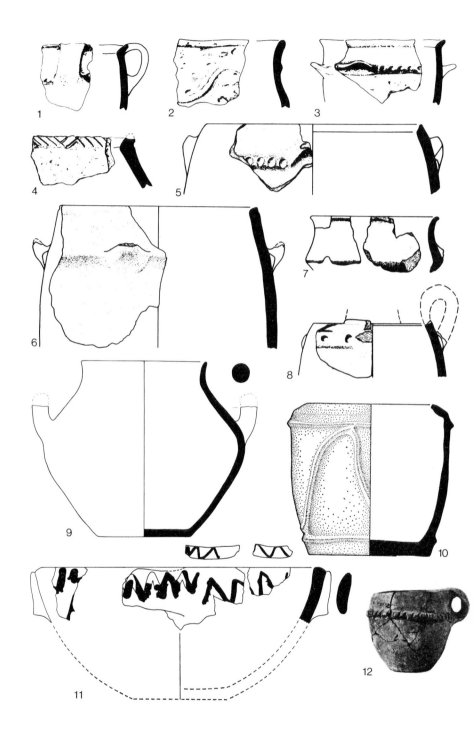

1 2 3

4 5

6 7

8

9 10

11 12

from earlier prehistoric levels, enough good modern excavations have taken place for it to be clear by now that this ware does not occur in the background in earlier Mycenaean phases. Rutter is sure of this for Korakou, and Catling for the Menelaion.[8]

The precise stratigraphic context and associations of barbarian ware are published for only a few sites. With a few rather dubious exceptions, accompanying Mycenaean pottery is of LH IIIC date (where adequate study has taken place). At Tiryns, the 1978–1979 excavations found vessels of this ware in levels attributed to transitional LH IIIB2 to C and pure LH IIIB2,[9] but I am grateful to Professor J. Rutter for the observation that the published "LH IIIB2" at Tiryns is later than LH IIIB2 as classically defined at Mycenae, relating more closely to earliest LH IIIC as in the Iria house or Athens Acropolis North Slope Stairway houses. Some possible sherds seem also to have been present earlier than IIIC at Mycenae,[10] but generally their appearance is placed following the LH IIIB2 destructions—as very clearly at the Menelaion. In all cases but one, the barbarian ware is found along with ordinary Mycenaean wares, but at Aigeira the excavators reported this "non-Mycenaean" material below the earliest Mycenaean level (early IIIC) in depressions in the rock, unaccompanied by Mycenaean material.[11] The ware seems to continue in use throughout the LH IIIC period—it is not, as was formerly thought, restricted to the earliest part of that period.[12]

It is not yet known whether the clays used for making the "barbarian ware" were local or not, though this should be readily ascertainable. Catling has observed that at the Menelaion

> a majority of the 'Barbarian' ware shows in the composition of its clay an aggregate of features . . . all of which can be matched at the Menelaion. . . . This is seen particularly clearly in the choice of additives as temper, notably crushed schist and quartz, which are standard in the coarse domestic pottery found on the site throughout its history.[13]

Rutter has argued the same for Korakou. One might go further and say that importation over anything other than the smallest distances seems most unlikely and would run counter to all we know of pottery manufacture and distribution mechanisms, especially as this pottery could have had no conceivable interest as pottery to potential importers. Wardle's published opinion is similar.[14] On the other hand, analytical evidence does now document that cooking vessels could be exported as well as fine wares.[14a]

So far we have established, then, that the "barbarian" ware was locally made and generally occurs in early LH IIIC levels along with Mycenaean

FIG. 52 ☐ "Barbarian ware" from various sites in Greece. (1–4) Sparta, Menelaion; (5–8) Tiryns, Unterburg; (9–11) Korakou; (12) Lefkandi. (After Catling, 1981; Kilian, 1981; Rutter, 1975; Popham and Sackett, 1968.)

wares. We now turn to much the most difficult and controversial aspect of the whole business, namely the area where its closest analogies are to be found. A number of general points may be made here. In the first place, it would be surprising if pottery of such crudity could be tied down very closely as far as parallels and analogies are concerned. The forms are simple, the fabric commonly found in later prehistory (even if not in Mycenaean Greece), the surface treatment and ornament widespread in time and place. Whereas a vessel of characteristic Mycenaean style is highly distinctive and can often be recognized from very small sherds, the only remarkable thing about the "barbarian ware" is its findspots. "Parallel-chasing" is a popular sport, and in the world of central and south-east European archaeology is carried out *de rigueur*. It was predictable, however, that it would lead to a plethora of suggested analogies, without conclusive proof being available for any one interpretation.

The second preliminary point concerns the habit of Aegean archaeologists of deriving everything inexplicable by traditional archaeological models from outside the Aegean, preferably from an area whose archaeology is poorly known, at any rate to them. Renfrew made the same point in his discussion of the rise of Aegean palace civilizations, for which external stimuli have traditionally been assumed. In the present case, the natural tendency has been to look not to the south or east (where material culture around 1200 B.C. is not known to show comparanda to the pottery in question)[15] but to the north and west, where the chronological framework is sufficiently hazy, the general level of pottery production sufficiently poor, and the availability of well-published corpora of material sufficiently low, for parallels to be safely drawn in the knowledge that detailed rebuttal is, at present, impossible. This is not to deny, however, that valuable comparative work has been done by those scholars who have dared to commit themselves on the issue.[16]

The surveys by Rutter and by Deger-Jalkotzy have examined parallels over a wide area before settling for their favoured points of origin. Kilian, on the other hand, whose knowledge at first hand of material in Italy and the Balkans is extensive, has preferred to point directly to one area as the likely source. Other scholars have pointed to analogies in particular areas for individual vessels.[17] In broad terms the scene encompasses Italy, north-west Greece and Albania, Jugoslavia and the Balkans generally, Thrace and Thasos, the Troad, and Romania; hardly surprising that plenty of parallels present themselves.

The task of pin-pointing the origins of the "barbarian ware" is actually an impossible one, for two reasons. First, too little of it is adequately recorded and published in Greece. In particular, the Mycenae material along with its precise stratigraphic position and associations remains unpublished. Secondly, in few of the areas mentioned above is there an adequate corpus of published material from which to draw parallels. Pottery parallels are in any case notoriously unreliable: potters have demonstrably created identical forms in quite unrelated areas of time and space, for their art is one that is conditioned by considerations of function, of materials, and by the basis of mental preconceptions about the final appearance of a pot that each potter had. Pottery parallels must be absolutely specific to be at all reliable; but in the last resort only constituent analysis of the clay can unequivocally tie down the place of origin of particular vases. In the present case, where not importation but immigration is claimed, no such help from the natural sciences can come to our aid.

Italy

A number of pieces from Lefkandi find their closest parallels in Italy. The cordoned one-handled cup[18] cannot be precisely tied down for context (Italian examples cover a span of time over Late Bronze and Early Iron Ages, but Proto-villanovan pieces are perhaps closest);[19] the carinated cups with high handle have close parallels on Late Bronze Age sites in southern Italy.[20] Rutter has mentioned parallels to Korakou material of his group I at Porto Perone/Saturo (Leporano), and Deger-Jalkotzy has discussed their wider context, stressing however that the features which best parallel the Greek pieces are themselves a new element in the period in question (Late Apennine and Subapennine of R. Peroni). It is also worth mentioning the curious cylindrical knob handle from Pylos which has been seen, possibly with some justification, as Italian-inspired.[20a]

The crucial weakness, to my mind, of any direct derivation of the Greek "barbarian ware" from Italy is the selective nature of the items represented. A full picture of southern Italian material culture around 1200 B.C., as far as it is known, may be seen at Leporano, Torre Castelluccia, and the Lipari acropolis, and is no doubt represented among the Scoglio del Tonno material. Although parallels in shape and decoration for the Greek pots are present, the absence in Greece of the most characteristic Italian forms is much more striking: the elaborate handles, biconical vases, low hemispherical cups, incised decoration, and so on. Of the Italian specialized forms only the portable hearth, represented by a few scrappy fragments at Tiryns, appears. I find it hard to believe that if the makers of "barbarian ware" were Italians they should not have made use of their most characteristic hallmark, the handle, and this objection applies even if the odd example should turn up in Greece.[21]

Troy

Good parallels for the Korakou material were observed by Rutter in the Coarse Ware of Troy VIIb, but the Troy VIIb assemblage is scrappy and few shapes are reconstructable. The apparent absence of the various forms of one- and two-handled cup which occur at Troy and seem very Bulgarian in appearance[22] may be the result of inadequate sampling, for there are many points of coincidence. The precise form of the Lefkandi cup is not paralleled at Troy, nor are the finer hand-made wares of that site.

Thrace, Bulgaria and Romania

Much play has been made of a group of vessels found on Thasos, mostly in tombs.[23] Unfortunately, too little of this material is published for any reasoned approach to the problem to bear fruit. Many individual features such as finger-impressed cordons or groovings below the rim are found on this pottery, but the general range of shapes and decorative techniques, as shown in the rather limited collection of whole or restorable vases, is not found in central and southern Greece, being essentially of north Aegean affinity.

Of Late Bronze Age Bulgaria little was known until recently. For Hänsel[24] the years around 1200 B.C. are filled by material of the "Čerkovna" group, the pottery of which includes globular shapes, notably jugs and bowls with high rounded handles; decoration, where present, is incised or impressed. This material is in fact part of a wider grouping, including groups usually named (north of the Danube) Tei, Gîrla Mare and Verbicioara (by Hänsel "Govora"), extending from central Bulgaria to the Carpathians, and having clear relatives in Greek Macedonia.[25] This complex has little or nothing in common with the "barbarian ware". It is perhaps all the more surprising, then, that claims have been made for regarding cultural groups north of these, in the Dobrogea and south-east Muntenia (Coslogeni) and even Moldavia (Noua, Sabatinivka), as being ancestral to the wares found in LH IIIC Greece.[26]

Rutter, who first put forward this suggestion, bases his hypothesis on similarities in the material and on the chronological priority of the northern groups. Specifically, he mentions the deep jar shape, horseshoe lug handles, applied cordons sometimes decorated with finger impressions or oblique slashes, and one or two other forms which appear in the Coslogeni or Noua repertoire. He also makes several references to material from Babadag (in the Dobrogea) as parallels for his Groups II, IV and "Miscellaneous".

While it is quite true that the deep jars, finger-impressed cordons, and lug handles are similar between the two areas, it must be stressed that these are all widespread and more or less unspecific features which recur time and again in the repertoire of the prehistoric potter. The original article defining the Coslogeni group illustrated rather little material, much of it fragmentary;[27] more has now been published,[28] and it is clear that the range of shapes and techniques is much wider than was at first apparent. The features supposedly introduced into Greece are only a few of a much wider range, from which it is reasonable to ask why some of the other really characteristic ones did not come as well; kantharos and jug shapes, or rounded and knob handles for instance. It is also clear from the published accounts, and from my personal inspection, that two separate fabrics occur: a coarse one with coarse temper and porous surface, usually grey; and a fine one with polished surface, in a brick or maroon colour. The shapes which are alleged to have been introduced to Greece are mostly the storage jars, which are in the coarse, unpolished, fabric: yet in Greece they are burnished.

Chronologically the position is far from being as clear as Rutter suggests. The Coslogeni material compares, though not particularly closely, with the Zimnicea-Plovdiv (Čerkovna), Tei and Monteoru groups, and is in a general sense attributable to the local "Late Bronze Age". The process of deriving absolute dates for these groups is extremely tortuous, and they were in any case long-lived. There are no radiocarbon dates. Little is known of what precedes Coslogeni, and what succeeds it is material of the Babadag group, which is usually put parallel with Troy VIIb2. Thus while Coslogeni material does in all probability span the time around 1200 B.C., there is no firm dating evidence and certainly no indication that its forms were in existence substantially earlier than that.

Macedonia

Rutter stated, and it remains true with the publication of more Macedonian material, that no connection with Macedonian Late Bronze Age material is discernible.

North-western Greece and Albania

Rutter pointed to a number of parallels between the Korakou sherds and material from these areas, notably the horseshoe lug, plastic decoration with cordons, and deep jar shapes. Deger-Jalkotzy further drew attention to the pottery from Gajtan and the Mati valley in Albania decorated with channels, plastic bands and knobs.[29] But the most detailed account advocating a connection between the "barbarian ware" and the north-west has been that of Kilian,[30] who parallels the cordons, knobs, ledges and barbotine bosses in the pottery of Metaxata and Mavrata on Kephallenia, and Dodona, Kalbaki, Elaphotopos, Astakos and Polis in Epirus, as well as in the material of certain southern Italian sites.

It is certainly true that Epirote sites have produced pottery decorated in these techniques, but again the problem lies not so much in what is similar as in what is not included from the Epirote repertoire (which is in any case very poorly known).[31] In particular the lack of one-handled cups and specialized handle forms in the "barbarian ware" seems a somewhat strange omission which, however, a larger sample may yet rectify.

Discussion

Acceptable parallels for the various features of "barbarian ware" can be cited from several areas of southern and south-eastern Europe, but they are without exception unspecific and of such widely occurring forms that little or no significance can be attached to the fact. On the other hand, all authorities agree that the ware is a novelty when it occurs in Greece; it is not part of the repertoire of coarse and cooking wares that occur in all Bronze Age periods. Equally it would seem incredible that pottery of this crudity could have been an object of trade, and several indications bear out the view that the manufacture was local.

If this is so, the question must be answered, why and by whom was a distinctively "non-Mycenaean" ware produced at this particular period? In particular, we must address ourselves to the hypothesis, several times advanced, that an intrusive population group was responsible for its manufacture. Pottery production in the Mycenaean world was clearly a matter for specialists and was therefore presumably organized along group specialization lines. Ethnographically, pottery as fine as this is almost always produced by specialists; as we saw in Chapter 2, the distribution and use of pottery may or may not be distinctive of other human characteristics, e.g. race, language, class or occupation.

Mycenaean pottery production was of a regularized nature in both technological and stylistic terms. From both site evidence (e.g. the Berbati kiln) and theoretical considerations, the conditions of manufacture seem clear: the range of wares from very fine to very coarse implies differences in clay preparation and building techniques, as well as in the skill of the potters involved. The fine wares must have required clay that had been extensively treated prior to its arrival in the potter's workshop, involving settling in tanks over a considerable period of time. Even some of the cooking wares had standardized tempers which imply the repeated use of long-established formulae at each stage of the operation. Production of these wares must have been by specialists, or at the very least by one specialist with the help of part-timers. On the other hand very large coil-built heavily-gritted storage vessels may have involved an element of home production: certainly some storage vessels are so large that they must have been built actually in the room they occupied. But the great majority of pottery on Greek Late Bronze Age sites emanated not from the home but from workshops, whose workers probably did little else than make pots, both "mass-produced" and "custom-built". In such a situation a highly formulaic mode of production would be the norm, while not excluding a degree of experimentation and divergence on the part of individuals, either to satisfy particular functional requirements or simply for its own sake.

In this framework the appearance of a quite distinct semi-standardized element of material culture like the "barbarian ware" may be seen as a response to pressures in the pottery supply system. It is hard to imagine, though it remains conceivable, that the "barbarian ware" would actually be preferred to standard Mycenaean ceramics if the latter were available, unless the former was intended for some specific purpose which could not be served by the normal range. Jan Bouzek has suggested that it could have been intended for the preparation and consumption of particular forms of food and drink; this may be a possible explanation, but the chronological problem, i.e. the sudden appearance of the pottery, is not thereby resolved. Rutter also points out[32] that the range of "barbarian ware" is considerable: not just the coarsest vessels but some finer pastes, small shapes, even painted ware, so that its function cannot be attributed to *one* special purpose.

The fact that the ware appears quite separate from Mycenaean pottery has led to the supposition that this was not the product of an indigenous group in the population unable to obtain standard Mycenaean wares, especially as the latter continue to be available in much the same forms as hitherto. If this were the case, it is argued, one might expect imitation of Mycenaean forms, crudely executed copies of particular originals. In fact the latest findings from Tiryns have produced this feature, even if it is at present rare;[33] but even if they had not it seems to me wrong to imagine that non-specialist potters (at any rate non-specialists in producing Mycenaean pottery), using coil-building techniques and only moderately prepared clays, would even attempt to imitate the fine table wares of the Mycenaean repertoire, which were made from well-prepared clays, thrown on the wheel, and fired to a high temperature in a quite sophisticated purpose-built kiln. Against this must be set the strange fact that the pottery in question has many elements that recur on several sites, and that the only analogies to it lie outside the main Mycenaean area.

In any case, how widespread was access to fine Mycenaean pottery? One tends to believe, on the basis of the frequency with which the pottery turns up on most sites, that it was commonplace, and access was free to all. More than 60 intramural pit-graves have been found in the Unterburg at Tiryns, however, from various phases of LH IIIC, without grave-goods (datable only by context).[34] Comparable graves have occurred on a number of other sites.

Indeed, less and less pottery was deposited with the dead in LH IIIB, which can be interpreted either in cultural or in socio-economic terms. It seems to me no less plausible to assert that access to fine burial pottery was differential than it is to say that some people did not feel the need to put pots with the dead. In fact uniform access seems to me to be most *unlikely* in a complex society such as that of the Mycenaeans.

Interpretations at this stage must necessarily be provisional, but certain crucial points stand out. Whatever the precise mechanism by which the mixture of wares in LH IIIC settlements came about, it does show a number of remarkable similarities to comparable wares in widely separated areas such as Italy, north-western Greece, and Troy. On the other hand, the supposition of population movements, and the presence of "northern [or any other] invaders" in LH IIIC Greece on the evidence of this pottery seems an unlikely explanation of the available facts, given the ambiguity of the evidence for a close correlation between pot styles and ethnic groups. Even if examples can be quoted where close correlations are observed, difficult questions remain. Why is barbarian ware present in such small quantities of the total ceramic assemblages? Why is it mainly restricted to the coarser end of the range? If it genuinely does represent an intrusive population, why are the better products not also represented? To my mind, this last objection weighs heavily against the supposition of any direct movement of potters from Italy, at any rate. At present we know little of how or why particular fashions in material culture are adopted by particular human groupings. Similarities in metal objects must relate closely to the activities of individual smiths, to the conceptions of particular artefacts that they held and to the technological means at their disposal, both factors conditioned by the breadth of their experience. Potting, however, is a more basic skill which can none the less produce widespread homogeneity of style and form over large areas, even where the mode of production is domestic, as is surely the case for the "barbarian ware". The means by which such homogeneity occurs, whether in "unified" populations or not, are unknown in detail but seem likely to relate in equal proportions to function, technology and conceptualization.

The problems of interpreting "barbarian ware" are thus currently insoluble.[35] With the discovery, recognition and publication of more groups of material it may become possible to answer questions such as: Was "barbarian ware" a unitary phenomenon all over Greece? How closely does it relate to comparable products in Italy, north-western Greece and elsewhere? What is its true time-range? Is it invariably made of local clays, or can importation be demonstrated? Answers to these questions can reasonably be expected. More problematical remains their interpretation, whether solutions should be sought in intrusive populations, in special purpose vessels, in the inability of the Mycenaean pottery industry to supply all sectors of society, or in differential access to standard ceramic forms.

By far the strongest case for a connection with alien ceramic traditions can be made for Italy and north-western Greece. Pottery production is hardly analogous to metalworking, and the products of each process tend to receive altogether different treatment; yet it is necessary to point out that the twelfth century was also the time when the metal industries of Greece and Italy shared many common features. If this is to be explained in terms of regular interchange between populations on either side of the Adriatic (as seems certain for smiths and smithing products), it may be that by some as yet ill-understood process certain elements of domestic material culture were also transmitted. It must be a prime task to identify possible means by which such transmission can take place.

Notes

1. Karo (1930a, pp. 160ff., 198, Taf. 95, 927–928 and Abb. 79, 930); Hachmann (1957a, pp. 166ff., 216 no. 592, Taf. 68, 1); first studied by H. Schmidt, *Prähistorische Z.* **4**, 1912, 35.

1a. H.-G. Hüttel, *JbRGZM* **27**, 1980, 159–165. Its affinities are unclear.

2. A. Hochstetter, *Germania* **59**, 1981, 239–259.

3. Ibid., pp. 255–256.

4. The discussion in this section owes much to the friendly exchange of views with Drs J. Rutter, S. Sherratt, H. W. Catling, K. Kilian and J. Bouzek.

5. Rutter (1975); cf. *AJA* **81**, 1977, 111–112 and in E. N. Davis (ed.), *Symposium on the Dark Ages in Greece*, 1977 (New York, Arch. Inst. of America), pp. 1–20, esp. pp. 5–6; E. French, *Arch. Anzeiger* 1969, 136.

6. Lefkandi: Popham and Sackett (1968, p. 18, fig. 34); M. Popham and E. Milburn, *BSA* **66**, 1971, 338, fig. 3, 6–7. Aigeira: Deger-Jalkotzy (1977). Tiryns: Kilian (1978, p. 316, Abb. 1, 1–2); *Arch. Anzeiger* 1979, 406, Abb. 31, 3–6; *Arch. Anzeiger* 1981, 165ff., Abb. 19–21; *Arch. Anzeiger* 1982, 399, Abb. 7; R. Avila, *Tiryns IX*, 1980 (Mainz, Zabern), p. 384, Taf. 25. Menelaion: H. W. and E. A. Catling, *BSA* **76**, 1981, 71–82. Kalapodhi: Schachermeyr (1980, pp. 70, 86); R. Felsch, *Arch. Anzeiger* 1980, 46–47. Teichos Dymaeon: Deger-Jalkotzy (1977, p. 38 with refs). Delphi: Rutter (1975, p. 29). Perati: Iakovidis (1970, **I**, p. 157, no. 35 pl. 45c). Athens: Rutter (1975, p. 29, fig. 16). Iria: H. Döhl, *Tiryns VI*, 1973 (Mainz, Zabern), pp. 186–189.

7. J. Tsedakis and A. Kanta, *Kastelli Chanion*, 1966 (Rome, Edizioni dell'Ateneo), pl. 1, 3; Schachermeyr (1980, pp. 86–87).

8. J. Rutter, *AJA* **80**, 1976, 187; Catling, *loc. cit.*, p. 74.

9. Kilian (1981, p. 170, Abb. 40, 2).

10. K. A. Wardle, *BSA* **68**, 1973, 323, Abb. 15 no. 111; not certainly Barbarian ware.

11. Deger-Jalkotzy (1977, pp. 10ff.).

12. J. Rutter, *Hesperia* **48**, 1979, 348ff., 391, published sherds of a handmade and burnished class of cooking ware from late LH IIIC levels at Corinth, but remarked that it "evidently has nothing to do with the broad range of hand-made and burnished wares

which occur in early LH IIIC contexts". S. Sherratt, *The Pottery of LH IIIC and its Significance* (Oxford, Ph.D. thesis, 1981), pp. 589ff., uses the evidence from Mycenae, Citadel House, and elsewhere to suggest that the barbarian ware did, in fact, continue through the period, albeit in very small quantities.

13. Catling, *loc. cit.*, p. 74; Rutter (1975, pp. 29f.).

14. Wardle (1977, pp. 188–189).

14a. For example, J. A. Riley, *BSA* **76**, 1981, 335–339.

15. S. Hood has discussed the hand-made wares of Kaloriziki, Bamboula and Idalion in *Eastern Mediterranean*, 1973, 45ff.

16. Principally S. Deger-Jalkotzy, J. Rutter and K. Kilian. J. Bouzek has also kindly communicated to me his (so far unpublished) views. An earlier attempt to tie down the origins of "non-Mycenaean" ware in Greece was by S. Hood in *Europa: Festschrift für Ernst Grumach*, 1967 (Berlin, de Gruyter), pp. 12–31.

17. So Popham and Sackett (1968); Hood, *loc. cit.*

18. Popham and Sackett (1968, p. 18, fig. 34).

19. Cf., e.g. Grottaferrata, *Not. Scavi* 1901, 180, fig. 87. This cemetery covers the Protovillanovan and early Villanovan phases.

20. M. Popham and E. Milburn, *BSA* **66**, 1971, 338–340, fig. 3, 6–7; many examples in Italy, e.g. Coppa Nevigata and Termitito: Magna Graecia (1982, tav. VI, 1, 6, tav. XXVII, 1).

20a. C. W. Blegen *et al.*, *The Palace of Nestor at Pylos*, **I**, 1966, 362 shape 16, figs. 355–356, nos. 664–665; apparently imitating handles on bronze vessels, e.g. Matthäus (1980a, nos. 166–185).

21. K. Kilian and M. Popham inform me that a couple of possible examples are known. H. W. and E. A. Catling, *BSA* **76**, 1981, pl. 7, 29; cf. Magna Graecia (1982, tav. III, 2). Horned handles were apparently present at Teichos Dymaeon.

22. C. W. Blegen *et al.*, *Troy IV*, 1958 (Princeton, University Press), pl. 267 upper.

23. Ch. Koukouli-Chrysanthaki, *Arch. Eph.* 1970, Chronika 16–22, pls I–IB; *Arch. Delt.* **26**, 1971, Chronika 414–415, pls 409–410; *Arch. Delt.* **27**, 1972, Chronika, 520ff., fig. 3, pls 452, 455, 457–458; *Arch. Delt.* **28**, 1973, Chronika, 447ff., fig. 3, pls 400, 402; *Arch. Delt.* **29**, 1973–4, B'3, 780ff.

24. Hänsel (1976, pp. 76ff.).

25. Cf. Coles and Harding (1979, pp. 141ff.). For Macedonia, Heurtley (1939).

26. Rutter (1975).

27. V. Leahu, *Studii şi cercetări de istoria veche* **20**, 1969, 17–32; S. Morintz and N. Anghelescu, *Studii şi cercetări de istoria veche* **21**, 1970, 373–415.

28. Hänsel (1976, pp. 73ff., Taf. I; 8, 3–9; 31–33).

29. Deger-Jalkotzy (1977, p. 48 with refs).

30. Kilian (1978, pp. 312ff.).

31. Most systematically, and best illustrated, in Wardle (1977, pp. 181ff.).

32. Letter of 9.1.82.

33. Kilian (1981, p. 166, n. 62, p. 180, n. 93; and pers. comm. (from LH IIIB2 on)).

34. K. Kilian, *JbRGZM* **27**, 1980, 176f., Abb. 5 and pers. comm. (from LH IIIB1). This fact was first drawn to my attention by Professor J. Rutter.

35. A recent attempt: Sandars (1983, pp. 60ff.).

9

The Mycenaeans overseas

Hitherto we have been concerned with the evidence for Mycenaean overseas enterprise on the basis of individual classes of material and it will be evident that this evidence varies greatly between different areas and types of object. This chapter surveys each area in turn where Mycenaean export or influence has been claimed, from the Greek borders to the furthest corners of Europe. We begin, however, by considering the nature of Mycenaean overseas enterprise in the East Mediterranean, where the quantity of exported Mycenaean pottery is much greater than anything known even in Italy. Since there must be some relationship, however vague, between the exports in the east and those in the west, this preliminary step is a necessary preamble to our main theme. If the nature of the Mycenaean presence cannot be determined in the east, where the benefits of record-keeping and writing were present, there would seem to be little hope for a proper understanding of the situation when we turn to the west.

A crucial problem which must be mentioned at the start is that alluded to in Chapter 2, namely the use of painted Mycenaean wares to assess the diffusion of "Mycenaean culture". The pitfalls in such an approach need reiteration. Fine painted wares, some even made especially for export, can only serve as indicators of exchange activity and say nothing about the permanent presence of "Mycenaeans". Even when such pottery is locally made, as occurs in a number of outlying areas in LH IIIC, it is the presence of the relevant technology on the one hand, and the taste for such pottery on the other, that is being witnessed. Of more value is the presence or absence of the characteristic medium and coarse wares for cooking and storage, which are a standard part of the ceramic repertory in the "core area" of Mycenaean culture, representing the common domestic wares which were presumably to be found in every household. It can be argued that these wares, more than any other aspect of material culture, serve as a touchstone to indicate the ethnic or political status of their users. This view is certainly more acceptable than the use of painted wares alone, but still suffers from some of the problems of interpretation discussed above.

The problem of identifying the significance of Mycenaean pottery outside Greece is different in each area. In the Near East and usually in Italy, only fine wares were imported. In northern Greece, on the other hand, some parts, notably Thessaly, do seem to have had a tradition of using coarser wares as well. Such considerations will be important in our assessment of the status of Mycenaean pottery in each area.

The Mycenaeans in the east and south (Fig. 53)[1]

Mycenaean pottery has been found at numerous sites in Egypt and the Near East, and from the early days of Bronze Age research this fact has served as a lynch-pin of both chronological and politico-economic reconstructions. In general, the find-circumstances and dating are (within certain limits) well understood: their interpretation is more controversial. I shall not consider the eastern and southern connections in detail here, for several excellent surveys of the matter already exist and the subject lies somewhat removed from my main theme.

Comparison of published surveys (complete up to the early 1970s) indicates that Mycenaean pottery has been found on some 60 sites in Anatolia, 80 in the Levant, and 28 in Egypt (Fig. 53). Crucial to any understanding of the situation on the Asian mainland is, of course, a consideration of the situation in Cyprus, where huge quantities of Mycenaean pottery are known, especially from the later periods. The presence of what are assumed to have been Mycenaean towns on Cyprus, in close proximity to Anatolia and the Levant, makes the question of connections specifically with the Greek mainland difficult to resolve.

Most discussions of the significance of Mycenaean pottery in the Levant have proceeded on the basis that their presence is solely to be explained in terms of trade, not settlement. Actually, defined views on the nature of the contact are hard to find. The following points have been generally considered to be relevant. The range of shapes found in the east is very restricted, stirrup-jars being by far the most common form, with straight-sided pyxides, piriform jars and pilgrim flasks also occurring in some numbers.[2] The total quantity of Aegean material found in Egypt and the Levant seems substantial, but by comparison with what has been found in Cyprus is in fact relatively slight. Furthermore, Cypriot pottery frequently accompanies the Mycenaean, strongly suggesting that Cyprus acted as an intermediary in whatever type of contact was involved.

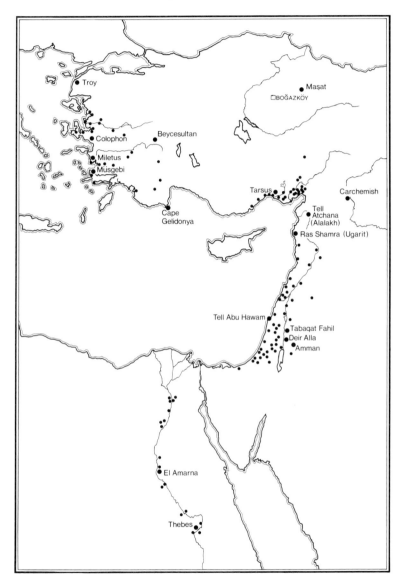

FIG. 53 ☐ Distribution of Mycenaean pottery in the Near East and Egypt (sites in Cyprus not mapped). (After Hankey, 1973.)

From these points it would appear that a restricted range of commodities, notably liquids (spices, perfumes, oils?), was being exported in the Mycenaean pots, and that their presence in Levantine sites, while numerically small, attests a regular economic presence in the East Mediterranean on the part of Mycenaean exporters. This "trade" has been seen as "radiating from a central source, Greece", and being directed primarily at Cyprus which had copper to trade in return. It has been argued that "Cypriote importers took the cream of the supply since it reached them first . . . and the Middle East in general got the left-overs."[3] Mycenaean pottery may thus have reached the Levant from Cyprus, and not directly from Greece: the frequency of Cypriot forms, both in the Mycenaean and the non-Mycenaean pottery, makes this an attractive hypothesis. How and why the Mycenaean pottery came to be in Cyprus in the first place is another matter. The most commonly accepted view is that until the end of LH IIIB it was imported, not manufactured on the spot,[4] whereas in LH IIIC actual Mycenaean settlement on Cyprus started. This contentious matter might be expected to be resolved by constituent analysis.[5]

The context of Mycenaean pottery in the Levant may be domestic, funerary, or—in rare instances—ritual. It is invariably in a tiny minority compared with local or Cypriot wares. At Tabaqat Fahil, for instance, east of the River Jordan, 11 rock-cut tombs contained over 3000 objects, among them 35–50 Mycenaean pots and much Cypriot Base-Ring II and White Slip II ware.[6] Fifty pots might seem a lot in an Italian context, but it is as nothing in a Palestinian one. It is much more difficult to assess the proportions of Mycenaean to local wares in sherd material on settlements. Only a few (e.g. Tell Atchana, Ras Shamra-Ugarit) have really substantial quantities, but even there they are vastly outnumbered by local and Cypriot wares. More usually only a few dozens of Mycenaean sherds turn up. Of particular interest are two "temples"—Amman and Deir Alla—in which Mycenaean vessels were found: at Deir Alla[7] the pots were in use at the time of the temple's destruction by fire following an earthquake. It would be wrong to read too much into this: the vessels were in a side-room, not in the temple cella, but presumably their contents were being used in the temple activities. The Amman site is remarkable more for its distance from the coast than for the quality or quantity of Mycenaean finds on it.[8]

The quantity of Mycenaean imports has been considered large enough on a few sites for the notion of a resident Mycenaean community to be tenable. This was Schaeffer's suggestion at Ras Shamra-Ugarit, for example, on the basis of the large quantities of Mycenaean pottery, found along with local and Cypriot wares, and especially of the figurines and ritual vessels found in tombs near the site—forms that are considered unlikely as trade objects in their own right, and obviously not traded for their contents.[9] Schaeffer further stressed the similarity between tomb form at Ugarit and the Aegean, and between certain cult installations (cups and channels, as at Dendra);[10] finally, he maintained that the physical type of the skeletons in some of the graves at Ugarit was of a non-Semitic, Mediterranean type. These views are today regarded with considerable scepticism.

At Tell Atchana (Alalakh), on the other hand, the excavator was definite that, in spite of the finding of "considerable" amounts of Mycenaean (and, of course, Cypriot) pottery,[11] "there was no colony of Mycenaean merchants such as at this time existed at Ugarit".[12] Actually, no figure is given for the number of Mycenaean sherds at Alalakh, but the clear indications are that they were in a tiny minority.

In Egypt, where far fewer find-spots of Mycenaean pottery are known than in the Levant, the nature of Aegean interests is perhaps more easily understood. It would be a strange claim indeed that this pottery represented Mycenaean settlement. Only at Tell el Amarna is the quantity great: perhaps 2000 sherds and six whole pots from the excavated areas, which are only a fraction of this huge site.[13] The contexts appear to be exclusively domestic, and 22 shapes have been identified, among them the globular flask in great profusion but also the stirrup-jar, small piriform jar, and pyxis or straight-sided alabastron. Closed shapes are thus more common but open ones of various types are also found (kraters, shallow one-handled cups, etc.). A point which distinguishes Tell el Amarna absolutely from the Levantine sites is the secondary position of Cypriot wares, which has been taken to indicate that Cypriots were not responsible in this instance for the presence of the Aegean pottery.[14] All in all, it seems clear that the Mycenaean pottery at El Amarna was in daily domestic use along with a lot of other, mainly local wares, and that it came to Egypt by some kind of exchange— "perhaps the result of an Egyptian mission to the Aegean, undertaken late in the reign of Amenophis III".[15]

Too little is known about the context and precise nature of most finds of Mycenaean pottery in Anatolia for any clear picture to be obtained.[16] At some sites on the Ionian coast, like Miletus and Müsgebi, Mycenaean pottery seems to have played a dominant role; Müsgebi is an Aegean-style cemetery comparable to those on adjacent islands. Equally, on other sites (like Troy) Mycenaean pottery was in a minority and the sites are regarded as "Anatolian". Beycesultan on the upper Menderes, one of the greatest tells of its age, has produced only a single Mycenaean sherd and some putative imitations, a picture borne out by the meagre finds from other inland Anatolian sites. Of these by far the most interesting is Maşat, north-east of Boğazköy in Amasya province, where Mycenaean sherds in some quantity were found in Hittite levels with hieroglyphic *bullae* (sealings).[17] The situation in Cilicia is also interesting, as the pottery from Tarsus and Kazanlı is apparently of local manufacture; almost all of it is LH IIIC in date, an interesting reflection on the situation in Cyprus.[18]

The Cape Gelidonya shipwreck lies in Turkish waters and may be recalled in passing here, though its importance has more to do with its cargo, its origin and its destination, than with its having foundered where it did. The south coast of Anatolia is virtually devoid of finds of Mycenaean pottery, but then prehistoric sites are hardly known there either. On the other hand a few finds in Lycia show that mechanisms did exist for the inhabitants of the interior to obtain exotic goods.

Composition analysis, by emission spectrography or neutron activation, clearly has an important role to play in identifying the sources of the Mycenaean pottery of the Levant, as elsewhere. Controversy has raged over the source of the pictorial kraters, a number of which have been found in the Levant (e.g. Tell Dan, Ras Shamra) and which might on archaeological grounds be attributed to Cyprus where they occur most frequently; but spectrographic analysis seems to demonstrate a mainland Greek origin.[19] More helpful are the results of neutron activation analysis on Greek, Levantine and Cypriot fabrics,[20] which have demonstrated that Mycenaean pottery in the Levant may be of Mainland, Cretan, Cypriot or local provenance. A majority of sampled sherds at Tell Abu Hawam, for instance, showed a "typical Argolid composition"; three match a Cretan grouping. At Kouklia and Tell Ashdod most of the LH IIIC 1 sherds were clearly of local clays.[21] On the other hand, analyses of sherds from Tell el Amarna and Tell Atchana showed, as expected, the characteristic east Peloponnesian composition type.[22]

The overall pattern of Mycenaean exportation of ceramics to the Levant is, because of somewhat haphazard find circumstances and details, not clear or consistent. If a fall-off with distance ("monotonic decrement") is to be expected, it is not always found: only Ras Shamra of the coastal cities is really prolific in Mycenaean pottery, while sites like Amman and Tabaqat Fahil, 100 km or more inland, were able to receive considerable quantities. The situation in northern Syria might be taken to exemplify the distance-decay model: large amounts of imported Aegean and Cypriot pottery at Ras Shamra, a good quantity at Tell Atchana, a few sherds at Khan Sheikhoun, Tell Mardikh and—most distant of all—Carchemish on the Euphrates. Finds from other parts of Mesopotamia have yet to be made. In the south, on the other hand, larger distances were encompassed: sherds have been reported from Saudi Arabia,[23] and predictably in the Nile Valley a certain amount of Mycenaean pottery reached Thebes, but Minoan wares penetrated much further south: the 131st Necropolis (160 km south of Aswan, where Kamares Ware is recorded), and Sesebi in Nubia, between the Second and Third Cataracts, over 1500 km from the mouth of the Nile.

Mee has suggested, to account for the presence of Mycenaean pottery in Troy, that seasonal fishing for mackerel and tunny could have brought the Mycenaean fishing fleet to the area, to encamp in the Troad for catching and drying the fish in the summer months.[24] The Bosphorus and Hellespont were famous for this purpose in antiquity, and tunny bones appear in all levels at Troy. It would be surprising if the seasonal movements of fish were not so exploited; whether elements of material culture, such as the presence in some quantity of foreign, i.e. Mycenaean, pottery, are thus explicable is another matter, though the existence of locally imitated Mycenaean is worthy of record. Elsewhere in Asia Minor no one theory is universally applicable, according to present evidence. In general the amount of Mycenaean pottery, especially of the earlier period, is not great. At Miletus, the lower levels have both local and imported Minoan, Minoan-style houses, and frescoed walls— but also monochrome pottery of local tradition. Miletus has usually been considered an actual Minoan settlement. In later levels considerable quantities of Mycenaean occur with some local wares, but too little is yet published for the situation to be at all clear; certainly in the third, latest phase the Mycenaean pottery is in the local micaceous fabric, while it is a Hittite vase that is clearly an import,[25] and Anatolian wares are not reported. The presence of chamber tombs of Mycenaean type is also suggestive. The same is clearly true of the cemetery at Müsgebi, and may hold for other sites on the Ionian coast.

In summary, the presence of Mycenaean pottery in Anatolia, Egypt and the Levant does not in general support the idea of settlement by Mycenaeans except on the Ionian coast. The extent to which a pottery style is uniquely representative of a given ethnic element is in any case highly dubious (cf. Chapter 2). Most arguments for the presence of Mycenaean in the Levant hinge on the quantity and range of shapes of the pottery, as at Ugarit. But even there other explanations can be advanced for the presence of the wares, particularly in view of their rather specialized nature. The absence of the characteristic cooking and storage vessels of Mycenaean type further speaks against any presence of "ethnic Mycenaeans". The one-way nature of the pottery export, together with the evidence for export-oriented production,[26] certainly implies that the pots themselves may have been valued, as well as whatever they may have contained. They fit most easily into a regular and widespread framework of reciprocal exchange networks in which Cyprus plays a crucial role.[26a]

The northern frontier of the Mycenaean world

The problem to be faced in central and northern Greece is that Bronze Age settlement was more or less continuous across it. Whereas in the Near East we have been concerned to decide whether or not "colonies" were involved, in Greece the problem is to decide at what point the Mycenaean "home area" stopped and the "non-Mycenaean" area started, in other words where the border between the two lay. Consideration of how borders may be defined archaeologically, and to what, if anything, they correspond in terms of human groupings, have been major preoccupations of archaeological theoreticians in recent years, and a number of possible methods have been suggested.[27] Rather than embark on a discussion of the relative merits of each of these, I will indicate in the examination of the specific material in hand which methods seem to offer the most useful complement to the pragmatic approach adopted here.

Criteria for defining the northern Mycenaean border have hitherto been explicitly considered only by Feuer,[28] who adopts the terms "core area" (centred on the Argolid), "border zone" ("that area of sedentary sociocultural system extending from the limits of its core area to the limits of its expansion"), and "frontier zone" (the zone immediately beyond the border zone, by definition beyond the "limits of its expansion" and hence lacking in the characteristic material culture of the core area). These terms are easy enough to create theoretically, but much harder to apply systematically, and though Feuer illustrates various possible ways of defining a Mycenaean boundary he concludes that a combination of natural features (e.g. topography) and settlement density (that is, those settlements with Mycenaean material) provides the best indicator—a result which differs little, if at all, from subjective viewpoints on the matter adopted previously. The crucial question is to decide what constitutes a "Mycenaean settlement", and what a "local" settlement with Mycenaean elements. As the discussion in Chapter 2 attempted to show, such questions are inappropriately framed in that material culture does not bear a one-to-one relationship with ethnic or linguistic groups, and in some situations none at all. Yet it is material culture that archaeologists have to work with, and it would be foolish to ignore the fact that most of central and southern Greece and the islands were united in the Late Bronze Age by very many material culture features, notably by the range of ceramics we call Mycenaean pottery. To this extent, therefore, the fall-off in use of Mycenaean pottery with distance from the "core area" may be presumed to reflect a human situation in which material culture preferences are as valid an object of study as any other aspect. In other words, a border in the distribution of Mycenaean pottery is as much a border as any other kind, even if it tells us little about its workers and users.

At least two different borders are, therefore, in question. One, perhaps the easier to define, is the absolute limit in the distribution of the artefact type. Even here, though, problems arise because of the scattered nature of distributions at the limits, and (especially with pottery) because of local production and imitation as well as importation. The other border is that of regular, widespread use of the type in question. In theory, such use might be reflected in quantifiable values for the occurrence of one type as against all other types of similar function, e.g. the percentage of Mycenaean pottery in a ceramic assemblage. In practice this is extremely hard to apply, especially where the majority of sites are only known from surface indications, and in the end subjective impressions have to play a part. My own position on the significance of Mycenaean pottery in the northern border area is a "minimalist" one: it will be clear from this and discussions in previous chapters that I attribute much less importance to the presence of Mycenaean pottery as an indicator of Mycenaean culture than do most observers. In several areas of northern Greece the quantity of Mycenaean pottery is no greater than it is at Troy, and often it is less; all we know about Troy from myth, history and legend suggests that whatever else it was, it was not Greek! The theoretical prediction that the use of particular objects of material culture will decline in proportion to the distance from the "core area" of their use certainly seems to hold good for Mycenaean pottery; it also means that the role of that pottery in the cultures of northern Greece can only be assessed in terms of fine, one might almost say luxury, tableware which had little or nothing to do with ethnic affinity.

In the light of these remarks, our discussion of the northern frontier of the Mycenaean world takes on rather a different complexion. Particularly in the absence of quantifiable estimates of the proportion of Mycenaean ceramics to the rest, we labour under considerable difficulties.[29] The publication of several important sites (Argissa, Assiros, Kastanas) will no doubt help in this respect, but I fear the time for a realistic assessment of the situation is a long way off. Only when excavation in Thessaly, Macedonia and Thrace has reached a comparable stage to that presently achieved in the Argolid and Messenia will the picture become noticeably clearer.

The fall-off pattern in the distribution of Mycenaean pottery may be observed in all provinces north and west of Boeotia, Locris and Phocis. In the early Mycenaean period, the fall-off begins correspondingly further south. The distribution of Mycenaean pottery covers most of Thessaly and large parts of Macedonia (Fig. 54), though there are puzzling gaps in the distribution (e.g. northern Thessaly, south-west Macedonia), whose explanation may be geographical. On the other hand, a recent article has suggested that the matt-painted ware of Late Bronze–Early Iron Age Macedonia is influenced by Mycenaean pottery-painting, and thus appears where Mycenaean wares do not.[30] In the north-west the distribution is much more sporadic, no doubt partly because of the uneven distribution of research, and the influence of topography. It is worth mentioning here, however, that it is in the north-west that Mycenaean ceramics actually penetrated furthest, turning up on several sites in Albania and, possibly, one in Bosnia. There is still no certain instance known to me of their presence in Bulgaria or Turkish Thrace.

In Thessaly, the quantity of Mycenaean pottery, both local and imported, suggests a regular usage, that is, it was fully integrated into local material culture. In Macedonia this might be true for the central area (Vardar-Axios valley), though there is little information yet on the relative proportions of Mycenaean to other fabrics. Furthermore, at least in some parts of Thessaly there is plain Mycenaean ware or "Helladic" ware deriving from the Middle Bronze Age material related to Middle Helladic; in Macedonia there is none

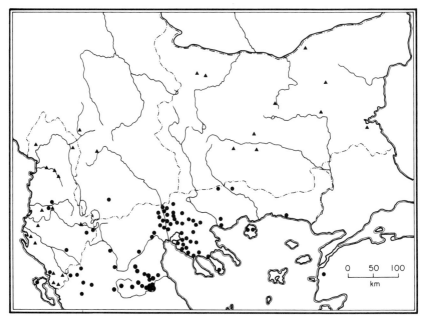

FIG. 54 ☐ Distribution of Mycenaean objects in the northern border area. ●, pottery; ▲, bronzes. (Pottery sites south of the R. Peneios and bronzes within Greece not mapped.) (After Kilian, 1976; French, 1967; Wardle, 1977 and others.)

(I owe this observation to Dr Oliver Dickinson). It has been known since Heurtley's work between the wars[31] that at tell sites like Vardino and Vardaroftsa Mycenaean pottery has a longish history covering LH IIIB and C. With the excavations at Assiros and Kastanas these observations can now be verified. At Assiros,[32] the earliest Mycenaean is attributed to late LH IIIA2 with local production beginning "during the latter part of the LH IIIB period" and continuing through LH IIIC. At Kastanas[33] the earliest is LH IIIB1 in levels 16 or 15, with local production also attributed to late LH IIIB and C; here a legacy of Mycenaean designs and forms continued well into Iron Age levels. The material from smaller investigations on other sites conforms with this chronological picture, and in the thirteenth to twelfth centuries the Mycenaean element in material culture was strong in central Macedonia.[34] Not so, however, in eastern Macedonia and Thrace, where very little Mycenaean material is known:[35] only from Thasos did even local Mycenaean imitations extend any way eastwards[36] with the exception of a single sherd from the cave of Maroneia south of Komotini.[37]

The situation in the north-west resembles that in the north, but there is no area of dense distribution at all. Aitolia-Acarnania, with Lefkas, has a handful of sites with Mycenaean pottery, of which only Thermon and Ay. Ilias are either early or important.[38] In Epirus and Kerkyra this situation is continued: only Dodona has any quantity of Mycenaean, all of it decorated wares, and the total number of sites with Mycenaean is a mere half-dozen.[39] On the other hand, the presence of a small tholos tomb at Parga, and the distribution of bronze swords and double-axes of Mycenaean type, indicates a sharing of Mycenaean material culture which pottery does not document. There is no material earlier than LH IIIA in Epirus, but the LH IIA Vapheio cup from Pazhok in Albania (below) suggests this may be coincidental.

Although one may not regard the modern Greek frontier as anything other than an arbitrary line drawn on a map, it is none the less striking how the distribution of Mycenaean pottery stops abruptly at it. While this may be due to political factors, such as the difficulty of conducting fieldwork close to the borders of Albania, Jugoslavia and Bulgaria, it is nevertheless surprising that Mycenaean wares did not penetrate further north. In the Vardar valley for instance, they occur up to the Greek frontier but barely beyond. On the other hand, quite a few Mycenaean bronzes have been found north of Greece, mainly swords but also knives, spearheads and double-axes (Fig. 54).

The following Mycenaean objects have been found in areas immediately north of Greece.

Albania

Pottery

Bajkaj[40]
Barç: stirrup-jar, skyphos and amphoriskos, LH IIIC, in tumulus burial.[41]
Elbasan area: ?LH IIIB-C sherds shown to participants in First Colloquium of Illyrian Studies, Tirana 1972.[42]
Gramsh: possible Mycenaean sherds with painted bands in Elbasan Museum, seen 1972.
Pazhok, tumulus 1: LH IIA Vapheio cup.[43]
Piskovë (Përmet), graves 88, 103: two imported Mycenaean vases, the only illustrated piece a LH IIIC oinochoe.[44]
Plaka, Cape Treporti: 2 LH III sherds picked up by Hammond.[45]
Tren cave: monochrome kylix stem and bowl handle, possibly Mycenaean.[46]

Bronzes[47]

Bruç (Mati valley): sword, type D.
Buthrotum: double axe.[48]
Gërmenj (Lushnjë): swords, types Ci, D.[49]

Kënetë (Kukës): knife (EIA context).[50]
Maliq, level IIIC: knives of north-west Greek type.
Mati valley: knives of north-west Greek type.
Nënshat (Shkodër): sword, type Di.
Pazhok (Devoll valley): spearhead, dagger.
Qafë e Marinzës (Fier): double-axe.
Qeparo (Vlorë): double-axe.
Rrethe Bazjë (Mati valley): sword, type Di.
Sarandë (Butrint): double axe.[51]
Vajzë (Vlorë), tumulus A, grave 12: sword, type A; knives of north-west Greek type; spearhead.
Vodhinë grave 16: dagger of Early–Middle Minoan type.
Xarë (Butrint): double-axe.

Other objects

Vajzë (Vlorë): beads of "glass-paste" from tumuli A and C may perhaps be Mycenaean, but there is no strong reason for supposing this to be the case for the gold leaf from tumulus B.[53]

Jugoslavia

Pottery

Beranci, Visoj (Bitola), grave 37: skyphos of Late Mycenaean character.[54]
Debelo Brdo (Sarajevo): two joining sherds of band-decorated closed vessel (? jug).[55]
Djevdjelija (Vardar valley): 10 sherds from the region.[55a]

Bronze

Iglarevo (Metohije): sword, type A (modified), knives.[56]
Tetovo (Skopje): sword, type Ci.[57]
?Serbia: knife of north-west Greek type.[58]

Bulgaria

Bronze[59]

Galatin (Vraca): sword, type Cii.
Dolno Levski (Pazardžik): spearhead, group D var. II.[60]
Peruštica (Plovdiv): spearhead, group D var. II.

River Vjača at Kričim (Plovdiv): spearhead, group H.
Krasnogradište (Gabrovo): spearhead, group D var. II.
Sokol (Sliven): spearhead (Mus. Plovdiv no. 3220).[61]
Lesura (Vraca): spearhead, group H.
Vardyn (T'rgovište): spearhead, group H.
Bylgarovo (Burgas): double-axe.
Semerdžievo (Ruse): double-axe.

Two other groups of Bulgarian bronzes may show the influence of Aegean traditions, though they are not themselves Mycenaean: the "horned" swords, and the little double-axe models.[62] Of the spearheads listed above it should be said that not all need be of Mycenaean manufacture, given the finding of spearhead moulds in Bulgaria; but so far these have no exact Bulgarian parallels and fit well into the Mycenaean sequence. The presumptive occurrence of these types in Macedonia suggests that this notion is reasonable.[63] Also of importance are the finds of ox-hide ingots (p. 49) off the Bulgarian coast, though whether or not these are of Aegean manufacture is naturally open to question. The finding of (apparently) three such ingots, along with stone anchors that may go back into the Bronze Age, naturally makes the "Bulgarian connection" especially interesting.[64]

The scarcity of Mycenaean pottery north of Greece, and the rapid fall-off of all kinds of Mycenaean material with increasing distance from the "core area" suggests that with few exceptions there was little desire or ability to participate in the material culture of southern Greece. The differential adoption of Mycenaean pottery in different areas may relate to topographical factors, for instance the impenetrable mountains of the Ossa-Olympos range in Pieria, and the presence of rolling corn-land in Thessaly and central Macedonia; but in southern Greece sites are often densely distributed with little exclusive access to subsistence resources, so this explanation cannot be the whole truth. The importance of the Vardar-Axios valley as a communication route to the interior must be stressed, though there is little sign that in the Bronze Age the route was actually used. On the other hand, the importance of first Pella and later of Thessaloniki shows that the area was a crucial one in historic times, the latter town becoming, and remaining, the most important city and port in the northern Aegean. In view of the landscape changes believed to have taken place since antiquity, it is even possible that the southern Axios sites were serving as direct recipients of sea-borne goods.[65] Given the existence of a sizeable hinterland, and of a chain of sites up the Axios to provide the possibilities for local and regional exchange, the situation in central Macedonia seems to be fairly represented by a picture of thirteenth to twelfth century expansion of shipping activity, with southern goods finding their way into the local exchange systems, and, in due course, being copied by local potters with the technical knowhow necessary for such production. The effects of exchange in less favoured regions were correspondingly smaller, though the mechanisms may have been similar. At all events, there can be little doubt that where imported Mycenaean wares appear in Macedonia, sea-borne trade brought them there.

The same may be true for the bronzes as well, some of which are rather earlier in date. On the other hand, swords and spears are precisely the sorts of finds which the movement of individuals could bring about. The relatively high number of weapons in the Greek border area could support such a view; equally, the desire of local warlords to keep up with the Agamemnons may also be invoked. Without contexts, or even with them, there is no way of knowing. The presence of local bronze workshops for particular objects is noteworthy: in Epirus, double axes and type F swords may have been a local speciality,[66] and in Bulgaria and Macedonia Kilindir-type axes were being produced.[67] These created dispersal areas for bronze types on both sides of the Greek border, but relate to local smithing traditions rather than international relations.

Feuer has suggested for Thessaly that Mycenaean material culture correlates with a particular form of economic regime, and that it will appear in strength only in areas where that regime can be successfully continued. Beyond that, increasing degrees of adaptation are necessary. Specifically for Thessaly, the percentage of arable land decreases rapidly as one leaves the plains, and the mountains that fringe them only offer potential for rough grazing. I have long felt that much the same correlation should account for the situation in Macedonia and perhaps to a lesser extent Epirus. The traveller on the road between Thessaloniki and Skopje, a distance of 240 km, passes rapidly from the eu-Mediterranean zone, characterized climatically by its hot, dry summers and wet winters, with Mediterranean red and brown soils, scrub-covered hills and fertile plains, to the humid continental zone with warm, moist summers and cold, dry winters, covered (in Macedonia) with mountain soils that are easily eroded and often very stony, and a vegetation that includes areas of grassland and deciduous forest. Present-day agricultural regimes are correspondingly different in the two areas, though cereals are main crops everywhere the terrain allows. But on the Aegean they are accompanied by olives and citrus fruit, and pastoral agriculture in the rough grazing areas, whereas north of Titov Veles mixed arable and livestock farming is possible. A critical factor in any "geographical" account would be the harshness of the winter, which climatic figures can bring out with dramatic effect.[68] The simple fact is that only the mountain-dwellers of Greece ever experience really cold weather, with temperatures below zero for substantial periods. It would hardly be surprising if economic and social adaptation to different conditions was sluggish or non-existent.

This brings us back, however, to the potential of pottery as a means of documenting the presence of "the Mycenaeans" in the various areas in which it is found. It in itself does not necessarily document the presence of the Mycenaean socio-economic formation such as we imagine to have been present in central and southern Greece. It is a reflection of exchange conditions and, when locally made, technological capacity, as well as the force of fashion. Mycenaean pottery in Macedonia no more attests the presence of "Mycenaeans" than it does in Egypt or the Levant. What then, can be used as an expression of "ethnicity" or religion? The latter element is the easier to deal with. Several authors have suggested that a useful means of defining a group boundary should be the distribution of non-utilitarian culture, particularly those elements that relate to belief systems or group-specific practices in dress. Using these criteria, the distribution of typically Mycenaean burials, of cult objects such as figurines, and of dress fasteners or attachments such as jewellery and buttons should be considered. The result of this is that Thessaly qualifies for inclusion in the Mycenaean world (tholos, chamber and built tombs, figurines, jewellery), but Macedonia does not: no "Mycenaean" burials, few items of material culture other than utilitarian ones. The situation in Epirus is unclear. Dodona may have been used as a religious focus in the Bronze Age as well as the Iron Age, but there is too little material to tell and nothing that specifically suggests it; the tholos tomb at Parga, on the other hand, the most remote example known, has usually been explained as "the tomb of a ruling family, either native and 'Mycenaeanised', or possibly immigrant".[69] If this tomb is to be interpreted as evidence of "Mycenaeans", its isolation suggests that no great implications for the "Mycenaeanising" of Epirus follow.

It remains to consider an aspect of the Macedonian Late Bronze Age situation which has consistently found a place in the literature, namely the fluted wares and twisted handles that Heurtley, following Childe, called "Lausitz". By this was apparently meant pottery of Urnfield type, as known from (among other places) the areas of eastern Germany, Poland and Czechoslovakia, where the "Lausitz culture" is centred.[70] These wares were found by Heurtley in a burnt destruction level at Vardaroftsa along with Mycenaean pottery attributed to the Granary Class, and many scholars have assumed that both here and at Troy, where the Knobbed Ware of Troy VII b2 follows—not directly—the destruction of Troy VII a, an arrival of new population elements—invaders—is the explanation.[71] These matters will become much better known shortly, when the excavations at Assiros and Kastanas are published, and only a few general remarks need to be provided here. Wardle has already indicated that Heurtley's stratigraphic and typological indications are ambiguous, and at both Assiros and Kastanas, the "Lausitz wares" (hereafter "Iron Age") postdate the Mycenaean levels, perhaps by a considerable margin.[72]

The more general point should be made, however, that the true significance of the appearance of these wares is far from clear. Ultimately they form part of a cultural grouping extending over the entire Lower Danubian-east Balkan province, the Trojan examples being outliers of this grouping.[73] Such fluted wares, though not all the other characteristics, also appear in Hungary in the Gáva and Vál groups, and these in turn relate to forms found in central Europe. In this sense a connection with the Lausitz culture is acceptable.[74] The tendency of similar forms to occur in widely separated areas at the same time is, however, well-known (the Urnfield culture as a whole is an extreme example of it) and there is no reason to suppose a specific connection between Macedonia and central Europe. Especially in view of the new dating evidence referred to above, with the implication of a considerable length of time between the main LH IIIC occupation of the tells and the adoption of the Iron Age wares, it would be rash to draw historical conclusions concerning the roles of the "Sea Peoples" and Urnfield cultures. Since, with a lowering of the dates, sites such as Vergina may be brought into the same time bracket, it is clear that a thorough analysis of the situation in Early Iron Age Macedonia is overdue.

The Central Mediterranean (Fig. 55)[75]

The first Mycenaean objects found in the West were the two vases found in a rock-cut tomb at Matrensa (Syracuse) in 1871. These were followed in 1880 by the two stirrup-jars from S. Cosimo, Oria (Brindisi), which emanated from a tomb discovered by chance and emptied without systematic recording.

The numerous excavations of Paolo Orsi in the Bronze Age cemeteries of Sicily turned up substantial numbers of Mycenaean vessels, while the excavations of Quagliati at Coppa Nevigata, Scoglio del Tonno and Porto Perone produced sherd material in Bronze Age layers. Orsi's excavations turned up by far the largest amount of Mycenaean material ever found in the west, and that in the best condition: between 1890 and 1920 he found Mycenaean pottery in all the more important Middle and Late Bronze Age cemeteries in which he excavated, half-a-dozen sites, and bronzes and beads plausibly to be connected with the Aegean in half-a-dozen more. The situation on Sicily has remained remarkably constant since that time: only another four sites with Aegean pottery have turned up. In Apulia a rather higher percentage of material has been recovered in the last 30 years; in all other parts of Italy the picture has been transformed completely by finds made during that period, and in some areas (e.g. Sardinia, northern Italy) the transformation has occurred only in the last few years. There is every likelihood that this trend will continue.

The nearest landfall in Italy for ships sailing from Greek shores is Apulia, and it is hardly surprising that a substantial number of sites—17 at the latest

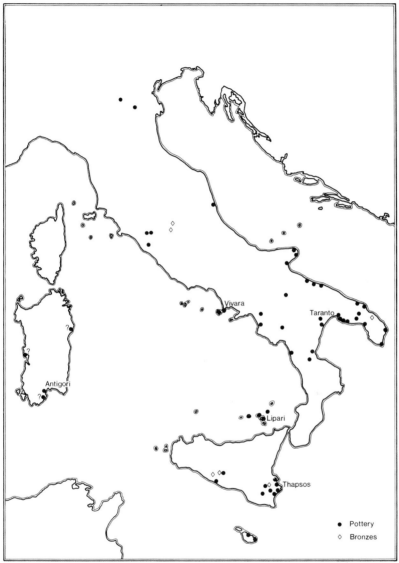

FIG. 55 ☐ Distribution of Mycenaean objects in Italy and adjacent areas. (After Vagnetti, 1980.)

count—have produced Mycenaean pottery, with a bronze sword from Surbo making an eighteenth. Very little of this material comes from funerary contexts,[76] and the vast majority is found on a mere handful of sites. Most of the find-spots, and all the important ones, are coastal. Of these, the trio of sites facing the Gulf of Taranto seem, from the quantity of imported material, to have enjoyed especial importance. More than 750 sherds of Aegean pottery were found on the ill-fated site of Scoglio del Tonno (Taranto) along with local and Apennine wares and an important collection of bronzes. The material also included figurines, which have commonly been regarded as an important indicator of Mycenaean presence at Taranto. The time-span covered is the entire LH III period; there is no early material.[77] The same is probably true, in spite of the excavator's statements to the contrary, of the twin site of Porto Perone-Saturo (Leporano), where a few hundreds of sherds are known, those identifiable of LH IIIB–C;[78] Dickinson accepts one plain goblet sherd as early. Little is known of Torre Castelluccia, but the material is also late in date. Most of the remaining finds are of a few sherds only, none certainly early; only Coppa Nevigata on the Gargano has a more substantial quantity, along with plentiful local material.

The virtual absence so far of proven early Mycenaean material is puzzling, but the pace of discovery is so great that this situation may quickly change. By the middle Mycenaean period Apulia was clearly well integrated into the Graeco-Italian exchange network. The question of "colonization" by Mycenaean Greeks could only affect Scoglio del Tonno, and the evidence there is insufficient to form a judgement. Vagnetti's negative assessment is surely correct.[79]

Further up the Adriatic coast, a good LH IIIB sherd comes from Treazzano di Monsampolo in the Tronto valley (Ascoli Piceno), together with material of "subapennine" type, including a wheel pin-head.[80] This piece is to date the only find on the Adriatic north of Apulia. Three sherds, attributed to LH IIIC, come from Frattesina and Fondo Paviani between the Po and the Adige; the northernmost of any Mycenaean finds in good contexts anywhere. The importance of Frattesina, given its glass, ivory, metals and other exotica, is assured, though it can only cover the final part of the Mycenaean period; but during that period several bronze types, as well as amber beads of Tiryns type, demonstrate the strength of trans-Adriatic contacts. Why such contacts were not present earlier is hard to explain; to attribute their absence to adverse sailing conditions in the Adriatic seems oversimplistic.[81] Mention should also be made here of the supposed Vapheio cup imitation among the Polada-culture material at Ledro in the Trentino.[82] I have indicated elsewhere that I believe this vessel to fit into its local context and to have nothing to do with Aegean pottery.

Only five sites in the Basilicata and Calabria are known to have produced Mycenaean pottery, all of them found or excavated in the last few years. It was always surprising that Calabria and the coast south-west of Taranto had not produced Mycenaean material, in view of its frequency in Apulia and in Sicily, and the fact that later Greek colonization encompassed those regions;

this can now be seen to have been entirely a function of inadequate exploration. Indeed, virtually no Bronze Age sites of importance were known anywhere in Calabria until the recent survey conducted by Professor Renato Peroni of the University of Rome. This survey, in and around the plain of Sibari, located many Bronze Age sites previously unknown; the only one so far to be tested by excavation, Broglio, has produced Mycenaean pottery in surprising quantities—greater by volume of earth dug than in better-known locations like Vivara.[83]

Much the same is true of the Basilicata, where admittedly more sites were known previously. But only with the recent excavations at Termitito (Montalbano Ionico) did Mycenaean material turn up, and in surprising quantity. The isolated sherd from Toppo Daguzzo shows that the odd vase was exchanged inland; its chronological position in relation to Apennine ceramics may turn out to be important, and there are radiocarbon dates from the site (unfortunately reversed in relation to the stratigraphy). The situation in these provinces at present attests a rather weak degree of contact between Apulian coastal stations and inland sites.

In Sicily, Mycenaean pottery has been found on ten sites, mostly cemeteries. Morgantina (Serra Orlando) is the only certain non-funerary site,[84] and the three sherds of Mycenaean pottery from there came from a disturbed context: they were "associated" with post-holes.[85] Also on the site was pottery of Ausonian II type (as known from Lipari; Cassibile type in the south-east of Sicily). Elsewhere on the site Apennine-type ware decorated with incised geometric designs occurs.

It is instructive to consider where Mycenaean pottery has *not* been found. Very little was found, for instance, on the "palace" site at Thapsos, although it occurs in quantity in the nearby rock-cut tomb cemetery.[86] The dating of this site is very uncertain; some of the material from it indicates a late (Cassibile period) date, but there are also Thapsos-period structures. Mycenaean pottery was not found, either, in the "anaktaron" at Pantalica, though one vase and other possible Aegean objects came from the tombs. It is not found in such other Middle and Late Bronze Age settlements as have been investigated, like Ognina (Syracuse) in the south-east, Monte Castellazzo (Poggioreale) or Boccadifalco (Palermo) in the west. Though Bronze Age settlements in Sicily are still inadequately known from excavation, it might be expected that if Mycenaean pottery were present in any significant quantity on them some of it would have turned up by now.

Instead, a number of the rock-cut cemeteries of the Middle Bronze Age (Thapsos period) produce Mycenaean material. At Thapsos itself over a dozen tombs had Mycenaean vases, usually a single vessel but occasionally more. One of the recently excavated tombs (Tomb D), containing not less than 49 burials, had as grave-goods a collection of ten Mycenaean vessels, three Cypriot vessels, a Maltese jug, numerous vessels of local ware, seven amber beads, six gold beads or pendants, numerous beads of bone, glass-paste and stone, and a bronze rapier (Fig. 56): this is one of the finest "Mycenaean" tomb groups outside the Aegean.[87] Also of the Thapsos period are the cemeteries or tombs at Milena, Matrensa, Cozzo del Pantano, Molinello, Floridia, Buscemi and Plemmyrion, where glass-paste beads were found. These sites have produced pottery of LH IIIA and B. By contrast the great cemeteries at Pantalica, of the succeeding periods of the Bronze Age, have produced only a single Mycenaean vessel.[88] Equally clearly the rock-cut tombs of the Sicilian Early Bronze Age (Castelluccio period) have no Mycenaean pottery at all, though they have produced glass-paste beads that have been quoted as being of Aegean provenance (cf. p. 92).

Mycenaean pottery in Sicily is thus localized in time and space, mainly in the south-east in LH IIIA and B. Thapsos in particular was the destination of much of the imported pottery: its position on the Magnisi promontory, pointing eastwards into the Ionian Sea, makes this less than surprising. The promontory offers a good landing place (though not an ideal harbour of the sort offered by Syracuse or Taranto), and is today the centre of an international maritime commerce—in oil (cf. the position of Antigori, below).

No certain indications of early Mycenaean trade have yet been recovered from Sicily. A cup from Monte Sallia (Ragusa) has been variously considered a Middle Helladic import, and a variant of local, Castelluccian, painted wares.[89] Only fabric analysis will be able to resolve this matter. Taylour noted that "although there are several other cups of the same period in the Syracuse Museum from south-eastern Sicily, which are somewhat similar in shape and decoration, our specimen stands out among them by reason of its greenish white clay and by its superior craftsmanship".[90] Personal inspection of this vase in 1978 confirmed this impression. Form, fabric, colour and design do stand out from the rest of the Castelluccio pottery, even though general parallels for all except fabric can be adduced: cross designs, for instance, are quite common, and the general syntax of the piece is not dissimilar to that of other Castelluccio vessels. Moreover, the chronological position of Castelluccio (i.e. pre-Thapsos) would render such a link possible. The non-ceramic material may lend some plausibility to this notion: two cemeteries (Valsavoia and Cava Cana Barbara, Syracuse province) have produced glass-paste beads of definitely Aegean type (as opposed to the rather simple forms known in faience in other parts of Europe and on Malta), while the bossed bone plaques have wider Mediterranean parallels.[91] The bone dagger pommel from Monte Sallia, on the other hand, is a standard pommel form and is remarkable mainly for having survived intact.[92] There is no pressing reason why this should be considered an Aegean piece, for daggers everywhere needed pommels.

FIG. 56 ☐ Grave-goods from Thapsos, tomb D. (After Voza, 1973.)

Contact between Sicily and the Aegean before the LH IIIA period cannot be taken as certain, but since early LH material was present in the Aeolian Islands and Vivara, it seems reasonable to accept the possibility of such contact.

It remains to consider a number of non-ceramic objects found mainly in Sicilian tombs which have been taken as evidence of Aegean contact. Chief among these are a group of rapiers, up to 60 cm long, with simple rhomboidal section and rounded shoulder, short pointed tang and three large rivets, in a flat triangular formation (Fig. 56.8). Both typologically and chronologically a connection with Aegean type A rapiers is excluded. Much more similar are the rivetted daggers or short swords found on both sides of the Adriatic (p. 170), and a single, unusual piece from Crete (Zapher Papoura gr. 44), of LM IIIA1 date.[93] On balance, however, these Sicilian pieces are likely to be part of a local tradition. Much the same may be said for the group of signet rings in silver and gold from Caltagirone, Pantalica, Monte Dessueri and S. Angelo Muxaro,[94] which bear a vague resemblance to Aegean rings but appear by comparison crude, and are anyway constructed in a different fashion.

On the other hand, the two fine bronze vessels from Caldare (Agrigento) and another from Milena (Agrigento) certainly appear to be of eastern, Aegean or Cypriot, manufacture,[95] and the same can probably be said of the bronze mirrors from Pantalica (North, graves 37 and 140; South, grave 173; North-West, graves 23 and 3), which find good parallels in Greece and Crete from LM II on.[96]

The two claimed Mycenaean sherds on Malta, from Borǵ in-Nadur and Tas Silg, do little to amplify the picture. The context of the Borǵ in-Nadur piece is less than satisfactory and almost certainly indicates redeposition;[97] it tells us little about the nature of the Mycenaean presence (if any) on Malta. Primary deposition contexts, such as the graves in the Tarxien Cemetery, the dolmens, and the few sites that do show occupation after the Temple period, have no Mycenaean material: the situation is clearly different from that in, for instance, south-eastern Sicily. On the other hand, there are several cases of Maltese pottery being found in Sicily, on the Thapsos palace site and tomb, for example, in Castelluccio tombs, and on the peninsula or island site of Ognina south of Syracuse, so that contact between Sicily and Malta undoubtedly took place.[98]

By contrast to the situation on Sicily, all the imported Aegean material on the Aeolian Islands comes from settlements, with the added advantage of a long and secure stratigraphical succession being attested at the Lipari Acropolis. This sequence, now published in full,[99] is one of the most important in the entire Bronze Age world, since four successive phases of occupation, from Early to Late Bronze Age, were accompanied by Mycenaean pottery, perhaps also Minoan, covering the entire Late Bronze Age. The correlations seen at Lipari also apply at Capo Graziano and Milazzese (islands of Filicudi and Panarea respectively). Sherds of Mycenaean pottery occurred at two sites on Salina, where house F at La Portella also included amber and glass-paste beads, the latter probably Aegean.[100] Amber and glass-paste, though no imported pottery, also occurred in the Ausonian II cremation cemetery of Lipari-Piazza Monfalcone.[101] The finding of a piece of LH IIIA-B stirrup-jar from a second century A.D. wreck off Capo Graziano deserves mention.[102]

The remarkable fact that Mycenaean pottery has been found in the Bronze Age levels of virtually every relevant site in the Aeolian Islands leads one to wonder what their special significance was. They are small islands of volcanic origin whose only conceivable natural resource worthy of export is obsidian. The Western Mediterranean, indeed, is known to have made extensive use of Lipari obsidian in the Neolithic and Chalcolithic, though little found its way to the Aegean. Vagnetti[103] has suggested that the role of Lipari as a trading-station could have continued from the Neolithic into later times, especially as far as contacts with peninsular Italy were concerned. It may be that other specialist services, such as potting, took over in importance when that of obsidian died down.[104]

While at first glance it might seem that there is little reason to visit the Aeolian Islands, since they lie at a significant remove from the main land route through peninsular Italy to Sicily (Vulcano, the nearest to Sicily, lies some 25 km north-west of Milazzo; Stromboli, the nearest to Italy, lies 55 km west of Cape Vaticano but—perhaps more significant—70 km north-west of the Gioia plain), in fact the islands are not so remote as one might think. The conical mound of Stromboli is a useful navigation mark, especially at night when its ejections of glowing ash and lava light up the whole area in a spectacular firework display. The islands can easily be seen from Sicily, less so from Italy, but provide a natural stopping place on the route from Naples or further north to the straits of Messina. Their role in the movement of goods and shipping to the Tyrrhenian Sea is likely to have been crucial.

Three sites are now known in Campania with Mycenaean material, two of them restricted to one or two sherds each. All of the material is attributed to LH IIIC. At the Polla cave in the Vallo di Diano occurred a bronze "wheel" with branching spokes (cf. p. 143), the type that occurs also in Greece. By contrast, the more famous and richer cave of Pertosa produced only bronze knives of Aegean type, and no pottery.[105] The presence of imported pottery on two sites on the margins of the plain of Paestum might suggest the existence of a localized exchange network in this area.

The relative wealth of material on Ischia and Vivara, and its early date, is in complete contrast to this. Vivara, with an area of only 0·32 km², has four find-spots of Mycenaean pottery, including a substantial amount of LH I–II (possibly also MH and MM), and some LH IIIB-C;[106] the material is from post-built houses, and from fill or scattered material. That Vivara was able to take part in exchange systems involving the Mycenaean world over a long period, perhaps in the same way as Lipari, seems assured; the special attraction of this stretch of coast for Greeks is confirmed by the fact that early colonies were founded there. Speculation about the full extent of prehistoric occupation on this coast is unlikely to be put on a surer footing given the nature of modern land use.

For central Italy, the finding of five Mycenaean sherds at Luni sul Mignone by the Swedish Expedition opened up the possibility of Mycenaean penetration into this area. Since then other sites have produced sherds, notably San Giovenale (near Luni) and Monte Rovello. A sherd from Narce described as belonging "to a subMycenaean tradition of painted wares" and coming from phase IV (Protovillanovan) was in fact, because of its mineral inclusions, locally made.[107] Sherds from the Sant' Omobono area of Rome, in a layer above the destruction of the archaic temple and therefore indisputably secondary, are now considered to be Geometric in date.[108]

A recent find that is not yet known beyond a brief mention is that of Telamone near Grosseto (allegedly LH IIIC). Alleged finds from Poggio di Castellonchio (Firenze), on the other hand, are now known to be the result of a misunderstanding.[109]

Another important find is the Piediluco/Contigliano hoard, which contains fragments of a tripod of Cypriot type, a four-spoked wheel, and a cauldron fragment with circular handle—the latter plausibly seen as of Greek type.[110]

Finally, we come to Sardinia. The sensational discovery of Mycenaean pottery, first from an unknown site in Nuoro province, and then from the Antigori *nuraghe*, has provided the natural complement to the now quite numerous fragmentary and whole ox-hide ingots known from the island for many years, confirming beyond all doubt that Sardinia was within the orbit of exchange with the East Mediterranean. To the well-known ingots from Serra Ilixi bearing signs of Aegean form and that from Sant' Antioco di Bisarcio must now be added a series of further find-spots, mainly of very fragmentary ingot pieces; this shows that the ingots were used for local metallurgy as well as in the international movement of raw copper. Though it is presumed that the copper in these ingots is local, this remains to be proven.

Further evidence for such contacts comes from finished bronzes. With many of the tool forms it is not easy to tell which are ancestral and which derivative, but certainly some of the Aegean metalworking hammers and other tools correspond very closely to examples on Sardinia.[110a] More definite, and certainly more spectacular, are finds like the tanged daggers in the Ottana hoard,[111] metal-worker's tongs of Cypro-Levantine type from Siniscola,[112] and handle-attachments from the Su Benticheddu cave and Sa Sedda 'e Sos

Carros,[113] with their best parallels in Enkomi. At least the latter would appear to be actual imports.

Although Mycenaean pottery was known from "clandestine" operations prior to 1980,[114] the discovery of stratigraphically provenanced sherds in the *nuraghe* at Antigori near Sarrok (Cagliari) (Fig. 57) in that year has confirmed

FIG. 57 ☐ Mycenaean landfalls in the West. (upper) Nuragic complex of Antigori, Sardinia (Photograph by the author.) (lower) Torre Castelluccia, Apulia (Photograph by Thyrza Smith.)

the picture of trans-Tyrrhenian movement in the most remarkable way. The site lies on a limestone knoll about 70 m in height and 500 m from the sea.[115] It commands a fine view of the bay of Cagliari, which is the natural seaward focus of southern Sardinia. The oblong area of the summit is rocky and uneven, and covered with archaeological remains in the form of standing and tumbled walls, with, in places, deep stratified deposits. The site has long been known, but never previously investigated. The main tower of the site is at the eastern end of the hilltop, and the deposits under excavation lie towards the west. On the south side the complex is surrounded by a substantial wall, with a narrow entrance-way visible. The whole site is rather difficult of access because of the steepness of the slopes. The main excavated area so far is a narrow area on the north side of the hill, above a steep drop: here a squarish sounding, following a pit dug by looters, was sunk to a depth of some 1·5 m, comprising 11 layers, the bottom one being sterile but not natural: it is thus not known how deep the deposits really are. Mycenaean sherds were found, along with local, nuragic pottery in levels 9 and 10; there was also a little lead double-axe. Datable pieces belong to LH IIIB. An interesting adaptation of local skills to foreign materials is seen in the lead rivets, commonly used to mend cracks on nuragic pottery in Sardinia, and here found also on a Mycenaean vessel.[116]

While the full context of these finds is not yet clear, it is at least certain that the Aegean sherds were actually found in a nuragic building, and, therefore, imported to Sardinia in antiquity. When one considers that there are some 7000 nuraghi in Sardinia and that only a small number have even been recorded satisfactorily, let alone excavated systematically, it is clear that the sample available is quite inadequate.

In this connection one may note that it is often very difficult to distinguish Mycenaean from other wheel-thrown, band-decorated, buff or pinkish wares. Only a detailed knowledge of the fabrics in a particular area can adequately assign sherds to their correct place in space and time. In Sardinia, for instance, band-decorated or monochrome-painted buff wares are common throughout the Phoenician and Punic periods, and the possibility that non-patterned Mycenaean sherds could have found their way into collections labelled "Punic" must be considered.[117] Equally, sherds may have been identified as Mycenaean when in fact they are later: this is almost certainly the case for two sherds from Barumini,[118] and cannot be ruled out for three band-decorated pieces recently published from the Nuraghe Domu s'Orku.[119]

Another often-repeated connection between Sardinia and the Eastern Mediterranean, at a particular period of the Late Bronze Age, is the presence in the latter area of the *Shardana*, at first fighting as mercenaries in the Egyptian army, later fighting with the "Sea Peoples" against Egypt.[120] There has frankly never been much more than the name to link the two, though attempts have been made[121] to see correspondences between the round shields, horned cap-like helmets, and stout thrusting swords shown in the Egyptian reliefs, and the accoutrements of the bronze figurines of Nuragic Sardinia, where horned helmets and round shields occur, as on a well-known piece in the Pigorini Museum in Rome from Sulcis (Cagliari) and another from Uta in Cagliari. The presence on Corsica of statue-menhirs with swords and holes, perhaps for detachable horns, in the helmet has been taken as further evidence for such a connection,[122] but if one is looking for horned helmets, the Near East is a much more profitable hunting-ground, and in some parts (e.g. Meso-potamia) they have a long history.[123] A famous example from—unusually—the Aegean is one of the helmet-types on the Warrior Vase from Mycenae.

The philological and epigraphic evidence seems to suggest a connection between the Shardana and Sardinia. A Phoenician inscription from Nora (only 14 km south of Antigori), attributed to the ninth century B.C., gives the name of the island as *Shardan*.[124] It must be stressed, though, that any connec-tion of Sardinia with the Shardana of the Sea Peoples is purely speculative. A recent suggestion, which tries to reconcile these varying indications, is that the Shardana moved to Sardinia *after* the Sea Peoples' raids, and that pre-viously they are to be located in the Levant, perhaps "not far from the north-ern Syrian coast".[125] Archaeologically it is most unlikely that artefactual evidence will confirm or deny the picture obtained from the Egyptian sources.

Italy—discussion

Though Mycenaean pottery has been found on over 50 sites (Fig. 56) the quantity on most of them is very small—in some cases a single sherd. Only a handful have even a modest quantity (as far as is known at present), and only five (Lipari, Scoglio del Tonno, Thapsos, Antigori and Termitito) have appreciable quantities on which to base a systematic study of the origin and form of the pots. The distribution through time and space is very uneven. Only Vivara and the Aeolian islands have early Mycenaean material in any quantity, while the presence of genuine Middle Helladic imports in Italy is hotly disputed, and even if verifiable is only on a very limited scale. But by the later sixteenth century substantial quantities of Mycenaean pottery were reaching the Tyrrhenian shores of Italy, apparently to the exclusion of other areas: only Apulia (as might be expected) shows any sign of early material. In the middle period (LH IIIA-B), the distribution is at its most dense, especi-ally in Sicily and Apulia, but with all the areas of Italy discussed except the north being represented. Finds from Etruria and Sardinia complete the circuit of the Tyrrhenian sea. In LH IIIC the distribution is less dense but almost as far-flung, with the Po valley now being represented. Sicily, on the other hand, almost drops out though Lipari and Antigori continue to have imported pottery.

The great increase in the number of sites with Mycenaean pottery recorded in recent years makes predictions about the eventual state of its presence in Italy hazardous, but comparison of distribution maps of 1967 and 1982 suggests that to a large extent the new finds are an infilling of the older map in the same general areas as those where finds were already known. This is true for Apulia, for instance, while the situation on Sicily has changed very little except for the discovery of Cypriot pottery. In three areas we may record significant changes: the Gulf of Taranto (Termitito), Sardinia, and the North. The scatter of isolated sherds found elsewhere suggests that in most areas the filtering process of down-the-line exchange has brought about a weak representation of imported pottery away from the coastal stations of the south and south-west. For those areas one may predict that such central sites will increase in number, with Calabria being a prime candidate for our attentions—in the areas that were of interest later on, for instance, like Sibari, Crotone or Locri. Coastal sites up the Tyrrhenian shores of Italy might also be expected to have existed, with Rome-Ostia, Giglio-Monte Argentario, Elba and even Corsica being "prime suspects". On the other hand, unless something dramatic happens, one might expect the situation on inland sites to change rather little: projects like the Calabria survey will no doubt unearth more sites with a few sherds, but not the quantity found on the coast. The situation on the Adriatic is far from clear. To judge from the amber distribution, it would be likely that only in LH IIIC did the Adriatic route become important, and the apparently late date of the Po valley finds supports this view. A Protovillanovan "Spina" would not come as any surprise, but there is no evidence at present for penetration of the Adriatic on any scale before that date.

Local exchange mechanisms should be looked to in accounting for the pattern of Mycenaean finds in mainland Italy. Granted that the goods arrived there at particular coastal stations, of which Taranto, Porto Perone-Saturo, Thapsos and Lipari stand out as pre-eminent, the filtering process of the existing exchange networks would account for the presence of a pot or two on stations inland from or subsidiary to these ports. Thus sites only a few kilometres from the sea, such as Broglio, received a share of the goods arriving, while more remote places like the Polla cave acquired only a single vessel. The direction and strength of this "dilution" process should enable us eventually to locate the precise points of origin of the goods. On the other hand, certain sites may have had favoured access to such goods, to judge from the quantity and quality of material recovered there: Termitito, for instance. Care must be taken, however, to ensure that post-depositional factors are not responsible for this apparently differential pattern.

The situation on Sicily seems to have been different from that everywhere else because of the practice of putting Mycenaean pots in graves. Only the two Apulian examples parallel this. Admittedly tomb architecture was considerably more elaborate on Sicily than elsewhere, but this has the effect of attracting tomb robbers as well as suggesting special status. Assuming that pots are the personal property of the deceased in the afterlife, the communities of south-eastern Sicily were alone able to furnish their dead with the imported ceramics that elsewhere seem to have been so scarce. The implication that there was plenty of Mycenaean pottery around is a reasonable one, and given the situation of Thapsos on the Magnisi promontory, as well-placed for the receipt of sea-borne goods from the east as anywhere could be, is hardly surprising. The situation there comes as close to that of the East Mediterranean as anything does, and, given the scale of construction which is evident in the Thapsos and Pantalica "palatial" buildings, makes the supposition of salient degrees of ranking in local society a natural inference.

The processes by which the pottery actually arrived on Italian soil, or to which parts they went, are much harder to unravel. Traditionally it has been assumed that the reason for Aegean interest in Italy in the first place was because of its mineral resources: this means that only certain areas, notably Etruria and Sardinia, would have been the ultimate aim of Aegean attentions, and that the disposal of pottery in Apulian coastal stations was merely evidence of points of call along the route, for watering, shelter and the like. Aegean or East Mediterranean ships are assumed to have been the ones involved, able by superior technology in ship-building and navigation to reach their destinations, in metal extraction to acquire the copper they needed, and in weaponry to subdue any resistance to the enterprise. In return for shelter, food and water en route, fine pottery and other objects (e.g. jewellery) would be provided. Yet the discussion of the finds context in the different parts of Italy makes it evident that the situation was really much more complex than this.

We have seen that the presence of Mycenaean pottery in the East does not imply anything about the presence of "Mycenaeans" in that area, nor even about Mycenaean foreign interests. Regular and extensive exchange networks existed throughout the East Mediterranean in the Bronze Age; numerous commodities were moved about, and no doubt numerous different people did the moving—certainly trade and traders are well-attested in Near Eastern textual sources, though they were not involved, as a rule, in the movement of such mundane objects as pots. Rather than the pots being used as a medium of direct exchange between Mycenaeans and their Levantine exchange partners, it seems much more likely that such pots were part of the general flow of goods in the East Mediterranean, apparently valued as pots as well as for anything they may have contained, and almost universally accompanied by Cypriot wares. That both these ceramic types were in fact carried about may be seen from the finds on the Cape Gelidonya ship. I maintain that the situation in the West was similar. Local and longer-distance exchange is attested by the movement of pottery between different parts of the Central Mediterranean world. At Lipari, for instance, were found both Sardinian and Apennine pottery as well as local and Mycenaean.[126] The intervisibility of all the different parts of the circum-Tyrrhenian land chain, with the exception of Sicily-Sardinia, makes it possible that one regional system was centred on the Tyrrhenian basin: Lipari and Vivara were important elements in this network. Another probably centred around the Gulf of Taranto and a third on eastern Sicily. Within each of these distinct areas, local traditions existed and local movement of goods brought about a greater or lesser degree of cultural homogeneity. Given an "input" of Mycenaean goods into these systems—an input which probably arrived at Taranto, Thapsos and Lipari, possibly other places as well—existing mechanisms would account for their dispersal. Such goods were brought by sea, of course, and the question of the nationality of the ships involved is both unanswerable and meaningless in a prehistoric context. Ships *were* plying the seas between Italy and Greece, probably on a regular basis as finds of stone anchors of East Mediterranean type also suggest;[126a] pots were being transported to Italy, and probably copper ingots were being transported to Greece. That, however, is the extent of the connection between the two events, and in my view it is quite wrong to imagine a one-to-one correlation between Mycenaean trading expeditions in search of copper, and the leaving behind in Italy of characteristic Mycenaean ceramics. The sophistication of cultural development in at any rate Sicily and Lipari strongly suggests that local communities were well able to articulate social and economic divisions by means of highly developed exchange systems, and there is no reason to suppose that nautical technology was not up to it.

So far we have considered mainly pottery and a certain amount of other material such as jewellery and copper ingots. There is, however, another aspect of the Greek–Italian connection that relates particularly to the late LH IIIB and IIIC periods, namely bronze production. I have indicated in each chapter which forms seem to show connections between the two countries, and the evidence taken all together is indeed very considerable. The implications of these close correspondences are what we must now consider.

Towards the end of the thirteenth century (LH IIIB), bronze forms appeared in Greece that are part of a wide family of European types but find their closest analogies in Italy. This is often called the Peschiera bronze industry after one of the largest collections of the period, but this name probably masks a wider distribution through many areas where the excellent preservation of Lake Garda is not available. The occupation of these sites probably goes back some way, to judge from Central European parallels, but it is the LH IIIB-C end that concerns us here. Some of the connections in bronze forms are extraordinarily close, notably in the fibulae: several pieces from Mycenae and from Peschiera are indistinguishable. Specifically supporting an earlier rather than a later dating for the first appearance of parallels in bronze types between Greece and Italy are the Mycenae axe-mould and possibly the Surbo sword (see Appendix 5). During the twelfth century the range of parallel bronze forms diversified, notable additions being the bird motif and, probably near 1100 b.c., the arc fibula. Similarities in fibulae continued, indeed, well into the Iron Age. A further link connecting the two sides of the Adriatic is amber, notably the beads of Tiryns type (p. 82).

It would be wrong to imagine that Italy and Greece were the only areas where such parallel developments were taking place. Many of the same bronze forms were appearing now throughout continental Europe, and some of them (notably flange-hilted swords) appear too in the Levant. Over many parts of the Late Bronze Age world, but specifically on either side of the Adriatic, smiths were turning out products of identical design. Even if the earlier examples are all made in one country or the other, by the twelfth century local production seems certain. Though this identity of production boils down in the end to the individual workmen, it suggests that the political climate was such as to allow the furthering of such contacts, whereas previously each region went its own way. However, such contact should not be exaggerated. The wide spread of particular bronzes in the Urnfield world shows that devices existed for transmitting the ideas for bronze types from one area to another. In the Late Bronze Age moulds were commonly made of clay, from a wax or metal original, and survive only where local preservation allows it. The transport of an original model or design for the creation of clay moulds would be a simple matter. This lies in the realm of speculation for Italy and Greece, for no clay moulds are known, but then moulds are virtually absent in mainland Greece altogether, and clay or sand[127] would be the natural substances to imagine being used in Mycenaean metallurgy.

It must be observed that for most of the bronze types it is not just a question of isolated imports from one area into another. Such is the case for the Surbo sword (Mycenaean in Italy) or the Mycenae winged axe mould (Italian in Greece), but these influences are exceptional. The same, or very similar, bronze types appear in quantity on both sides of the Adriatic, in many cases too numerous to be imports. Such is the case with flange-hilted swords and daggers, fibulae, "wheels", pins, some knives, and various ornaments and motifs, notably the bird motif. Prior to *c*. 1200 b.c., what bronzework there was in Italy was quite separate from that in Greece; after 1200 b.c., many (though very far from all) forms link the two areas. Some of these links continued down into the Iron Age, though our concern here is only with those involving LH IIIC and Protovillanovan.

Unfortunately, almost all the dating evidence for the bronze types in question rests on the Aegean chronology, so it is impossible to argue for a priority outside Greece without circularity. One of the classes of evidence for which this is not true is the sword. European flange-hilted swords developed in the Tumulus Bronze Age (Sombor-Smolenice-Ia/Ib), and the typologically earliest Greek form is the pan-European IIa type, Nenzingen in central Europe where the earliest dates are Br D. It is reasonable to suppose that the flange-hilted dagger is also a non-Greek type, though the dating evidence cannot at present prove this. Of the violin-bow fibula we can only say that it is not a standard Mycenaean type before *c.* 1200 B.C., which does not of course exclude the possibility that it was invented by the Mycenaeans at that time; on balance this seems unlikely.[128] The "wheels" are perhaps best omitted from the argument until the Kastanas material is published; certainly they were present on both sides of the Adriatic, and two different possible functions have been suggested. The situation with pins is equally unclear; the existence of long dress pins in the Tumulus Bronze Age has been taken as indicating an ancestry in Europe, but there would be a considerable time gap between the period of greatest popularity in Europe and their adoption in Greece. If, on the other hand, the appearance of long dress pins and fibulae in Greece does indicate new dress styles, as has been suggested, one imagines that the inspiration for the new accoutrements would come from someone or somewhere: in the absence of dress designers, from the popular traditions of some area as expressed in the products of bronzesmiths' workshops.

Most striking of all is the appearance of birds and bird motifs, most notably on the bronze bowl from Pylos with a design extraordinarily close to that on Protovillanovan metalwork and pots; there is also the appearance of knives with zoomorphic handle (Perati, Ialysos). Here marked disagreement is apparent in the recent literature, with one school of thought favouring an Aegean (and ultimately Near Eastern) ancestry for the design, and the other seeing these pieces as distinct from Aegean zoomorphic designs known prior to this period, and influenced ultimately by the art of the Urnfield world.[129] In spite of the dogmatic nature of certain recent pronouncements on the subject, this is a matter for subjective assessment, with hard fact—such as dating evidence—at a premium. The Pylos bowl is barely, if at all, earlier than the Italian pieces: the tomb it was in contained pottery of LH IIIB and C, but it was not associated with any particular burial. LH IIIB is thus a *terminus post quem*, and it could date to the thirteenth, twelfth or even eleventh century. In fact one cannot even be certain that it is not a later insertion altogether, though this would be a unique occurrence: a fragment of an iron pin occurred in the dromos, and the tomb is only 17 m away from the Protogeometric tholos.[130] There is no compelling reason for dating the violin-bow fibulae in the Coste del Marano hoard later than LH IIIC, even if the hoard does also contain arc fibulae which can hardly be earlier than 1100.[131] As discussed elsewhere (p. 205

and Appendix 5) this is an area of great uncertainty chronologically, with the subdivisions and chronology of LH IIIC very much under debate, and with no clear evidence for a terminal date. The interesting suggestion that Near Eastern prototypes should be sought for bird motifs and bird-handled knives would carry more weight if it could explain why such influences should be felt at just this time, and why the influences should have been so eclectic. In any case, the designs alleged to influence the Pylos double bird-protomes are neither particularly close nor much, if at all, earlier than the Greek piece.[132] Such considerations are anyway irrelevant to the problem in hand, that of identifying the context and orientation of the Adriatic bronze industries in the thirteenth to twelfth centuries. Wherever certain motifs ultimately hailed from, Italy in the Peschiera and Protovillanovan phases is clearly intermeshed via numerous products in bronze with the Urnfield world on the one hand, and the Aegean world on the other. Probably we do not yet have the earliest examples of any of the objects studied here, and anyway a detailed chronology is still impossible. What is of interest is the strong "Adriatic connection" of the decades around 1200 B.C., with bronzes, amber and pottery apparently being moved in both directions. This marked shift in orientation is one of the most obvious features of the twelfth century Aegean world, and has been noted already in northern Greece. On the reasons for such a shift we will have cause to speculate in Chapter 10.

Further afield

Tempting though it is to hope that Mycenaean trade with the West Mediterranean will one day be proven, and to look favourably on items alleged to be of Aegean provenance, there are in fact no such objects known from the West Mediterranean basin at present. Certain classes of artefact which occur there are considered further in other chapters—amber and faience, for instance. The history of the Minoan pots allegedly found in the Balearics is dubious, and the same goes for all other claimed connections with Iberia.[133] This is all the more surprising in that it would be perfectly reasonable to expect Mycenaean export items in the West, especially in view of the role later played by Phoenician trade.

The story that may be told for central Europe is rather more complicated, though no more positive. A variety of objects have been alleged to be of Aegean provenance, or inspiration. The cup found on the moor near Dohnsen, Kr. Celle, for instance, seems patently to be an Aegean product, but cannot be believed in as a genuine Mycenaean export (cf. p. 108). The Fritzdorf cup, along with its relatives like Rillaton, is most plausibly seen as deriving from local metallurgical and ceramic traditions, and to owe little to Aegean proto-types. Spirally-ornamented bone and antler objects (Chapter 7) have, in my opinion, little or nothing to do with the Aegean and are certainly not imported. Swords and daggers with T-hilt (Chapter 6) are made that way for functional reasons. Faience beads were locally produced, even if the technology came ultimately from the East Mediterranean. In any case, they are more likely to be connected with Egypt than with Greece. Only armour (Chapter 6) shows direct connections between central Europe and Greece, and even then this does not amount to importation. Like other areas, in fact, central Europe is notable above all for the absence of Aegean Bronze Age objects demonstrably imported in antiquity.

In Scandinavia, again, a few items have been alleged to be of Aegean origin. Spiral ornaments on bronzes we have already mentioned; a sword from Jut-land is clearly of local type, and an arrowhead that has been compared to Aegean types cannot in fact be tied down with the definiteness that has been suggested. On the other hand, folding stools known from Period II graves in Denmark and northern Germany might seem candidates for objects of ulti-mate East Mediterranean derivation, though there is no reason to suppose they were actual imports. At the same time it must be remembered that the Baltic was most probably the ultimate source of the amber found in Bronze Age Greece, and that a connection of some sort between the two areas is possible.

In the Ukraine and the Caucasus the position is unclear. The Borodino hoard shows some striking similarities to Mycenaean products, but certainly cannot be taken as being Mycenaean-derived. Only the rhomboid-headed pin with spectacle ornament provides any close link, and that motif can be paral-leled on local pottery of the Balta Verde group. The Ukrainian axes, provided their context really is irreproachable and they do not emanate from an early Russian excavation in a south Slav area, do seem to be Mycenaean double-axes, especially the axe of Kilindir type from Kozorezovo. But it would be reasonable to expect that ships went along the Black Sea coast: Mycenaean pottery from Troy shows that objects of "Greek" material culture reached near to the entrance to the Black Sea. Is it possible that these double axes were used as ingots, as similar non-functional pieces were in central Europe?

Several objects in the Caucasus bear a resemblance, sometimes rather remote, to Mycenaean pieces, e.g. arrowheads, horse-harness, spearheads and pins.[134] The faience industry was well-established there, too, in the later second millennium, but this probably reflects the influence of Mesopotamia rather than any connection with the Aegean. There is nothing in the Caucasus which can be taken as a Mycenaean product, and *vice versa*; the similarities in bronzework mentioned indicate a general connection of the East Mediter-ranean, Levant and Anatolia with the Caucasus, rather than a specific link with Greece.

Mycenaean contact with eastern Europe was thus negligible at all times. There are no imports or exports, and only a general similarity, first in artistic styles, then in bronze products, links the two areas. This suggests, however, that creative traditions in this period were remarkably sensitive to outside stimuli.

Britain

The case for believing that contacts existed between Mycenaean Greece and Wessex rests on a number of classes of objects believed to be foreign to the places in which they were found. Of those that apparently travelled from north to south the amber beads are of especial significance—indeed the only pieces for which a good case can be made—while of the objects found in Britain and supposedly of Aegean provenance particular mention may be made of the Pelynt sword-hilt, bronze double-axes, the crescentic ear-ring from Wilsford barrow G.8, faience beads, the Bush Barrow bone mounts, and Cypriot daggers.

The most satisfactory evidence for contact comes, as we have seen, from the amber spacer plates. It is hard to explain the identity of the Greek and British pieces except by supposing an identical place of manufacture. Much, if not all, of the amber from early Mycenaean Greece could, arguably, have come via Britain. There is a wide chronological horizon—the whole of LH I-II—in which this could have occurred, and the first occurrence of amber in Greece around 1550 B.C. is not incompatible with an Early Bronze Age date in England, as the discussion below (p. 277) makes clear.

With faience beads the situation is more difficult, and the evidence of scientific analysis contradictory. In any case the supposed connection would be with Egypt, and not with Mycenaean Greece, but as an indicator of trade with the East Mediterranean it is relevant here. The analogy of central Europe suggests that specific bead types occur in specific areas; this, together with the evidence of scientific analysis, supports local production in a number of localities. A similar situation obtains in Britain, where Wessex shapes are generally distinct from Scottish, suggesting at least two separate production centres. Against this must be set two factors: the Wessex beads do, in some instances, look very much like the Egyptian (but also the central European); and the total is, in numbers of beads, very small, which suggests they were a valuable and highly prized commodity. In any event, there is a case for maintaining that the faience beads of Wessex represent a short chronological horizon. They are mostly of the same type and occur in the same contexts; if, as seems likely, many of them came from the same production centre, they could all have been interred in a short space of time. This idea would agree with the notion of a "minimal" Wessex culture.[135]

The similarity between the Bush Barrow bone mounts and the pieces from the Shaft Grave Iota is undeniable and the number of pieces the same, though the Bush Barrow pieces, with a diameter of up to c. 2·6 cm, are rather smaller than the Mycenaean, which are c. 4–5 cm in diameter. The presence of local comparanda in both areas renders a direct connection less than plausible, and little reliance should be placed on them. The minute gold pins in the lost dagger pommel from Bush Barrow have been attributed[136] to East Mediterranean influence, since wire is not found in Britain until the Late Bronze Age. Parallels from Brittany and elsewhere, however, do not show the same technique, nor is any other parallel known in Mycenaean Greece.[137]

Double-axes, Cypriot daggers and gold ear-rings have been discussed in Chapters 4, 5 and 6, and their evidence was found to be inconclusive at best, and completely misleading at worst. The Pelynt sword-hilt (p. 160) is arguably Late Mycenaean in date, but presents insuperable problems of context and history. The Rillaton cup has been compared to Beaker and other handled cup shapes.

One oft-quoted parallel not yet discussed is Stonehenge and its daggers.[138] For the architecture of the monument itself, there can be little reason to suggest any connection whatsoever with Mycenaean Greece, especially as skill in massive stoneworking developed rather late in Greece. The main reason for calling it Mycenaean in inspiration was the discovery of carved daggers, said to be of Mycenaean type (Karo B), on stone 53. Though Atkinson "and his collaborators . . . [were] convinced that this identification is correct", it seems extraordinary that weathered carvings of such ambiguity should be compared with a rather rare type thousands of kilometres away. The general proportions of the Stonehenge daggers are different from those of Karo type B (wider), and they apparently have a T-shaped pommel, which is only assumed for the Shaft Grave daggers of Type B.[139] One explanation of these carvings has been that they depict two axes, one above the other; for the left-hand piece this is certainly a possibility, while the other looks much like a single axe. All in all, the eye of faith is needed to detect any genuine similarity to Mycenaean daggers.

Perhaps the most interesting, albeit ambiguous, piece of evidence from Britain is the tin ingot from Falmouth harbour (p. 55). Usually considered to be of Roman date, it has handles which attribute it to Buchholz type 2, rather than the standard Roman ox-hide shape, type 1. There is no means of dating this piece, nor is any parallel for it known, but it could just be Bronze Age in date; the implications are obvious.

The sum of evidence from Britain amounts to very little. The only reasonably certain export to Greece was amber, while the only possible imports, like the Pelynt dagger, the double-axes and the ear-rings, have no local context. In the light of these facts, one has no alternative but to reject the possibility of any regular contact between Britain and Mycenaean Greece, at least as expressed in the archaeological record. Sporadic contact, of a kind and by means which remain to be discussed, seems likely and can be accounted for by very few individual acts of exchange. The extent of Mycenaean contact with Britain, even if undeniable in view of the amber evidence, was limited; its effects must have been negligible.

Summary and conclusions

The export of Mycenaean material from the Mycenaean core area, which is loosely defined as central and southern Greece and the islands, proceeded at differential rates in different directions. Only Tyrrhenian sites received early Mycenaean pottery with the single exception of the Pazhok Vapheio cup; some exported bronzes are early. In the middle Mycenaean period a substantial number of Italian sites have imported pottery, which also appears in Macedonia for the first time. The late period shows the maintenance of links in the west, with the Adriatic coming into prominence, and the strengthening of them in the north. It is to the late period also that the majority of connections in bronzework belong. Documentation for Mycenaean export beyond Sardinia in the west and the border area in the north is poor or absent altogether.

Most observers hitherto have taken the view that Mycenaean exports, in east, west or north, represent the specific legacy of trading expeditions by East Mediterraneans, if not actually Mycenaeans, and this may indeed be the case. There is little doubt, however, that in Italy imported pottery on inland sites got there by means of local exchange mechanisms, and it is likely that the role of such mechanisms has been considerably underestimated. Especially in view of developments in tomb and settlement architecture on Sicily, and the manifest ability of local exchange to circulate Sardinian and Maltese pottery to Sicily and the Aeolian Islands, the scope and scale of developing socio-economic structures seems to have been considerable. Much the same is true of Macedonia in the late period, where, it is suggested, local mechanisms accounted for the dispersal of imported pottery that was brought by sea, perhaps to a single port. In the north-west, on the other hand, a filtering process was in operation, imported goods presumably acting as prestige goods in a prestige exchange chain.

The large and increasing amount of evidence of sea travel in the second millennium B.C. makes such sea-borne movement of goods less than surprising. What remains unclear is the real nature of the enterprise. Were metals really the source of interest for trans-Adriatic mariners? If so, how was control of metal sources maintained and organized? In my view metals do not account for the majority of Mycenaean exports anywhere. The density and nature of the export to Sicily, for instance, makes it clear that social factors played at least as important a role as did economic ones.

A glimpse of such social factors is also, perhaps, obtainable in the border lands, where Mycenaean weapons seem to have enjoyed a certain vogue, perhaps reflecting a role as status goods in communities for which there is little other evidence of social differentiation. Such a role would also be conceivable in areas further afield, if there were any evidence of the presence of Mycenaean objects. The rapid fall-off of such objects with increasing distance from the core area is a striking feature of the distribution.

The differential distribution of pottery and other objects is also striking. It is predictable that objects as fragile as pots will be less likely to be moved over long distances overland, whereas bronzes present less problems in this respect. The scatter of bronze tools and weapons in the border areas, some of them early, seem to exemplify this pattern. In the west, on the other hand, few Mycenaean bronzes are known and pottery is numerically preponderant, presumably reflecting the fact that the movement of goods was sea-borne and directed at specific localities.

The picture presented here must be regarded as a provisional one, for the tempo of discovery has been increasing in recent years. Parts of Italy, Albania, Macedonia, Thrace and Bulgaria undoubtedly still have secrets to yield up, and in some of those regions the political situation means it will be many years before they can do so. In the meantime, the pattern of finds allows a level of discussion and even prediction which was impossible 25 years ago.

Notes

1. Basic literature: Stubbings (1951); Hankey (1967); *The Mycenaeans in the Eastern Mediterranean*, Acts of the International Archaeological Symposium, Nicosia 1972 (1973) (hereafter *Eastern Mediterranean*); Buchholz (1974); K. Bittel, *Gymnasium* **83**, 1976, 513–533; Mee (1978); B. J. Kemp and R. S. Merrillees, *Minoan Pottery in Second Millennium Egypt*, 1980 (Mainz, Zabern).

2. Stubbings (1951, p. 69); Hankey (1967, p. 145).

3. Hankey (1967, p. 146).

4. For example, Catling (1964, pp. 40ff.).

5. I. Perlman *et al.*, *Eastern Mediterranean*, pp. 213ff.; H. W. Catling, E. E. Richards and A. E. Blin-Stoyle, *BSA* **58**, 1963, 94–115, for the analysis of a series of Cypriot sherds, and the identification of both "local" and "imported" types.

6. Hankey (1967, pp. 128ff.).

7. Hankey (1967, pp. 131ff.).

8. Hankey (1967, pp. 135ff.).

9. C. F. A. Schaeffer, *Syria* **17**, 1936, 111; **13**, 1932, 12; **14**, 1933, 104; *Ugaritica* **I**, 1939, 53ff., 67, 99; *Eastern Mediterranean*, pp. 363–364.

10. Persson (1931, pp. 100–101, pl. 29, fig. 76).

11. L. Woolley, *Alalakh*, 1955 (Oxford, University Press for Soc. of Antiquaries), p. 369.

12. L. Woolley, *A Forgotten Kingdom*, 1953 (London, Penguin Books), p. 156.

13. Stubbings (1951, pp. 90–92); Hankey (1973, 1981).

14. Hankey (1973, p. 130); Oxford Aegean Archaeological Seminar, 21 January 1982, Abstract, and Hankey (1981, p. 45).

15. Ibid.

16. Stubbings (1951, pp. 22–23, 88–89); Mee (1978); S. Mitchel and A. W. McNicholl, *Arch. Reports for 1978–9*, 63–64.

17. M. Mellink, *AJA* **85**, 1981, 466; **82**, 1978, 318; **81**, 1977, 294; **80**, 1976, 265; **79**, 1975, 208; **78**, 1974, 115.

18. French (1975); Mee (1978, pp. 131–132, 145).

19. H. W. Catling and A. Millett, *BSA* **60**, 1965, 212–224. This conclusion has been borne out by more recent work on the Mycenaean pottery of Rhodes, which shows that large numbers of pots, including some of types considered specifically Rhodian, were in fact of Peloponnesian origin: R. E. Jones and C. B. Mee, *J. Field Arch.* **5**, 1978, 461–470. The conclusion of a mainland origin repeated, now more guardedly, by Catling, Jones and Millett in *Report Dept. of Antiqs Cyprus* 1978, 70–90.

20. F. Asaro, I. Perlman, *Eastern Mediterranean*, 213–224.

21. F. Asaro, I. Perlman and M. Dothan, *Archaeometry* **13**, 2, 1970, 169–175: LH IIIC1 sherds from Tell Ashdod, analysed by neutron activation, clearly differed from (admittedly small) reference samples from Enkomi, Palaeopaphos and Kition, and closely resembled in composition Philistine ware from the same site. The conclusion (p. 175): "It is logical to ascribe the techniques which produced the Myc IIIC1 wares as those traditional for the potters and hence that we are dealing with a recently transplanted people."

22. H. W. Catling, E. E. Richards and A. E. Blin-Stoyle, *BSA* **58**, 1963, 94–115.

23. Hankey (1967, p. 143).

24. Mee (1978, p. 148).

25. Mee (1968, pp. 134–136, 149); M. Mellink, *AJA* **79**, 1975, 207, pl. 39, 9 for the Hittite vase.

26. Taylour (1958, pp. 128ff.) for the "Rhodian" (i.e. specialized) nature of the finds from Scoglio del Tonno; E. S. Sherratt, in Best and de Vries (1980, pp. 177–179).

26a. As shown, for example, by the evidence of stone anchors: H. Frost, *Report Dept. Antiqs. Cyprus* 1970, 14ff., 22; cf. D. E. McCaslin, *Stone Anchors in Antiquity: Coastal Settlements and Maritime Trade-Routes in the Eastern Mediterranean ca. 1600–1050 B.C.* (Studies in Mediterranean Archaeology **61**), 1980, Göteborg, Åstrom.

27. For example, T. Kimes, C. C. Haselgrove, and I. Hodder, *J. Anthrop. Arch.* **1**, 1982, 113–131.

28. Feuer (1981).

29. An indication of the proportion of Mycenaean pottery in levels 18–12 at

268 The Mycenaeans and Europe

Kastanas has been given by A. Hochstetter, *Prähistorische Z.* **57/2**, 1982, 209, fig. 4. From levels 18–13 it was 4% or less, and in level 12 around 11%.

30. A. Hochstetter, *Prähistorische Z.* **57/2**, 1982, 201–219.

31. Numerous reports in *BSA* in 1920s and 1930s, summarized in Heurtley (1939).

32. Wardle (1980, pp. 239, 250–251).

33. Hänsel (1979, p. 183); Podzuweit (1979).

34. Heurtley (1939); D. French, *Index of Prehistoric Sites in Central Macedonia*, privately circulated, 1967.

35. D. Theochares, *Prehistory of Eastern Macedonia and Thrace, 1968* (Ancient Greek Cities, **9**, Athens, Center of Ekistics), contains very little Bronze Age material and no Mycenaean. In addition to Coles and Harding (1979, n. 65)—cf. *Arch. Delt.* **26**, 1971, 429; *Praktika* 1972, 86–90; *BCH* **99**, 1975, 668, fig. 169 (Asar Tepe); D. Grammenos, *Arch. Delt.* **30**, 1975, Meletai, 193–234; D. Grammenos and M. Photiades, *Anthropologika* **1**, 1980, 15–53; Ch. Koukouli-Chrysanthaki, *Anthropologika* **1**, 1980, 54–85; *Thracia Praehistorica*, 1982, 231ff.; D. Grammenos in Hänsel (1982).

36. Ch. Koukouli-Chrysanthaki, *Arch. Delt.* **27**, 1972, 552, pl. 452 beta, 524, pl. 455 alpha; *Thracia Praehistorica*, 1982, 243ff., plates 17, 19.

37. E. Tsimpidis-Pentzos, *Praktika* 1971, 87, pl. 112 alpha.

38. Wardle (1977); Hope Simpson and Dickinson (1979, Maps B, E).

39. Wardle (1977); Hope Simpson and Dickinson (1979, Map K); Papadopoulos (1976). New material from tumuli at Ephyra: Th. Papadopoulos, *Praktika* 1979, 119f.

40. D. Budina, *Buletin Arkeologjik* **3**, 1971, 57ff., Tab. 4 (quoted in Kilian 1976, p. 128).

41. Andrea (1972, p. 82, Tab. III, 5, 7–8); *Iliria* **4**, 1976, 134, pl. III.

42. Mus. Tirana. N. Ceka, *Monumentet* **3**, 1972, 7, n.3.

43. Islami and Ceka (1964, pp. 95–96, Tab. VII, 1); Korkuti (1970, p. 46, Tab. IV, 3).

44. N. Bodinaku, *Iliria* **11**, 1981, 2, 243ff., 258, Tab. II, 7.

45. N. Hammond, *BSA* **32**, 1931–2, 136; 1967, 133, 313.

46. M. Korkuti, *Iliria* **1**, 1971, Tab. XII (not mentioned in the text).

47. Most recently Prendi (1977–8); Harding (1975); references in these works unless otherwise indicated; also F. Prendi in Hänsel (1982).

48. N. Valmin, *Das adriatische Gebiet in Vor- und Frühbronzezeit* 1939 (Lund, Gleerup), p. 218, Abb. 52, 6 (quoted Buchholz 1983).

49. Zh. Andrea, *Iliria* **11**, 1981, 1, 225 Tab. I, 4–5.

50. A. Hoti, *Iliria* **11**, 1981, 1, 217 Tab. III, 3.

51. D. Budina, *Iliria* **1**, 1971, 287 Abb. 8.

52. Museum Butrint, seen in 1971 and 1975.

53. Hammond (1967, pp. 346–348).

54. Mikulčić (1966, pp. 16, 89—9th–8th century dating); K. Kilian, *Prähistorische Z.* **50**, 1975, 78–79 Taf. 59, 15; *Arch. Iugoslavica* **20–21**, 1980–81, 58ff.

55. J. A. Sakellarakis and Z. Marić, *Germania* **53**, 1975, 153–156.

55a. M. Parović-Pešikan, *Arch. Iugoslavica* **20–21**, 1980–81, 56ff.

56. Kilian (1976).

57. Mikulčić (1966, p. 9, Taf. IId); Sandars (1963, pp. 145–146).

58. Garašanin (1954, p. 58, Taf. 37, 4).

59. Reference is to Hänsel (1970) and Černych (1978, pp. 228ff.) unless otherwise indicated.

60. After the divisions of Höckmann (1980).

61. Hänsel (1970, p. 30, n.5).

62. Fully documented in Černych (1978, pp. 204ff., 238ff.).

63. Höckmann (1980, p. 135, D20–24).

64. B. Dimitrov, *Int. J. Nautical Arch.* **8.1,** 1979, 70–79, fig. 3; Buchholz (1983, pp. 54, 128 n.47, Abb.11).

65. Cf. the discussion of changing coast-lines in Hammond (1972, pp. 142ff., map 15); J. Bintliff, *Proc. Prehist. Soc.* **41,** 1975, 81, fig. 3; **42,** 1976, 241–262. H. D. Schulz, *JbRGZM* **26,** 1979, 223ff.

66. Papadopoulos (1976, pp. 298ff., 307ff., pls 12–16).

67. Witness the moulds from Breznik (Černych 1978, p. 204, fig. 42, 3) and Malinica (Niš Catalogue 1971, p. 72, no. 232).

68. Climatic data for different stations (Mellor 1975, pp. 23ff., F. L. Wernstedt, *World Climatic Data,* 1972 (Lemont, Climatic Data Press):

Station	Elevation (m)	Mean Jan. temp. (°C)	Mean July temp. (°C)	Annual precip. (mm)	Wettest months
Skopje	245	−1·7°	23·3°	487·7	May June Oct
Kjustendil	525	−0·9°	21·1°	607·1	May June July
Korcë	889	0·5°	20·5°	721·4	Oct Nov Dec
Vlorë	1	8·9°	24·5°	1089·7	Nov Dec Jan
Athens	107	9·3°	27·6°	401·1	Nov Dec Jan
Thessaloniki	69	5·5°	27·5°	464·1	Oct Nov Dec
Larissa	73	5·4°	28·5°	501·9	Oct Nov Dec
Navplion	2	10·0°	28·7°	547·1	Nov Dec Jan

69. Hope Simpson and Dickinson (1979, p. 299).

70. Coles and Harding (1979, pp. 339ff.). The "Lausitz" itself is the area of hills around Bautzen in the south-east corner of East Germany.

71. For example, by W. Kimmig, *Studien aus Alteuropa* **I,** 1964 (Köln, Böhlau), pp. 220ff., 257ff.

72. Wardle (1980, p. 262); Hänsel (1979, pp. 191ff.), where the Iron Age wares appear in levels 9 and 10, after the destruction of the building in levels 11 and 12. The latter is attributed to a late phase of LH IIIC or even early Protogeometric: *ibid.* p. 189, Abb. 15, 2, 7, 9. The whole question of "Lausitz invaders" discussed by B. Hänsel, *Beiträge zur Ur- und Frühgeschichte* **1,** 1981, 207–223 (AFD Beiheft 16).

73. Hänsel (1976, pp. 88ff., Karte 3).

74. This viewpoint argued by, e.g. J. Bouzek, Der Vardar- und Morava-Bereich in seinem Verhältnis zu Griechenland zwischen 1200 und 900 v.u.Z., lecture given 1980

at Conference in honour of F. Schachermeyr. Cf. too Bouzek (1969, pp. 66–68) for a balanced view of possible connections.

75. Taylour (1958); Biancofiore (1967); Tinè and Vagnetti (1967); Marazzi and Tusa (1976); Vagnetti (1980); Magna Graecia (1982) (most up-to-date information).

76. Only the finds from Torre S. Sabina and Oria.

77. *Pace* Biancofiore (1967, pl. 2: 98, 101, 177, 212); Dickinson (1977, p. 104).

78. *Pace* Lo Porto (1963, pp. 333–334); Dickinson (1977, p. 104); Benzi and Graziadio (1982, pp. 19ff.).

79. Vagnetti (1980, p. 161); *contra* Taylour (1958).

80. Magna Graecia (1982, pp. 197ff., pls 73–74).

81. R. L. Beaumont (*J. Hellenic Studies* **56,** 1936, 160–161) discussed winds in the Adriatic, only to reject them as an important factor. I thank Professor C. F. C. Hawkes both for this reference and for further valuable information on the question of Adriatic navigation.

82. L. Barfield, *Antiquity* **40,** 1966, 48f., pl. 8b; cf. *Antiquity* **46,** 1972, 316–317.

83. The observation of Dr Lucia Vagnetti.

84. The vase from Agrigento said by Taylour (1958, p. 63) not to have come from a tomb but (according to Orsi) from the *marina* of Girgenti (Agrigento) did in all likelihood emanate from a tomb.

85. E. Sjöqvist, *AJA* **64,** 1960, 134, pls 29–30.

86. Voza (1972, p. 205). This is the only primary reference known to me for the finding of Mycenaean pottery on the settlement at Thapsos: it is described as "very scarce" in the area of the settlement, which implies that there was *some*.

87. Voza (1972, p. 192, fig. 12, p. 194 fig. 13, pp. 195ff.; 1973, pp. 31, 34ff., pls VI–VII). The definitive publication is awaited. Another tomb, Al, contained a Mycenaean and a Cypriot vase, not illustrated.

88. Tinè and Vagnetti (1967, p. 21, pl. XXIV, 118); the jug there attributed to LH IIIC, but a much more likely date is LH IIIA2, both for form and pattern (this observation confirmed by Dr O. Dickinson).

89. Bernabò Brea (1966, pp. 113–114, pl. 29); Dickinson (1977, p. 104); Benzi and Graziadio (1982, p. 23).

90. Taylour (1958, pp. 55–56).

91. J. D. Evans, *Antiquity* **30,** 1956, 80–93.

92. Bernabò Brea (1966, p. 109, pl. 43).

93. Evans (1905, pp. 108–109).

94. Tinè and Vagnetti (1967, p. 21, pl. XXV, pp. 121–122).

95. Tinè and Vagnetti (1967, p. 22, pl. XV, p. 59–60); Magna Graecia (1982, 127–129, tav. XLI, 2, XLII, 1). For the laver, Catling (1964, p. 153 fig. 17, 10, pl. 21, b-d); for the hemispherical bowl, pp. 147–149, fig. 17, 1–7, pl. 19, a-c (shape), p. 152, fig. 17, 9, pl. 21a (hinged handle). Matthäus (1980a, pp. 131f., 139f., Taf. 73, 3 with refs); the hemispherical bowl not accepted by him as East Mediterranean work, and the laver assigned only to "Cyprus or Greece"—cf. (1980b, p. 136).

Vagnetti (1980, p. 157) mentions a total of four bronze basins from Caldare and Milena, but the above references only account for three.

96. G. Italia, *Archivio Storico Siracusano* N.S. **4,** 1975; Catling (1964, pp. 226–227). Another Aegean mirror was found in the Lipari hoard (Bernabò Brea and Cavalier 1980,

p. 780, Tav. CCCXV, no. 283). I thank Robert Leighton, University of Edinburgh, for drawing my attention to this find.

97. The Borġ in-Nadur sherd was found "outside the limiting wall" of Chapel A (Room 17), part of the (originally) Copper Age building. M. Murray, *Excavations in Malta* **III**, 1929 (London, Quaritch), p. 8, pl. XX, 1; Evans (1971, p. 17, fig. 42, pl. 32, 6); the sherd is effectively unstratified. Tas Silg: F. Mallia, *Missione Arch. Italiana a Malta* 1966, p. 50, pl. 35, 20 (not available to me; quoted L. Vagnetti, *Parola del Passato* **134**, 1970, 361).

98. J. D. Evans, *Proc. Prehist. Soc.* **19**, 1953, 85ff.

99. Bernabò Brea and Cavalier (1980).

100. Bernabò Brea and Cavalier (1968) for the finds on Salina and Panarea; *BPI* **75**, 1966, 143–173 for Filicudi; new finds on Lipari: M. Cavalier, *Rivista di scienze preistoriche* **34**, 1–2, 1979, 72ff.

101. Bernabò Brea and Cavalier (1960, 1980, pp. 565, 600) (Mycenaean pottery mentioned, presumably incorrectly, in Tinè and Vagnetti 1967, p. 22).

102. L. Bernabò Brea and M. Cavalier, *BPI* **75**, 1966, 171. On the use of the north side of Capo Graziano as an anchorage from Roman times, and the problems of the bay, G. Kapitän, *Int. J. Nautical Arch.* **7.4**, 1978, 269–277, esp. 274.

103. Vagnetti (1980, p. 157, n.17).

104. The suggestion of Dr John Cherry.

105. U. Rellini, *Monumenti Antichi* **24**, 1916, 461–616.

106. Dr Oliver Dickinson has examined this material and kindly confirms the datings.

107. T. W. Potter, *A Faliscan Town in south Etruria*, 1976 (London, British School at Rome), pp. 209, 268, fig. 96, no. 780, and information from Dr L. Vagnetti.

108. Vagnetti (1980, p. 154).

109. Telamone: Professor R. Peroni informs me that a newspaper report on German excavations on this site refers to the finding of an LH IIIC sherd. Poggio di Castellon-chio: information from M. Benzi, Pisa.

110. Vagnetti (1980, pp. 152–153); *Mélanges de l'école française de Rome, Antiquité* **86**, 1974, 657–671.

110a. Harding (1975, p. 195), refers to hammer-heads with square shaft-hole in Sardinia, attributing the information to Dr E. Macnamara. In fact the Sardinian hammer-heads almost all have round shaft-holes; I apologize to Dr Macnamara for misquoting her.

111. F. Lo Schiavo, *Sardegna Centro-orientale dal Neolitico alla fine del mondo antico*, 1978 (Sassari, Dessi), pp. 75–79; *Atti XXII Riunione Scientifica del l'Istituto Italiano di preistoria e protostoria* (1978), 1980, 341–358.

112. F. Lo Schiavo, *op. cit.*, pp. 85–87.

113. Ibid. pp. 89–91, 99–101.

114. The full story is told by F. Lo Schiavo in Lo Schiavo and Vagnetti (1980, pp. 371–373), with addendum by M. L. Ferrarese Ceruti, pp. 391–393; M. L. Ferrarese Ceruti, *Rivista di Science Preistoriche* **34**, 1979, 243–253; "Documenti micenei nella Sardegna meridionale", in press.

115. I am very grateful to Dr Ferrarese Ceruti, of the Istituto Antichità Sarde of the University of Cagliari, for arranging a trip to the site and showing me some of the finds.

116. M. L. Ferrarese Ceruti, *Rivista di Scienze Preistoriche* **34**, 1979, 244ff.

117. Such sherds were found in a number of *nuraghi*: for instance, of the material on display in Sassari and Cagliari museums, the sites of Sant'Antine (Torralba SS) and Cucurru Nuraxi (Settimo S. Pietro CA) have produced them.

118. A band-decorated sherd, and another, monochrome red, from Barumini, Su Nuraxi, vano 23, found by Dr. Ferrarese Ceruti in the Barumini material recently (*op. cit.* p. 249), seemed to me on inspection not to be of Mycenaean fabric. Dr Vagnetti tells me she is of the same opinion.

119. Magna Graecia (1982, pp. 177–179, tav. LXIV, 10–12).

120. The general problem, and the sources, discussed by R. D. Barnett, *Cambridge Ancient History*, 2nd ed., II, 1969 (Cambridge, University Press), ch. 28, esp. pp. 12–13; W. Helck, *Jahresbericht des Inst. f. Vorgesch. Univ. Frankfurt* 1976, 7–21; Sandars (1978, pp. 105ff., 158ff., 198ff.).

121. For example, by Barnett., *op. cit.*

122. R. Grosjean, *Antiquity* **40**, 1966, 194ff.; *La Corse avant l'Histoire*, 1966 (Paris, Klincksieck), pp. 65ff., pl. 45; J. Arnal, *Les Statue-Menhirs, Hommes et Dieux*, 1976 (Toulouse, Ed. des Hesperides), pp. 146, 150, figs 56–57; G. Lilliu, *La Civiltà dei Sardi*, 1967 (Turin, ERI Edizioni RAI), pl. XL(b); *Sculture della Sardegna nuragica*, 1966 (Cagliari, La Zattera), nos 12–13, p. 60ff.: the round shield here has a pointed boss and projections on the upper edge; the sword is grotesquely heavy and wide-bladed, carried resting on the shoulder. Horns project from warriors' helmets on many other pieces, including such long examples as the "Miles cornutus", Lilliu no. 96, pp. 182–183. It is fair to point out that archers are much more common in the preserved finds than swordsmen.

123. Sandars (1978, pp. 106–107).

124. R. D. Barnett, *op. cit.*

125. Sandars (1978, p. 107).

126. Bernabò Brea and Cavalier (1980, pp. 551ff., 567ff., 600ff., 791ff., 827ff.).

126a. L. Quilici, *Arch. Classica* **23**, 1971, 1–11; V. Tusa, *Omaggio a F. Benoit* I, 1972; Buchholz (1974, pp. 346–347).

128. It is rejected, for instance, by J. Alexander and S. Hopkins, *Proc. Prehist. Soc.* **48**, 1982, 405ff., though the difficult problems of relative dating in Greece, Italy and the East Alps are not dealt with.

129. H. Müller-Karpe, *Germania* **41**, 1963, 9ff.; *Jahresbericht des Inst. f. Vorgesch. Univ. Frankfurt* 1975, 20f.; Matthäus (1980b, pp. 133ff.); Bouzek (1969, pp. 29ff., fig. 9); Harding (1975, p. 199).

130. Blegen *et al* (1973, pp. 230ff., fig. 291, 1a-e).

131. Matthäus (1980a, pp. 276, 294) accepted that the time difference between the two is slight, but elsewhere (1980b, p. 135) states baldly: "Chronologisch geht das pylische Becken diesen Funden (Coste del Marano, Monte S. Angelo) sicherlich voran."

132. R. M. Boehmer, *Die Kleinfunde von Boğazköy*, 1972 (Berlin, Mann), pp. 39–40, Taf. 3, 38 (decorated sheet fragment from border between Büyükkale levels II and III, 13th to 8th century); A. Rowe, *The Four Canaanite Temples of Beth-Shan* **I**, 1940 (Philadelphia, Univ. Museum), Taf. 40, 1 (cylinder seal from

temple of Amenophis III, doubtful as a true parallel); both quoted by Müller-Karpe, *op. cit.*

133. Buchholz (1974, pp. 357–358); Dickinson (1977, pp. 104–105).

133a. Chr. Strahm, *Arch. der Schweiz* **III,** 1971, 9–10, Abb. 6; *Helvetia Arch.* **3** (12), 1972, 99–112.

134. C. F. A. Schaeffer, *La Stratigraphie Comparée*, 1948 (Oxford, University Press), figs 273, 274.6, 291.11, 296.16.

135. Coles and Taylor (1971).

136. For example, by Piggott (1966, p. 120); McKerrell (1972, pp. 299f.).

137. Piggott (1966) quotes various local parallels, mainly from Brittany, and compares also inlaid daggers and swords from Shaft Grave IV.

138. R. J. C. Atkinson, *Proc. Prehist. Soc.* **18,** 1952, 236–237.

139. Karo (1930a, p. 96, Abb. 28).

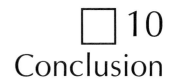

10
Conclusion

The Mediterranean lands were a series of regions isolated from one another, yet trying to make contact with one another. So in spite of the days of travel on foot or by boat that separated them, there was a perpetual coming and going between them, which was encouraged by the nomadic tendencies of some of the populations. But the contacts they did establish were like electric charges, violent and without continuity . . . . It may make it easier to understand how it is that each Mediterranean province has been able to preserve its own irreducible character, its own violently regional flavour in the midst of such an extraordinary mixture of races, religions, customs and civilisations.[1]

The north–south routes, although important, by no means totally conditioned the mass of countries and peoples they passed through. Distance and frequently relief made this impossible. The barriers lying between the Mediterranean and northern Europe played their negative role. So southern influence did not spread through the North in waves, although that might be the image that first comes to mind. When it penetrated deeply into a region, it was along narrow channels running northwards with the great trade routes and reaching with them the most distant lands. It is sometimes to these distant lands that we must go to explain the history of the sea.[2]

Braudel's words, written of the sixteenth century A.D., are so apt that they suggest to the reader that the situation he describes must have always existed. Certainly for the Roman period, arguably for the Iron Age, the "perpetual coming and going", the "narrow channels running northwards with the great trade routes" find a reflection in both history and archaeology. How far back did such contacts extend? Technically, socially and economically, was it even possible that the "north–south routes" should have existed in the Bronze Age?

We have completed the typological and geographic survey of the material culture evidence for contact between Late Bronze Age Greece and the rest of Europe, and are in a position now to consider the implications of the individual studies for our understanding of the situation as a whole. These conclusions fall into two broad categories: the implications for the chronology of the period, which is a matter of nuts and bolts rather than any deeper statement about the period itself; and the "historical" conclusions, relating to processes and events during the course of the Late Bronze Age. While a correct chronological framework is of course essential for a true appreciation of contacts between different cultures at any period, it is nevertheless statements about the structure and nature of the society and economy of the period that constitute our main goal, and correspondingly more space will be devoted to the latter than the former.

Chronology

Few issues have caused so much disagreement in Bronze Age studies as the chronology of the Early and Middle Bronze Age of continental Europe. In particular, the serious difference between traditional notions of chronology and radiocarbon dating, though only assuming prominence in relatively recent years, is a basic stumbling-block to progress. Our first task here, then, is an examination of the grounds advanced for the dating of the Early Bronze Age, particularly as far as central and eastern Europe is concerned.

As indicated in a number of places already in this book, the basis for the traditional chronology is the series of presumed correspondences between the material culture of Greece in the Shaft Grave period and central Europe. The discussion by Hachmann, which set out the traditional archaeological view with most clarity, may be taken as typical.[3] Hachmann relied particularly on the "halberd" from Shaft Grave VI, the Borodino hoard, and above all on the correspondences in spiral and spiral-related designs on Carpathian basin bone and metalwork to set the Apa-Hajdúsámson horizon and Br A2 parallel with the Shaft Grave period. At the same time he recognized possible contradictions and difficulties in the evidence of the amber and faience beads, concluding that in spite of the presence of amber spacers in Tumulus Bronze Age burials of Br B2 and later, it was in fact Wessex and therefore the Únětice culture, not the Tumulus period, which should be placed parallel with the Shaft Graves. Many of the supposed connections had been noted before,[4] and have indeed been used since. Mozsolics[5] preferred to set the period of close correspondence a little later, LH IIA in Aegean terms, mainly it seems because of the evidence of the finds from Kakovatos. Gimbutas[6] also preferred this position, though she argued too for contacts in LH I and, indeed, took a positive view both of Cypriot daggers in Europe and ingot torcs in the Near East (of which more below).[7] Hänsel[8] used the same lines of evidence to set his phase FD III (Early Danubian III), in which the first "mycenaeanizing" ornaments appear, as with Hajdúsámson and Tufalău, parallel with LH I.

Since the basis for this chronological structure is manifestly flimsy—as the more sober commentators have noted[9]—it is hardly surprising that it does not need to be pushed very hard to fall over. It is, indeed, remarkable that those scholars who lay great store by cross-dating for deriving dates for the Bronze Age see fit to use some "connections" and not others. The amber spacers are a case in point: although these appear in southern Germany in Br B2 the connections of the spiral designs in Br A2 have seemed to most people more important, and the amber evidence is therefore quietly ignored, refuge being taken in Hachmann's demonstration of a different function for the German and the Graeco-British spacers. Much the same is true for the ring ingots, the classic horizon for these appearing in Br A1 in central Europe. Examples that are indistinguishable from European pieces have been found in unimpeachable contexts in the Levant, where they date around 2000 B.C.[10] Schaeffer recognized the potential importance of these facts, and Gimbutas followed him in accepting a connection;[11] yet few have drawn the logical conclusion, which is to set the Br A1 period around 2000 B.C.

I have indicated in Chapter 7 that in my view little weight can be placed on the evidence of artistic motifs for chronological cross-comparison. Although there are undoubted similarities between motifs in the two areas there are no instances of actual importation of decorated objects, and good reasons to suppose that the cultural framework within which they appeared shows them to have been one aspect of a broad artistic tradition. If these objects are removed from consideration, little weight can be attached to any of the other single objects, such as the "halberd" from Shaft Grave VI. The evidence of faience beads is also notoriously difficult to use, since they were demonstrably made and used over a long period.

Taking instead as positive points for fixing cross-comparisons the ring ingots and the amber spacers, a perfectly acceptable Early Bronze Age chronology results. Br A1 covers the time around 2000 B.C., perhaps a little after it rather than before it. The period of amber spacer importation in Greece, LH I–II, or c. 1550–1400 B.C., corresponds to the Tumulus Bronze Age in central Europe and the Wessex Culture in Britain, at any rate in part. Br A2 and its related groups in the Carpathian basin fall between these two points at a time which cross-dating cannot yet fix more precisely.

When we turn to the later period, Müller-Karpe's demonstration that Br D corresponds, at least in part, to LH IIIB remains commonly accepted.[12] He placed the two periods more or less exactly parallel, i.e. c. 1300–1200 B.C. Sandars, on the other hand, saw "no compelling reason for beginning Reinecke D before the twelfth century, over most of which it extends".[13] Her grounds for believing this are complicated, but boil down to the idea that what objects there are in LH IIIB indicating Br D affinities are restricted to the very end of LH IIIB, while the "Peschiera" bronzes in Italy cannot be closely dated by means of finds like Scoglio del Tonno. It seems to me that the sum of evidence currently available suggests that Br D *did* overlap with LH IIIB, perhaps for some considerable time. Sandars herself quotes the type IIa flange-hilted swords from Enkomi and Kos, Langada T.21; there are also violin-bow fibulae from LH IIIB2 contexts at Tiryns, perhaps Kos, Langada T.20 and Metaxata T.132, as well as an LM IIIB example from Mallia. The median-winged axe mould from Mycenae has little close chronological value, being found in the fill of the destroyed LH IIIB1 House of the Oil Merchant; being of Bietti Sestieri's Ortucchio type,[14] which she places in the twelfth century on other grounds, this author has supposed that the axe is foreign to its context. On the other hand one of the closest parallels to the Mycenae axe-mould is the axe from the Surbo hoard, where the sword hilt is more likely to be of LH IIIB date than anything else.[15] None of these finds gives a very clear picture, but the cumulative evidence suggests that at any rate LH IIIB2 (as defined in the Argolid) corresponds to Br D, which should therefore begin in the second half of the thirteenth century. The position of Protovil-lanovan Italy in the scheme of things is hard to understand, particularly as its early phases are separated from the Peschiera phase on what seem to me to be very artificial grounds; if the above line of reasoning is followed, at least some groups currently assigned to the twelfth century should start even before that (cf. Appendix 5).

The extent to which the proposed chronology is supported or otherwise by radiocarbon dates is our next concern. In the first place it must be stated that radiocarbon dates from the Aegean area can play no part here. Several authors have indicated the difficulties and contradictions that the available dates introduce: not only do they not agree with the historical chronology, they are also inconsistent—sometimes wildly so—with each other. The prob-lems encountered in dating as (apparently) short-lived an event as the eruption of Thera suggest that little help is to be gained from radiocarbon dating for Aegean chronology at present. In view of this it might seem methodologically unsound even to consider the European dates, but in view of the uncertainties inherent in traditional dating methods little is lost by looking at them. In fact the picture they present is, with the arrival of an adequate number of dates, remarkably consistent.[16]

Table 1 gives the approximate duration of the main phases in central Europe, as known from all published dates, using both uncalibrated (b.c.) and calibrated (B.C.) dates. The Clark calibration is used.[16a]

It is abundantly clear from this that if radiocarbon dating is correct, and if these dates accurately reflect the periods they are supposed to belong to, then certain phases have to be removed altogether from the possibility of contact with the Greek Late Bronze Age. This is a point which was foreshadowed in 1968 by Renfrew, though at that time the quantity of available information was hardly sufficient. Thus Br A1 and A2 actually fall well before the

Table 1

Traditional		b.c.	B.C.
c. 1800	Start of Early Bronze Age (first appearance of cultural groups of EBA type) (Br A1)	c. 1900	c. 2300
c. 1600	Tin-bronze, rich graves, start (Br A1–A2)	c. 1700	c. 2100
c. 1500	Barrow-burial, start (Br B–C)	c. 1500	c. 1800
c. 1300	Cremation burial in regular use (Br D)	c. 1100	c. 1400
c. 1200	End of Br D, ?start of Ha A1	c. 950	c. 1200
c. 1100	Start of Ha A2	(?c. 1000)	(?c. 1250)
c. 1000	Start of Ha B1	?	?

sixteenth century, which is the time of the Shaft Graves and LH 1. Only with Br B does contemporaneity become demonstrable, and, indeed, likely. At the other end of the period, matters are confused because of the inadequate number of available dates, but at least for Br D there is an internally consistent series from the Padnal at Savognin,[17] indicating that the fourteenth and thirteenth centuries B.C. are involved: this agrees well with, for instance, the presumed time-span of the Peschiera bronze industry and embraces the one century (thirteenth) which Müller-Karpe assigned to Br D. After that, too few dates are available for any clear picture to be built up, but it is noteworthy that down to c. 1200 B.C. calibrated radiocarbon dates agree well with the historical chronology based on clear-cut cross-dating evidence (ring ingots and amber spacers). It is unfortunate that radiocarbon fails to make clear which central European phases are genuinely contemporary with LH IIIC in Greece.

Historical conclusions

It will be evident by now that the stance adopted in this book towards historical interpretations of archaeological data is essentially a negative one. I do not believe that assumptions of northern mercenaries in Greece, let alone Mycenaean architects at Stonehenge, are remotely justified by the artefactual evidence in a prehistoric period. Even in those instances where Bronze Age Europe verges on history, as with the Linear B tablets, it is evident that historical conclusions can rarely be drawn. It may not be stretching things too far to see in the coastguard tablet evidence for violent upheaval at the end of LH IIIB, especially in view of the fate which did actually befall Pylos; but the absence of the slightest direct evidence for trade and traders in the tablets strongly suggests that artefacts will help even less as far as writing history is concerned. The Linear B tablets represent our nearest approach to intelligible mind-to-mind contact with prehistoric Greeks; where signals of communication like these, which are designed to convey information from person to person, fail to provide evidence for trade, the coded information inherent in mute artefacts will hardly do better.

Nevertheless it would be foolish to pretend that there are no quasi-historical lessons to be learnt from the cumulative evidence for trade and communication discussed in this book. Such lessons concern three main phases of activity: the Shaft Grave period, the period of maximum dispersal of Mycenaean pottery, and the late period.

The evidence for Greek contact with far-off places in the Shaft Grave period is well-known and, at least in some instances, unimpeachable. This is not the place to discuss the significance of imports from or contacts with Crete, Egypt, Syria and Anatolia, though to some extent all the external connections of the Shaft Graves must be seen as an interrelated whole, effects in one area influencing or bearing on those in another. To the extent that the Peloponnese in LH I, and Mycenae above all, was able to exploit exchange networks linking Greece with distant lands, the northern connections of the Shaft Graves are as relevant as the southern and eastern.

In this connection a word must be said about Dickinson's suggestion of Mycenaean control of the copper trade and the supposed opening up of metal routes to Etruria, the Carpathians and even central Europe.[18] According to this, the need for metals brought about a situation whereby the Aegean world "plugged in", as it were, to the central and east European procurement network, ingot metal being exchanged for a certain amount of Mycenaean produce. Control of these newly opened exchange routes was then one way by which the Shaft Grave princes acquired their wealth, metal being a commodity in great demand throughout the East Mediterranean world by the Late Bronze Age. This theory has everything to commend it except archaeological evidence. While it remains possible that metal could have been moved from the Carpathian or Balkan sources to Greece without any trace surviving in the archaeological record, it would seem more likely—especially given the propensity of Aegean pottery to be moved around—that relevant finds of some kind would have been made by now. The Bulgarian ingots (p. 49) may be a step in the right direction, but there is no reason yet to connect these finds specifically with an early Late Bronze Age date.

The use of trade as a triggering mechanism in a process of social evolution is popular among many different kinds of archaeologist today. According to one model,[19] the rise of local élite groups to "paramount" status can proceed in just this way, the increased availability of goods from outside the socio-economic unit enabling control of the redistribution system to pass into the hands of the favoured few, with status obligations—such as tribute or taxes—becoming incumbent on those in an inferior position. The extent to which Shaft Grave Mycenaeans demonstrably drew on distant sources of both raw materials and manufactured goods shows that exchange connections, or procurement systems, must have played an important role in the LB 1 Aegean too, and can certainly be used as one variable in the set of complex equations which would characterize the rise to dominance of élite groups in this period. It remains, however, to be satisfactorily explained why this process took place when it did and not before, and why its effects were noticeable in particular restricted geographical areas, but this task lies beyond our present concerns.

Whether the opening out of exchange networks giving access to a range of commodities hitherto unobtainable preceded the ability to store and display wealth, and thus perhaps caused it, or succeeded it, in effect being a consequence of it, remains to be understood. Access to raw materials, especially gold, was clearly one way in which the Shaft Grave occupants manifested their status, but it does not automatically follow that those materials were the reason for that status. Since the northern connections of the Shaft Graves are no more developed than the southern and eastern, and considerably less so than the evidence for purely local processes, there is no reason, in my view, to suppose that links with the north were especially responsible for the development that the Shaft Graves represent.

The period of maximum dispersal of Mycenaean goods in both north and west were the middle and late periods, LH III. Amber and maybe copper were reaching Greece already in LH I–II, though in the case of amber, circulation was limited. In LH IIIB there is relatively little amber around; in LH IIIC there is something of a resurgence with good evidence for an Adriatic exchange system coming into play. If the Mycenaean sherds in Sardinia do reflect interest in metals, their LH IIIB–C date might suggest that this was one period when metals were being sought in the west by the suppliers of a metal-hungry Greece. Late IIIB and early IIIC are also the periods when "barbarian" ware occurred, and it will be recalled that an Adriatic connection for this pottery has been alleged.

The patterns of contact were probably never static, to judge from the distribution of finds over time and space. During LH IIIA and B, Mycenaean goods served as status objects in eastern Sicily, where individuals were buried in chamber tombs with a range of local and imported goods: almost the only area in the west where this is known to have happened, and without clear evidence for a point of entry for such imports (though sites like Thapsos are well-placed to serve as entrepôts). The ability of local élites to acquire such prestige objects, which apparently develops between the Castelluccio and Thapsos periods, implies social and economic conditions in which exchange is already a significant means of articulating social divisions. That settlements generally do not seem to have had Mycenaean pots in use on them throws the tomb finds into higher relief. It could even be that the imports were *not* landed on Sicilian shores by foreign merchantmen, but exchanged within local systems from Apulia or Lipari to Sicily. The emergence of elaborate domestic structures in eastern Sicily, probably in the Pantalica and Cassibile periods though conceivably earlier, suggests strongly that the indications from Thapsos-period tombs are correct, and that the development of élite groups with favoured access to imported goods was a major element in the course of the Middle and Late Bronze Ages in Sicily; the imported goods are one of the main ways in which they display their status. Perhaps it was precisely because eastern Sicily was not itself on the main axis of movement that such distinctions in burial provision arose, goods being channelled up through the system towards those who were able to claim them by right.

If this suggestion is one possible reading of the situation on Sicily, it will surely not do for the coastal stations of Apulia, for Lipari, or even for Sardinia. There, imported material was probably received direct from the ships which brought it, and was present in some considerable quantity, apparently being in daily use in the houses of at any rate some of these settlements (though on others, like Scoglio del Tonno, its context is less clear). The same should also be true for coastal stations in Macedonia, if any were known. In both cases, I have suggested that exchange via local systems would account for the observed distribution patterns.

In the last resort we are ignorant of the precise means by which goods travelled to or from Greece at any period, except that boats must have been involved. The Linear B archives give some idea of the social context of such exchange, rather less of the economic context; they document a "metallurgical system", but not who procured the necessary materials. By contrast, the frequent references to trade and traders in Near Eastern documents show that individual enterprise was a common force behind trade,[20] though state and collective enterprise occurred too. Elaborate devices for carrying on and controlling trade also existed. All well as entrepreneurs working mainly in one spot there were also travelling merchants; the Cape Gelidonya shipwreck is reconstructed as having carried one such. It is a fair, though currently unprovable, assumption that trade between Greece and the west and north was carried on by people of this sort.

What did they find when they reached "barbarian" shores? Most probably tribally-organized communities with already existing networks for the movement of goods, but organized in relatively small units. Sites like the Lipari acropolis were already ancient when vessels bearing Mycenaean pottery entered the scene. Lipari obsidian had been widely distributed in the Neolithic.[21] The ability of eastern merchants to link in to western trading networks was surely crucial to the success of such missions. How resources such as copper were controlled is a matter for speculation. On the whole, it is hard to imagine a free-for-all; but equally, rigid control by one particular "power" is unlikely too. Mining for metal ore is a long and dangerous business, usually carried out part-time by locals anxious to improve or maintain their economic lot.[22] Expeditions from distant lands by foreigners bringing their own work-force are not normally encountered, and in the case of possible Mycenaean exploitation of Italian ore sources seem most unlikely. Instead, the harnessing of local forces and the circulation of ingot metal in local systems are much more plausible as mechanisms for the creation and distribution of metal wealth, and a means by which eastern merchants could have acquired such metal.

The extent to which these matters have anything to do with the "decline and fall" of Mycenaean civilization is equally unknown. What is likely is that pre-existing exchange networks, such as we have just described, enabled the transfer of technology and artefact forms from 1200 B.C. on in a way which had hitherto not been the case, perhaps under the stimulus of increased commercial intercourse with the Aegean. By this means concepts such as the flange-hilted sword and dagger or the safety-pin became, for a time, identical on both shores of the Adriatic, and by whatever mechanism, certain pottery traditions of household production also exhibit a remarkable homogeneity. A "second wave" of common bronze forms has been held by some observers to be responsible for, or at any rate to accompany, the final destruction or abandonment of Mycenaean sites in LH IIIC, as invaders from the north swept in bringing their material culture and religious practices (cremation burial) to Greece. There is little or nothing to commend such a view today. Partly as a result of modifications in dating (e.g. of the "Lausitz" wares of Macedonia), more as a result of an increased awareness of the limitations of material culture evidence, today explanations of the end of Mycenaean Greece in these terms raise more questions than they answer.

Are there then any connections between the northern exchange and the end of the Greek Bronze Age? To the extent that during the twelfth century substantial realignments in trading orientations took place, one can perhaps talk of a general connection. The destruction of the Near Eastern cities is, after all, archaeological fact, and it must surely have entailed disruption to existing trading patterns. The switch to the movement of goods to the north, particularly the Adriatic, might even be an effect rather than a cause of this disruption.

Figure 58 shows the schematic representation of the Mycenaean penetration of the Central Mediterranean in the period of maximum dispersal, according to two prominent recent writers on the subject.[23] Mycenaean goods are viewed as entering the system at a number of coastal sites, which are connected by exchange networks to other areas; these relate in turn through a series of "regional connections", to more distant cultural blocks in northern Italy and central Europe. We might view the process of goods entering the local system as shown in Fig. 59, where coastal stations at which trading vessels call are responsible for the injection of foreign goods into the system; they are linked by existing exchange networks with other coastal sites, with hinterland farmsteads, and with more distant, perhaps seasonally occupied, upland settlements. Pottery, metals and foodstuffs will already be circulating within such a system, which can distribute small quantities of exotica without difficulty. Figure 60 shows the suggested extent of local exchange networks in the west, and the entry points for Mycenaean goods; a similar diagram could probably be created to express the situation in Macedonia. But within such a framework there are clearly alternative routes that material can pursue, as Figs 61–62 represent. Figure 61 portrays the situation where imported goods serve a prestige role, being preserved as treasured objects in local households and eventually being deposited, unbroken, in tombs. This is the situation suggested for eastern Sicily. On the other hand, Fig. 62 shows the case where a supply of goods is filtered down an exchange line, the goods perhaps being used by households who receive them, but eventually being broken and ending up as part of the debris on a deserted site; this is the more usual situation encountered in both north and west.

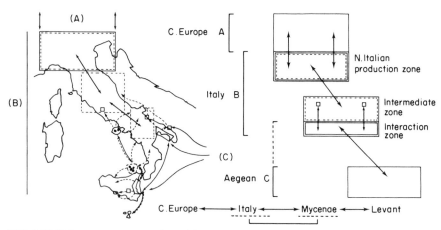

FIG. 58 ☐ Mycenaean penetration of the central Mediterranean, schematic representation, according to Marazzi and Tusa (1979).

Further considerations which must be borne in mind are the interplay of intensity versus duration of contact, and the rise of local production of ceramics in imitation of imported wares. In fact, few sites provide evidence of both intense and long-lived contact. Lipari is probably the only case where this

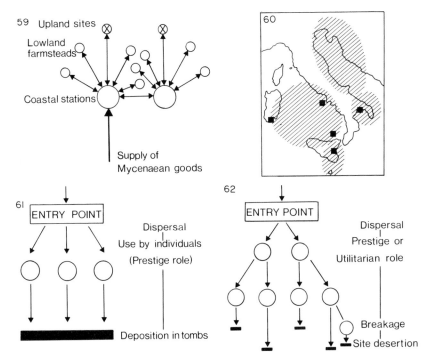

FIG. 59 ☐ Model depicting entry of Mycenaean pottery into local exchange network via coastal station.
FIG. 60 ☐ Suggested extent of local exchange networks in the West in the Late Bronze Age.
FIGS 61 and **62** ☐ Alternative routes for imported Mycenaean goods. Figure 61. Imported goods as prestige objects, deposited in tombs. Figure 62. Imported goods as prestige or utilitarian objects, broken and incorporated in site debris.

occurs, though Scoglio del Tonno perhaps had the more intense contact in the middle and late periods. On the other hand, Vivara had brief but intense contact in the early period, Porto Perone the same in the late period. In the west the question of local production in imitation of Mycenaean ceramics is uncertain, except perhaps at the very end of the period. In Macedonia, on the other hand, as in Thessaly and also in Troy, such production started fairly soon after the first importation from southern Greece, and must have affected attitudes to fine Mycenaean ceramics in general, though the fate of both was probably the same. The fact of imitation seems good evidence that the pottery was valued in itself in those areas, but also that it was not plentiful. Both these aspects of the export of fine painted ceramics deserve more detailed attention, which, one hopes, will soon become possible with the increased scale of activity in both excavation and publication.

Prospects

At the conclusion of this book it seems worthwhile to consider how the subject under investigation is likely to develop in the foreseeable future. Although speculation of this sort is rash, and the pace of discovery fast enough to confound the most rational forecasts, the clear implication of the foregoing discussion is that a pattern does exist, that progress can and will be made, and that clear answers will eventually be given to some of the questions raised here.

Potentially the most revolutionary development that is in prospect at present is that analytical characterization of materials will solve once and for all problems of provenience, particularly of metals. The signal failure of emission spectrography to relate artefacts to sources at last looks like being made good by the lead isotope technique, which has already recorded notable successes in the Aegean area. Unfortunately it is all too likely that resistance will be met from museum curators who have already given permission for their objects to be sampled once by the Stuttgart team. The analysis of ceramics, especially Mycenaean pottery, will also be important in tying down imports to particular production areas. This work will no doubt go hand in hand with the examination of the exported pottery by the acknowledged experts in the field, and by the two means together a great deal more should become established than was the case until recently. Analysis of glass can also be expected to prove important, for unlike faience, finds of glass in parts of Europe prior to the Late Bronze Age are in all probability imported from the East Mediterranean.

The future of chronological studies is easier to predict in some areas than others. Without a lucky breakthrough, Aegean chronology seems likely to stay put for quite some time. Most adjustments to the historical chronology depend on what is happening in Egypt, but in any case most are quite minor. In time, firmer fixed points may be hoped for in the Aegean cross-dating. Radiocarbon dating in the Aegean is, frankly, in a terrible muddle and seems unlikely to regain credibility for many years. In Europe, on the other hand, the signs are distinctly hopeful at any rate down to Br D. The accumulation of more and better samples, and the publication of more determinations already carried out (e.g. by the Berlin laboratory), are matters of urgency. Tree-ring studies will also make progress, though their applicability to the task in hand may be questioned: the confirmation of the chronological sequence for northern Italy is a task which could be carried out by this means, quite apart from the value of tree-rings for radiocarbon calibration.

On the technological side, much more needs to be known about the processes of Bronze Age production, particularly of metals and pottery but also in other productive aspects such as agriculture. The exchange of materials assumes a technological framework within which such exchange is important, and may have led too to the exchange of technology and concepts. These aspects relate also to the economic framework within which production took place. Aspects of this are discernible in the Linear B archives, but only at one time and in very fragmented form. Attempts at quantifying the role of metal-working in the overall economic structure of Bronze Age communities have made some progress, but should be taken much further if the real significance of metals to those communities is to be understood.

The goals described so far relate to specific research that can be or is being undertaken. For the question of Mycenaean contacts, however, much of the information which we need is unlikely to be found simply by creating research projects. If it were, we would be creating them. Unfortunately, much depends on the chances of discovery. It is likely that Mycenaean pottery will eventually turn up in Corsica, Thrace, Macedonia and Bulgaria, but it is most *unlikely* to be found by proposals just to go and find it, for practical and political reasons. I remain confident, however, that at least some of these gaps on the map will be filled before the end of the century. We might also hope for a "lucky break", such as the finding of another shipwreck, or a new series of informative Linear B tablets, or better site evidence for metallurgical practices. These might transform the situation overnight in a way which more finds of Mycenaean pottery are unlikely to do.

Yet much of the help is already at hand. If adequate study were to have taken place of all the relevant material that already lies in museum stores, much of the speculation in this book could probably be removed. From Stonehenge at one end of Europe to Mycenae at the other, ignorance and misinformation prevail where the simple expedient of publication of the evidence could have removed it. Partly gaps in publication are attributable to a lack of appreciation of the importance of particular classes of material, as is the case with the "barbarian" ware, but in other cases no such excuse is at hand. These lapses, however, serve to highlight the magnificent achievement of those who have crowned their field research with exemplary publication of the results. These, alas, are all too few: too often the basic corpora of material to which reference must be made are those classic excavations of the 1920s and 1930s published 50 or more years ago.

There is, of course, another aspect of publication which has been far from slow in coming forward, namely studies of general or particular aspects of the Mycenae–Europe link. Here the field may be divided into two parts, on the one hand systematic studies of particular classes of material, on the other gen-eralizations, often speculative, on Mycenaean trade and foreign interests— usually on the basis of tiny amounts of material in equivocal situations. To my mind there is little doubt that the Mycenae–Europe link has suffered from over-exposure. It was built up on a rickety framework in days when such things were acceptable. Today they are not, yet the fact that the framework has collapsed seems to have escaped the notice of some scholars altogether. What is needed are systematic studies of particular classes of material over as many areas as possible, as the magnificent series *Prähistorische Bronzefunde* is doing, albeit at inordinate length and expense. What should be halted are general studies of small parts of many different classes of evidence, which attempt to create correlations without an adequate overall framework in which to test them. The road to a better understanding of the situation is littered with the ruins of such attempts, from the daggers of Stonehenge to the rapiers of Romania and the "Lausitz" pottery of Macedonia.

In the last resort, it must be remembered that the Bronze Age was a prehistoric period, even in Greece, and specific historical events are rarely reconstructable from archaeological material alone. The growing realization that material culture can be a good guide to certain aspects of behaviour but a very poor one to others is leading to a more sober assessment of what we can legitimately hope to reconstruct. In the Anglo-Saxon world this is today less of a problem than in some other quarters, but there are pockets of resistance, and well-placed pockets at that, for whom archaeology is history or it is nothing. Archaeological facts do not need to apologize for themselves; there are plenty of approaches for which they are ideally suited, but writing history is not one of them.

The study of the Mycenaeans in Europe, then, is more properly the study of Mycenaean material in Europe, and *vice versa*. Unlike the era of Greek colonization, when literary evidence comes to our aid, only legends and myths are available with which to compare the archaeology, with the brief exception of the phases illuminated by archival material. I have tried to make it clear in this book that I regard the important question as being not: "Were there Mycenaeans in Europe?" but: "What was the significance of the export of Mycenaean material to Europe, in social, economic and technological terms?" In spite of the many problems which remain, it is possible to feel reasonably optimistic that these questions will receive answers in the foreseeable future.

Notes

1. F. Braudel, *The Mediterranean and the Mediterranean World in the Age of Philip II*, 1966/1972 (London, Collins), p. 161.

2. Ibid., p. 223.

3. Hachmann (1957a, pp. 165–180).

4. For example, on the significance of the designs on the Ţufalău discs, V. Milojčić, *Actes de la IIIe Session, Congrès International UISPP* (Zürich), 1950, p. 277; Mozsolics (1950, p. 21); the trail leads back to Reinecke, e.g. *Mitt. Anthrop. Ges. Wien* **32**, 1902, 111.

5. Mozsolics (1967, p. 123); cf. *Mitt. Anthrop. Ges. Wien* **93–4**, 1964, 111; Mozsolics (1965–6).

6. Gimbutas (1965, pp. 47–70).

7. Ibid., pp. 32–35.

8. Hänsel (1968, pp. 160, 170).

9. For example, Hachmann (1957a). H. Schickler (1974) has also concluded (in my view correctly) that the evidence for the traditional parallelization of Br A2 and the Shaft Graves is quite inadequate.

10. Cf. above, p. 54.

11. Gimbutas (1965, pp. 32ff.).

12. Müller-Karpe (1959, pp. 183ff.).

13. Sandars (1971, pp. 12ff.).

14. Bietti Sestieri (1973, pp. 396ff.).

15. K. Branigan, *Proc. Prehist. Soc.* **38,** 1972, 278ff.

16. Harding (1980).

16a. Clark (1975).

17. Harding (1983).

18. Dickinson (1977, p. 55); *Bull. Inst. Classical Studies* **19,** 1972, 146–147.

19. S. Frankenstein and M. Rowlands, *Bull. Inst. Arch.* **15,** 1978, 73–112.

20. *Iraq* **39,** 1977, 1–231 (= *Trade in the Ancient Near East*, Proceedings of the XXIII Rencontre Assyriologique International, Birmingham 1976), with additional refs.

21. B. Hallam, S. E. Warren and C. Renfrew, *Proc. Prehist. Soc.* **42,** 1976, 85–110.

22. For example, D. Birmingham in Gray and Birmingham, 1970, 166–167; I. Blanchard, *Economic History Review* **31,** 1978, 1–24.

23. Marazzi and Tusa (1979, fig. 4b).

Bibliography

Adams, R. McC. (1974). Anthropological perspectives on ancient trade. *Current Anthropology* **15** (3), 239–258.

Alexandrescu, A. (1966). Die Bronzeschwerter aus Rumänien. *Dacia* **10**, 117–189.

Andrea, Zh. (1972). Kultura e timave të pellgut të Korcës dhe vendi i saj në Ballkanin juglindor. *Studime Historike* **26** (9), 4, 81–105.

Andreou, I. (1978). Kivotioschimos tafos sto Romano Ioanninon. *Athens Annals of Archaeology* **10/2**, 168–174.

Andronikos, M. (1969). *Vergina. I. To nekrotapheion ton timvon*. Athens: Greek Archaeological Society.

Aner, E. and Kersten, K. (1973–9). *Die Funde der älteren Bronzezeit des nordischen Kreises in Dänemark, Schleswig-Holstein und Niedersachsen*, Vols 1–6. Neumünster: Wachholtz/Copenhagen: National Museum.

Annable, F. K. and Simpson, D. D. A. (1964). *Guide Catalogue of the Neolithic and Bronze Age Collections in Devizes Museum*. Devizes: Wiltshire Archaeological Society.

Aspinall, A. and Warren, S. E. (1976). The provenance of British faience beads: a study using neutron activation analysis. in *Applicazione dei metodi nucleari nel campo delle opere d'arte* (Roma-Venezia 1973), Accademia dei Lincei, Atti dei Convegni Lincei **11**: 145–152.

Aspinall, A., Warren, S. E. and Crummett, J. G. (1972). Neutron activation analysis of faience beads. *Archaeometry* **14**: 27–40.

Åström, P. (1977). *The Cuirass Tomb and other Finds at Dendra, Vol. 1, The Chamber Tombs*. Studies in Mediterranean Archaeology **4**. Göteborg: Åström.

Barfield, L. (1966). A Bronze Age cup from Lake Ledro (Trento). *Antiquity* **45**: 48–49.

Barfield, L. (1971). *Northern Italy before Rome*. London: Thames and Hudson.

Bass, G. F. (1967). *Cape Gelidonya: a Bronze Age Shipwreck. Transactions of the American Philosophical Society* **57**, part 8. Philadelphia.

Bass, G. F. (1973). Cape Gelidonya and Bronze Age maritime trade. In *Orient and Occident: Essays presented to Cyrus H. Gordon on his sixty-fifth birthday*, edited by H. A. Hoffner (Alter Orient und Altes Testament 22), pp. 29–38.

Batović, Š. (1959). Iz ranog željeznog doba Liburnije. *Diadora* **1**: 37–86.

291

Baumgartel, E. (1953). The cave of Manaccora, Monte Gargano. Part II: the contents of the three archaeological strata. *Papers of the British School at Rome* N.S. **8**: 1–31.

Beck, C. W. (1970). Amber in archaeology. *Archaeology* **23**, 1: 7–11.

Beck, C. W., Southard, G. C. and Adams, A. B. (1968). Analysis and provenience of Minoan and Mycenaean amber, II: Tiryns. *Greek, Roman and Byzantine Studies* **9**: 5–19.

Beck, H. C. and Stone, J. F. S. (1936). Faience beads of the British Bronze Age. *Archaeologia* **85**: 203–252.

Benac, A. and Čović, B. (1956). *Glasinac. Katalog der Vorgeschichtlichen Sammlung des Landesmuseums in Sarajevo, Teil I: Bronzezeit*. Sarajevo: Zemaljski Muzej.

Benzi M. and Graziadio, G. (1982). Note sulla provenienza delle ceramiche egee rinvenute in Italia meridionale. In *Aparchai. Nuove ricerche e studi sulla Magna Grecia e la Sicilia antica in onore di Paolo Enrico Arias*, pp. 19–33. Pisa: Giardini.

Bernabò Brea, L. (1966). *Sicily before the Greeks* (2nd edition). London: Thames and Hudson.

Bernabò Brea, L. and Cavalier, M. (1960, 1968, 1980). *Meligunìs-Lipára*. Vols I, III, IV. Palermo: Flaccovio.

Best, J. G. P. and de Vries, N. M. W. (eds) (1980). *Interaction and Acculturation in the Mediterranean*. Amsterdam: B. R. Grüner.

Betzler, P. (1974). *Die Fibeln in Süddeutschland, Österreich und der Schweiz I*. Prähistorische Bronzefunde, Abt. XIV, 3. Munich: Beck.

Biancofiore, F. (1967). *La Civiltà Micenea nell'Italia Meridionale, I. La Ceramica* (2nd edition). Rome.

Bianco Peroni, V. (1970). *Le Spade nell'Italia continentale*. Prähistorische Bronzefunde, Abt. IV, 1. Munich: Beck.

Bianco Peroni, V. (1976). *I coltelli nell'Italia continentale*. Prähistorische Bronzefunde, Abt. VII, 2. Munich: Beck.

Bietti Sestieri, A. M. (1973). The metal industry of continental Italy, 13th to the 11th century B.C., and its connections with the Aegean. *Proceedings of the Prehistoric Society* **39**: 383–424.

Blegen, C. W. (1937). *Prosymna, The Helladic Settlement preceding the Argive Heraeum*. Cambridge: Cambridge University Press.

Blegen, C. W., Rawson, M., Lord William Taylour and Donovan, W. P. (1973). *The Palace of Nestor at Pylos in Western Messenia. Vol. 3. Acropolis and Lower Town, Tholoi, Grave Circle, and Chamber Tombs. Discoveries outside the Citadel*. Princeton: University Press.

Blinkenberg, C. (1926). *Fibules grecques et orientales*. Lindiaka 5. Copenhagen: Høst.

Boardman, J. (1961). *The Cretan Collection in Oxford*. Oxford: Oxford University Press.

Bočkarev, V. S. (1968). Problema Borodinskogo klada. In *Problemy Archeologii* **1**: 129–154.

Borchhardt, H. (1977). Frühe griechische Schildformen. In *Kriegswesen, Teil I. Schutzwaffen und Wehrbauten*, edited by H.-G. Buchholz and J. Wiesner (*Archaeologia Homerica*, Band 1, Kapitel E), pp. 1–56.

Borchhardt, J. (1972). *Homerische Helme*. Mainz: Zabern.

Bouzek, J. (1966). The Aegean and Central Europe: introduction to the study of cultural interrelations. *Památky Archeologické* **57**: 242–276.

Bouzek, J. (1968). *Homerské Řecko a střední Evropa*. Unpublished habilitation dissertation, Charles University, Prague.

Bouzek, J. (1969). *Homerisches Griechenland*. Prague: Charles University.

Branigan, K. (1970). Wessex and Mycenae—some evidence reviewed. *Wiltshire Archaeological Magazine* **65**: 89–107.

Branigan, K. (1974). *Aegean Metalwork of the Early and Middle Bronze Age*. Oxford: Oxford University Press.

Briard, J. (1965). *Les Dépôts Bretons et l'Age du Bronze Atlantique*. Rennes: Travaux du Laboratoire d'anthropologie préhistorique de la Faculté des sciences.

Buchholz, H.-G. (1959). Keftiubarren und Erzhandel im zweiten vorchristlichen Jahrtausend. *Prähistorische Zeitschrift* **37**: 1–40.

Buchholz, H.-G. (1974). Agäische Funde und Kultureinflüsse in den Randgebieten des Mittelmeers. Forschungsbericht über Ausgrabungen und Neufunde, 1960–1970. *Archäologischer Anzeiger* 1974, 325–462.

Buchholz, H.-G. (1983). Doppeläxte und die Frage der Balkanbeziehungen des ägäischen Kulturkreises. In *Ancient Bulgaria* I, edited by A. G. Poulter, pp. 43–134. Nottingham: Department of Archaeology.

Carancini, G. L. (1975). *Die Nadeln in Italien/Gli Spilloni nell'Italia continentale*. Prähistorische Bronzefunde, Abt. XIII, 2. Munich: Beck.

Catling, H. W. (1956). Bronze cut-and-thrust swords in the East Mediterranean. *Proceedings of the Prehistoric Society* **22**: 102–126.

Catling, H. W. (1961). A new bronze sword from Cyprus. *Antiquity* **35**: 115–122.

Catling, H. W. (1964). *Cypriot Bronzework in the Mycenaean World*. Oxford: Oxford University Press.

Catling, H. W. (1968). Late Minoan vases and bronzes in Oxford. *Annual of the British School of Archaeology in Athens* **63**: 89–131.

Catling, H. W. (1977a). Panzer. In *Kriegswesen, Teil 1, Schutzwaffen und Wehrbauten*, edited by H.-G. Buchholz and J. Wiesner. *Archaeologia Homerica* Band 1, Kapitel E, pp. 74–118.

Catling, H. W. (1977b). Beinschienen. In *Kriegswesen, Teil 1, Schutzwaffen und Wehrbauten*, edited by H.-G. Buchholz and J. Wiesner. *Archaeologia Homerica* Band 1, Kapitel E, pp. 143–160.

Catling, H. W. and Catling, E. A. (1981). "Barbarian" pottery from the Mycenaean settlement at the Menelaion, Sparta. *Annual of the British School of Archaeology at Athens* **76**: 71–82.

Černych, E. N. (1978). *Gornoe delo i metallurgija v drevnejšej Bolgarii*. Sofia: Bulgarian Academy of Sciences.

Chadwick, J. (1976). *The Mycenaean World*. Cambridge: Cambridge University Press.

Childe, V. G. (1927). The Minoan influence on the Danubian Bronze Age. In *Essays in Aegean Archaeology Presented to Sir Arthur Evans*, pp. 1–4.

Childe, V. G. (1929). *The Danube in Prehistory*. Oxford: Oxford University Press.

Childe, V. G. (1948). The final Bronze Age in the Near East and in temperate Europe. *Proceedings of the Prehistoric Society* **14**: 177–195.

294   The Mycenaeans and Europe

Clark, R. M. (1975). A calibration curve for radiocarbon dates. *Antiquity* **49**: 251–266.

Clarke, D. L. (1970). *Beaker Pottery of Great Britain and Ireland*. Cambridge: Cambridge University Press.

Coles, J. M. (1962). European Bronze Age shields. *Proceedings of the Prehistoric Society* **28**: 156–190.

Coles, J. M. and Harding, A. F. (1979). *The Bronze Age in Europe. An introduction to the Prehistory of Europe c. 2000–700 B.C.* London: Methuen.

Coles, J. M. and Taylor, J. J. (1971). The Wessex culture: a minimal view. *Antiquity* **45**: 6–14.

Cowen, J. D. (1955). Eine Einführung in die Geschichte der bronzenen Griffzungenschwerter in Süddeutschland und den angrenzenden Gebieten. *Bericht der Römisch-Germanischen Kommission* **36**: 52–155.

Cowen, J. D. (1966). The origins of the flange-hilted sword of bronze in Continental Europe. *Proceedings of the Prehistoric Society* **32**, 262–312.

Crouwel, J. H. (1981). *Chariots and other Means of Land Transport in Bronze Age Greece*. Amsterdam: Allard Pierson Series, 3.

Curwen, E. C. (1954). *The Archaeology of Sussex*. London: Methuen.

Dakaris, S. I. (1956). Proistoriki taphi para to Kalbaki-Ioaninnon. *Archaeologiki Ephimeris* 1956: 114–153.

Dalton, G. (ed.) (1967). *Tribal and Peasant Economies. Readings in Economic Anthropology*. Austin: University of Texas Press.

Dalton, G. (1975). Karl Polanyi's analysis of long-distance trade and his wider paradigm. In *Ancient Civilization and Trade*, edited by J. A. Sabloff and C. C. Lamberg-Karlovsky, pp. 63–132. Albuquerque: University of New Mexico Press.

Deger-Jalkotzy, S. (1977). *Fremde Zuwanderer im spätmykenischen Griechenland*. Wien: Österreichische Akademie der Wissenschaften.

Desborough, V. R. d'A. (1964). *The Last Mycenaeans and their Successors*. Oxford: Oxford University Press.

Desborough, V. R. d'A. (1965). The Greek mainland, c. 1150–1000 B.C. *Proceedings of the Prehistoric Society* **31**: 213–228.

Desborough, V. R. d'A. (1972). *The Greek Dark Ages*. London: Benn.

Deshayes, J. (1966). *Argos, les fouilles de la Deiras*. Etudes peloponnésiens, 4. Paris: Librairie philosophique J. Vrin.

Deshayes, J. and Dessenne, A. (1959). *Mallia, Maisons II. Exploration des maisons et quartiers d'habitation (1921–48)*. Etudes Crétoises XI.

Dezort, J. (1946). Styky Moravy jihovýchodem v době bronzové. *Obzor Prehistorický* **13**: 57–63.

Dickinson, O. T. P. K. (1977). *The Origins of Mycenaean Civilisation*. Studies in Mediterranean Archaeology, 49. Göteborg: Åström.

Dörpfeld, W. (1902). *Troja und Ilion*. Athens: Beck and Barth.

Dumitrescu, V. (1961). *Necropola de incinerație din epoca bronzului de la Cîrna*. Bucharest: Edit. Academia R.S.R.

Evans, A. J. (1905). The prehistoric tombs of Knossos. *Archaeologia* **59**: 391–562.

Evans, A. J. (1914). The 'Tomb of the Double Axes' and associated group, and the Pillar Rooms and ritual vessels of the 'Little Palace' at Knossos. *Archaeologia* **65**: 1–94.

Evans, J. D. (1971). *The Prehistoric Antiquities of the Maltese Islands; a Survey.* London: Athlone Press.

Feuer, B. A. (1981). *The Northern Mycenaean Border in Thessaly.* Ph.D. dissertation, UCLA. University Microfilms.

Foster, K. P. (1979). *Aegean Faience of the Bronze Age.* New Haven: Yale University Press.

French, D. H. (1967). *Index of Prehistoric Sites in Central Macedonia.* Unpublished typescript.

French, E. (1975). A reassessment of the Mycenaean pottery at Tarsus. *Anatolian Studies* **25**: 53–75.

Gale, N. H. and Stos-Gale, Z. (1982). Bronze Age copper sources in the Mediterranean: a new approach. *Science* **216**, no. 4541: 11–19.

Garašanin, D. (1954). *Katalog Metala.* Belgrade: National Museum.

Gerloff, S. (1975). *The Early Bronze Age Daggers in Great Britain and a Reconsideration of the Wessex Culture.* Prähistorische Bronzefunde, Abt. VI, 2. Munich: Beck.

Gimbutas, M. (1965). *Bronze Age Cultures in Central and Eastern Europe.* The Hague: Mouton.

Godelier, M. (1977). *Perspectives in Marxist Anthropology.* Cambridge: Cambridge University Press.

Goldman, H. (1931). *Excavations at Eutresis in Boeotia.* Cambridge (Mass): Harvard University Press.

Goldmann, K. (1980–1). Die mitteleuropäische Schwertentwicklung und die Chronologie der Altbronzezeit Europas. *Acta Praehistorica et Archaeologica* **11–12**: 131–181.

Gray, R. and Birmingham, D. (eds) (1970). *Precolonial African Trade. Essays on Trade in Central and Eastern Africa before 1900.* Oxford: Oxford University Press.

Guido, C. M. (1978). *The Glass Beads of the Prehistoric and Roman Periods in Britain and Ireland.* London: Society of Antiquaries, Research Report 35.

Guilaine, J. (1972). *L'âge du bronze en Languedoc occidental, Roussillon, Ariège.* Memoires de la Société préhistorique française, 9. Paris: Klincksieck.

Hachmann, R. (1957a). *Die frühe Bronzezeit im westlichen Ostseegebiet und ihre mittel- und südosteuropäischen Beziehungen.* Beihefte zum Atlas der Urgeschichte, Band 6. Hamburg: Kartographisches Institut, Flemmings Verlag.

Hachmann, R. (1957b). Bronzezeitliche Bernsteinschieber. *Bayerische Vorgeschichtsblätter* **22**: 1–36.

Hall, E. H. (1914). *Excavations in Eastern Crete. Vrokastro.* Pennsylvania Anthropological Publications, III, no. 3, pp. 77–185.

Hammond, N. G. L. (1967). *Epirus. The Geography, the Ancient Remains, the History and Topography of Epirus and Adjacent Areas.* Oxford: Oxford University Press.

Hammond, N. G. L. (1972). *A History of Macedonia. I. Historical Geography and Prehistory.* Oxford: Oxford University Press.

Hampel, J. (1886, 1892, 1896). *A Bronzkór emlékei Magyarhonban.* 3 Vols. Budapest.

Hankey, V. (1967). Mycenaean pottery in the Middle East: notes on finds since 1951. *Annual of the British School of Archaeology at Athens* **62**: 107–147.

Hankey, V. (1973). The Aegean deposit at El Amarna. In *The Mycenaeans in the*

Eastern Mediterranean. Acts of the International Archaeological Symposium, Nicosia 1972, Department of Antiquities: Cyprus, pp. 128–136.

Hankey, V. (1981). The Aegean interest in El Amarna. *Journal of Mediterranean Anthropology and Archaeology* 1/1: 38–49.

Hankey, V. and Warren, P. (1974). The absolute chronology of the Aegean Late Bronze Age. *Bulletin of the Institute of Classical Studies* 21: 142–152.

Hänsel, B. (1968). *Beiträge zur Chronologie der mitt leren Bronzezeit im Karpatenbecken*. Beiträge zur ur- und frühgeschichtliche Archäologie des Mittelmeerkulturraumes, 7–8. Bonn: Habelt.

Hänsel, B. (1970). Bronzene Griffzungenschwerter aus Bulgarien. *Prähistorische Zeitschrift* 45: 26–41.

Hänsel, B. (1973). Eine datierte Rapierklinge mykenischen Typs von der unteren Donau. *Prähistorische Zeitschrift* 48: 200–206.

Hänsel, B. (1976). *Beiträge zur regionalen und chronologischen Gliederung der älteren Hallstattzeit an der unteren Donau*. Beiträge zur ur- und frühgeschichtliche Archäologie des Mittelmeerkulturraumes, 16–17. Bonn: Habelt.

Hänsel, B. (1979). Ergebnisse der Grabungen bei Kastanas in Zentralmakedonien 1975–1978. *Jahrbuch des römisch-germanischen Zentralmuseums Mainz* 26: 167–202.

Hänsel, B. (ed.) (1982). *Südosteuropa zwischen 1600 und 1000 v. Chr.* Prähistorische Archäologie in Südosteuropa, 1. Berlin/Bad Bramstedt: Moreland Editions.

Harding, A. F. (1975). Mycenaean Greece and Europe: the evidence of bronze tools and implements. *Proceedings of the Prehistoric Society* 41: 183–202.

Harding, A. F. (1980). Radiocarbon calibration and the chronology of the European Bronze Age. *Archeologické Rozhledy* 32: 178–186.

Harding, A. F. (1983). The Bronze Age in central and eastern Europe: advances and prospects. *Advances in World Archaeology* 2: 1–50.

Harding, A. F. and Hughes-Brock, H. (1974). Amber in the Mycenaean world. *Annual of the British School of Archaeology at Athens* 69: 145–172.

Harding, A. F. and Warren, S. E. (1973). Early Bronze Age faience beads from central Europe. *Antiquity* 47: 64–66.

Hawkes, C. F. C. (1961). Gold earrings of the Bronze Age, East and West. *Folklore* 72: 438–474.

Hencken, H. (1971). *The Earliest European Helmets, Bronze Age and Early Iron Age*. Harvard: Peabody Museum.

Heurtley, W. (1939). *Prehistoric Macedonia*. Cambridge: Cambridge University Press.

Höckmann, O. (1980). Lanze und Speer im spätminoischen und mykenischen Griechenland. *Jahrbuch des römisch-germanischen Zentralmuseums Mainz* 27: 13–158.

Hodder, I. (ed.) (1978). *The Spatial Organisation of Culture*. London: Duckworth.

Holste, F. (1951). *Hortfunde Südosteuropas*. Marburg/Lahn: Vorgeschichtliches Seminar der Phillipps-Universität.

Holste, F. (1953). *Die bronzezeitlichen Vollgriffschwerter Bayerns*. Munich: Beck.

Hood, S. and Coldstream, J. N. (1968). A Late Minoan tomb at Ayios Ioannis near Knossos. *Annual of the British School of Archaeology at Athens* 63: 205–218.

Hood, S., Huxley, G. and Sandars, N. (1958). A Minoan cemetery on Upper Gypsades. *Annual of the British School of Archaeology at Athens* **53–4**: 194–262.

Hope Simpson, R. and Dickinson, O. T. P. K. (1979). *A Gazeteer of Aegean Civilisation in the Bronze Age, Vol. 1: the Mainland and Islands*. Studies in Mediterranean Archaeology **52**. Göteborg: Åström.

Horedt, K. (1960). Die Wietenbergkultur. *Dacia* **4**: 107–137.

Hüttel, H.-G. (1981). *Bronzezeitliche Trensen in Mittel- und Osteuropa*. Prähistorische Bronzefunde Abt. XVI, 2. Munich: Beck.

Iakovides, S. (1970). *Perati. To nekrotapheion*. Vols 1–3. Athens: Archaeological Society.

Islami, S. and Ceka, H. (1964). Nouvelles données sur l'antiquité illyrienne en Albanie. *Studia Albanica* **1**: 91–137.

Jacobsthal, P. (1956). *Greek Pins and their Connections with Europe and Asia*. Oxford: Oxford University Press.

de Jesus, P. S. (1980). *The Development of Prehistoric Mining and Metallurgy in Anatolia*. British Archaeological Reports, S74. Oxford.

Karo, G. (1930a). *Die Schachtgräber von Mykenai*. Vols 1–2. Munich: F. Bruckman.

Karo, G. (1930b). Schacht von Tiryns. *Athenische Mitteilungen* **55**: 119–140.

Kiefer, C. and Allibert, A. (1971). Pharaonic blue ceramics: the process of self-glazing. *Archaeology* **24**: 107–117.

Kilian, K. (1975). *Fibeln in Thessalien von der mykenischen bis zur archäischen Zeit*. Prähistorische Bronzefunde, Abt. XIV, 2. Munich: Beck.

Kilian, K. (1976). Nordgrenze des ägäischen Kulturbereiches in mykenischer und nachmykenischer Zeit. *Jahresbericht des Instituts für Vorgeschichte, Universität Frankfurt a/M*. 1976: 112–129.

Kilian, K. (1978). Nordwestgriechische Keramik aus der Argolis und ihre Entsprechungen in der Subappenin-facies. *Atti della XX Riunione Scientifica del l'Istituto Italiano di Preistoria e Protostoria*, Basilicata 1976: 311–320.

Kilian, K. (1981). Ausgrabungen in Tiryns, 1978, 1979. Bericht zu den Grabungen. *Archäologischer Anzeiger* 1981 Heft 2: 149–194.

Kilian-Dirlmeier, I. (1979). *Anhänger in Griechenland von den mykenischen bis zur spätgeometrischen Zeit: griechisches Festland, Ionische Inseln, dazu Albanien und jugoslawisch Mazedonien*. Prähistorische Bronzefunde, Abt. XI, 2. Munich: Beck.

Korkuti, M. (1970). Rapports de civilisation illyro-égéens à l'âge du bronze. *Studia Albanica* **7**: 43–59.

Kossack, G. (1954). *Studien zum Symbolgut der Urnenfelder- und Hallstattzeit Mitteleuropas*. Römisch-Germanische Forschungen, **20**. Berlin: de Gruyter.

Kraiker, W. and Kübler, K. (1939). *Kerameikos. Ergebnisse der Ausgrabungen. I. Die Nekropolen des 12. bis 10. Jahrhunderts*. Berlin: de Gruyter.

Kurti, D. (1977–8). Përhapja e tumave ilire në Mat. *Iliria* **7–8**: 311–316.

Lo Porto, F. G. (1963). Leporano (Taranto)—La stazione protostorica de Porto Perone. *Notizie degli Scavi di Antichità* (8th series) **17**: 280–380.

Lo Schiavo, F. (1980). Wessex, Sardegna, Cipro: nuovi elementi di discussione. *Atti della XXII Riunione Scientifica dell' Istituto Italiano di Preistoria e Protostoria* (1978): 341–358.

Lo Schiavo, F. (1981). Ambra in Sardegna. *Studi in onore di F. Rittatore Vonwiller*, part 1, pp. 3–22. Como.

Lo Schiavo, F. and Vagnetti, L. (1980). Micenei in Sardegna? *Rendiconti della Classe di Scienze morali, storiche e filologiche, Accademia Nazionale dei Lincei*, Serie 8, **35**, fasc. 5–6: 371–393.

Lucas, A. and Harris, J. R. (1962). *Ancient Egyptian Materials and Industries*. 4th edition. London: Arnold.

McKerrell, H. (1972). On the origins of British faience beads and some aspects of the Wessex-Mycenae relationship. *Proceedings of the Prehistoric Society* **38**: 286–301.

McKerrell, H. (1976a). Prehistoric trade in blue glazed faience. In *Applicazione dei metodi nucleari nel campo delle opere d'arte* (Roma-Venezia 1973), Accademia Nazionale dei Lincei, Atti dei Convegni Lincei **11**: 297–316.

McKerrell, H. (1976b). The application of X-ray fluorescence and neutron activation analysis in archaeological research. In *Proceedings of the Nordic Conference on Thermoluminescence and other Archaeometric Methods*, pp. 117–133. Uppsala.

Macnamara, E. (1970). A group of bronzes from Surbo, Italy: new evidence for Aegean contacts with Apulia during Mycenaean IIIB and C. *Proceedings of the Prehistoric Society* **36**: 241–260.

Maczek, M., Preuschen E. and Pittioni, R. (1953). Beiträge zum Problem des Ursprungs der Kupfererzverwertung in der Alten Welt. II. Teil. *Archaeologia Austriaca* **12**: 67–82.

Maddin, R., Wheeler, T. S. and Muhly, J. D. (1977). Tin in the Ancient Near East: old questions and new finds. *Expedition* **19**/2: 35–47.

Magna Graecia (1982). *Magna Graecia e Mondo Miceneo, Nuovi Documenti*. XXII Convegno di Studi sulla Magna Graecia, Taranto 7–11 October 1982.

Maiuri, A. (1923–4). Jalisos—scavi della Missione Archeologica Italiana a Rodi. *Annuario della Reale Scuola Archeologica di Atene* **6–7**: 83–341.

Marazzi, M. and Tusa, S. (1976). Interrelazioni dei centri siciliani e peninsulari durante la penetrazione micenea. *Sicilia Archeologica* **9** (31): 49–90.

Marazzi, M. and Tusa, S. (1979). Die mykenische Penetration im westlichen Mittelmeerraum: Probleme und Voraussetzungen bei der Gestaltung einer Forschung über die italienischen und sizilianischen Handelszentren. *Klio* **61**, 2: 309–351.

Marinatos, S. (1960). Lausitzer Goldschmuck in Tiryns. In *Theoria (Schuchhardt Festschrift)*, pp. 151–157.

Matthäus, H. (1977–8). Neues zur Bronzetasse aus Dohnsen, Kr. Celle. *Die Kunde* **28–29**: 51–69.

Matthäus, H. (1980a). *Die Bronzegefässe der kretisch-mykenischen Kultur*. Prähistorische Bronzefunde, Abt. II, 1. Munich: Beck.

Matthäus, H. (1980b). Italien und Griechenland in der ausgehenden Bronzezeit. Studien zu einigen Formen der Metallindustrie beider Gebiete. *Jahrbuch des deutschen archäologischen Instituts* **95**: 109–139.

Mee, C. (1978). Aegean trade and settlement in Anatolia in the second millennium B.C. *Anatolian Studies* **28**: 121–156.

Meillassoux, C. (ed.) (1971). *The Development of Indigenous Trade and Markets in West Africa*. 10th International African Seminar, Freetown 1969. Oxford: Oxford University Press.

Mellor, R. E. H. (1975). *Eastern Europe: a Geography of the Comecon Countries*. London: Macmillan.

Merhart, G. von (1952/1969). Studien über einigen Gattungen von Bronzegefässen. In *Festschrift Römisch-Germanisch Zentralmuseum Mainz*, Vol. 2, pp. 1–71 (reprinted in *Hallstatt und Italien*. Mainz).

Mikulčić, I. (1966). *Pelagonija u svetlosti arheoloških nalaza. Od egejske seobe do Avgusta*. Beograd/Skopje: Archaeological Society of Jugoslavia/Archaeological Museum.

Milojčić, V. (1948–9). Die dorische Wanderung im Lichte der vorgeschichtlichen Funde. *Archäologischer Anzeiger* **63–64**: 12–36.

Milojčić, V. (1955). Einige "mitteleuropäische" Fremdlinge auf Kreta. *Jahrbuch des römisch-germanischen Zentralmuseums Mainz* **2**: 153–169.

Montelius, O. (1895, 1904, 1912). *Civilisation primitive en Italie depuis l'introduction des métaux*. Vols 1–3. Stockholm: Imprimerie royale/Berlin: A. Asher.

Montelius, O. (1924). *La Grèce préclassique*. Stockholm: Haeggström.

Morricone, L. (1965–6). Eleona e Langada: sepolcreti della tarda età del bronzo a Coo. *Annuario della reale scuola archeologica di Atene* **27–28**: 5–312.

Mozsolics, A. (1950). *Der Goldfund von Velem-Szentvid*. Basel: Prometheus Druck (Praehistorica 1).

Mozsolics, A. (1953). Mors en bois de cerf sur le territoire du basin des Carpathes. *Acta Archaeologica* (Budapest) **3**: 69–111.

Mozsolics, A. (1964). Der Goldfund aus dem Kom. Bihar. *Mitteilungen der anthropologischen Gesellschaft in Wien* **93–94**: 104–114.

Mozsolics, A. (1965–6). Goldfunde des Depotfundhorizontes von Hajdúsámson. *Bericht der römisch-germanischen Kommission* **46–47**: 1–76.

Mozsolics, A. (1967). *Bronzefunde des Karpatenbeckens. Depotfundhorizont von Apa und Hajdúsámson*. Budapest: Akadémiai Kiadó.

Mozsolics, A. (1971). Some remarks on "Peschiera" bronzes in Hungary. In *The European Community in Later Prehistory. Studies in Honour of C. F. C. Hawkes*, edited by J. Boardman, M. A. Brown and T. G. E. Powell, pp. 59–76. London: Routledge and Kegan Paul.

Muhly, J. D. (1973, 1976). *Copper and Tin. The Distribution of Mineral Resources and the Nature of the Metals Trade in the Bronze Age*. (and *Supplement*). *Transactions of the Connecticut Academy of Arts and Sciences* **43**: 155–535; **46**: 77–136.

Muhly, J. D., Wheeler, T. S. and Maddin, R. (1977). The Cape Gelidonya shipwreck and the Bronze Age metals trade in the eastern Mediterranean. *Journal of Field Archaeology* **4**: 353–362.

Müller-Karpe, H. (1950). Grünwalder Gräber. *Prähistorische Zeitschrift* **34–35**: 313–325.

Müller-Karpe, H. (1959). *Beiträge zur Chronologie der Urnenfelderzeit nördlich und südlich der Alpen*. Berlin: de Gruyter.

Müller-Karpe, H. (1961). *Die Vollgriffschwerter der Urnenfelderzeit aus Bayern*. Munich: Beck.

Müller-Karpe, H. (1962). Die Metallbeigaben der früheisenzeitlichen Kerameikos-Gräber. *Jahrbuch des deutschen archäologischen Instituts* **77**: 59–129.

Mylonas, G. (1972). *Ho taphikos kyklos B ton Mykinon*. 2 Vols. Athens: Archaeological Society.

Negroni Catacchio, N. (1970). La problematica dell'ambra nella protostoria italiana. Parte I: Diffusione dell'ambra in Italia e suoi rapporti col mondo culturale preistorico. *Sibrium* 10: 275–288.

Newton, R. G. and Renfrew, A. C. (1970). British faience beads reconsidered. *Antiquity* 44: 199–206.

Niš Catalogue (1971). *Les Civilisations préhistoriques de la Morava et de la Serbie orientale*. Catalogue de l'exposition, Musée National Niš.

Noble, J. V. (1969). The technique of Egyptian faience. *American Journal of Archaeology* 73: 435–439.

Novák, P. (1975). *Die Schwerter in der Tschechoslowakei I*. Prähistorische Bronzefunde Abt. IV, 4. Munich: Beck.

Panajotov, I. (1980). Bronze rapiers, swords and double axes from Bulgaria. *Thracia* 5: 173–198.

Papadopoulos, A. J. (1979). *Mycenaean Achaea*. Vols 1–2. Studies in Mediterranean Archaeology, 55. Göteborg: Åström.

Papadopoulos, Th. I. (1976). Hi epochi tou chalkou stin Ipeiro. *Dodoni* 5: 271–338.

Pástor, J. (1978). *Čaňa a Valalíky. Pohrebiská zo staršej doby bronzovej*. Košice: Vychodoslovenské Muzeum.

Patek, E. (1968). *Die Urnenfelderkultur in Transdanubien*. Budapest: Akadémiai Kiadó.

Paulík, J. (1968). Panzer der jüngeren Bronzezeit aus der Slowakei. *Bericht der römisch-germanischen Kommission* 49: 41–61.

Peroni, R. (1956). Zur Gruppierung mitteleuropäischer Griffzungendolche der späten Bronzezeit. *Badische Fundberichte* 20: 69–92.

Peroni, R. (1959). Per una definizione dell'aspetto culturale "subappenninico" come fase cronologica a se stante. *Memorie (scienze morali, storiche, e filologiche) dell' Accademia nazionale dei Lincei*, series 8, 9, fasc. 1: 3–253.

Persson, A. W. (1931). *The Royal Tombs at Dendra near Midea*. Lund: Gleerup.

Petrescu-Dîmboviţa, M. (1977). *Depozitele de bronzuri din România*. Bucharest: Academia de Ştiinţe.

Petrescu-Dîmboviţa, M. (1978). *Die Sicheln in Rumänien, mit Corpus der jung- und spätbronzezeitlicher Horte Rumäniens*. Prähistorische Bronzefunde, Abt. XVIII, 1. Munich: Beck.

Píč, J. L. (1899, 1900). *Čechy předhistorické*. Vols 1–2. Prague: Nákladem vlastním.

Piggott, S. (1938). The Early Bronze Age in Wessex. *Proceedings of the Prehistoric Society* 4: 60–106.

Piggott, S. (1966). Mycenae and barbarian Europe: an outline survey. *Sborník narodního muzeja v Praze (Historie)* 20, 1/2: 117–125.

Podzuweit, C. (1979). Spätmykenische Keramik von Kastanas. *Jahrbuch des römisch-germanischen Zentralmuseums Mainz* 26: 203–223.

Polanyi, K., Ahrensburg, C. M. and Pearson, H. W. (eds) (1957). *Trade and Market in the Early Empires. Economies in History and Theory*. New York: Free Press/Macmillan.

Popham, M. and Sackett, L. H. (1968). *Excavations at Lefkandi, Euboea 1964–66*. London: Thames and Hudson.

Potratz, J. A. H. (1966). *Die Pferdetrensen des alten Orient*. Rome: Pontificium Institutum Biblicum.

Poursat, J.-C. (1977). *Catalogue des ivoires mycéniens du Musée National d'Athènes*. Bibliotheque des Ecoles françaises d'Athènes et de Rome, 230 bis. Athens: Ecole française.

Prendi, F. (1958). Trouvailles illyriennes de l'Albanie septentrionale. *Buletin i Universitetit Shtetëror të Tiranës*, Seria shkencat shoqerorë, 1958/2: 109–136.

Prendi, F. (1966). La civilisation préhistorique de Maliq. *Studia Albanica* **3**: 255–280.

Prendi, F. (1977–8). L'âge du bronze en Albanie. *Iliria* **7–8**: 27–58.

Prendi, F. and Budina, D. (1970). La civilisation illyrienne de la vallée du Drino. *Studia Albanica* **7**: 61–87.

Randsborg, K. (1967). Aegean bronzes in a grave in Jutland. *Acta Archaeologica* (Copenhagen) **38**: 1–27.

Renfrew, C. (1968). Wessex without Mycenae. *Annual of the British School of Archaeology at Athens* **63**: 277–285.

Renfrew, C. (1972). *The Emergence of Civilisation. The Cyclades and the Aegean in the Third Millennium B.C.* London: Methuen.

Renfrew, C. (1975). Trade as action at a distance: questions of integration and communication. In *Ancient Civilization and Trade*, edited by J. A. Sabloff and C. C. Lamberg-Karlovsky, pp. 1–60. Albuquerque: University of New Mexico Press.

Renfrew, C. (1977). Alternative models for exchange and spatial distribution. In *Exchange Systems in Prehistory*, edited by T. K. Earle and J. E. Ericson, pp. 71–90. London and Orlando: Academic Press.

Říhovský, J. (1972). *Die Messer in Mähren und dem Ostalpengebiet*. Prähistorische Bronzefunde, Abt. VII, 1. Munich: Beck.

Rottländer, R. C. A. (1970). On the formation of amber from *Pinus* resin. *Archaeometry* **13**: 35–52.

Rottländer, R. C. A. (1973). Der Bernstein und seine Bedeutung in der Ur- und Frühgeschichte. *Acta Praehistorica et Archaeologica* **4**: 11–32.

Roudil, J.-L. and Soulier, M. (1976). La Grotte du Hasard à Tharaux (Gard). 1. La salle sepulchrale IG et la commerce de l'ambre en Languedoc-oriental. *Gallia préhistoire* **19**: 173–200.

Rutter, J. (1975). Ceramic evidence for northern intruders in southern Greece at the beginning of the Late Helladic IIIC period. *American Journal of Archaeology* **79**: 17–32.

Säflund, G. (1939). *Le Terremare delle provincie di Modena, Reggio Emilia, Parma, Piacenza*. Lund: Skrifter utgivna av Svenska Institutet i Rom, VII.

Safronov, V. A. (1968). Datirovka Borodinskogo klada. In *Problemy archeologii* **1**: 75–128.

Sandars, N. K. (1955). The antiquity of the one-edged bronze knife in the Aegean. *Proceedings of the Prehistoric Society* **21**: 174–197.

Sandars, N. K. (1959). Amber spacer-beads again. *Antiquity* **33**: 292–295.

Sandars, N. K. (1961). The first Aegean swords and their ancestry. *American Journal of Archaeology* **65**: 17–29.

Sandars, N. K. (1963). Later Aegean bronze swords. *American Journal of Archaeology* **67**: 117–153.

Sandars, N. K. (1971). From Bronze Age to Iron Age: a sequel to a sequel. In *The European Community in Later Prehistory*, edited by J. Boardman, M. A. Brown and T. G. E. Powell, pp. 3–29. London: Routledge and Kegan Paul.

Sandars, N. K. (1978). *The Sea Peoples. Warriors of the Ancient Mediterranean.* London: Thames and Hudson.

Sandars, N. K. (1983). North and South at the end of the Mycenaean Age: aspects of an old problem. *Oxford Journal of Archaeology* **2** (1): 43–68.

Sapouna-Sakellarakis, E. (1978). *Die Fibeln der griechischen Inseln.* Prähistorische Bronzefunde, Abt. XIV, 4. Munich: Beck.

Schachermeyr, F. (1980). *Die Ägäische Frühzeit. Die Ausgrabungen und ihre Ergebnisse für unser Geschichtsbild.* 4. Band. *Griechenland im Zeitalter der Wanderungen, vom Ende der mykenischen Ära bis auf die Dorier.* Mykenische Studien, **8.** Vienna: Verlag der Öst. Akademie der Wissenschaften.

Schauer, P. (1971). *Die Schwerter in Süddeutschland, Österreich und der Schweiz. 1. Griffplatten-, Griffangel- und Griffzungenschwerter.* Prähistorische Bronzefunde, Abt. IV, 2. Munich: Beck.

Schickler, H. (1974). Review of Hänsel 1968. *Fundberichte aus Baden-Württemberg* **1**: 705–734.

Schliemann, H. (1878). *Mycenae and Tiryns.* London: Macmillan.

Schmidt, H. (1902). *Heinrich Schliemann's Sammlung trojanischer Altertümer.* Berlin: Reimer.

Schmidt, H. (1904). Troja-Mykene-Ungarn. Archäologische Parallelen. *Zeitschrift für Ethnologie* **36**: 608–656.

Seddon, D. (1978). *Relations of Production: Marxist Approaches to Economic Anthropology.* London: Frank Cass.

Snodgrass, A. (1964). *Early Greek Armour and Weapons from the End of the Bronze Age to 600 B.C.* Edinburgh University Press.

Snodgrass, A. (1971). The first European body-armour. In *The European Community in Later Prehistory*, edited by J. Boardman, M. A. Brown and T. G. E. Powell, pp. 31–50. London: Routledge and Kegan Paul.

Sprockhoff, E. (1931). *Die germanischen Griffzungenschwerter.* Berlin: de Gruyter.

Sprockhoff, E. (1952). Ein Grabfund der nordischen Megalithkultur von Oldendorf, Kr. Lüneburg. *Germania* **30**: 164–174.

Spyropoulos, Th. (1972). *Hysteromykinaiki Helladiki Thisavri.* Athens: Archaeological Society.

Stone, J. F. S. and Thomas, L. C. (1956). The use and distribution of faience in the ancient East and prehistoric Europe. *Proceedings of the Prehistoric Society* **22**: 37–85.

Stubbings, F. H. (1951). *Mycenaean Pottery in the Levant.* Cambridge: Cambridge University Press.

Sulimirski, T. (1966–8). Handel Troi z Europa. *Tęki Historiczne* **15,** 3–27, 357–358.

Sulimirski, T. (1968). *Corded Ware and Globular Amphorae north-east of the Carpathians.* London: Athlone Press.

Sulimirski, T. (1970). *Prehistoric Russia: an outline.* London: Baker.

Sulimirski, T. (1971). Aegean trade with eastern Europe and its consequences. In *Mélanges offerts a André Varagnac*, pp. 707–728. Paris: Sevpen.

Sundwall, J. (1943). *Die älteren italischen Fibeln.* Berlin: de Gruyter.

Symeonoglou, S. (1973). *Kadmeia I: Mycenaean Finds from Thebes, Greece; excavation at 14 Oidipou Street.* Studies in Mediterranean Archaeology, **35**. Göteborg: Åström.

Tallgren, A. M. (1926). *La Pontide préscythique après l'introduction des métaux.* Eurasia Septentrionalis Antiqua, **2**.

Taylor, J. J. (1980). *Bronze Age Goldwork of the British Isles.* Cambridge: Cambridge University Press.

Taylour, Lord W. (1958). *Mycenaean Pottery in Italy and Adjacent Areas.* Cambridge: Cambridge University Press.

Tihelka, K. (1965). *Hort- und Einzelfunde der Úněticer Kultur und des Věteřover Typus in Mähren.* Fontes Archaeologicae Moravicae, **4**. Brno: Archaeological Institute.

Tinè, S. and Vagnetti, L. (1967). *I micenei in Italia.* Taranto: Museo Archeologico.

Točík, A. (1959). Parohová a kostěná industria mad'arovskej kultúry na juhozápadnom Slovensku. *Študijní Zvestí* **3**: 23–53.

Tufnell, O. and Ward, W. A. (1966). Relations between Byblos, Egypt and Mesopotamia at the end of the third millennium B.C. A study of the Montet Jar. *Syria* **43**: 165–241.

Tylecote, R. F. (1976). Properties of copper ingots of Late Bronze Age type. In *Festschrift für R. Pittioni zum siebzigsten Geburtstag. II. Industriearchäologie und Metalltechnologie*, pp. 157–172. Archaeologia Austriaca, Beiheft **14**.

v. Uslar, R. (1955). Der Goldbecher von Fritzdorf bei Bonn. *Germania* **33**: 319–323.

Vagnetti, L. (1980). Mycenaean imports in central Italy. Appendix II, in E. Peruzzi, *Mycenaeans in Early Latium.* Rome: Edizioni dell'Ateneo.

Ventris, M. and Chadwick, J. (1973). *Documents in Mycenaean Greek*, 2nd edition. Cambridge: Cambridge University Press.

Vinski-Gasparini, K. (1973). *Kultura polja sa žarama u sjevernoj Hrvatskoj.* Zadar: Filozofski Fakultet.

Vinski-Gasparini, K. (1974). Fibule u obliku violinskog gudala u Jugoslaviji. *Vjesnik arheološkog muzeja u Zagrebu* **8**: 1–28.

Vladár, J. (1973). Osteuropäische und mediterrane Einflüsse im Gebiet der Slowakei während der Bronzezeit. *Slovenská Archeológia* **31/2**: 253–357.

Vokotopoulou, I. (1969). Nei kivotioschemi taphi tis YE IIIB–G periodou ex Ipeirou. *Archaiologiki Ephimeris* 1969: 179–207.

Voza, G. (1972). Thapsos, primi resultati delle piu recenti ricerche. *Atti della XIV riunione scientifica del l'Istituto Italiano di preistoria e protostoria*, 13–16 Ottobre 1970: 175–205.

Voza, G. (1973). Thapsos. In *Archeologia nella Sicilia sud-orientale*, pp. 30–52. Naples: Centre Jean Bérard.

Wace, A. J. B. (1932). *Chamber Tombs at Mycenae.* (*Archaeologia* **82**).

Wace, A. J. B. (1953). Mycenae 1939–1952. *Annual of the British School of Archaeology at Athens* **48**: 3–93.

Wardle, K. A. (1977). Cultural groups of the Late Bronze and Early Iron Age in North-West Greece. *Godišnjak* (Sarajevo) **15**: 153–199.

Wardle, K. A. (1980). Excavations at Assiros, 1975–9. A settlement site in central Macedonia and its significance for the prehistory of south-east Europe. *Annual of the British School of Archaeology at Athens* **75**: 229–267.

Werner, J. (1952). Mykenae-Siebenbürgen-Skandinavien. *Atti del I° Congresso di preistoria e protostoria Mediterranea* : 293–308.

Willvonseder, K. (1937). *Die mittlere Bronzezeit in Österreich*. Vols 1–2. Vienna: Schroll.

Woytowitsch, E. (1978). *Die Wagen der Bronze- und frühen Eisenzeit in Italien*. Prähistorische Bronzefunde, Abt. XVII, 1. Munich: Beck.

Yalouris, N. (1960). Mykenische Bronzeschutzwaffen. *Athenische Mitteilungen* **75**: 42–67.

Zaharia, E. (1959). Die Lockenringe von Sărata-Monteoru und ihre typologische und chronologische Beziehungen. *Dacia* **3**: 103–134.

Zwicker, U., Virdis, P. and Ceruti, M. L. (1980). Investigations on copper ore, prehistoric copper slag and copper ingots from Sardinia. In *Scientific Studies in Early Mining and Extractive Metallurgy*, edited by P. T. Craddock, pp. 135–163. British Museum Occasional Paper **20**.

Appendix 1: Amber finds in Greece, Italy, Jugoslavia and the Near East

Additions since 1974.

This list includes all finds that have come to notice since the compilation of the lists in Harding and Hughes-Brock (1974). References designated (H.H.-B.) have been kindly provided by Helen Hughes-Brock. No attempt is made here to provide a full list of corrections and additional sources.

Mainland Greece and islands

Chios, Emborio. Three small fragments of amber from Area F, one possibly part of a spacer. LH IIIC. S. Hood, *Excavations in Chios 1938–1955, Prehistoric Emporio and Ayio Gala* **II,** 1982, p. 677, no. 66, pp. 727–730, fig. 306.

Cos, Langada T. 35. Seven formless fragments. LH IIIB–C. L. Morricone, *Annuario* **43–44,** N.S. 27–28, 1965–6, 169, fig. 173, right (H.H.-B.).

T. 57. One fragment of an elongated fusiform bead, dark red, length (L) = 9 mm, diameter (D) = 5 mm, LH IIIA–C. L. Morricone, *op. cit.*, p. 249, fig. 274 middle right (H.H.-B.).

Kara Hymettou, Attica. J. Crouwel, *Babesch* 1973, 99, no. VI 7 (H.H.-B.).

Kallithea, Achaea, T. Theta. Beads reported. Praktika 1977, 184f. (O. Dickinson).

Mycenae, chamber tomb 91. J. Sakellarakis, *Die kretisch-mykenische Glyptik und ihre gegenwärtige Probleme*, 1974, p. 117, n. 14 mentions a "Vöglein mit Kopf als Vierfüssler aus Bernstein" from this tomb, which on other evidence he assigns to LH II (H.H.-B.).

Nichoria, Messenia, tholos. The context of these beads has now been published in a preliminary report. "A few beads" (those illustrated are discoid, with possible fragments of other shapes) came from the tholos floor, LH IIIA2/B1; a single bead and frags of six or more others came from Pit 2, probably LH IIIB1; from Pit 4, but "without certain associations", were found "fragments of a very large, oblate amber bead", perhaps original diameter of 50 mm. *Hesperia* **44** (1975), 78–79, pl. 20c. An amber "ring bead" (?annular) has also been reported from Pit 1: N. C. Wilkie, *Temple University Aegean Symposium* **6**, 1981, 59.

Orchomenos. Grave with four small vases and amber beads reported in cemetery north of the Treasury of Minyas, which contains late MH and LH I–(II) pottery. *Ta Nea* 11 October 1972; cf. Hope Simpson and Dickinson (1979, pp. 236–237). This reference kindly supplied by Dr O. Dickinson.

Thebes, Gerokomeion. Th. Spyropoulos, *Arch. Delt.* 1970, B'1, 219. Lentoid bead from chamber tomb dated LH II–IIIB (H.H.-B.).

Tiryns, chamber tombs. Grave VI (=C): found in north-east corner west of bench-like projection, with bones and faience beads. "Eine zylindrische [= Tiryns type] und ein paar runde Bernsteinperlen". LH IIIB stirrup-jar nearby, but pottery from chamber covers LH IIIA–C.

Grave VII (=B). Probably six beads: two flattened spherical, two small spherical. One ?spacer, one oblong. Tomb contents cover LH II–IIIC.

Grave XV. One irregular spherical bead, D. 16 mm. LH II–IIIC.

W. Rudolph, *Tiryns* **VI**, 1973, 42, 48 no. 30, Taf. 25, 3; 54 no. 24, Taf. 29, 2; 77 no. 48, Taf. 46, 3.

Crete

Archanes, tholos Delta. Among the rich finds from a woman's burial are "beads of amber". LM IIIA2. *Ergon* 1975, 169.

Knossos, Sellopoulo T. 4. Necklace with burial III, "found near the lower jaw", consisting of four snail beads of glass paste, two spherical beads of banded glass, one faience scarab with engraved face, and "1 oval bead, much decayed, probably amber", L. 20 mm. Latest burial in tomb: LM IIIA1. Scarab gives *terminus post quem* of *c.* 1417 B.C. M. R. Popham, *BSA* **69**, 1974, 203 fig. 6c, 211, 214, 224, J14.

Knossos, Lower Gypsadhes. One elongated oval bead, round in section, L. 27 mm, D. 10 mm. LM IIIA1. M. R. Popham, *BSA* **75**, 1980, 171ff., fig. 6E, pl. 17C.

Kydonia, 14–21 Manu St. U. Jantzen in F. Matz, *Forschungen auf Kreta*, 1942, p. 77 (H.H.-B.).

Milatos. Reports of amber in an LM III tomb (H.H.-B.).

Cyprus (cf. L. Åström, *Swedish Cyprus Expedition* **IV**/**1D** (1972), 556, 616)

Enkomi. Sondage 24, champ 333. One broken amber bead. Material from sounding includes "rebord d'un vase peint, probablement du Chypriote Recent III", but find is not really datable.—French Tomb 11. Necklace of seven beads, in glass-paste, amber, cornelian and faience, mixed with human teeth. LC IIA. C.F.A. Schaeffer, *Enkomi-Alasia* (1952), 16, 153.

Hala Sultan Tekke. Area 8, Layer 4, "Feature" 1045. One oval bead, L. 40 mm, W. 35 mm, D. of string-hole 10 mm. LC III (twelfth century B.C.). P. Åström, G. Hult, M. Strandberg Olofsson, *Hala Sultan Tekke* **3**, 63, 139 (*Stud. Med. Arch.* **45**: 3, Göteborg 1977).

Kition, Tomb 9. The preliminary report (*Report Dept. Antiqs Cyprus* 1963, 5) mentions amber but there is no reference to it in the final publication: V. Karageorghis, *Excavations at Kition* **1**, 1974. This is confirmed by Dr Karageorghis.

Egypt and Near East

F. Daumar (*Chronique d'Egypte* **46**, 1971, 50–58) has discussed the textual evidence for amber in ancient Egypt, using a passage of Pliny (*Hist. Nat.* XXXVII, 36) to support the translation of *škr* as amber. I thank J. R. Harris for this reference and for the advice that this conclusion is dubious.

J. D. Muhly (1973, p. 414, n. 35) discusses the suggestion by B. Landsberger (*Hebräische Wortforschung, Festschr. W. Baumgartner*, Leiden 1967, pp. 190–198) that Akkadian *elmešu* and Hebrew *hasmal* are to be translated "amber". The first references date from the post-Ur III period, which would imply an early second-millennium date. (H.H.-B. adds that this suggestion goes back at least to 1895: *Dict. de la Bible*, s.v. "ambre", where earlier refs are given.)

The amber statuette in Boston is published by G. Garbini in *Orientalia* **28**, 1959, 208–212, pls XLIII–XLIV (H.H.-B.).

Italy

North and Central

References in Negroni Catacchio (1970, p. 278):
Lagazzi di Vho (Piadena-Cremona)
Cattaragna (Lonato-Brescia)
Monte Castellaccio (Imola-Bologna)
Franzine de Villabartolomea (Verona)
Peschiera palafitta (Verona), Middle to Late Bronze Age
Lucone (Polpenazze-Brescia)
Bande di Cavriane (Brescia)
Varese lake, palafitta
Brabbia torbiera (Varese)
Colombare di Bersano (Piacenza)
Parma, terramara, Middle to Late Bronze Age
Quingento (Parma)
Redù (Modena)
Pragatto di Crespellano (Bologna)
Marmore (Terni)
Titignano (Orvieto-Terni)

Populonia (Tiryns type): Lo Schiavo (1981, p. 16, n. 34)
Fondo Paviani (Tiryns type): Lo Schiavo (1981, p. 20, n. 9)
Panicarola sul Trasimeno (Tiryns type): Lo Schiavo (1981, p. 20, n. 9)
Frattesine (previously referred to as Fratta Polesine) (Rovigo): Protovillanovan finds;
   preliminary report now in A. M. Bietti Sestieri, *Padusa* **11**, 1975, 1–14.

South and Sardinia

References in Negroni Catacchio (1970, pp. 278–279):
Castelluccio (Siracusa)
Valsavoia (Catania)
Molina della Badia, Grammichele (Catania)
Vaste (Lecce)
Sardinia: ten or more sites, Lo Schiavo (1981, tav. IX)

Jugoslavia (cf. J. M. Todd, M. H. Eichel, C. W. Beck, A. Macchiarula, *J. Field Arch* **3**, 1976, 313–327)

Vrčin (Croatia), gr. 3. One bead, lentoid, D. 13 mm, H. 5 m, D. of hole 3 mm.
   Cemetery dated to Br D. T. Malinowski, *Fontes Arch. Posnanienses* **21**, 1970, 220,
   figs 3–4.
Sokolac, Glasinac plateau. Todd *et al.*, *op. cit.*

Appendix 2: Amber spacer-plates

Additional to Gerloff (1975).

Britain

Wessex, find-place unknown. Three + specimens in Devizes Museum, examined in 1972.

France

Grotte du château du Diable, Ollioules (Var): Guilaine (1972, p. 206).

Moidons, Salins (Jura), Tum. 7. Guilaine (1972, p. 207).

Saint-Fiacre, Melrand (Morbihan). Guilaine (1972, p. 207).

Grotte du Hasard, Tharaux (Gard). Three complete or nearly complete spacers and fragments of at least five others. Oblong; simple perforations, up to five per piece. Middle Bronze and Late Bronze I. Roudil and Soulier (1976, pp. 179ff., fig. 9).

Grotte des Duffaits, La Rochette (Charente). "Une dizaine de fragments". Final Middle Bronze Age, with elements of Br.D. C14 date from this cave: 1210±100 b.c. (Gif-2263) and 1020±100 b.c. Roudil and Soulier (1976, pp. 181, 187, 191).

Grotte de la Madeleine, Villeneuve-les-Magnelonne (Hérault): one or two spacers. P. Cazalis de Fondouce, in *Géographie générale du département de l'Hérault*, 1900, **III/1,** 151; Roudil and Soulier (1976, pp. 183, 190, 198).

Bois-Bas, Minerve (Hérault), dolmen 11. One spacer. J. Arnal, *Préhistoire* **15,** 1963, 91; Guilaine (1972, pp. 162, 384); Roudil and Soulier (1976, pp. 183, 190, 198).

Viols-le-Fort, (Hérault), "grand dolmen". One or more spacers. E. Teissier, *BSPF* **45,** 1948, 229–249, mentions two beads of amber, but not a spacer. It seems possible that some confusion over the contents of the different dolmens in the area has arisen. Roudil and Soulier (1976, p. 183, 190, 198).

Viols-le-Fort (Hérault), dolmen de la Draille. Two spacers. Roudil and Soulier (1976, pp. 183, 198).

Lozère, site unknown. One spacer, in one-time Prunières collection; not seen by Roudil and Soulier (1976, p. 190).

Grotte des Fées, Tharaux (Gard). Two broken spacers, perhaps amber. Roudil and Soulier (1976, p. 197).

Germany

Omitted by Gerloff from Hachmann's (1957b) list:
Bernloch-Wiesenfeld (Münsingen). Hachmann (1957b, no. 24).
Erpfingen. Hachmann (1957b, no. 28).
Grossengstingen (Reutlingen), Tum. 2 gr 2. Hachmann (1957b, no. 30).
Heilbronn, Tum. 1. Hachmann (1957b, no. 31).
Huldstetten-Tigerfeld, Tum. 1. gr. 1. Hachmann (1957b, no. 32).

(The finds from Böttingen, Hachmann nos 25–26, are probably correctly omitted as not being spacers.) Gerloff also mentions:
Allendorf (Marburg). Spacers in hoard of late Urnfield date. Thick pieces, simple perforations. O. Uenze, *Prähistorische Z.* **34–5**, 1949–50, pt. 2, 213f., fig. 3.

Greece (Harding and Hughes-Brock, 1974)

Mycenae, Shaft Grave V
Peristeria, tholos 2.
Khaniale Tekke, Knossos, Crete (Iron Age re-use)
(Routsi, Gerloff no. 55, is doubtful as a spacer.)

Italy

Cles (Trentino). Harding and Hughes-Brock (1974, p. 168). Context not known to me, but perhaps Urnfield or Iron Age date.

Switzerland

Savognin, Padnal (GR) J. Rageth, *Jahrb. Schweiz. Ges. f. Ur- und Frühgeschichte* **50**, 1976, 172ff., Abb. 41

Appendix 3: Faience beads

Additions since 1971

Listed here are finds of faience beads additional to those catalogued by me in *Archeologické Rozhledy* **23**, 1971, 188–200. Some are new finds, others were simply missed in the original listing. A number of finds catalogued there have now been fully published, notably those in West Slovakia excavated by A. Točík, and in East Slovakia by J. Pástor. Since a systematic search of the literature is virtually impossible this list can make no pretension to completeness; but it seems likely that the main areas of density of distribution have now been identified.

A few corrections arising from changing international boundaries since the Second World War, and listed in 1971 according to the pre-1939 names (which at that time were still prevalent in the literature), are also included.

USSR

Perejezdnaja, Bachmut, Kurgan 1, grave 4. A necklace of "beads of blue Egyptian paste" round the neck of a child in a ?Pit Grave. Tallgren (1926, p. 113); Sulimirski (1966–8).

Rajskoje, Bachmut, Kurgan 2. Three beads of "white paste" with other beads in Catacomb Grave. Tallgren (1926, p. 68); Sulimirski (1966–8).

Stadniki, Ostrog. Biconical bone and faience beads from cist burial with Early Bronze Age bronzes. Sulimirski (1968, pp. 23, 42, 195 and refs).

Strelica, Gomel. Beads (?material) reported in barrows of the Dnieper-Desna group. Sulimirski (1968, pp. 52, 66 with refs).

Suvorovskaja, Stavropol. "Paste" beads from kurgan graves of North Caucasian and Precaucasian groups, notably nine cylindrical and segmented beads from Kurgan 13, grave 10. A. L. Nečitajlo, *Suvorovskij Kurgannyj Mogil'nik* 1979, 65.

Torčin, Luck. Faience beads with cord-decorated pottery from flat inhumation graves excavated in 1938. Sulimirski (1968, pp. 23, 160 with refs).

Glass beads are reported by Sulimirski (1968, 1970) from the Verteba Cave at Bil'če Zolote, Komarov barrow 33, and Zielence, Terebovlja.

Romania

Periam (Perjamos), Arad. According to T. Kovacs (Budapest) there are beads from graves 5 and 111 on this site (Pecica group).
Poiana. Examination of this bead in Bucharest suggested that it is made of clay, not paste or faience, and should be deleted from the list.

Slovakia

Abrahám, Galanta. Beads found here according to A. Točík (pers. comm.).
Borša, Trebišov. Pástor (1978, p. 91) (unpublished).
Čaňa, Košice. Faience beads found in 27 graves out of 162, segmented, cylindrical, and annular. Pástor (1978, p. 90).
Dreveník, Spišská Nová Ves. Oral information from J. Pástor in 1970, and
Dúbravka, Michalovce.   shown on map of faience beads in Pástor
Haniska pri Košiciach   (1978, p. 119).
Lastovce, Trebišov. Pástor (1978, p. 91) and orally in 1970.
Rusovce, Bratislava. Formerly Oroszvár, Moson (Hungary): see 1971 list under Hungary.
Pástor (1978, p. 91) further quotes a reference to faience beads at Hula (A. Loubal, *Sborník MBS* 13, 1935, 347–375) but I have been unable to check this.

Poland

Horodysko, Chelm. Segmented, annular and cylindrical beads in hoard of material of Strzyżów culture. J. Machnik, *Frühbronzezeit Polens*, 1977, 97–98, fig. 15, 4.
Pieczeniegi, Miechów. A. Krauss, *Mat. Arch.* 9, 1968, 159–165, esp. p. 164, pl. I, 4.
Raciborowice, Hrubieszów. Segmented and other beads from cemetery of Strzyżów group. Sulimirski (1968, pp. 23, 159).
Strzyżów, Hrubieszów. Twenty-one faience beads in a child's burial. Sulimirski (1968, pp. 23, 160 with refs).

Hungary

Battonya (Békés), A. Gazdapusztai, *Acta Antiqua et Archaeologica* 12, 1968, 35. "Einige Fayence-Perlen", graves not listed. M. Girić, *Mokrin* I, 1971, 225, is not correct in attributing these to grave 68 on the basis of this reference.

Dunaújváros, Fejér. Annular, segmented and cylindrical beads from eight graves in Nagyrév cemeteries in various parts of the town (formerly known as Sztalinváros and Dunapentele). Mus. Dunaújváros; I. Bóna, *Alba Regia* **1**, 1960, 12, pl. VIII, 7.

Hernádkak, Borsod-Abaúj-Zemplén. NM Budapest, 52. 337. Five beads from graves 46 and 78.

Kisapostag, Fejér. A. Mozsolics, *Der frühbronzezeitliche Urnenfriedhof von Kisapostag*, 1942, 54, pl. V, 46, 48.

Kulcs, Dunaújváros, Fejér. Annular beads in three Nagyrév graves in a large cemetery of Early and Middle Bronze Age date. I. Bóna, *Alba Regia* **1**, 1960, 7–15, pl. VII.

Tószeg-Ökörhalom, Szolnok. Facetted annular beads, originally described as stone, from Nagyrév contracted burial. J. Banner, L. Martón and I. Bóna, *Acta Arch.* (Budapest) **2**, 1959, 139, fig. 29, no. 4; I. Bóna, *Alba Regia* **4–5**, 1963–4, 33.

Jugoslavia

Mokrin, Kikinda. M. Girić, *Mokrin, Nekropola ranog bronzanog doba* **I**, 1971, 225. Biconical, star and "oval" shapes, many examples. Mus. Novi Sad.

Italy

L. Barfield, *Antiquity* **52**, 1978, 150–153, with list and refs.

Spain and France

R. J. Harrison *et al.*, *Madrider Mitteilungen* **15**, 1974, 95ff. See also text in this volume, p. 94.

British Isles

Complete catalogue and study has been carried out by Paul Peek and Stanley Warren, University of Bradford. They have listed 109 find-spots in Britain and over 350 beads from the British Isles.

Appendix 4: The sword from Ørskovhede

Ørskovhedehus, Balle, Bredsten parish, Vejle county, S.E. Jutland. Sprockhoff (1931, p. 68); Randsborg (1967).

Flange-hilted sword from coffin in Early Bronze Age tumulus, with arrow-head, three bronze studs or bosses, fragments of wooden "ring" and scabbard with leather adhering, and pot probably of period II.

Since Randsborg republished this piece it has been widely accepted as—if not actually of Aegean derivation—at any rate evidence of Aegean influence on northern swordsmiths and an important cross-link for dating. The sword was assigned by Sprockhoff to his group Ib since (broadly speaking) the tang is straight-sided and the shoulders angular. Randsborg, on the other hand, drew attention to features alleged to be characteristic of Aegean swords of type Di: "first and foremost the three very large rivet holes in the tang, the strongly outward curved, square shoulders and the wide oval opening where the hilt is joined to the blade", but further the "slight concavity of the tang edges", "the detail that the midrib has steep, concave sides", and the alleged inward curvature of the upper part of the blade. Randsborg also saw the arrowhead as an Aegean type.

Since Aegean type D swords were flange-hilted and of roughly the same length and configuration as the European Type I, it is not surprising that particular examples of the one will resemble the other in some details. Before one can show a definite affinity to an "exotic" group, however, it is necessary to rule out the possibility of a local attribution. Since Randsborg's article only illustrates Aegean swords as parallels its reader is almost bound to conclude that Randsborg must be right. Reference to the corpora of swords now available readily shows that the Ørskovhede piece fits into the Ib class without any difficulty: Schauer (1971) assigns it to his Asenkofen type, Gusen variant. Let us consider Randsborg's detailed points one by one.

(1) "The three very large rivet holes." The first question is, how many rivet holes were there originally, and how big were they? To this we can answer, *at least* three and

probably more, since the end of the tang is broken off, perhaps where the metal was weakened by another hole. What is more, the one surviving rivet, recorded as having been found in the lowest hole, is only 4·5 mm (4·9 mm according to my own measurement) in diameter, the holes being about 9 mm in diameter. With these facts in mind, it is clear that there is no lack of local parallels for the piece: Sprockhoff (1931, p. 8) remarked that swords with four tang rivets were almost as common as those with none, but his lists show great variation in the numbers present, and he himself attributed it to "reiner Willkür". Other pieces in Schauer's Gusen and Braunau variants are closely comparable: Gusen itself, Essenbach, Braunau (Schauer 1971, pl. 49).

(2) "The strongly outward curved, square shoulders." The angle of outward curvature is c. 130°. Compare this with the following values for Ib swords: Toppenstedt 135°, Molgyer 150°, Nechtelsen 140°, Norby 130°, Podejuch 150°, Skanderborg 140°, Mejlby Hede 130°, Sem 140°, Hövede 140°, Nindorf 150°, Dornsode 140°. Aegean type Di swords have values between c. 100° and 115°, that is markedly squarer than Ib swords. It is thus clear that there is no substance in this remark.

(3) "The wide oval opening where the hilt is joined to the blade." Randsborg's drawing shows the "Omega" hilt-plate formation, but inspection of the piece in 1979 showed that it is not so pointed at the ends. Even if it were, there is absolutely no reason to see this as an Aegean feature. *All* swords of this type have it, in one form or another. Let us imagine the Ørskovhede sword complete with its hilt: it will of course look like a *Vollgriffschwert*. The quickest of references to corpora of *Vollgriffschwerter* (e.g. Holste 1953, Müller-Karpe 1961) shows that virtually all have a semicircular or oval opening at the base of the hilt-plate, which is frequently omega-shaped.

(4) "The slight concavity of the tang edges." This concavity is very slight, and may readily be seen on other swords of type I: cf. for instance Czech swords of early form like Kobeřice, Libotenice and Sedlec (Novák 1975, pls 6–7, Smolenice in his typology but Ib in J. D. Cowen's) or certain northern examples, e.g. Skanderborg (Sprockhoff 1931, p. 67, pl. 2, 14). The feature is in any case so slight as not to be worth detailed remark.

(5) The "steep, concave sides" of the midrib. Inspection of blade sections of type I swords in Schauer (1971) and Novak (1975) shows plenty of examples very similar to the Ørskovhede section. Sprockhoff (1931) did not include drawings, but from the illustrations it seems certain that the midrib type is well-represented in the north, too. Inspection of the Ørskovhede and Muldbjerg swords revealed identical blade sections.

(6) The inward curvature of the upper part of the blade. This point, if proven, would be an important one because Aegean Di swords do have a markedly tapering blade, in contrast to the European type I which has a blade that is parallel-sided for most of its length. When we inspect the Ørskovhede piece the first thing we notice is that the upper part of the blade is damaged, as is much of the rest of it. What seems quite clear from the drawings is that it does not taper in the upper two-thirds. There is one small area where the blade edge is preserved just below the shoulder (fig. 3, right-hand side in Randsborg's photo) which clearly shows that this is a normal type Ib blade.

Not mentioned by Randsborg, but in my view the feature providing much the most persuasive argument for an Aegean derivation, is the rounded point of the shoulder, not unlike the lobate shoulder of Aegean Di swords, whereas Ib shoulders tend to be angular and pointed. Examples of a more rounded form can be found, however, and one crucial feature of the Di shoulders is definitely *not* present—namely the continuation of the flange round to the lower part of the shoulder.

Randsborg listed those features that he considered linked the Ørskovhede sword positively with Aegean Di swords. He also listed those features of Di swords which are absent. These are: the shoulder flanges already mentioned, the rivet-holes in the top of the blade, the narrow raised flat or rounded midrib, sometimes ridged, and the pommel tang, which in the case of Ørskovhede we can make no judgement about. Metallographical analysis has also borne out the differences between the Ørskovhede and Greek swords, the former being cast without subsequent hammering and studied examples of the latter being cold and/or hot-forged (Randsborg 1967, pp. 26–27; Sandars 1983, pp. 52–53).

In the light of this it is surely incorrect to attribute the Ørskovhede sword to specifically Aegean influence. All its features appear within the European type I series, and there it should remain. An attribution to "the period before 1400 (B.C.)" cannot, on typological grounds alone, be sustained, even if that is the general period when the type was produced.

Appendix 5: The date of the early Protovillanovan bronze industry

The dating of particular bronze types in the Protovillanovan period is crucial for a full picture of Greek–Italian contact in this period. At present there are widely differing views on the matter. Müller-Karpe, for instance, placed Peschiera in the fourteenth to thirteenth centuries, Protovillanovan (PVN) I in the twelfth and PVN II in the eleventh centuries. Sandars moved the entire structure down almost a century, not starting PVN until shortly before 1100 B.C. Bietti Sestieri, on the other hand, has updated a number of hoards that Müller-Karpe had relegated to the eleventh or even tenth centuries.

Since the available fixed points are so few, it is strange that students of the problem have not kept a close eye on them. We may enumerate them as follows:

(1) Mould for axe of Ortucchio type, Mycenae, House of the Oil Merchant, LH IIIB context (though not on a floor level—see below).
(2) Fragmentary sword of type F ii, Surbo (Apulia) hoard, with winged axe of Ortucchio type, two shaft-hole axes, two hammer-heads, and a chisel; the sword on typological grounds allegedly an early type, but really only datable LH III B-C.
(3) Violin-bow fibulae in LH IIIB contexts in Greece, e.g. Tiryns (LH IIIB2).
(4) Arc fibulae in LH IIIC contexts in Greece, e.g. Argos, Perati, etc.

These indicators are of different sorts and have different implications. For the first, LH IIIB1 would appear to offer a *terminus post quem* for the axe's deposition—it cannot be dated automatically to the LH IIIB1 destruction of the House of the Oil Merchant since it was not part of the floor deposit, and may have got into the debris after the destruction. Nevertheless, the excavators explicitly described the fill as being of LH IIIB date and would have recognized an LH IIIC presence; LH IIIC sherds *were* found, "above the ruins of the house" (Wace 1953, p. 15), and since the mould is specifically described as being "in the burnt debris" there is no reason to doubt its IIIB

317

date. From my knowledge of excavating destruction deposits at Mycenae, where large amounts of debris filled up buildings prior to levelling and re-use (not in this case), I would say it is highly unlikely that the mould "might have fallen among its ruins long after the destruction" (Bietti Sestieri 1973, p. 399). For the Surbo hoard, LH IIIC is a *terminus ante quem* for the making of the sword, and LH IIIA a *terminus post quem* for the deposition of the hoard. For the last two indicators, LH IIIB2 and LH IIIC are *termini ante quos* for the adoption of the fibula types, and bearing in mind that the earliest examples of a phenomenon are the hardest to spot archaeologically, it is quite reasonable to assume that the types were in fact well-established in the periods in question. Indeed, given the fact that violin-bow, stilted and arc fibulae overlap both in Italy and in Greece, there is no particular reason why arc fibulae should not have become current in Greece as early as 1150 B.C.

Given these pointers, it is hard to understand such statements as "the axes from Ortucchio, Piano di Tallone and Osternienburg all seem to belong to the twelfth century" or "the group [Mottola hoard] can be dated to the eleventh century". Admittedly the term "Protovillanovan" is a rag-bag, containing everything that is not recognizably Peschiera/Terremare on the one hand, or Villanovan on the other, but there is clearly a substantial overlap between the mainstream Peschiera industry and the characteristic Urnfield type of hoard like Poggio Berni or Casalecchio. Thus "pure Peschiera" material probably dates solely to the thirteenth century and no later, but that does not exclude the possibility of other types, especially types for special purposes like metalworkers' tools, starting before 1300 B.C. as well. The true Peschiera industry is, after all, found only in the north of Italy, and its contemporaries further south are assumed rather than demonstrated.

Of the PVN bronze groups studied by Bietti Sestieri, then, we may conclude that a dating around or soon after 1200 B.C. would be possible (desirable!) for Surbo, Gualdo Tadino, Ortucchio, Piano di Tallone and the Fucino group. Acceptable in the twelfth century are Mottola and Coste del Marano. Hoards such as Poggio Berni and Casalecchio contain a mixture of pieces and cannot therefore be closely dated; an eleventh century date is probably correct.

Subject index

Page numbers in *italics* refer to figures in the text

Index of place names

Page numbers in *italics* refer to figures in the text